Hitler's Austria

Hitler's

Austria

Popular Sentiment in the Nazi Era,

1938-1945

Evan Burr Bukey

The University of North Carolina Press

Chapel Hill and London

© 2000

The University of North Carolina Press

All rights reserved

Set in Monotype Garamond and Modula types
by Keystone Typesetting, Inc.

Manufactured in the United States of America

The paper in this book meets the guidelines for permanence
and durability of the Committee on Production Guidelines for
Book Longevity of the Council on Library Resources.

Library of Congress Cataloging-in-Publication Data

Bukey, Evan Burr, 1940–

Hitler's Austria : popular sentiment in the Nazi era, 1938–1945 /
by Evan Burr Bukey.

   p. cm.

Includes bibliographical references and index.

ISBN 0-8078-2516-6 (alk. paper)

ISBN 0-8078-5363-1 (pbk.: alk. paper)

1. National socialism—Austria. 2. Hitler, Adolf, 1889–1945.

3. Austria—History—Anschluss, 1938. 4. Antisemitism—Austria.

I. Title.

DB99.B87   1999   99-21475

943.605'22—dc21   CIP

cloth 05 04 03 02 01   7 6 5 4 3

paper 05 04 03 02 01   5 4 3 2 1

For Anita,

and for Ellen and David

CONTENTS

TABLES & MAPS

PREFACE

This book represents an attempt to reconstruct the political attitudes and day-to-day preoccupations of ordinary Austrians under Nazi rule, an empirical effort to glimpse the mental world of those men and women who inhabited what was both Hitler's homeland and between 1938 and 1945 an integral part of his Greater German Reich. It seeks to address questions that have long vexed historians of Central Europe. How popular was the Anschluss? What aspects of National Socialism engendered mass support or opposition? Did traditional religious and political groups remain largely impervious to Nazi ideology? How did the general populace respond to the German war effort? To what extent did Austrians distinguish themselves in the killing machinery of the Third Reich? Were most people neither victims nor perpetrators, a populace that simply "stood aside, undefined"?[1]

Before examining the main themes of this book, a few words need to be said about the term "popular sentiment," an expression that is much discussed but difficult to define. For our purposes, it refers to the collective dispositions of society or what is sometimes called civilian morale. It consists of long-standing assumptions, shared beliefs, and common attitudes. It includes habits of conduct and behavior. It tends to be reactive, subconscious, and politically inert. Popular sentiment differs markedly from "public opinion," a term that usually refers to the convictions of those concerned with civic affairs—the "politically conscious minority."[2]

In the nineteenth century Karl Marx clearly recognized the importance of mass or popular sentiment in his pungent observation that "the tradition of dead generations weighs like a nightmare on the minds of the living."[3] He was hardly the first to consider the force of amorphous opinion, but he was followed by figures like Emile Durkheim, Lucien Lévy-Bruhl, and Marc Bloch who were more interested in surveying collective attitudes than in changing the world. The result has been an increasing preoccupation with the "history of mentalities," an enterprise that attempts to chart the patterns of behavior, the habits of thought, and the everyday concerns of ordinary people; it is an effort that seeks to measure the "attitudes and values of everyone living in a given society,"[4] to "map the mental universe which furnishes a culture with its essential characteristics."[5]

Historians, however, are relative newcomers to the study of mass opinion. Throughout the ages those most interested in understanding it have been rulers and politicians. They have been the ones most eager to ferret out the views of "simple folk," recognizing that political success depends to some degree on popular consent. Plato and Aristotle both called attention to the importance of popular sentiment, and Machiavelli hectored princes to pay due regard to it. While few potentates followed the example of the medieval caliph Harun-al-Rashid, who disguised himself to overhear the complaints and grievances of his subjects, most invariably relied on informers and spies to detect sedition and social unrest.[6]

Still, it was not until the eighteenth century that European monarchs commissioned forces of secret police to oversee the state bureaucracy and to prepare reports on the behavior of individuals. Among the most eager to organize a system of wider surveillance was the Austrian emperor Joseph II, the famous enlightened despot who between 1765 and 1790 tried to streamline the Habsburg monarchy. Thereafter, the French Revolution gave enormous power to state security forces, so that both radical revolutionaries and traditional monarchs utilized their secret police to root out subversion and dissent.

Between 1815 and 1860 the Austrian secret police were commonly regarded as the most effective in Europe. Under the direction of Count Joseph Sedlnitzky they censored the media, intercepted the mail, and monitored the conversations of individuals. "One doesn't dare lift his voice here," Beethoven once wrote; "otherwise the police find lodging for you."[7] Although Sedlnitzky's agents were few in number, the public was cowed by fear of their omnipresence.[8] This was a minimalist system of surveillance, one that declined with the liberalization of the monarchy after 1860 but which survived until the dissolution of the Habsburg state in 1918. Two decades later a similar system of observation would be reinstated by the Nazis.

When Hitler seized Austria in 1938, he set his sights on perceived ideological adversaries, primarily Communists, Marxists, Freemasons, Ultramontaines, the Christian churches, and aristocratic reactionaries. At the same time, he endeavored to mobilize the general population to support his vast plans of conquest. His regime sought to detect popular grievances and to root out their sources, either by crushing cells of ideological resistance or by responding with answers or real solutions.[9]

In incorporated Austria, as in Germany, the Nazis placed the entire population under surveillance, assigning party members the task of reporting suspicious or hostile activity to the Gestapo.[10] On the residential level the NSDAP acted as the eyes and ears of the regime, but in individual cases only.[11] The larger mission of tracking down organized resistance groups and measuring overall morale fell to the Sicherheitsdienst (SD) of the SS. By 1938 the SD had developed into a domestic intelligence agency that regularly prepared comprehensive reports on popular sentiment for Hitler and the Nazi leadership. Relying on a network of informers, agents, and reporters, the security agents sought to provide "factual information" on "opponents" and the "general mood and situation."[12]

This book, like other examinations of popular sentiment in Nazi Europe, is based largely on the surviving station reports of the Security Service as well as on those of the Landräte, or county executives, and the more irregular observations of the judicial authorities. Reliance on these and other Nazi sources raises obvious methodological challenges, a problem scholars have long recognized and tried to take into account.[13]

One of the most difficult of the obstacles is what the British historian Ian Kershaw has called the "problem of intimidation."[14] Under Hitler's dictatorship ordinary Germans and Austrians generally kept their mouths shut or did not say what they actually thought; in public they tended to gravitate toward people having similar views or to accommodate their conversation to the immediate situation. Besides, most Austrians were hardly strangers to surveillance.[15] Added to this was the fact that many individuals held split-minded views, looking in opposite directions at the same time or divorcing specific Nazi policies from the regime, especially from the person of Hitler himself.[16]

Closely related to the "problem of intimidation" is that of uneven coverage or lacunae. "The silences of the reports are, in fact, more evocative than what is said in them."[17] Part of the reason for this may be attributed to the intimidation factor, the other to the individual concerns or subjective feelings of the SD observers at any given time. Nonetheless, there is general agreement that the SD reports provide a remarkably accurate assessment of popular sentiment in Greater Germany, a primary source comparable with the records of the wartime Mass-Observation teams in Great Britain, a collection of documents regarded as among the best raw data concerning the social history of the Second World War.[18]

For the study of Nazi Austria a final difficulty lies in the disparate and scattered nature of the surviving SD records.[19] Many of the highly confidential station reports have been presumed lost or remain classified in provincial archives.[20] Research for this investigation, however, has uncovered entire collections both in Europe and the United States. These include virtually complete files from both Upper and Lower Austria, records from Vienna for the period 1939–40, and a complete dossier of SD situation re-

ACKNOWLEDGMENTS

It is a pleasure to acknowledge the aid and assistance of those who have helped me research and write this book. First, I wish to thank two scholars I have never met: Ian Kershaw of the University of Sheffield and Marlis Steinert of the Institute of Higher International Studies in Geneva. Their pioneering studies of popular opinion in the Third Reich provided both an inspiration and an analytic framework to present my findings in a logical, coherent way. So many of their insights have found their way into the general literature that it is impossible for any scholar to escape their influence.

I am also indebted to numerous colleagues and friends in the United States, Great Britain, and Europe. Among them are the staffs of the Mullins Library of the University of Arkansas, Fayetteville; the Military Archives Division of the National Archives, Washington, D.C.; the Public Record Office, London; the Allgemeines Verwaltungsarchiv (now a division of the Archiv der Republik), Vienna, especially the general director of the Austrian State Archives, Dr. Lorenz Mikoletzky, and his most amiable wife, Dr. Julianne Mikoletzky; the Dokumentationsarchiv des österreichischen Widerstandes, Vienna, especially Dr. Heinz Arnberger, Dr. Elisabeth Klamper, and my old friends Dr. Jonny Moser and Dr. Sigwald Ganglmair.

I have gained many insights from numerous conversations with individuals who lived in Nazi Austria, including supporters and opponents of the regime: Josef Wolkerstorfer, Dr. Arthur and Elisabeth Weber, Josef and Elisabeth Eisenhut, Josef Kick, Dr. Herbert Steiner, and especially Alfred Kessler.

For institutional support I am indebted to the University of Arkansas for an off-campus-duty assignment that enabled me to undertake my research in Vienna. I am especially grateful to Wolfson College, Cambridge, for awarding me a Visiting Fellowship in 1993–94 that allowed me to pursue my project in an atmosphere of uncommon tolerance and civility. In particular, I wish to thank Sir David Williams, Gordon Johnson, Graham Pollard, Roland Huntford, Julie Jones, and Hugh and Mary Bevan. I also extend my heartfelt gratitude to the Cambridge Faculty of History for their stimulating company and cordiality, most especially to Jonathan Steinberg, T. C. W. Blanning, Chris Clark, and Brendan Simms.

Of those friends and colleagues who generously read and suggested revisions of various drafts I owe special thanks to Todd Hanlin, Bruce F. Pauley, Jay Baird, Jonathan Petroupolos, Ernst Hanisch, and Günter Bischof. To the late Fred Parkinson I am extremely grateful for many kindnesses and editorial suggestions, to James Briscoe for stylistic criticism, and to Henry Friedlander for compelling me to rethink my original conclusions.

I am beholden to William Wright and Michael Gehler for publishing portions of this study elsewhere.

Many others have provided help and encouragement over the past decade. In particular, I wish to thank Radomir Luza, Johnpeter Horst Grill, Robert Knight, Jill Lewis, Sybil Milton, Peter Steiner, David Hopper, and Suzanne Smith.

To John Lukacs gratitude is due for unstinting support and sage advice.

Among my colleagues at the University of Arkansas I should like to thank the late Stephen F. Strausberg, Randall B. Woods, Donald Engels, and Daniel Sutherland. To my friend and collaborator Kurt Tweraser I extend immense gratitude for everything he has taught me about his native Austria. In addition, I want to thank Lewis Bateman, the executive editor of the University of North Carolina Press, for his support of this project. All errors and shortcomings must be regarded, however, as mine alone.

Finally, I wish to thank my wife and children, to whom this book is dedicated. Their love and devotion have sustained me through difficult years. Anita has, with patience, borne more than her share of distress; Ellen and David, now adults, have even developed an interest in their father's work.

ABBREVIATIONS & GLOSSARY

The following abbreviations are used in the text.
For abbreviations used in the notes, see page 235.

Bund Deutscher Mädel	League of German Girls
CV	Cartellverband (Alliance of Catholic Students)
DAF	Deutsche Arbeitsfront (German Labor Front)
DAP	Deutsche Arbeiterpartei (German Workers Party)
DÖW	Dokumentationsarchiv des österreichischen Widerstandes (Documentation Archives of the Austrian Resistance, Vienna)
FPÖ	Freiheitliche Partei Österreichs (Freedom Party of Austria)
Gauleiter	district leader(s) of the Nazi Party
GDVP	Grossdeutsche Volkspartei (Greater German People's Party)
Gendarmerie	rural constabulary
Gestapo	Geheime Staatspolizei (secret state police)
Hitler Jugend	Hitler Youth
KPD	Kommunistische Partei Deutschlands (Communist Party of Germany)
KPÖ	Kommunistische Partei Österreichs (Communist Party of Austria)
Kraft durch Freude	Strength through Joy
Kreisleiter	circuit leader(s) of the Nazi Party
NSDAP	Nationalsozialistische Deutsche Arbeiterpartei (National Socialist German Workers Party, Nazi Party)
NSKK	Nationalsozialistisches Kraftfahrer Korps (National Socialist Motor Corps)
NSV	Nationalsozialistische Volkswohlfahrt (National Socialist People's Welfare Organization)

OSS	Office of Strategic Services
Ostmark	Eastern March; Nazi name of incorporated Austria (changed in 1942 to Alpen- und Donau-Reichsgaue, but commonly employed until 1945)
ÖVP	Österreichische Volkspartei (Austrian People's Party)
RAD	Reicharbeitsdienst (Reich Labor Service)
RM	Reichsmark
SA	Sturmabteilung (storm troopers)
SD	Sicherheitsdienst (security service of the SS)
SDAP	Sozialdemokratische Arbeiterpartei (Social Democratic Party of Austria)
Sipo	Sicherheitspolizei (security police)
SPÖ	Sozialistische Partei Österreichs (Socialist Party of Austria)
SS	Schützstaffel (elite guard of the NSDAP)
VdU	Verband der Unabhängigen (League of Independents)

I

The Road to Greater Germany

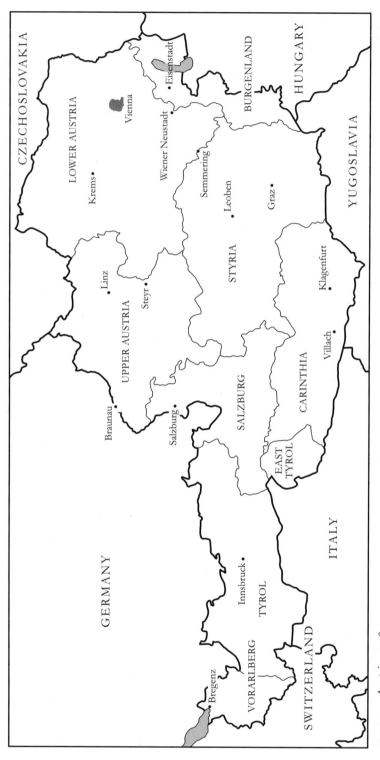

MAP 1. *Austria, 1938*

1 BEFORE THE OSTMARK

The attitudinal terrain of modern Austria owes much to the state-building process that began in the seventeenth century, an endeavor that left a legacy of myths, customs, and composite feelings that continue to shape popular sentiment. At the heart of the campaign was a crusade against the foreign and domestic enemies of the Habsburgs: the Turks and the Protestants. While the dynasty fought the Ottomans on the field of battle, it entrusted the Roman Catholic Church with the task of imposing religious and cultural unity throughout the family's far-flung domains, including Bohemia, Moravia, and the Habsburg Hereditary Lands. This entailed what Charles Ingrao has aptly called a "graduated process of persecution."[1] It included the expropriation of Protestant churches and assets; the expulsion of Protestant preachers and educators; the burning of heretical books and literature; and the indoctrination of the populace by militant religious orders. The Roman Church also sought to awe the masses by giving art and architecture symbolic representation in grandiose new basilicas, monasteries, and palaces. In addition, it encouraged devotional rituals, promoted sacramental pilgrimages, and placed renewed emphasis on the cult of the Blessed Virgin.[2]

As entire provinces of what is now the Republic of Austria had been Lutheran or Calvinist for over a century, the emotional impact of the Counter-Reformation on the lives of countless individuals was devastating. In the eyes of the authorities everyone was suspect, everyone subject to the inquisition of the confessional booth. At least 40,000 persons fled the Habsburg Hereditary Lands, among them 754 noble families. As for the rest, many remained clandestine Protestants, living in secluded Alpine valleys—particularly in Styria and Carinthia—or conforming outwardly to the dictates of the Roman Church. Nevertheless, the overwhelming majority of the Austrian populace embraced the restoration of Catholicism.[3]

There is no exact way of measuring the effect of the Counter-Reformation on the attitudes and behavior of subsequent generations of Austrians, but recent scholarship has demonstrated that the psychic legacy was both substantial and abiding.[4] Re-Catholicization reinforced a Manichaean view of the world in which an unforgiving God sanctioned violence against clearly defined enemies: Protestants, Turks—and Jews. It imposed a dogma so uncompromising and rigid that it encouraged split-minded thinking and evasive discourse, qualities that persist to this day in Viennese conversation and behavior. The Counter-Reformation both stirred and bureaucratized spiritual life. It placed emphasis on ornamentation, color, and sensuality. It exalted hierarchy, ceremony, and splendor.[5]

These and other numinous elements added distinctive features to Austrian political culture. Among them were a predilection for florid language and ritual; an emphasis on the theatrical and aesthetic; a premium on personal relationships for protection, patronage, and advancement. All in all, the legacy of the Counter-Reformation weighed heavily on the "minds of the living" well into the twentieth century. During the First World War Friedrich Adler justified his murder of Prime Minister Karl von Stürgkh as an act of revenge against a "state made Catholic by fire and sword during the Counter-Reformation," an order perpetually contemptuous of the thinking individual and his personal convictions.[6] Viewed dispassionately, Robert Kann, the foremost historian of the Habsburg monarchy, concludes "the chief and far-reaching consequences of the reformatory process consisted not so much in the memories of the injuries done but in those to be avoided by a cultivation of conformism and expediency."[7]

THE THERESIAN-JOSEPHINE LEGACY

In 1740 the self-confidence of the Habsburgs was severely shaken by Prussia's conquest of Silesia. The challenge of an upstart Protestant power compelled the Habsburgs to undertake reforms aimed at transforming their inheritance into a uniform and efficient society, a process that both exposed their subjects to the rationalist ideas of the Enlightenment and modified the entrenched values of the Counter-Reformation. The reforms were numerous and varied. They included curtailing the labor services of the peasantry or replacing serfdom with free labor, taxing the domanial assets of the nobility, and introducing standards of merit in the armed forces and the civil service. Significant changes in education also established a tripartite system of public schooling.[8]

At the heart of the reform movement lay a recognition of the need to reassess the relationship of the Habsburgs to their subjects.[9] This meant that Maria Theresa (1740–80) and her son Joseph II (1780–90) sponsored measures to favor manufacturers, tradesmen, and bankers and to improve the lot of the rural masses. Joseph II also sought to stanch the emigration of Protestants from the monarchy and to channel the Roman Church's activities into ventures useful to the state. Beginning in 1781 he issued a series of decrees emancipating non-Catholics and granting a measure of civic equality to the Jews. Thereafter, the impetuous emperor quarreled with the pope, secularized one-third of the monarchy's "utterly useless" monasteries, and directed the clergy to assume the tasks of social workers and teachers.[10]

If the psychic legacy of the Counter-Reformation was one of conformity, that of the Theresian-Josephist reform movement was one of ambiguity.[11] On the one hand, the effort indisputably stimulated education, self-improvement, and even individual thinking; it also widened opportunities and bettered the lives of the poor. Joseph II's creation of a civil service based on merit brought government and people closer together. On the other hand, the Theresian-Josephist system meant benevolent despotism; it connoted an "enlightened police state" dominated by a monarch who ruled on behalf of the people but insisted on their active cooperation. Maria Theresa and Joseph II left a legacy of reform from above, not below.[12]

During the nineteenth century the political concept of Josephinism mingled with notions of representative government to constitute an "autocratic theory of the Liberal state."[13] Central European liberals identified with the enlightened emperor as an exemplar of their own reform program. They placed particular emphasis on his nationalization of the church, misrepresenting imperial measures curtailing papal prerogative as initial steps toward the establishment of a secular, anticlerical state.[14]

Even more consequential was their invocation of Joseph's Germanization program, an attempt to standardize the language of the monarchy by making German the official tongue of government and commerce. When the emperor issued his linguistic decree of 1784, he was driven primarily by expediency; his argument was that German was spoken in more provinces than any other dialect or idiom and that it was more up-to-date than Latin, the official language of Hungary.[15] While Joseph II may have deemed German culture superior to others of his realm, he was by no means an ethnic German nationalist. By the mid-nineteenth century, however, both German and Austrian liberals claimed to be fulfilling his mandate by demanding a unitary state in Central Europe, a constitutional German empire that would transform or supplant the polyglot Habsburg monarchy. For the German-speaking inhabitants of Austria these demands marked the beginning of an identity crisis that would bedevil them and their descendants for a century to come.[16]

Before the revolutions of 1848 the German-speaking inhabitants of the multinational Habsburg monarchy saw no contradiction in feeling both German and Austrian. During that tumultuous year students and liberal bourgeoisie enthusiastically supported the efforts of the Frankfurt Parliament to unify Germany into a nation-state. Thereafter, German nationalist feeling moderated only slightly. This was partly because of the near success of the Frankfurt Parliament, partly because other Austro-Germans had been jolted into awareness of their own minority status by the unexpected aspirations of Italians, Czechs, and Hungarians. Suddenly, the German subjects of the emperor felt both isolated and threatened by the nationalistic aims of others. A subsequent influx of large numbers of Jewish immigrants to Vienna further irritated xenophobic sensibilities. Still, it was not until Otto von Bismarck expelled Austria from German affairs after the Austro-Prussian War of 1866 that Austro-Germans suffered a real crisis of identity. Thereafter, both public and private life would be suffused by what the Social Democratic leader Otto Bauer called "the conflict between our Austrian and German character."[17]

The most influential exponent of Germanic nationalism in the Austrian monarchy was Georg Ritter von Schönerer. He founded a Pan-German movement that was at once anti-Habsburg, antiliberal, anti-Catholic, anticapitalist, antisocialist, and, above all, anti-Semitic. Resorting to fiery rhetoric and extremist behavior, he attracted large numbers of university students as well as members of the preindustrial middle strata (*Mittelstand*) of artisans and shopkeepers who felt threatened by Jewish competition or technological modernization or both. Under Schönerer's influence anti-Semitism became much more central to German nationalism in Austria, especially because it seemed to provide a scientific explanation of societal woes to a generation already steeped in Darwinian and Wagnerian ideas.[18]

At the same time, Schönerer failed to expand his political base to mobilize peasants and industrial workers, although in Upper Austria and the Waldviertel there was some success among farmers. His failure was due partly to the persistence of the restricted franchise until 1907. It was due also to his own autocratic, intemperate character, a personality that tended to alienate close associates and outrage potential voters, most notably in 1888 when he stormed into the offices of the *Neues Wiener Tagblatt* to assault the editor with a walking stick—an incident that cost Schönerer both a jail sentence and the loss of his parliamentary seat.[19]

By 1901 the Pan-German movement had largely faded into oblivion, able to garner only 40,000 votes in the parliamentary elections of that year. All the same, Schönerer had left a lasting impact in German-speaking Austria, exalting a vituperative "sharper tone" in politics and giving respectability to antipatriotic ideas of populist nationalism and ethnic hatred. He also inspired a generation of devoted followers who achieved success as attorneys, civil servants, politicians, and businessmen, especially in the provinces.[20] For nearly a quarter of century they and other German Nationalist notables dominated the municipal life of cities such as Innsbruck, Graz, and Linz, where they both exploited and molded popular attitudes.[21] That Hitler derived many of his ideas from Schönerer is well known by scholars; that in Linz he grew up under the auspices of patrician elites espousing similar views is less well known although absolutely essential in understanding part of the mental world of his homeland.[22]

Schönerer's teachings also survived in the clubby associational subculture of urban Austria, particularly in fashionable athletic clubs like the Deutscher Turnerbund and Deutsche Turnschaft, organizations whose statutes promoted martial values and excluded Jews. Much the same was true of more specialized sporting groups and mountaineering societies such as the Austrian Alpenverein. Nor was the cult of Germanic nationalism confined to the playing fields and locker rooms of the small-town bourgeoisie; choral societies, literary circles, and civic-minded groups also paid homage to the German Reich and German race. In mixed-ethnic areas or border regions, where German speakers had good reason to feel besieged, school boards and teachers associations were particularly outspoken and shrill in their hostility to outsiders, particularly Jews.[23]

THE GERMAN WORKERS PARTY

Invariably, Schönerer's gospel of prejudice and ethnic hatred trickled down to nonsocialist elements of the working classes. In the 1880s the sudden migration of desperately poor Czech workers into the rapidly developing towns of northern Bohemia led to the spontaneous founding of unions of German-speaking miners, textile workers, typesetters, and railwaymen. Adopting "Aryan" paragraphs, they demanded protective legislation against "unskilled" Czech labor and the nationalization of certain key industries. In 1904 representatives of these unions met in Trautenau (Trutnou) on the Bohemian-Silesian frontier. Here they founded the German Workers Party (Deutsche Arbeiterpartei, or DAP), a radical nationalist labor movement and direct precursor of the Austrian Nazi Party.[24]

A genuine labor party, the DAP was composed and led by workingmen. It differed from the Marxist Social Democratic movement in its rejection of internationalism, its dismissal of theory, and its willingness to accept white-collar employees. The DAP placed emphasis on the fusion of nationalism and socialism. It demanded the nationalization of monopolies, the elimination of unearned increment, and a strong stand against foreigners, clericals, Jews, capitalists, and Marxists. Finally, it demanded expansion of the living space of the German people to the east.[25]

Despite the DAP's success in expanding membership and activities between 1904 and 1918, it remained primarily a regional movement, confined largely to the ethnic borderlands of northern Bohemia. On the territory of what later became the Republic of Austria it established only a handful of scattered chapters or Ortsgruppen: fifteen in Styria, four in Carinthia, and one each in Upper Austria and Salzburg.[26] As the local groups were generally associations of Bohemian railwaymen stationed far from home, it is unlikely that they had much influence on Hitler or on local sentiment. On the other hand, it is fairly certain that DAP railwaymen from the hypernationalistic town of Eger, near Bayreuth, played a key role in the founding of the Munich branch of the German Workers Party—the original German Nazi movement discovered by Hitler in 1919.[27]

THE FIRST REPUBLIC

In 1918 the defeat and disintegration of the Austro-Hungarian monarchy threw the people of the Habsburg Hereditary Lands into emotional turmoil. The abrupt transition from imperial power to dwarf state curtailed jobs and opportunities, sharpened divisions between town and country, and ushered in two decades of rancorous political conflict. It also intensified the problem of national identity, exacerbating the emotional struggle between the country's Austrian and German character.

At first, there was a sense of release and elation, an odd euphoria that crystallized into strong support for the establishment of a German-Austrian Republic.[28] On 10 September 1919, however, the victorious Allies forced the new Austrian government to sign the Treaty of St. Germain, a settlement that compelled Vienna to shoulder the burdens of the lost war, including a war guilt clause and liability for reparations. As in Weimar Germany, the people in Austria experienced universal shock and indignation, most notably at the loss of border territories, especially South Tyrol, and at Article 88, the clause prohibiting union or Anschluss with Germany "except with consent of the Council of the League of Nations."[29]

All this meant that the Austrian Republic lost its raison d'être in the minds of its populace. It became a "state nobody wanted,"[30] a "hydrocephalic monster," a grotesque betrayal of the much-touted principle of national self-determination. To all but a handful of traditionalists and industrial manufacturers, the idea of an independent Austria was simply inconceivable. Given the economic hardships confronting the German-Austrian lands, particularly the specter of impoverishment, both elites and ordinary people judged the new state "nonviable." From today's perspective they appear to have been unduly pessimistic. At the time, however, they faced chronic food shortages, financial collapse, and a barrier of high tariffs erected by neighboring states—including democratic Czechoslovakia. These factors combined with high unemployment after 1923 lent credence to the consensus view of nonviability, undermining both the will to develop the country's resources and the legitimacy of the new order.[31] Handicapped by a permanent identity crisis, the First Austrian Republic found it daunting, if not impossible, to develop a representative system commanding popular allegiance.[32]

While a majority of Austrians openly yearned for Anschluss with the Weimar Republic, few of them thought of themselves as Germans in the radical sense propounded by Schönerer and his followers. In October 1919, for example, seventeen nationalist parties combined in the Greater German People's Party (GDVP), a movement strongly influenced by Schönerer's Pan-German ideas. Despite vigorous agitation, the party never garnered more than 17 percent of the vote in electoral contests between 1919 and 1933, attracting primarily, students, teachers, and civil servants—the same groups that had flocked to the German messiah years before. As for those composing the remaining four-fifths of the population, they divided their loyalties between the Social Democrats and Christian Socials, two ideologically driven movements dedicated to conflicting worldviews every bit as uncompromising as those of the German Nationalists. In the aggregate, the three political parties constituted warring "camps" (*Lager*), movements that placed allegiance to respective subcultures above allegiance to the state.[33]

The history of the First Republic was a turbulent one, a stormy experience that deeply divided and demoralized the Austrian people.[34] Between 1920 and 1932 the country was governed by various bourgeois coalitions of Christian Socials in league with the Greater Germans or the Peasant League. Although the Social Democrats never assumed the seals of office, they dominated Vienna where they dispensed patronage and launched an ambitious program of low-cost housing construction and municipal services resulting in perhaps the most successful socialist experiment ever undertaken in Europe.[35] The Social Democrats remained confident of someday winning the absolute majority of votes needed to bring them to power, a projection based on rising success at the polls. This was a prospect, needless to say, that alarmed the governing parties. While the Christian Socials were originally committed to the cause of political democracy, they represented a constituency of middle-class elements and farmers undergoing severe economic dislocation or hardship or both. As members of a Catholic party still partially loyal to the Habsburg dynasty, many Christian Socials so feared a Socialist victory that they increasingly threw their support to private armies known as the Heimwehr, formations organized initially as local militias that eventually sought the destruction of the republic.[36]

When the Great Depression arrived in Austria, the impact was calamitous. The collapse of the country's banking system culminating in the spectacular failure of the Viennese Credit-Anstalt on 11 May 1931 both drained the treasury of foreign exchange and gold reserves and triggered an international banking crisis. Within a year the country was bankrupt. Between 1929 and 1932 production fell by 39 percent, foreign trade by 47 percent, and wholesale prices by 17 percent. During the same period unemployment rose to well over a third of the workforce. With Austria on the verge of civil war and the parties hopelessly divided among themselves, little attempt was made to grapple with the crisis, let alone to seek a collective solution.[37]

Yet, it cannot be said that the Austrian people were ready to abandon the democratic system. In elections held on 9 November 1930, only two months after Hitler had achieved a stunning electoral breakthrough in Germany, 90 percent of the Austrian electorate voted for the three establishment parties. Further, the Heimwehr, which had won only eight parliamentary seats, began to disintegrate. In order to stem the extremist tide likely to sweep the country from Germany, there was even serious talk of the Social Democrats and Christian Socials forming a coalition government. In the spring of 1931 both camps put out feelers, but the distrust and cleavages dividing the two subcultures proved too deep-seated to overcome.[38]

Furthermore, the Christian Socials had no intention of relinquishing control of the ship of state, even though they had won only 36 percent of the votes in the elections of 1930. For nearly two years they managed to continue governing in partnership with the Greater Germans, or more precisely with factions of the splintering GDVP. On 24 April 1932 the Austrian Nazi Party scored significant gains in local elections in Vienna, Lower Austria, Styria, Carinthia, and Salzburg, in effect capturing the German Nationalist camp. Instead of resigning or joining forces with the Social Democrats, the Christian Social government of Engelbert Dollfuss, formed on 20 May, turned to the Heimwehr and Fascist Italy for support. With the legislature hopelessly deadlocked, the chancellor increasingly resorted to authoritarian measures, including rule by decree. When the parliament met on 4 March 1933 to deal with the incipient constitutional crisis, Dollfuss prorogued it on a technicality. Thereafter he placed restrictions on the press, dissolved the Constitutional Court, and announced his intention of creating a Christian Corporative state—an improvised dictatorship backed by the army and bureaucracy, the Catholic Church, and Mussolini's Italy.[39]

THE ANSCHLUSS MOVEMENT

Meanwhile, large numbers of Austrians continued to hold out hope for union with Germany—even in the face of Hitler's dramatic rise to power in Berlin. In the immediate postwar period, as we have already seen, there had been an extraordinary outpouring of Anschluss sentiment, a fervor representing more an emotional response to the collapse of the Habsburg monarchy and the Paris peace treaties than a genuine manifestation of German nationalism. For the Social Democrats the prospect of Anschluss meant forging a Socialist order in Central Europe, a Marxist Greater Germany in which the Austrian proletariat would play a prominent role and Vienna would function as an alternate federal capital. For the Christian Socials, on the other hand, there was little enthusiasm for joining a "Red Germany." Once word of the harsh provisions of the Treaty of St. Germain became known in 1919, however, popular outrage was so great that Anschluss agitation spread to the Catholic provinces, where in 1921 over 90 percent of the electorate of Tyrol and Salzburg voted to secede from the Austrian Republic in order to join Germany. This ringing endorsement of the Anschluss by largely Christian Social voters was primarily a protest plebiscite—an expression of both economic despair and resentment of Red Vienna. Thereafter, Allied pressure rendered the entire question moot.[40]

Throughout the next decade the Anschluss movement lost some of its emotional intensity in the political life of both Austria and Germany. Yet on the local level incessant Anschluss propaganda exposed hundreds of thousands of Austrians to the cult of ethnic-German nationalism. Most Austrians regarded national self-determination as a matter of justice and accepted the notion that their country was "nonviable." Admiring German military prowess in the Great War and experiencing a stagnant or declining standard of living, countless individuals responded favorably to lectures, demonstrations, and cultural exchanges. They also applauded symbolic changes such as the adoption in 1926 of a German field-gray army uniform or the coordination of Austro-German railroad regulations and probate law. After 1918, German nationalism "captured broad segments of the Austrian population, not only rightist nationalists, but also liberal, democratic circles, which were traditionally devoted to the concept of German national unity, and also Social Democrats, who had spearheaded the Anschluss movement in the immediate postwar period."[41]

The spread of the Great Depression to Austria generated a powerful surge of Anschluss sentiment. Given the country's dependence on foreign trade and foreign loans, the crash had a particularly devastating impact on tourism and the outmoded manufacturing sector. In early 1931 the Austrian and German governments tried to negotiate a customs union in the desperate hope of stimulating the economy and containing radicalism in both countries. When the project became known on 21 March, the French government withdrew its assets from the Viennese Credit-Anstalt, both ruining Austria's financial system and, as we have already seen, precipitating an international banking crisis. The humiliating failure of the plan discredited the democratic Anschluss cause in both Vienna and Berlin, leaving the field almost uncontested to Hitler's National Socialists.[42]

THE NAZI TEMPTATION

That the Nazis would emerge as the chief torchbearers of the Anschluss movement in Austria was not without irony: despite a strong start in the monarchy, Hitler's movement had scarcely shaped or even touched the political contours of the First Republic. Before 1931 it was an obscure fringe group, rent by feuding and division. In 1928 there were only 4,446 members. Even after Hitler's spectacular electoral breakthrough in Germany, his followers in Austria could win no more than 110,638 votes in the parliamentary elections of 9 November 1930, 3 percent of the total.[43]

Even so, the brown flood soon began rising in the Danube and its tributaries. In May 1931 the Nazis captured 9.1 percent of the vote in municipal elections in Eisenstadt and 25.9 percent in Klagenfurt. Shortly thereafter, the Austrian NSDAP made a "real breakthrough."[44] On 24 April 1932 it garnered over 16 percent of votes cast in provincial elections in Vienna, Lower Austria, and Salzburg and in communal balloting in Styria and Carinthia. A year later—three months after Hitler's "seizure of power" in Germany—it won a spectacular 41 percent of the municipal vote in Innsbruck, an outcome almost equal to the 43.9 percent won by the German party in the Reichstag elections of 5 March 1933. At the grass-roots level, according to the police, the National Socialists were still unable to win over or penetrate the Catholic subculture in the provinces, especially Tyrol, but were otherwise making "astonishing" progress capturing the hearts and minds of the general population, particularly in Carinthia and Styria.[45]

Nevertheless, the Nazi momentum did not extend much beyond the German Nationalist *Lager*. For that reason it is unlikely that the Austrian party could have built the sort of mass base to equal Hitler's stunning electoral triumphs in Germany or to assume power in the Ballhausplatz. In Vienna the Nazis did capture one-fifth of their total vote from the Christian Socials and approximately 8 percent from the Social Democrats; in Salzburg and other provincial towns they attracted roughly one-fifth of traditional Social Democratic voters.[46] "In a curiously delayed fashion," Bruce Pauley has noted, "the Nazi vote in Austria nearly duplicated that in Germany."[47]

Still, while the Austrian Nazis attracted a socially heterogeneous following, even mobilizing about a fifth of traditional nonvoters, they confronted a political environment fundamentally different from that of the Reich. Perhaps the most distinctive feature of Austrian political topography was the sharp contrast between the civic affairs of metropolitan Vienna and the rural provinces. Unlike Germany there were few middle-size cities, the sort of urban milieu that provided fruitful recruiting grounds for Nazi voters. This meant that the relatively self-contained worlds of Red Vienna and the Christian Social countryside remained generally impervious to Nazi penetration. In the first instance, the Social Democratic organization retained the loyalty of most of the working-class population; in the second, the Catholic Church with its politically active priesthood still wielded tremendous influence among the farming populace.[48] The fact that three-fourths of the Austrian electorate continued to place a subcultural allegiance above loyalty to their country provided an ironic but effective barrier against the spread of Nazi ideology. Put another way, Austria's unresolved identity crisis unwittingly helped preserve the state that nobody wanted and that the Nazis vowed to destroy.

On the other hand, Hitler's consolidation of power in Berlin accompanied by regional electoral breakthroughs in Austria certainly conveyed the *impression* of an imminent Nazi takeover. When Dollfuss suspended the Austrian parliament on 4 March 1933, the National Socialists responded by demanding national elections and unleashing a wave of terrorist bombings. On 26 May Hitler imposed a 1,000-mark fee on German tourists visiting Austria, hoping through economic pressure to overthrow the Austrian government and force new elections, the outcome of which, he calculated, would lead to amalgamation with the Reich. Two weeks later Dollfuss outlawed the NSDAP. He felt that he had no other choice, but he yearned for a modus vivendi with elements of the Nazi movement.[49] Like Kurt von Schleicher and Franz von Papen in Germany, he hoped to throttle the radicals within Hitler's fold while enlisting the support of those he considered moderate. Like Schleicher (and nearly Papen) he would find the ploy both wrongheaded and fatal.

Shortly after dissolving the National Assembly in 1933, Dollfuss announced his intention of establishing a "social, Christian, German state of Austria on the basis of estates and under a strong authoritarian leadership."[50] Although his Christian Corporative regime turned out to be little more than a throwback to the bureaucratic absolutism of the nineteenth century, it provided a new twist by dramatically affirming the viability of the Austrian state and appealing to traditional patriotic sentiment for support. At the same time, Dollfuss also stressed the Teutonic character of his regime. This was both an expression of firm conviction and a rationalization of the embarrassing patronage of Fascist Italy, the nation commonly regarded as Austria's "hereditary enemy." In many ways, Dollfuss embodied the ambiguities and split-mindedness of Austrian sentiment in the interwar period.[51]

Given his dependence upon both the Heimwehr and Mussolini, it is hardly surprising that Dollfuss regarded the Social Democrats as more dangerous opponents than the National Socialists. In February 1934, under intense pressure from Mussolini, he unwittingly precipitated a bloodbath when workers in Linz took up arms to resist months of unlawful, arbitrary measures aimed at crushing the labor movement. After four days of savage fighting in the industrial centers of the country, nearly 200 civilians lay dead. Thereafter, ten "ringleaders" were sent to the gallows, several hundred others were imprisoned, and thousands of participants were dismissed from their jobs. Compared with most civil wars, the February clash had been mild, even relatively bloodless. Nonetheless, it left a legacy of bitter hatred that would persist for decades and discredit the cause of Austrian patriotism preached by the Christian Corporative regime.[52]

Before the outbreak of armed conflict, Dollfuss had tried to shore up his position by enrolling the populace in a mass party called the Patriotic Front. His government, however, clearly represented the "dictatorship of one camp over the other two camps."[53] It enjoyed the support of the army, the bureaucracy, and the Catholic Church. It could also rely on the rural masses, various Habsburg loyalists, and most of Vienna's large Jewish population. Nevertheless, the regime required foreign backing to survive. To this end Dollfuss negotiated an alliance with Italy and Hungary. He also sought to reach a settlement with the Reich, even putting out feelers to the German Nationalist wing of the underground Austrian Nazi Party.[54] Hitler's Alpine followers reacted, however, with scorn. On 25 July 1934, 154 Nazis stormed the Chancellor's Office in Vienna and, in a bungled attempt to seize power, gunned down Dollfuss. The conspirators surrendered at the end of a long hot afternoon, but their revolt spread to Styria, Carinthia, Tyrol, Salzburg, and parts of Upper Austria. In contrast to the February fighting, the Nazi uprising was both more widespread and less intense. In only a few days it was put down by well-trained units of the Austrian army.[55]

SCHUSCHNIGG AND THE ANSCHLUSS

Reaction to the aborted coup, especially to the shooting of Dollfuss, who in his death agony had been denied both a doctor and a priest, was one of near universal horror and condemnation, both foreign and domestic. In a dramatic show of force Mussolini even rushed troops to the Brenner frontier to demonstrate his support for Austrian independence against German aggression. The Duce's move so unnerved Hitler that he beat a quick retreat, cutting nearly all ties to his Austrian paladins, appointing the conservative Franz von Papen ambassador to Vienna, and postponing the Anschluss indefinitely. As for the Christian Corporative regime, it emerged from the twin civil wars of 1934 in a much stronger position with a real opportunity to consolidate its control and through magnanimous, conciliatory measures to win the general population to its cause. Under the leadership of the new chancellor, Kurt von Schuschnigg, this was a road not taken.[56]

Unlike Dollfuss, the new chancellor was a political bureaucrat, a decent but myopic man who lacked the common touch and saw little need to broaden his own narrow political base. He was also a zealous Catholic, but to a much greater degree than his fallen predecessor he regarded German identity as an essential component of the Christian Corporative order. Dreading an Austro-German conflict, he tended to be more receptive to Nazi deceit than might otherwise have been the case.[57]

So long as Schuschnigg could depend on Italian support, he managed to govern Austria with a degree of administrative aplomb. But with Mussolini's shift to Hitler at the end of the Ethiopian War in May 1936, Schuschnigg found himself alone confronting both a sullen population and renewed German pressure. In almost every respect his country's international position was much more precarious than it had been before. Whether Schuschnigg might have done more to strengthen Austrian independence through imaginative diplomacy or the extension of an olive branch to his domestic opponents must forever remain an open question. The latest research suggests that he might have done more to shore up Austria's position.[58] Instead, he sought a settlement with Nazi Germany.[59]

On 11 July 1936 Schuschnigg signed a gentlemen's agreement with Reich ambassador Papen. According to it, Berlin recognized Vienna's independence and agreed to lift all economic sanctions in exchange for an understanding that Austria would conduct its foreign policy as a "German state."

There was also a secret clause providing amnesty for imprisoned Austrian Nazis and the granting of cabinet portfolios to members of the National Opposition, a coalition of pro-Nazi Catholics and German Nationalists.[60]

Although Schuschnigg thought that the July Agreement temporarily stabilized his position, its effect was quite the opposite: the pact gave quasi-official status to a terrorist organization that the Austrian government had brought under control only with great difficulty, thus enabling the Nazis to conduct operations both legally and illegally at the same time. In the months that followed, Schuschnigg made some attempt to widen his domestic support, for example, by promoting a growing monarchist movement, but in the face of escalating Nazi agitation, he refused to move to the left. Abandoned by Italy on the diplomatic stage, he issued only halfhearted appeals to the West and to the Little Entente.[61]

By November 1937 Austria was completely isolated, a fact that did not go unnoticed in Berlin. On the fifth of that month Hitler met with his generals to discuss his strategy for military expansion, a scheme that included the seizure of both Czechoslovakia and Austria. Although the Nazi dictator had paid relatively little attention to his homeland in the sixteen months since the July Agreement, he was thoroughly pleased by the progress of his "evolutionary" course. He intended to get control of the country, much as he had in Germany, through a cabinet coup on the part of the National Opposition. On 12 February 1938 he summoned Schuschnigg to Berchtesgaden and, in the course of a stormy meeting, browbeat the Austrian chancellor to accept terms that included the appointment of the Viennese Nazi lawyer, Arthur Seyss Inquart, as minister of the interior. On 9 March Schuschnigg tried to pull his chestnuts out of the fire by calling a plebiscite on the question of Austrian independence, even agreeing to make peace with the underground Socialists. But it was too late. Unwilling to tolerate a further postponement of the Anschluss, Hitler gave Austrian Nazis the signal for a domestic uprising and, after some additional confusion, on 11 March ordered German forces to invade Austria at dawn the next day.[62]

ECONOMIC TRENDS AND REALITIES

Of the many problems afflicting the Austrian people in the interwar period, recurring economic crises were the most wrenching. In the hectic years following the collapse of the monarchy there were acute shortages of food and fuel, hyperinflation, and a draconian stabilization of the currency that in 1923 led to the dismissal of 85,000 civil servants and public employees. By 1929 industrial production stood at only 95 percent of the prewar level and a mere 80 percent of overall capacity.[63]

The world economic crisis ruined the Austrian banking system, left a third of the working population without jobs, and led indirectly to the destruction of both organized labor and the democratic republic. The Depression also produced a level of unemployment that was higher and more persistent than in most other European countries. By 1934, 44.5 percent of all Austrian industrial workers had been laid off and 34.8 percent in all nonagricultural vocations. Regionally, the slump had its greatest impact in Vienna, in older industrial cities such as Wiener Neustadt and Steyr, and in a whole string of textile, mining, and steel communities in the deep valleys of Styria. In some factory towns of Carinthia and Salzburg the entire population was unemployed.[64]

By contrast, the agricultural sector declined only 2 percent between 1929 and 1933. Nevertheless, the farming population hardly escaped the ravages of the Depression. While food prices remained high, to the detriment of all but the wealthiest producers, there was a sharp decline of income on the land, especially among already impoverished Alpine farmers, herdsmen, and loggers. The result was massive indebtedness, followed by a profusion of foreclosures. Between 1933 and 1937, in fact, 71,135 holdings fell under the auctioneer's hammer—16.7 percent of all Austrian farmland.[65]

In tackling the economic crisis the Dollfuss-Schuschnigg dictatorship pursued harsh deflationary policies designed to balance the budget and stabilize the currency. The government's program featured severe spending cuts, high interest rates, and frozen wages. From an orthodox economic point of view there was considerable success: by 1937, both industrial and agricultural production had surpassed the levels of 1929; trade was more favorably balanced; the National Bank had liquidated most of its foreign debt and even accumulated substantial reserves of gold and foreign exchange.[66] In a sense, the Christian Corporative regime demonstrated the viability of the Austrian state, but it did so at the cost of alienating a majority of the Austrian people. On the eve of Anschluss a third of the population was still out of work, while those fortunate enough to have jobs were bringing home paychecks considerably smaller than before the Great War.[67] No one could deny that the tourist trade was recovering or that orders for heavy industrial goods were accelerating. Still, the price of foodstuffs remained high and consumer production showed no signs of emerging from stagnation. Further, it was all too clear that the economic upswing of 1937 was closely tied to both the July Agreement and the rearmament boom in Germany, a development that, although promising, could hardly be credited to the Schuschnigg government.[68]

Throughout most of the interwar period Austria bore a striking resemblance to Bavaria, a land with which it shared both a common border and a similar culture and heritage. Geographically smaller and more diverse, the Alpine republic (in 1934) contained 6,760,233 inhabitants, while its neighbor (in 1933) had 7,681,584. Excluding Vienna, both lands were divided into eight administrative districts, both were predominately Roman Catholic (90.5 and 62.7 percent respectively), and both were largely agrarian in nature. While it is true that Vienna with its population of 1.9 million gave Austria a distinctive character and cosmopolitan reputation, most of the country, including entire provinces, was rural or heavily forested. Outside the metropolis, there were only two cities with a population of over 100,000: Graz with 152,841 inhabitants and Linz with 108,970; these two provincial capitals had little industry other than small-scale, nonmechanized enterprises. There were also eight towns of between 20,000 and 60,000 inhabitants and nineteen of between 10,000 and 20,000. Of these, Salzburg (63,231), Innsbruck (61,005), and Klagenfurt (29,671) were provincial capitals, Wiener Neustadt (36,768) and Steyr (22,208) modest industrial hubs, and the rest small towns, market centers, or, in the case of Donawitz in Styria or Hallein in the province of Salzburg, gritty steel or mining communities. Including Vienna, in other words, only a third of the Austrian people (35.9 percent) lived in cities of more than 20,000 inhabitants, a proportion roughly comparable with that of Bavaria (30.5 percent).[69]

At first glance, the economic structure of both Austria and Bavaria in the 1930s appears to have been well balanced with an even distribution of jobs into primary, secondary, and tertiary sectors (Table 1). Closer scrutiny reveals, however, two very traditional societies dominated, for the most part, by agriculture and small-scale manufacturing. In the case of Austria, 1,003,961 persons normally made their living in agriculture and forestry, 1,100,441 in industry and crafts, and 1,065,870 in the service sector.[70] Apart from Vienna, however, every province was predominately rural, even Styria with its heavy industry in the Iron Mountain region and its medium-size capital, Graz. Further, because of Austria's legacy of empire, the number of government bureaucrats, state pensioners, and nondependents without occupation was abnormally high.[71] Even within the realm of commerce, the position of the tourist trade meant that private and domestic service was overrepresented.

Industrial manufacturing, as mentioned earlier, was particularly hard hit by the Depression. Nearly two-thirds of all jobs lost were in the industrial sector. Of those persons normally working in industry and crafts (including

TABLE 1. *Population Distribution into Main Economic Sectors*

Economic Sector	Bavaria 1933		Austria 1934	
	N	%	N	%
Agriculture and forestry	2,419,352	31.5	1,842,450	27.2
Industry and crafts	2,582,116	33.6	2,100,461	31.1
Trade and commerce	1,024,449	13.3	1,019,034	15.1
Public and private services	533,128	6.9	452,779	6.7
Domestic service	151,604	2.0	193,375	2.9
Nondependents without occupation	970,935	12.7	1,152,134	17.0
Total	7,681,584	100.0	6,760,233	100.0

Sources: Kershaw, *Popular Opinion*, 12; *Statistisches Handbuch für die Republik Österreich* (1936), 16:11.

the unemployed), 264,359 (25 percent) had positions in clothing or textile firms, 217,252 (21 percent) in iron or metalworking enterprises, 163,888 (16 percent) in construction trades, and 131,658 (13 percent) in food-processing plants. Only 33,262 (3 percent) were employed in modern chemical industries, a mere 10,634 (1 percent) in electrotechnical firms.[72]

The major characteristic of Austria's industrial structure in 1934 was, therefore, traditional small-scale manufacturing and consumer goods production. Like Bavaria before Hitler's rise to power, the country was—to borrow Kershaw's language—"very much the land of small industry, characterized by workshops run by independent craftsmen and their assistants and by branches such as textiles, clothing, [and] food production."[73] By 1938, there had been no structural changes, despite a trend favoring raw materials and finished goods for export. With the consumer industry still mired in recession, a large proportion of the unemployed thus comprised well-trained, highly skilled workers, a group resentful, alienated, and yearning to go back to work.

Much the same thing could be said of the Austrian people as a whole. Throughout the Depression or, for that matter, throughout most of the entire interwar period they had every reason to feel discouraged and demoralized. The severe dislocations caused by military defeat, civic strife, and economic hard times made it difficult, if not impossible, to lead a normal life. Despite a decline in infant mortality, the number of live births rose by only a few thousand. There was something approaching an epidemic of tuberculosis and other infectious diseases. There were also exceptionally large numbers of suicides.[74] Before 1934, Austrians could find solace, even hope, within their respective "camps."[75] After the twin civil wars of that year, however, they confronted a regime that had done away with democracy, shot civilians in the street, and demanded emotional loyalty to an authoritarian system that, however moderate in practice, a majority of them despised and rejected. Even government supporters exhibited considerable division and little optimism.

By all accounts, popular attitudes hardened noticeably under Schuschnigg's chancellorship.[76] Although government encouragement of a Habsburg restoration movement briefly raised spirits among groups of peasants, civil servants, retired officers, and middle-aged women, especially in Tyrol, the effort failed to attract mass support. As early as 1935 the police were reporting the spread of hopelessness and despair within the farming population, the social group that had supported Dollfuss with the most spontaneity and enthusiasm. From Carinthia came word of great "distress," from Vorarlberg of "ever growing impoverishment in the mountain districts." The following year the security director in Upper Austria wrote that the mood of the local population was "indifferent," primarily because of the "dissatisfaction of the peasants with insufficient sales and low prices and of the workers with continuing unemployment."[77] Nevertheless, most farmers and peasants remained generally loyal to the regime. This was made clear by outpourings of genuine support for Schuschnigg in 1938. At the same time, there were exceptions: destitute mountain farmers and most of the rural population of Carinthia and Styria, two border provinces with a long tradition of anticlericalism and ethnic-German solidarity against outsiders, intensified since 1918–19 when embattled farmers had taken up arms against marauding Yugoslavs. Here entire regions openly expressed sympathy with the National Socialists, a sentiment that was increasingly reinforced by glowing reports from local boys who had gone to Germany as migrant workers.[78]

Not surprisingly, it was among the small-town and urban populace that bitterness and resentment of the Dollfuss-Schuschnigg dictatorship became most intense. We have already seen that most of the German Nationalist camp went over to Hitler before 1934 and that in Vienna at least a fifth of the Christian Social electorate switched to Nazi candidates in 1932. That the Viennese outcome was not simply an aberration or protest vote was evident in the subsequent emergence of a strong pro-Nazi Catholic bloc under Seyss-Inquart. To what extent other social groups were willing to throw their support to the National Socialists between 1933 and 1938 will never be completely known. Careful reconstruction of the underground party's profile by Gerhard Botz reveals a movement of middle-class activists, primarily from the professional and bureaucratic strata of society, who appealed to the young of all classes, especially students; mobilized some rural support, particularly in anticlerical bastions like Carinthia, the Salzkammergut, and the Enns Valley; and made greater inroads into the industrial working class than is commonly thought.[79]

After the February civil war the Austro-Marxist labor movement had gone underground.[80] For the Nazis the defeated Socialists constituted an enormous target group of 40 percent of the Austrian people. Once the guns fell silent in February 1934, Hitler's followers quickly stepped forward to defend February fighters in court, to provide aid in common detention centers, and, in one spectacular case, to spirit the Upper Austrian militia commander, Richard Bernaschek, and two of his aids to Germany. Relying on anti-Catholic and anti-Semitic arguments, Nazi propaganda claimed that the Social Democrats had been betrayed by pusillanimous Jewish leaders in Vienna and that only by supporting the NSDAP could the hated Christian Corporative regime be destroyed. To what degree blue-collar workers responded to such appeals is difficult to say. But it does appear that roughly a third of those in the provinces were willing to cast their lot with the National Socialists as well as a smaller proportion in Vienna, where entire units of February fighters, for example, in Ottakring, actually joined the SA.[81]

By 1938, then, millions of Austrians had grown weary of the Christian Corporative system, an authoritarian regime most of them had never supported in the first place. Driven by hatred and economic despair, they looked longingly toward Germany where Hitler's government was generating jobs, confidence, and an affluence that was spreading rapidly among all classes of an increasingly classless society. This is not to say that free parliamentary elections would have produced a landslide victory or even a plurality for the Nazi cause. Despite defections, subcultural loyalties remained firm, the opposition of Socialist and Catholic elites implacable. Furthermore, the Austrian NSDAP was still riven by so many internal rivalries, conflicts, and divisions that it is difficult to see how the party could have mounted an effective electoral campaign. That Hitler eventually chose the military option was, in part, to restore order among his homeland followers.[82]

And yet, while it is unlikely that Austrians would have given Nazi candidates sufficient support to bring them to power under democratic or even semidemocratic conditions, there can be no doubt that most of the populace looked favorably on a merger with Germany, even under Hitler's leadership. It is true, of course, that in 1933 both Socialist and Catholic "camps" had discarded the Anschluss planks in their respective platforms. It is also certain that the leaders of both *Lager* were ideologically opposed to Nazism, even willing to fight against it in the streets. Nevertheless, Social Democratic elites still believed in union with the Reich as essential to their Marxist fantasy of an all-German revolution, while the Christian Socials regarded themselves as part of a Catholic Germany dating from the Middle Ages. In contrast, the Christian Corporative system tried to foster a new sense of Austrian patriotism, but the regime's shortcomings and failures discredited both it and the cause of traditional patriotism. Paradoxically, only the Communists gave serious thought to Austria as a distinctive nation-state, but they were a marginal fringe group without influence or power.[83]

The available evidence, although anecdotal and impressionistic, indicates that by 1938 most Austrians were seeking dramatic political change. Impelled by economic misery, disdain for the existing political system, and growing awe of the German Reich, a significant number saw amalgamation as the only way out of their misery.[84] Within the welter of confusing, multifaceted, and oscillating attitudes, however, there was no consensual commitment to the ideological tenets of National Socialism. At the very most, no more than a third of the Austrian people had become true believers. Schuschnigg's estimate of two-thirds support for his plebiscite on Austrian independence was, therefore, probably correct: once Socialist and Catholic elites approved the referendum, they could be counted on to deliver the votes. Conversely, when the plebiscite was canceled and the Anschluss actually took place, the issue of Austrian identity seemed settled forever. This helps to explain why there occurred such an astonishing outpouring of euphoria and support for the new Greater Germany, meaning a mighty union of Germanic peoples under the leadership of Adolf Hitler, himself an Austrian.[85]

THE ANTI-SEMITIC CONSENSUS

The enormous crowds that would welcome the German invasion also represented the collective endorsement, even by individuals and groups otherwise opposed to National Socialism, of specific aspects of Hitler's program, most notably his promise to settle accounts with the Jews. In contrast to Germany where large numbers of individuals disapproved or ignored Nazi anti-Semitic restrictions, a majority of Austrians stood ready to carry them out. "With the very important exception of the Anschluss question," Bruce Pauley has written, "it is doubtful whether any other single issue in Austria, even the hated Treaty of St. Germain, appealed to so large a cross-section of the Austrian population as anti-Semitism."[86]

Judeophobia was deeply rooted in the Austrian psyche. Ever since the Middle Ages there had been waves of persecution and expulsions, more often than not encouraged by the church. During the eighteenth century Joseph II's famous Patent of Toleration had suspended medieval restrictions on Jews, but it was not until the reign of Francis Joseph (1848–1916) that legal discrimination was abolished altogether. Between 1857 and 1910 the numbers of Jews living in Vienna increased dramatically to 8.63 percent of the municipal population. Almost from the beginning, ordinary people, especially small businessmen and artisans, reacted with envy and resentment to the astonishing economic and cultural success of the new immigrants, who by 1910 constituted "71 percent of Vienna's financiers, 63 percent of its industrialists, 65 percent of its lawyers, 59 percent of its physicians, and over half of its journalists."[87] The new anti-Semitic rage that began in Vienna and spread rapidly through German-speaking Austria was exploited by well-known Jew baiters such as Schönerer and the Viennese political boss, Karl Lueger. It was also blessed by the Roman Catholic hierarchy and given dangerous intellectual prestige by Social Darwinian apostles of "scientific racism." Nevertheless, following two decades of vicious abuse, anti-Semitism started to fade around 1900 and by the outbreak of the Great War appeared to be in remission.[88]

This was a deceptive trend. During the war the influx of tens of thousands of impoverished Jewish refugees from Galicia and Bukovina exacerbated already acute shortages of food, housing, and fuel. When the monarchy collapsed in 1918, it was accompanied by an eruption of anti-Semitic incidents that grew exponentially with the democratization of Austrian politics and continued well into the 1920s. The newspapers were filled with accounts of physical attacks, brawls, and even murders, for example, in 1925 of the Jewish writer Hugo Bettauer. Between 1926 and 1930 incidents of anti-Semitic violence receded and virtually disappeared. But with the advent of the Great Depression the political parties and media resumed a drumfire of abuse, calling for discriminatory legislation and holding the Jews accountable for a bewildering variety of political, economic, and social ills. The charges were diffuse and multifarious, of course, but the most common one held that 6 million German-Austrians were being held hostage by a tiny minority of an alien race. That even the respectable Catholic *Reichspost* purveyed such views provides substantial evidence that virulent Judeophobia was by no means confined to the lunatic fringe. Indeed, as Pauley soberly notes, the Nazis differed from the other parties "only in their willingness to use violence against Jews."[89]

Under the Dollfuss-Schuschnigg regime the Jewish community recovered a measure of governmental protection it had not enjoyed since the days of the Habsburgs. The public was outraged, despite the fact that the government kept mild discriminatory laws on the books. One of the most frequent charges leveled against the Christian Corporative system was that it was in

2

THE AUSTRIANS AND
THE ANSCHLUSS

Those familiar with the story of the Anschluss know that it was a complicated affair. So much has been written about it that little can be added here.[1] After Hitler's tempestuous meeting with Schuschnigg at Berchtesgaden on 12 February 1938, events unfolded much more rapidly than anyone anticipated. Schuschnigg did little to improve Austria's international position or to shore up his domestic following. On 24 February he delivered a speech in parliament that appealed to large crowds of patriotic supporters, but aside from granting an amnesty to imprisoned Socialists and Communists, offered little else. Simultaneously, Nazi demonstrations erupted in the provinces. On 18 February there was an enormous celebration in Linz as "Storm Troops in full uniform marched through the streets and drove in lorries with huge Swastika flags."[2] The following day members of the National Socialist Soldiers' Ring staged a raucous parade in Graz. In both instances, the police looked on in silence.

Within a week Graz was in Nazi hands. A British correspondent reported that an outsider "would imagine he has entered a German Nazi city. The majority of the people in the streets this afternoon wore the Swastika emblem, some of them just metal Swastika badges, others the official German party sign. Young boys greeted each other with the Hitler greeting and some of them were singing the Horst Wessel song."[3] On 1 March, Arthur Seyss-Inquart, Schuschnigg's pro-Nazi minister of the interior, traveled to Graz on the pretense of reasserting governmental control. After perfunctory negotiations with local officials, he reviewed a torchlight parade from the apartment of a prominent Styrian Nazi. "A deafening roar of triumph rose up from the marchers and the dense crowd of onlookers," another British correspondent recorded.[4]

Seyss-Inquart fancied he was stage-managing the creation of a Catholic-Nazi Austria.[5] What he failed to grasp was that neither he nor Hubert Klausner, the head of the underground NSDAP, could contain the spreading brownshirt revolt. As for Schuschnigg, he abruptly announced a snap plebiscite to be held within four days. On Sunday, 13 March, all Austrians over the age of twenty-four were asked to vote "in favor of a free and German, an independent and social, a Christian and united Austria."

In Berlin Hitler was taken completely by surprise. The following day he huddled with party officials, diplomats, and generals. After considerable discussion and debate, he ordered the mobilization of the Eighth Army in Bavaria, gave the Austrian Nazi Party complete "freedom of action," and told Seyss-Inquart to convince Schuschnigg to call off the plebiscite. Early Friday afternoon the Austrian chancellor gave way. At 3:05 P.M. there was a long-distance call from Göring demanding Schuschnigg's immediate resignation and replacement by Seyss-Inquart. The weary chancellor concurred, but federal president Wilhelm Miklas refused to accept his letter of resignation.[6]

Elsewhere storm troop formations were on the march. With Styria and Carinthia already constituting a "Nazi republic," Hitler's followers seized public buildings and railroad stations in Innsbruck, Linz, Salzburg, Graz, and Klagenfurt. By suppertime most of the country was in their hands. At 7:47 P.M. Schuschnigg went on the radio to announce that he was stepping down, "resolved not to spill German blood." Almost immediately the streets of Vienna filled with brownshirts and crowds. Seyss-Inquart then telephoned Göring to report that although the Nazis were taking charge, Miklas still refused to appoint him chancellor. This provided the pretext for Göring—the driving force in Berlin—to argue for German intervention. After thirty minutes of intense discussion, he persuaded Hitler to sign a directive ordering the Eighth Army to cross the Bavarian frontier at dawn. He also arranged for Vienna to send a telegram under the guise of legality imploring Berlin "to restore order." Facing a real invasion Miklas at last gave way; shortly before midnight he entrusted Seyss-Inquart with the seals of office.[7]

Once in power, the Austrian Nazis tried to stop German troops from marching into the country and appealed to both the Reich Chancellery and the Armed Forces High Command to call a halt to the invasion. Even General Wolfgang Muff, Hitler's military attaché in Vienna, agreed.[8] But Hitler had made one of his "unshakable decisions." Not only did he think it "immoral to allow such a [magnificent] army to stand idle";[9] he also considered the bungling Austrian Nazis undependable.[10] What he did not take into account was the tumultuous welcome he would receive from the Austrian people, an outburst of frenzied acclamation seldom seen since the days of the Caesars.

Early Saturday morning Hitler flew from Berlin to the headquarters of the Eighth Army in Munich. His coup de main was unfolding in three stages: a pseudorevolutionary uprising from below, a semilegal transfer of power from above, and a powerful military invasion from outside. In all phases it was his word that had been decisive.[11] What ordinary Austrians (and Germans) made of these events can be gauged from a variety of sources—the testimony of eyewitnesses, memoirs, newsreels, photographs, after-action reports of the invading Wehrmacht. Still, Carl Zuckmayer, the distinguished German playwright forced to flee Hitler for a second time, left behind words of caution: "What it was like in reality (or rather, in the lived dreams which we want to call reality), how it actually happened—this is something that only those who went through it can possibly know."[12]

By the time Hitler touched down at Oberwiesenfeld air base, the Nazi uprising had been under way for nearly twenty-four hours, in some provinces for days, in Styria for weeks. Vienna was the last "bastion" to fall, but it was here that the masses commanded the streets in revolutionary numbers. The previous afternoon huge crowds began to converge on the inner city, gathering on the Graben, at St. Stephen's Cathedral, and before the State Opera. By sunset they were packing municipal squares, choking off traffic and shouting "One People, One Reich, One Leader, One Victory!"[13]

As news of the cancellation of Schuschnigg's plebiscite spread, the American journalist William L. Shirer ran into a "hysterical mob" gathered outside St. Charles Church, the baroque basilica dedicated to the memory of St. Charles Borromeo, the seventeenth-century scourge of heretics and unbelievers. "Crowds moving about all the way," the newsman scribbled. "Singing now. Singing Nazi songs. A few policemen standing around good naturedly."[14] He accompanied the throng into the fashionable Kärntnerstrasse to see "young toughs heaving paving blocks into the windows of Jewish shops."[15] Astonished by the roaring approval of the crowd, he later wrote, "The Brownshirts at Nuremberg had never bellowed the Nazi slogans with such mania."[16]

Elsewhere, in the plaza between St. Stephen's Cathedral and the Kärntnerstrasse, another correspondent, G. E. R. Gedye, pushed his way through swarms of storm troopers, boys "barely out of the school room marching side by side with police turncoats," accompanied by a "stream of humanity . . . hooting furiously, trying to make themselves heard above the din, men and women leaping, shouting and dancing in the light of the smoking torches which soon began to make their appearance, the air filled with a pandemonium of sound in which intermingled screams of 'Down with the

Jews! Heil Hitler! Sieg Heil! Perish the Jews! Hang Schuschnigg! Heil Seyss-Inquart! Down with the Catholics! Ein Volk, ein Reich, ein Führer.'"[17]

The Nazi brawlers—tens of thousands of them—fanned out into Jewish neighborhoods, looting shops and beating hapless passersby. Their savage revelry continued until long after midnight. Carl Zuckmayer recorded:

> That night hell broke loose. The underworld opened its gates and vomited forth the lowest, filthiest, most horrible demons it contained. The city was transformed into a nightmare painting by Hieronymous Bosch: phantoms and devils seemed to have crawled out of sewers and swamps. The air was filled with an incessant screeching, horrible, piercing, hysterical cries from the throats of men and women who continued screaming day and night. People's faces vanished, were replaced by contorted masks, some of fear, some of cunning, some of wild, hate-filled triumph.[18]

Reflecting on his experience in the Great War and the Weimar Republic, he continued:

> What was unleashed upon Vienna had nothing to do with the seizure of power in Germany, which proceeded under the guise of legality and was met by parts of the population with alienation, scepticism, or an unsuspecting nationalistic idealism. What was unleashed in Vienna was a torrent of envy, jealousy, bitterness, blind, malignant craving for revenge.[19]

At dawn, motorized units of the German Eighth Army converged on the Austro-Bavarian frontier, seizing bridgeheads and border posts at Lindau, Mittenwald, Kiefersfelden, Freilassing, Burghausen, and Schärding. Trimmed with swastika banners and spring foliage, the reconnaissance vehicles and motorcycles sped past gathering crowds of cheering onlookers. Behind them came the infantry, proceeding not in battle formation but with flags and martial music.[20] Along the roads enormous crowds of Austrians pelted the soldiers with flowers. An astonished staff officer reported that "German troops haven't been welcomed so warmly since the triumphal procession following Bismarck's founding of the Reich. It is simply impossible to describe what is happening along the route of march."[21] At 11 A.M. another officer recorded that "people have walked off their jobs to greet the German soldiers with incredible enthusiasm."[22] Shortly before noon General Heinz Guderian's Second Panzer Division reached Linz. "The flags and decorations on the tanks proved highly successful," he later wrote. "The populace saw that we came as friends, and we were everywhere joyfully received."[23]

As Guderian's tankers prepared to resume the advance toward St. Pölten,

Himmler, Seyss-Inquart, and Glaise-Horstenau showed up. They informed Guderian that Hitler was scheduled to arrive in Linz within three hours. It was not, however, until 3:50 P.M. that the Führer crossed the Inn River at Braunau. The streets were so choked by cheering crowds that Hitler's chauffeur had to downshift his three-axle, cross-country, open Mercedes to avoid injuring the well-wishers. To the tune of peeling bells and thunderous applause the motorcade proceeded to Linz, arriving at 7:30 P.M. When Hitler stepped onto the Rathaus balcony to address the throng, between 60,000 and 80,000 Austrians roared their approval.[24]

As the Eighth Army's most important goals were to secure the Italian and Czech frontiers, its columns moved rapidly toward the Brenner Pass and Vienna. Nearly everywhere the advancing troops were greeted with enthusiasm. Elite mountain rangers tramped into Salzburg to find its towers and churches bedecked with Nazi streamers, provincial pennants, and municipal banners. The narrow passages and spacious squares of the picturesque city, were crammed with "lively crowds," enraptured by "delirious enthusiasm," shouting "euphoric cheers that seemed to never end."[25] Even in Tyrol, well known for its hostility to National Socialism, the overall reaction was one of "boundless popular jubilation";[26] in Kufstein cheering town dwellers welcomed the Sixty-first Regiment with flowers and cigarettes.[27]

Meanwhile, along the main route of advance, Guderian's armored vehicles drove through an evening snowstorm to reach Vienna around midnight. Despite the hour crowds broke into "frantic rejoicing" at the first sight of German armored cars rumbling onto the Ringstrasse. After an improvised parade past the State Opera, "renewed cheering and rejoicing broke out again."[28] The revelers hoisted Guderian to their shoulders, tore "souvenir" buttons from his greatcoat, and carried him to his headquarters. "We were treated with great friendliness," he laconically observed.[29]

The vast crowds welcoming the invading Wehrmacht were not without influence. Hitler had originally envisioned a "personal union" of Germany and Austria, but he was so moved by his hometown reception that the following afternoon, Sunday, 13 March, he signed a law incorporating his native land into the German Reich. He also charged Gauleiter Josef Bürckel of the Saar-Palatinate with the task of organizing a plebiscite to sanction the new statute.[30] In the meantime, the Luftwaffe scattered 300 million leaflets from the skies as the Wehrmacht continued its triumphal advance. Since both Protestant and Catholic churches had issued pastoral letters calling on the faithful "to thank God in their prayers on Sunday for the bloodless course taken by the great upheaval and to pray for a happy future for Austria," Hitler's soldiers moved into towns and villages to the acclaim of churchgoers.[31]

Originally, neither the Führer nor the Armed Forces High Command saw any point in occupying Styria or Carinthia. Once military teleprinters started chattering news of the Eighth Army's thunderous reception in Upper Austria, Hitler changed his mind. On Saturday afternoon he ordered token contingents of paratroops, motorized infantry, and mountain rangers into the twin territories "so that those provinces to which the German and National Socialist cause is particularly indebted may soon have reason to rejoice."[32] In issuing this order it is likely that the dictator wanted to bolster local morale. His adherents in Styria and Carinthia were so thoroughly dedicated to him that there was no reason to worry about the sort of "autonomist tendencies" existing elsewhere. What is indisputable is that troops of the Second Airborne Regiment landed in Graz on 13 March to a frenzied reception. They were followed by companies of other soldiers rolling or tramping into Styria over roads lined by cheering spectators.[33] As for Carinthia, only a small number of paratroops and reconnaissance vehicles entered the province together with some 1,000 uniformed police. To their astonishment, they were bombarded by flowers, even in the streets of Slovenian-speaking hamlets near the Yugoslavian frontier.[34]

On Monday, 14 March 1938, Hitler left Linz. His motorcade proceeded along the fabled Nibelungenstrasse, driving through crowds chanting Nazi slogans and shouting "Sieg Heil!" Two and a half hours later the dictator paused at Melk to take the salute of the local Austrian garrison. After another stop at St. Pölten, his procession slowed to twenty kilometers an hour to please the howling masses. At 5:40 P.M. the Führer's Mercedes swung onto Vienna's Ringstrasse to the sound of cheers and peeling bells.[35] The correspondent of the *Manchester Guardian* reported that the imperial boulevard was so densely lined with spectators that "the German police and SA, who had kept order along the route, had to make repeated efforts to keep back the crowd which often broke through at different places."[36] Other writers indicated that "there were people at every window and even enthusiastic supporters sitting on the rooftops."[37] Accompanied by two dozen police cars, Hitler's motorcade swept past the Gothic Rathaus, the classical Greek parliament, the Museums of Art and Natural History, the Hofburg, and the State Opera. At the Hotel Imperial, once home to Richard Wagner, it came to a halt. Here the conqueror of Vienna stepped from the running board to receive Seyss-Inquart's cabinet.[38]

G. E. R. Gedye described the "roaring crowds" as "the greatest I have ever seen in Vienna." He reported that "they refused to go home despite warnings from the loud-speakers that the Führer was 'too tired' to speak to them."[39] Thousands of men and women continued to sway back and forth outside the Hotel Imperial, chanting "We want to see our Führer!" Finally, Hitler appeared at a balcony to deliver a brief address that concluded "no one will ever again divide the German Reich, as it exists today."[40]

The following day Vienna awoke to see thousands of men, women, and children streaming into the city from the surrounding countryside to glimpse the native son who now controlled their destiny. "Old Austria seemed to be returning in this prodigal son of Austria," Joachim Fest later wrote, "however illegitimate and vulgar he might be."[41] By midmorning more than a quarter of a million people packed the Inner City—jamming roads and thoroughfares, crowding narrow streets and passages, and converging on Heroes Square. In some places the mass of humanity was so dense that the Berlin police had to deploy cordons three-men-deep.[42] "Stately trees on the side walk were literally bowed down with the weight of numbers trying to get a better view," an English correspondent wrote.[43]

Shortly before 11:00 A.M. Hitler strode through the Castle Gate of Heroes Square to take the salute of massed formations of the SA, SS, Hitler Youth, and League of German Girls. In the shadow of the equestrian statues of Archduke Charles and Prince Eugene of Savoy tens of thousands of Viennese yelled and chanted "We thank our Führer!"[44] Hitler, ascending to the terrace of the Hofburg, delivered a spellbinding address. In it he proclaimed a "new mission" for Austria, one that corresponded to the "precept that once summoned the German settlers of the [Holy Roman] Empire of Old to come here. The primeval Ostmark of the German people shall henceforth constitute the youngest bulwark of the German nation and thus of the German Reich."[45]

Upon completing his "report to history," Hitler stood to attention, stared into space, and saluted. The response was a roar of applause, punctuated by endless shouts and chants.[46] After lunch the dictator returned to the Ringstrasse to review a military parade that began with the flypast of 400 aircraft, followed by 42 tanks, 35 armored cars, 100 light artillery pieces, 75 infantry cannon, 2,000 motorized infantry, 40 antiaircraft guns, 120 motorcycle troops, and 10 infantry battalions.[47] Although many of the troops were Austrian, the correspondent of the *Manchester Guardian* noted, "officers and men of the German Army came in for much cheering. Strangely enough, there was less for the rather considerable number of Austrian troops."[48]

Another British observer wrote that the crowd "was composed of all classes. For once workers and bourgeois stood side by side with undivided enthusiasm. My predominant impression was of young faces and rather shabby clothes. This was no host of reactionaries assembled to greet a reactionary triumph. Whatever their motive, it was the people of Vienna who lined the streets."[49]

Even after Hitler left the reviewing stand around 4:00 P.M., the din continued. Tens of thousands of Viennese followed him to the Hotel Imperial where they jeered and cursed Theodor Cardinal Innitzer, the Austrian primate who had come to make a courtesy call.[50] That evening the multitude invaded Leopoldstadt, the Jewish district along the Danubian Canal. G. E. R. Gedye accompanied the mob. The triumphant rabble, he observed, "called families from their houses and forced them to kneel and try to scrub from the pavements slogans such as 'Heil Schuschnigg!'" But he added, "The crowds were composed, particularly as dusk approached, of some of the worst elements of the population, assembled to jeer at the Jews and shouting 'Perish Jewry!' 'Out with Jews!' and 'Who has found work for the Jews? Adolf Hitler!'"[51]

In the meantime, the soldiers of the Eighth Army moved forward to complete the occupation of "the youngest bulwark of the German nation." During the first days of the invasion there had been massive traffic jams, twenty-five fatal accidents, and the breakdown of hundreds of tanks and vehicles. On Wednesday, 16 March, divisional commanders ordered all but a handful of units to return their stocks of live ammunition and to slow to twenty-five kilometers per day. With the Austrian people welcoming their conquering cousins as liberators, the invaders decided that spit and polish should replace raw muscle.[52]

Popular reaction to the arrival of German troops continued to be delirious right up to the end of the operation. A stream of military reports recounted scenes of "unbelievable euphoria," "songs and humor," and "indescribable rapture." Even in industrial enclaves thousands of blue-collar workers turned out to cheer the advancing troops. From the Iron Mountain district of Styria the commander of the 100th Mountain Regiment wrote he had seen "not one clenched fist, only eager faces."[53] After occupying a billet in Floridsdorf, the tenement district of Vienna, an ordnance officer filed a report on the squalor and poverty of the local residents. "It's understandable that the neighborhood has been a stronghold of Marxism until recently," he wrote. "Nevertheless, our soldiers have experienced neither insults nor overt hostility, but rather have been welcomed as liberators."[54]

Still, popular enthusiasm was by no means universal. When the first German aircraft flew over Wels on Saturday 12 March, an eight-year-old boy found himself playing in the home of a retired Habsburg officer. "I remember hearing a lot of noise and going out on the balcony to see what happened," he recalled a half century later. "There were lots of people in the streets shouting and happy. But inside that house, I saw the colonel with tears in his eyes. I remember that vividly. I remember wondering what could have happened to make people in the streets so happy and him so sad."[55]

How many tears were shed behind closed doors is impossible to say. Among the millions of photographs taken during the Anschluss, only a single snapshot of an unhappy face has come to light.[56] The invading forces were not always welcomed with blossoms, however. In Steyr the population was "cooler and less interested" than elsewhere. In Melk, Ybbs, and Pöchlau the reception "left something to be desired"; in Wörgl there was "obvious antipathy toward the German soldiers." Throughout Tyrol many peasants simply stood by "detached" or "aloof." In parts of Lower Austria villagers made little attempt to hide their "dislike of the German Armed Forces" or to remove pictures of Dollfuss from their homes.[57] As for Vienna, the center of Austria's large Jewish population, perhaps as many as half a million persons reacted to the Anschluss with disbelief, dismay, and dread. Among them were 170,000 Jews, 80,000 "hybrids," and an undetermined number of civil servants, Catholic priests, monarchists, Social Democrats, and solitary individuals.[58]

What accounts for the euphoria with which most Austrians greeted the loss of their country's independence, a rapture remarkably similar to that with which most East Germans hailed the collapse of the German Democratic Republic a half century later?[59] First, there can be no doubt that the initial enthusiasm was both genuine and spontaneous; Reich German cameramen and broadcasters certainly provided extensive coverage of the Anschluss, but neither they nor Propaganda Minister Goebbels had sufficient time to stage-manage events.[60] Second, it is clear that the populace was profoundly relieved that bloodshed had been avoided. For most people the intervention of German troops thwarted the outbreak of civil war and provided a security shield against foreign aggression. The sight of well-equipped Landsers marching through the country revived memories of wartime solidarity and evoked a sense of satisfaction that the humiliations of 1918 had at last been overcome. Third, nearly all hoped for a dramatic improvement in the material conditions of everyday life; most Austrians were aware of Hitler's economic achievements and had good reason to believe that their expectations would soon be fulfilled. Fourth, there can be little doubt that millions of people welcomed the Anschluss as a chance to put an end to the so-called Jewish Question. The anti-Semitic violence that followed Schuschnigg's valedictory was perpetrated by the Austrian Nazis and their accomplices, not by the German invaders. That the new regime openly sanctioned persecution and Aryanization, in other words, could only enhance its popularity.[61]

This does not mean that the masses had suddenly embraced all the doctrines of National Socialism. As already mentioned, no more than a third of the populace could be considered dyed-in-the-wool believers. Most Austrians were therefore hailing the collapse of the Old Regime; they viewed the Anschluss as both a powerful "agent of change" and the fulfillment of an ancient dream.[62] On the other hand, mass demonstrations and revolutionary violence had not brought down the Christian Corporative system; Austria's venerable tradition of servility ensured that popular loathing had to await the arrival of the German armed forces before finding release against the weak and helpless, especially the Jews.

THE APRIL PLEBISCITE

On 13 March, Hitler ordered Gauleiter Josef Bürckel of the Saar-Palatinate to organize a "free and secret plebiscite" to be held on Sunday, 10 April, a referendum in which all Germans and Austrians over the age of twenty would be asked to endorse the Anschluss. The election would scarcely qualify as a democratic contest. Nevertheless, it represented more than a "thoroughly rigged vote."[63] Hitler sincerely believed that "all state power must emanate from the people and [be] confirmed in free state elections."[64] Plebiscitary acclaim buttressed the Nazi regime and provided some measure of the popular pulse; it also worked to stifle opposition and to strengthen the dictator's hand in the eyes of foreign powers. Hitler thus threw himself into the campaign as if he were running against a real opponent; for two and one-half hectic weeks he barnstormed through Greater Germany, paid minute attention to each and every rally, and even fretted about the outcome of the vote.[65]

As for the Austrian people, the April plebiscite both shaped and reflected popular attitudes. The available evidence suggests that a substantial majority of the populace welcomed the opportunity to participate in the electoral process to resolve the question of national identity and to exercise the right to vote denied for over half a decade.[66] The Nazis were well aware that the Anschluss euphoria rested on an ephemeral emotional base and sought to maintain the popular enthusiasm through massive, ongoing mobilization.[67] For nearly a month they staged rallies, canvased voters, and subjected the Austrian populace to spectacular pageantry, dramatic radio broadcasts (for which 20,000 receivers were made available), and a campaign tour by Hitler himself.[68]

Goebbels's publicity machine pursued a two-track approach during the "electoral struggle," featuring stories of both mass celebrations and mass arrests, a technique that drew a "fine line between urging the Austrians to support Hitler and hinting that it would be unwise to oppose him."[69] In addition, party speakers, editors, and broadcasters emphasized Hitler's historical achievements, pledged the fulfillment of national destiny, and promised an immediate end to unemployment. Their language stressed "tradition," "hearth and home," and the "bond of German blood"; it also drove home the theme of German unity.[70]

On 21 March Gauleiter Bürckel began the formal campaign by delivering an address to a packed house in Vienna's famous Concert Hall. G. E. R. Gedye observed that his frequent "attacks on the Jews were applauded with great enthusiasm."[71] In the weeks that followed a parade of Reich German dignitaries crisscrossed Austria, urging voters to cast their ballots for Greater Germany. Among them were Göring, Goebbels, Himmler, and Hitler himself. Newspaper accounts indicate that the stormiest applause erupted after promises to rid the country of Jews.[72]

On 2 April, John C. Wiley, the American chargé d'affaires, wrote that Vienna was "red" with swastika flags, that "every conceivable sort of National Socialist organization has paraded through the streets," and that "even in the normally quiet suburbs one hears the hoarse voices of party orators together with more or less thunderous 'Sieg Heils' from loud speakers thoughtfully attached to convenient telephone poles."[73] After portraying the city as a sea of banners, posters, and illuminated slogans, he explained the concrete measures already taken by the Nazis to lend substance to their "propaganda of the word," efforts touted by Goebbels's publicity managers as "propaganda of the deed."

If actions speak louder than words, the noise must have been deafening. On 26 March, Göring announced the immediate transfer of 60 million marks for industrial development and agricultural modernization. His pledge was followed by the extension of German social security benefits to Austria, the resumption of relief payments to the unemployed, and the dispatch of 100,000 schoolchildren and 25,000 adults on recuperative holidays to the Reich.[74] To the poor the National Socialist People's Welfare Organization (NSV) distributed "1,000 quintels of smoked fish . . . , 300,000 pounds of coffee, 40,000 pounds of vegetables, 80,000 oranges, 39,000 lemons [and] 80,000 cans of fish."[75] The new masters also set up soup kitchens, did away with an unpopular bicycle fee, and put an end to the tax auction of indebted farmsteads.

In addition to pageantry and economic aid, the Nazis took pains to court the Roman Catholic hierarchy and the remnants of organized labor. Both proved receptive. The primate of Austria, Theodor Cardinal Innitzer, was an enthusiastic nationalist who welcomed the Anschluss as the fulfillment of the age-old dream of German unity. He personally welcomed Hitler to Vienna and on 18 March persuaded his bishops to issue a pastoral letter urging the faithful to vote for the Führer in the plebiscite. As will be explained in greater detail, the credulous archbishop also authorized the draping of swastika banners from churches, wrote a preamble to his draft, and signed an accompanying letter with the words "Heil Hitler!" On 28 March all three documents appeared in newspapers and posters throughout the Ostmark, the official term for incorporated Austria.[76]

The Socialists proved even easier to win over. Roughly a third of them had already cast their lot with the Nazis. The rest the new regime resolved to convert by appealing to national unity, by emphasizing the social and economic failures of the Christian Corporative regime, and by taking concrete steps to end unemployment. Among the propaganda attacks on the Jews and the church there were also speeches, posters, and newspaper columns crafted to attract the blue-collar vote.[77] The results were not long in coming. On 3 April Karl Renner, the most prominent Social Democrat remaining in Austria, endorsed the Anschluss; in the pages of the *Neues Wiener Tagblatt* he reminded readers of his own efforts to unite Austria with Germany in 1919, concluding with the words "I will vote yes!"[78]

Once the Nazis had secured the support of the leaders of both the Catholic and Socialist "camps," there seemed little reason to vote against the Anschluss. Late in the afternoon of 31 March, Bürckel's office conducted an initial survey of the attitudinal landscape. In a two-hour conference call— surely one of the first in Austrian history—regional campaign managers reported their impressions of the popular mood.[79]

From Salzburg came word that most meeting halls were filled to overflowing, that Göring's program of economic development was being widely hailed, and that the bishops' pastoral letter had made a "profound impression" on regular churchgoers, although less so on their priests; electoral observers stressed that members of the lower clergy were still keeping their distance: some vicars remained reserved, others disdainfully aloof. The reports from Vorarlberg and Upper Austria were less informative; both forecast voter support of 100 percent. In Lower Austria Bürckel's agents claimed that the overall mood was "exceptionally good, especially among those engaged in industrial production." But they added, "The rural populace is here and there undecided." In Styria, by contrast, most farmers were considered generally enthusiastic.[80] From Carinthia the campaign manager boasted that morale in his province was "exceptionally favorable." In staccato sentences he asserted that the "enthusiasm among voters in Central Carinthia is enormous," that there was "no opposition to the referendum," and that "even the Slovenians have been won over."

From Innsbruck, Dr. Robert Schueller, the deputy director of propaganda, was more cautious. He explained that while the government's message was getting through to the general populace, most radio broadcasts could not reach the inhabitants of deep Alpine valleys, let alone countless shepherds, lumbermen, and impoverished mountain peasants. Further, only a handful of towns had projection facilities to show propaganda films such as Leni Riefenstahl's *Triumph of the Will*. To offset the technological deficit Schueller recommended the greater distribution of flyers, brochures, and other illustrated material. While predicting an electoral triumph, he emphasized that most priests would cast an affirmative vote only at the behest of the Roman Catholic hierarchy.[81]

That the Nazis kept a sharp eye on their enemies along the campaign trail scarcely needs to be mentioned. Within moments of Schuschnigg's resignation speech, gangs of storm troopers and vigilantes had emerged from hiding to settle accounts with Hitler's opponents, both real and imagined. The initial victims, according to G. E. R. Gedye, were a "medley of princes, peasants, and paupers, world famous bankers, obscure proletarians, Jews from the highest rank to the lowliest, army officers, police officials, and the Communists and Socialists."[82] Early in the morning of 12 March Heinrich Himmler touched down at Aspern aerodrome to coordinate and orchestrate the arrests; behind him followed some 40,000 German security police. Exactly how many Austrians landed in Gestapo custody, fell prey to abuse or murder, or passed through concentration camps in early 1938 has never been determined, but at least 20,000 persons were seized or arrested.[83] Whatever the number, it was sufficient both to delight and to intimidate the populace.

Hitler's propaganda production became a "morality play, staged for the masses, in which forces of evil and treason were represented by those voting no, and the honest German people, by those voting yes."[84] Eyewitnesses and historians alike have commented on the baroque theatricality of the "electoral struggle," in which rallies took place at night, illuminated by blazing bonfires or beams of shimmering searchlights. The Nazis thus came close to the total "aestheticizing of politics," a major goal of their movement. They also achieved a Nietzschean "transvaluation of values," reversing the norms of the Lenten season, the forty-day period of fasting and penitence preceding Good Friday. Instead of abstinence and contrition they offered ambrosia and revelry, a Dionysian Mardi Gras of Germanic orgies and pagan ecstasies. For propagandists and voters alike it was to be a "springtime without end."[85]

In response the masses appear to have experienced a flush of liberation not unlike that felt in 1914 at the outbreak of the Great War. Despite the horrific memory of that conflict, they did not react with foreboding to the

Nazi glorification of violence.[86] In Gmunden thousands even cheered Gauleiter August Eigruber's pledge to erect a concentration camp in Upper Austria.[87] When Hitler reentered his homeland on 3 April the plebiscitary contest reached a fever pitch. Each campaign appearance became a state visit with solemn ceremonies, formal receptions, and mass rallies. There were also inspiring speeches, usually delivered in shuttered factories, abandoned rail stations, or other large facilities ravaged by the Depression. On Saturday, 9 April, the Führer arrived at the West Train Station in Vienna; an hour later he stepped onto the balcony of the city hall to proclaim the Day of the Greater German Reich.[88]

That evening Hitler delivered a closing address in the Northwest Train Station. In it he presented a liturgical history of the NSDAP, boasted of his achievements in restoring Germany to greatness, and dwelt on those events leading to the Anschluss. Repeatedly invoking Providence, he concluded: "I would now give thanks to Him who let me return to my homeland in order that I might now lead it into my German Reich! Tomorrow may every German recognize the hour and measure its import and bow in humility before the Almighty, who in a few weeks has wrought a miracle upon us!"[89]

The next morning, at 7:00 A.M., town criers throughout the Third Reich called voters to the polls. It was to be Hitler's last plebiscite. Most polling stations were manned by uniformed storm troopers. Although individuals had the option of entering a voting booth, most marked their ballots in public—much as voters do in parts of the American South to this day. The official returns indicated a huge turnout and nearly unanimous affirmative vote; they also showed that approval of the Anschluss was higher in the Ostmark (99.73 percent) than in Germany (99.08 percent). Still, 11,929 Austrians had voted no; another 5,776 had invalidated their ballots.[90]

Analysis of the results of the April plebiscite requires great caution. Some 360,000 persons or 8 percent of the electorate had been excluded from the ballot box; many others bent with the wind. While the elections were technically "free and secret," their setting made it risky to vote against the Anschluss.[91] That said, the returns provide some indication of prevailing attitudes, a point Gerhard Botz has argued for two decades.[92] First, since both Cardinal Innitzer and Karl Renner had endorsed the Anschluss, at least two-thirds of the electorate could be counted on to approve it. Second, Nazi propaganda had obviously made an impact on voters, especially those who beheld Hitler or experienced the captivating stare of his porcelain-blue eyes.[93] Third, the affirmative vote was greatest in provinces with the highest Nazi membership: Burgenland (99.93 percent), Styria (99.81 percent), and Lower Austria (99.74 percent). Conversely, negative ballots were most numerous in provinces with the strongest sense of Austrian identity: at one extreme rural Roman Catholic Tyrol (.70 percent); at the other, working-class Red Vienna (.59 percent).[94]

In what specific ways the April plebiscite reflected the desires and wishes of the Austrian population must remain a matter of speculation. What is perhaps most striking is that the loss of independence was attended by so little protest or resistance. With all this in mind, Botz is surely correct in arguing that popular reaction to the Anschluss cannot be characterized simply as credulity, opportunism, or hope of economic betterment. The enthusiasm of 1938 corresponded at a more basic level to the excitement of the moment; it represented a genuine outpouring of German nationalist feeling that was shared by virtually everyone in the interwar period. Although Hitler's foreign policy goals remained open, scarcely anyone objected to his authoritarian system or to his intention of ridding Austria of undesirable minorities and social outcasts. If nothing else, the prevailing anti-Semitic consensus ensured that a "majority" of Austrians stood ready "to fulfill their 'duty' in the Greater German Reich."[95]

II

From Anschluss
to War

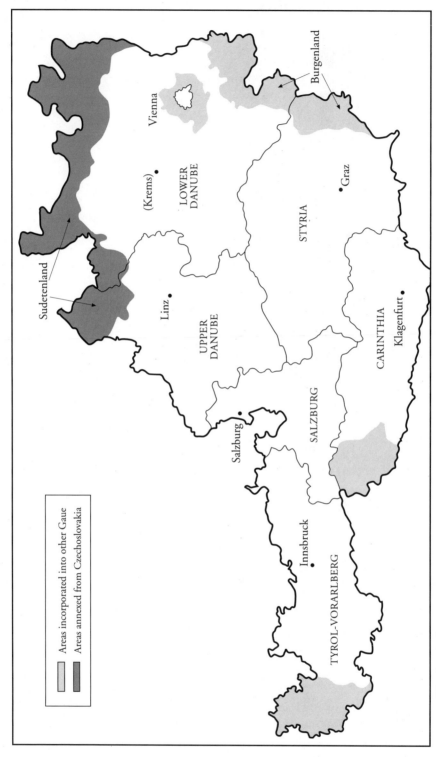

Burgenland

Sudetenland

Vienna

LOWER
DANUBE

(Krems)

Graz

STYRIA

Linz

UPPER
DANUBE

CARINTHIA

Klagenfurt

SALZBURG

Salzburg

Innsbruck

TYROL-VORARLBERG

MAP 2. *The Ostmark, 1938–1945*

3

THE NAZI POPULACE
Between Acclamation and
Disappointment

The Austrian Nazis who surged to power in the Dionysian rising of 1938 had every reason to celebrate a triumph without parallel in living memory. In three decades they had evolved from a small group of Sudeten German malcontents into a catchall party that constituted "a representative sample of Austrian society."[1] While it is true that German intervention ensured final victory, the Austrian NSDAP momentarily enjoyed wide popular support. Between 1938 and 1943 party leaders would enroll proportionately more members in Austria than their associates in the Altreich (Germany in the frontiers of 1937). And while their countrymen made up only 8 percent of the population of Greater Germany, by 1945 they would comprise 14 percent of the SS and 40 percent of those involved in killing operations from the T4 euthanasia program to Auschwitz.[2]

The most obvious problem in surveying the attitudes of the Nazi populace in Austria is that of differentiation. Much like the German NSDAP (and the Bavarian *Mittelstand*), the Austrian party embraced "extremely variegated strata of the population with apparently unrelated group interests."[3] At the same time, the industrial working class and the Catholic farming population remained largely identifiable subcultures. A second and more difficult obstacle is the lack of documentation. Although various agencies of the German party had once submitted reports on the morale of Nazi rank and file, both the regime and the security organs saw little point in gathering intelligence on the attitudes of those charged with the surveillance of the larger population. On 5 October 1936 Deputy Führer Rudolf Hess even issued a directive, explicitly prohibiting "snooping" or "spying" on party members.[4]

Examination of the sentiments of the "brown masses" requires analysis of exiguous data and imaginative extrapolation. Nevertheless, an effort must be made in order to glimpse the mental world of those 693,007 Austrians who eventually joined the NSDAP and who—with their families—conditioned the attitudes of the rest of the population. One place to begin is with the membership structure of the indigenous party.

STRUCTURE AND MEMBERSHIP OF THE AUSTRIAN NSDAP

Careful research has revealed that between 1904 and 1945 Austrian Nazism experienced significant changes in its social and regional composition[5] (see Tables 2 and 3). For two decades the movement was comprised primarily of railwaymen, postal workers, and various employees in the public sector. Once it captured the German Nationalist base in 1932, the party's social profile became representative of the "new" middle class of civil servants and employees, a group that also included thousands of officials forced into early retirement by the Austrian government in 1923.[6]

After the NSDAP was banned by the Dollfuss government on 19 June 1933, some 10,000 activists fled to Germany where they organized the so-called Austrian Legion; the following year they were joined by a new wave of refugees from the July Putsch. In the subsequent restructuring that took place among underground cadres still in Austria the number of civil servants and public employees declined. Despite police surveillance and arrests, overall membership continued to increase, however, rising from 67,000 in June 1933 to 127,000 in February 1938. Within the ranks of the reorganized and expanding movement the number of professionals and self-employed rose notably higher than in the past. There were also many more industrial workers, especially in the provinces.[7] In terms of geography, membership continued to swell in Carinthia and Styria, grew steadily in Vienna and Lower Austria, and expanded slightly in Salzburg, Tyrol, and Vorarlberg. In Upper Austria there were scarcely any gains—at least until shortly before the Anschluss.[8]

Shortly after the April plebiscite, Hitler promoted his election manager, Josef Bürckel, Reich commissioner for the reunification of Austria with the German Reich. The new chief began to screen and register Austrian party members and to process the applications of those claiming to have aided the Nazi movement before 11 March 1938. Working closely with the Brown House, home office of the NSDAP in Munich, Bürckel's staff issued 207,095 provisional green membership cards within the next eight months. The number of registered members then rose from 221,017 in March 1939 to 693,007 exactly four years later.[9]

While the rolls of the post-Anschluss movement have yet to be fully quantified, sample studies and postwar data reveal a significant change in social composition.[10] Whereas the pre-Anschluss NSDAP could claim, with a certain degree of justification, to represent all groups of Austrian society,

TABLE 2. *Nazi Party Occupational Composition, 1923–1933 (in percentages)*

	Linz 1923–33	Vienna 1926–33	Austria 1923–33	Bavaria 1923
Farmers/peasants	—	.8	—	2.0
Private employees	24.7	23.8	26	24.0
Civil servants/ public employees	30.8	19.7	9	14.8
Professionals	8.9	8.2	2	8.4
Self-employed	5.5	11.5	8	3.5
Workers	19.2	21.3	44	27.9
Students	2.7	4.9	9	10.7
Military	6.8	—	2	—
Other	1.4	9.8	—	8.7
(Sample size)	(146)	(122)	(167)	(1,126)

Sources: Botz, *Nationalsozialismus in Wien*, 218; Bukey, *Hitler's Hometown*, 88.

after 1938 the proportion of professionals, civil servants, and urban self-employed rose significantly. The many working-class boys conscripted into the armed forces may account for part of this structural shift; a more likely explanation is that those middle-class elites, especially civil servants and public employees who had been vulnerable to governmental pressure during the period of "illegality," simply emerged from the shadows to dominate the Austrian cadres.[11]

Between 1938 and 1945 the social configuration of the Austrian NSDAP came to approximate the larger German model—as might be anticipated in an increasingly totalitarian state (Table 4). Nonetheless, those individuals and groups who predominated in Austria represented the bureaucratic and professional strata of society to a greater degree than in the Altreich, where peasant proprietors, artisanal producers, and petit bourgeois shopkeepers had made a major, often disruptive, impact on party life.[12] The Austrian Nazis were not immune to antimodernist sentiments, but they generally stood apart from those of their countrymen who dreamed of resurrecting the medieval guild system and had, for the most part, supported the Christian Corporative order. The NSDAP continued to attract and integrate diverse and varied social groups, but it remained "first of all a movement of the new middle class [of managers, technicians, and government employees] and secondly of the non-agrarian older middle sector."[13]

In terms of generational structure, the registration process revealed that 20.8 percent of the active membership had joined the NSDAP prior to

TABLE 3. *Nazi Party Occupational Composition, 1933–1938 (in percentages)*

	Linz Activists 1933–38	Vienna Activists 1933–38	Vienna Party Members 1938
Farmers/peasants	1.4	—	0.4
Private employees	13.5	19.6	21.5
Civil servants/ public employees	18.9	18.1	18.9
Professionals	16.2	1.4	4.6
Self-employed	13.5	7.3	9.2
Workers	26.2	29.0	25.4
Students	2.7	2.2	3.5
Military	4.0	—	—
Other	1.3	22.4	16.5
(Sample size)	(74)	(138)	(260)

Sources: Botz, *Nationalsozialismus in Wien*, 218; Bukey, *Hitler's Hometown*, 160.

30 January 1933, 12 percent in the six months before its ban on 19 June, and a further 10.1 percent in the year preceding the Dollfuss Putsch of 25 July 1934. Between that abortive uprising and the gentlemen's agreement of 11 July 1936 some 13 percent had entered the underground movement. Thereafter, an additional 22.2 percent enlisted in the run-up to the Anschluss. Put another way, some 43,000 Austrian Nazis could claim to be "Old Fighters," veteran militants who had supported the Führer before his rise to power, and felt entitled to some reward for their service. At the same time, a much larger group of 94,000 to 121,000 "Illegals," many of whom who had risked life and limb as underground fighters, contended that the spoils of victory belonged to them alone.[14]

While the Anschluss may have constituted a provincial uprising against Vienna, Bürckel's enrollment figures indicated that with 64,919 registered members the capital city actually boasted the largest number of party activists. The second largest concentration of card-carrying members was in Lower Austria (57,171), followed by Styria (37,409) and Carinthia (30,735). In the remaining provinces the registration figures were much lower with Tyrol-Vorarlberg (7,893), Upper Austria (6,500), and Salzburg (2,468) together comprising only 8.1 percent of the total membership. While the foremost historian of Nazi Austria urges caution in approaching these statistics, the figures do reveal territorial strongholds that played a notable role in the larger contest for spoils and power.[15]

TABLE 4. *Occupational Proportion of Nazi Party Members in Selected Segments of Austrian Society, 1933–1941 (in percentages)*

	1933	1938	1941
Students	14.2	20.6	47.5
Professionals	14.2	18.0	60.0
Civil service	3.9	7.7	38.0
Employees	3.2	7.0	28.9
Workers	1.6	3.7	14.6
Self-employed	1.6	4.8	18.0
Agriculture	2.3	5.3	25.7
Total of Nazi employed	2.3	5.1	21.2
(*N*)	(68,400)	(164,300)	(688,300)

Source: Botz, "Zwischen Akzeptanz und Distanz," 439.

THE INTRA-NAZI FACTIONS

Austrian Nazism, it bears repeating here, was always a more diverse, heterogeneous, and fissiparous coalition than its German counterpart.[16] The issues at stake were ones of leadership, tactics, and immediate goals. They did not involve ideology.[17] In this important respect the party faithful in Austria never questioned the precepts of German National Socialism, the populist creed for which they were prepared to lay down their lives. Devoted to Hitler, they believed in radical Germanic nationalism, colonial expansion, and anti-Semitic racialism. They were antiliberal, anticapitalist, anti-Marxist, and, above all, anticlerical. Viewing humanity as a species divided into superior and inferior strains, they proposed to reward achievement and to resolve conflict within the framework of an Aryan National Community (*Volksgemeinschaft*), a biological utopia they intended to create through eugenic engineering and military conquest.

In contrast to the German NSDAP, the Austrian party never produced an outstanding personality to unite and lead it. There were many reasons for this, but subservience to Hitler (and to Germans in general) made it improbable that any provincial chieftain would ever aggregate a base larger than those of contending rivals. Moreover, once the party was outlawed by the Viennese government, Nazi functionaries either fled the country or faced arrest, imprisonment, and surveillance. The disastrous July Putsch of 1934 deepened divisions, but the Austro-German Treaty of 11 July 1936 paradoxically crystallized the cleavages into several identifiable though also overlapping factions. This was because a secret paragraph of the accord retained the government's prohibition of the NSDAP while inviting representatives of the movement to accept political responsibility on an individual basis.[18]

The first of the identifiable factions consisted of the pre-1933 Old Fighters, many in German exile, who claimed pride of place on the basis of prior service and seniority. The second—and largest—was the underground apparatus under Captain Josef Leopold, the titular head of the entire Austrian movement between 1935 and February 1938. Popular in Lower Austria, Leopold was considered headstrong and rebellious by rivals and the Christian Corporative regime. In truth he was not the radical depicted even today by some historians. He accepted Hitler's "evolutionary" approach to the Anschluss adumbrated in the gentlemen's agreement, albeit reluctantly and in the face of considerable opposition from party hotheads. Convinced that he was following orders from Berlin, Leopold repudiated bombs and bullets to negotiate a settlement with the Schuschnigg regime that would legalize the entire Austrian NSDAP. Such an approach, Leopold felt, would inevitably lead to free elections, followed by a Nazi takeover. That Austria itself might then vanish was a probability he seems not to have foreseen.[19]

The fantasy of an autonomous Austria coexisting with or within Greater Germany was an illusion shared by many, but most of all by a second group, the Catholic Nationals—a clique of radical conservatives, largely professionals and intellectuals, who were newcomers to Nazism but regarded themselves as a natural elite. Small in number, their leader was Seyss-Inquart. Much like the German reactionaries who had undermined the Weimar Republic, the Catholic Nationals sought to "build bridges" to the National Socialists. They hoped to fashion a Greater Germany in which Austria would retain a large measure of autonomy. One of them, the military historian Edmund Glaise-Horstenau, openly considered himself a "particularist."[20]

A third faction, large and amorphous, consisted of hard-core activists who rejected the July Agreement. Regarding the accord as a betrayal to the hated "system," they refused to accept Leopold's leadership and continued to pursue terrorist tactics, most notably in Vienna and Styria. A motley collection of plebeians, working-class youngsters, and hoodlums, they regularly marched through squares and streets, vandalized property, and took their cues from SA functionaries or neighborhood bosses. In February and April 1937 they revolted against the party leadership, demanding an end to all negotiations with the hated Schuschnigg regime. Leopold responded by quelling the mutinies, but he paid a heavy price in prestige, a loss that did not go unnoticed in Berlin.[21]

The principal beneficiaries of these disputes were a small coterie of Carinthian Nazis who perceived with extraordinary clarity what "Hitler and von

Papen had in mind when the July Agreement was signed."[22] Under the leadership of two highly intelligent and utterly ruthless activists, Dr. Friedrich Rainer and Odilo Globocnik, both in their early thirties, the Carinthians realized that Schuschnigg would never legalize a mass movement of roughnecks and ruffians. As confidants of Austrian SS chief Ernst Kaltenbrunner, with whom Rainer had studied law in Graz, the two men grasped that Hitler's major objective was to buy time, a point made later to their face by Hitler himself. Unlike Leopold and his followers, the Carinthian faction decided to join forces with the Catholic Nationals in negotiating with the Viennese government. Their goal was to infiltrate the regime, to undermine Leopold, and to wrest control of the party from his supporters. The Carinthians recognized that the key to success was German pressure, not the Austrian NSDAP.[23]

The cooperative efforts of the Rainer-Seyss coalition induced Hitler to dismiss Leopold on 21 February 1938. This meant that the subsequent uprising of the Austrian Nazis was undertaken by hostile factions. When Bürckel received authorization to reorganize the Austrian NSDAP he faced the daunting task of reconciling the conflicting interests of half a dozen contentious groups, each of which expected a substantial share of the spoils.

THE DISPOSITION OF POWER AND BOOTY

That there should be a relatively equitable allocation of power and rewards was a matter upon which the new masters concurred. It was Hitler's intention to liquidate the institutions of Austrian civil society and to transform his homeland into a laboratory for the eventual establishment of a full party state, a totalitarian polity not unlike that being fashioned in the Soviet Union. Frustrated by the persistent quasi autonomy of his own armed forces as well as that of the civil service, private industry, and the Christian churches, the Nazi dictator resolved to dissolve Austria as a territorial entity, to detach its provinces from Vienna, and to keep the Danubian capital for a transitional period under tight Reich German control. In the seven Reichsgaue taking shape in the provinces, Austrian National Socialists were to assume command as native tenants in chief. Hitler intended that they should enrich themselves and wield near absolute power on the local level. But he also insisted that their factional strife should be regulated on a territorial basis.[24]

Following these guidelines, Bürckel and his staff deliberated a general settlement. The key proposals were made, however, by Christian Opdenhoff, the senior personnel manager of the German Nazi Party. Opdenhoff was a man of uncommon vigor and a shrewd judge of character, who pored over dossiers, conferred with party bigwigs, and undertook an inspection tour of the Ostmark. Impressed by the intensity of anti-Viennese sentiment in the provinces, he recommended the full eradication of Austrian autonomy and the appointment of Gauleiter from each of the contending forces of the Austrian NSDAP. He also advised balancing the interests of the SA and the SS, even though the SS held nearly all the cards.[25]

On 23 May 1938 Hitler summoned Bürckel, Seyss-Inquart, and Keppler (his economic advisor for Austrian affairs) to Munich where, in the corridors of the Brown House, he revealed his decisions on the future of Austria. First, he enhanced Bürckel's mandate by subjecting virtually all agencies and bureaus in Austria—including Keppler's office and Seyss's rump regime—to the Reich commissioner's control. The Führer's proconsul was required to heed directives from Göring and to negotiate with Reich ministers, but in all other matters he was to enjoy Cincinnatus-like power until the end of his charge. Second, Hitler reduced the number of federal provinces from nine to seven, partitioning Burgenland between Styria and Lower Danube and merging Vorarlberg and Tyrol. He also awarded East Tyrol to Carinthia and directed that through incorporation Vienna was to become the second largest city in the Reich. Although reorganized as Reichsgaue, the provinces generally retained their territorial integrity.[26]

Third, Hitler announced the commendation of his new vassals, the Gauleiter who would dominate party and state in the Ostmark. As might be expected, the Carinthian faction, emerged with the lion's share of the spoils: Friedrich Rainer received Salzburg, Odilo Globocnik procured Vienna, and Hubert Klausner, their close associate, took Carinthia. Dr. Hugo Jury, a onetime deputy Gauleiter who had deserted Leopold in 1937, secured Lower Danube. Elsewhere, greater attention was paid to diversity. Franz Hofer, an Old Fighter who had dominated Tyrol before 1933, returned to Innsbruck; Siegfried Uiberreither, an SA functionary, took over in Styria; and August Eigruber, the longtime Illegal Gauleiter of Upper Danube, retained his post in Linz.[27]

While the new barons might differ and quarrel over turf, most had a good deal in common. First, all were native Austrians, as were all but one of their deputies. Second, all but Uiberreither were high-ranking SS officers, five of whom were between thirty and thirty-six years old. What distinguished them as a group was talent, ability, and youth. As for Captain Josef Leopold, the longtime head of the Illegals, he was left out in the cold.[28]

THE RESPONSE OF THE RANK AND FILE

How did the Nazi rank and file react to these intrigues and rivalries? The evidence suggests complex and contradictory emotions. From the very beginning there was ambivalence about the German occupation, a sensation of both victory and defeat, an "amalgam of envy, admiration, and subservience."[29] There were reports of women kneeling in the streets before German soldiers, of storm troopers clicking their heels to Prussian war heroes, of Austrian Nazis groveling at the feet of Berlin officials.[30]

There were also expressions of disappointment, of injured pride, of feeling "like natives in a conquered country."[31] Within a week of the Anschluss an American diplomat reported that "rumors have it that disillusionment in Austrian Nazi circles has not been long in coming. The 'plums' are going to the German comrades."[32] So intense was the sense of foreboding that it spawned considerable anxiety and anguish among Hitler's disciples. But the Führer had not forsaken his followers; in entrusting the Ostmark to an indigenous elite he remained "the loyal Eckard of Austria."[33] The Anschluss system would mean, in other words, the "rule of Austrians by Austrians."[34]

At the same time, the dictator pursued a double-barreled policy bound to alienate individuals and groups of the party faithful. In favoring the provinces over Vienna, he deliberately snubbed the metropolitan NSDAP, leaving its members exasperated and angry. In resolving to eradicate all vestiges of Austrian autonomy, he infuriated those who had cast their lot with Seyss-Inquart or had anticipated the Anschluss in terms of home rule; indeed, even Rainer and Globocnik were "deeply shocked" by the course of events.[35] To carry out Hitler's orders, moreover, Reich commissioner Bürckel proceeded with "ruthless insensitivity," appointing Saar-Palatinal cronies to key positions and banishing rivals to desk jobs outside the country. While the Reich commissioner's populist style may have broadened his appeal to the general populace, his attacks on Nazi office seekers in the press and at outdoor rallies hardly endeared him to the targets of his scorn. Nor did the dispatch of 113 German Kreisleiter, or circuit executives, to tutor and assist local party cadres.[36]

Bürckel was not the only German official to bruise Austrian feelings. Even Hermann Göring, much admired in the Ostmark, could not resist patronizing his kinsmen, thundering to a crowd of 20,000 Viennese Nazis that they "should not imagine that we we have come from the Reich to do your work or set your table."[37] Even more disdainful was a lead article in the *Schwarzes Korps*, the official organ of the SS, that promised "in short order a Prussian will be standing behind every Austrian, both lazy and industrious, not mincing words when things go wrong."[38]

Contemporary observers, disgruntled Nazis, and postwar historians have made much of such taunting declarations, citing them as examples of what the American chargé d'affaires in Vienna called the "complete Germanization" of Austria.[39] With Reich Germans seemingly in charge of the highest offices in the land, there followed an understandable wave of disillusionment and discontent. "By the fall of 1938," one writer contends, "the Germans had managed to alienate virtually every social and political group in Austria."[40] A closer examination of the evidence reveals that it was the Austrian Nazis who were the most disillusioned.[41]

The most obvious reason for their indignation was Bürckel's imperious behavior. Charged with the elimination of all vestiges of Austrianism, he pursued his objective with relish. While leaving much of that dirty work to Seyss-Inquart's rump regime, the Reich commissioner kept all but a small group of German staffers at arm's length, frequently bypassed the Carinthians, and made most of the major decisions himself.[42] In a confidential report, Christian Opdenhoff even expressed sympathy with the Austrian Nazis.[43]

A second reason for anger and distress was the decisive victory of the Carinthian crowd in the intra-Nazi struggle for power, a triumph spelling defeat and disappointment for thousands of Leopold supporters, most of whom considered Rainer and Globocnik usurpers. The Nazi uprising that triggered the Anschluss was directed as much against them as it was against the Schuschnigg regime.[44] While it is impossible to recapture the sentiments of the rampaging masses in those halcyon days, Bürckel's difficulty in imposing discipline after the German invasion highlighted the volcanic fury of a "dispossessed class that claims its rights and cannot conceive them save in terms of empty violence, of killing, taking, suppressing."[45] On the other hand, many of the exultant brownshirts believed that Leopold might be restored to power or at last be given some share of the pie.

On one issue nearly all of the Illegals were united: those émigré Nazis living in Germany, especially the members of the Austrian Legion, deserved none of the spoils.[46] One Salzburg functionary stated bluntly that "while others left for the Reich to find lucrative jobs in 1933 and 1934, the leaders now in charge of the Gau were going to jail to languish for months or years."[47] In Tyrol the restoration of Franz Hofer, the pre-1933 Gauleiter residing in Berlin, provoked such a row that a delegation of provincial Kreisleiter traveled to Vienna to file a complaint, but to no avail. Most of the other Old Fighters, including 2,000 onetime dignitaries, either remained in the Altreich or returned to marginal or menial jobs. Hofer was the exception.[48]

The 8,000 members of the Austrian Legion received particularly shabby treatment. Their formation, an armed detachment of Nazi refugees stationed in Germany, was not allowed to accompany Hitler's triumphal invasion or to participate in the April plebiscite. Excluded by the formidable combination of Bürckel, Seyss-Inquart, and Himmler, the legion had to wait until 2 April to parade in Vienna. Even then, Bürckel snubbed its officers and men, denying them any further share of Nazi glory. Two weeks later the regime ordered a general demobilization, ending all pay allotments and discharging most of the officers. While many of the legionnaires returned to Germany, those opting to remain in Austria faced unemployment or low-paying work; by the end of July over 1,000 were loitering on the dole.[49]

Not all legionnaires fared so badly. In Carinthia the Gau leadership managed to provide jobs for most of the Nazi émigrés, although frequently as laborers or custodians. There were also a few who later made a career in the party bureaucracy.[50] For most exiles, however, the Anschluss meant a bitter homecoming: the shattering of dreams of power, glory, and social advancement. What they encountered was not only the opposition of those in power; they also found little room at the top of a modernizing society for a generation of semiliterates. The surviving evidence suggests that most of the Old Fighters accepted their fate with stoic grumbling. Some wrote (unanswered) letters to Bürckel; others drowned their complaints in alcohol. A few, such as Alfred Proksch, chief of the Austrian NSDAP between 1928 and 1931, received highly visible sinecures.[51] None made trouble for the regime. One down-and-out legionnaire returning to Vorarlberg simply observed that "these people haven't the faintest idea of National Socialism and its goals."[52]

The Catholic Nationals also found themselves out in the cold—but with much warmer clothing. Once Hitler had signed the Anschluss Act making Austria a "province of the German Reich," Seyss-Inquart appealed to him to preserve a measure of Austrian autonomy. Hitler responded on 15 March by designating Seyss-Inquart Reich procurator and governor of the Austrian Provincial Government. The twin appointments appeared to grant Seyss-Inquart's request, but they were largely ceremonial positions.[53] Throughout the following weeks, Seyss-Inquart, the members of his cabinet, and other prominent Catholic Nationals campaigned enthusiastically for the cause of Greater Germany. They may have assumed a prominent role for themselves in the new order, but the truth was not long in coming. Within days, Edmund Glaise-Horstenau, Seyss-Inquart's vain and snobbish vice-chancellor, recognized that Bürckel and the Carinthian Nazis were calling the shots. Appalled by their noisy pageantry and uncouth ostentation, he remarked that "it suddenly dawned on me how little I counted compared with the old guard and found myself everywhere pushed into the background."[54]

It took only a few more weeks for Seyss-Inquart to realize that he might soon be out of a job. Once Hitler promoted Bürckel to Reich commissioner on 23 April, Seyss-Inquart was relegated to carrying out measures integrating Austria into the Greater German Reich. On 23 May, as we have already seen, his Austrian Provincial Government was transformed into a lame-duck regime. While Hitler's decision to dissolve Austria into its provinces came as a shock to Seyss-Inquart, he felt consoled by the dictator's promise of a cabinet appointment in Berlin.[55]

Assuming that he had been charged with the formation of an "Austrian ministry," Seyss-Inquart drafted various schemes promoting Vienna as an economic and cultural center to extend German influence into the Balkans. He also entertained fantasies of "Austrianizing" Germany, presumably intending to add a dash of Viennese charm to the German way of life.[56] Because Hitler had proclaimed a special mission for the Ostmark, the dreams of the Catholic Nationals appeared close to fulfillment. There were certainly no tears when Seyss-Inquart declared, "We Austrians do not mourn the sovereignty of this country."[57]

Over the course of the following year, Seyss-Inquart became involved in innumerable turf wars with Bürckel, eventually yielding the field to the Reich commissioner and on 1 May 1939 departing the Ostmark for a position in Berlin. Most other prominent Catholic Nationals and German Nationalists experienced similar fates: some received assignments outside the country, a number resumed military careers, a few secured appointments to the Greater German Reichstag.[58] One veteran German Nationalist, Franz Langoth, an Upper Austrian politician much admired by Hitler, had several job opportunities: director of the Nazi welfare association, command of Sachsenhausen concentration camp (which he declined), and later lord mayor of Linz.[59] In short, for their services in undermining Austrian independence the respectable members of the National Opposition received a "golden handshake."

There seems little point in dwelling at length on the attitudes of these individuals, a privileged group who gloried in the Anschluss but disapproved particular aspects of it. Typical of the lot was Glaise-Horstenau, vice-chancellor of the Austrian Provisional Government, later Nazi plenipotentiary in wartime Croatia. Like most of his countrymen, Glaise stood in awe of Hitler. He relished invitations to the Führer's dining table for lengthy chatter, but disdained the dictator's entourage. Even more, he loathed the Austrian Gauleiter, dismissing Globocnik as a "gangster," Uiberreither as "disgusting," Eigruber as a "laborer," and Hofer as "a dubious man." Most of all, the sight of Nazi bosses seated in the gilded loges of the Vienna State Opera disgusted him, although not to the point of turning a lascivious eye from their glamorous wives and mistresses.[60]

Given his "particularist" perspective, it is hardly surprising that Glaise castigated Seyss-Inquart for failing to defend the "Austrian cause," especially against the "proletarian" Bürckel. The onetime Habsburg general-staff officer even went out of his way to express patrician sympathy for the Leopold faction. Still, he was most incensed by what he called the "Prussification" of the Austrian civil service.[61] Claiming that the Ostmark was being overrun by Reich Germans, Glaise expressed a sentiment that was spreading rapidly throughout Viennese society.

For countless numbers of the party faithful Hitler's policy decisions of 23 May 1938 came as a disappointment. Already angered by the triumph of the Carinthian faction, thousands of Illegals still loyal to Leopold felt double-crossed. Even before the Führer's ovation on Heroes Square, they had been stunned by the regime's refusal to purge the Austrian civil service.[62] Many now resumed their campaign of "wild Aryanization," expropriating 7,000 Jewish firms and countless dwellings. By the time Bürckel could restore order at least 25,000 Nazis had seized control of Jewish enterprises as "provisional managers." The Austrian Provincial Government reacted by establishing an Office for the Regulation of Jewish Property, an agency designed to restrict the number of "provisional managers" and to siphon Jewish assets into the coffers of the state.[63]

Announcement of these various changes pleased the provincial cadres but inflamed the Viennese NSDAP. In dispatches to Whitehall, the British consul general described their disillusionment, taking pains, however, to exempt the younger generation of university graduates, especially "doctors and lawyers [who] have thrown themselves heart and soul into the movement and are reaping a rich harvest as the Jew is eliminated from professional life." Other cohorts, less educated or more set in their ways, seemed unable to adjust to the rapid pace of change, expressing an "Austrian dislike of 'Prussian methods.'" But he added, "The true position is that the local National Socialists are quite incapable of serious administrative work."[64]

A bewildered German official assessed the situation in a slightly different way. He complained that the illegal fighters had "either assumed high-paying positions" for which they were unqualified or, in the case of those with doctorates, "tended to seek jobs doing guard duty, orderly work, or sorting mail." Even though individual performance rarely corresponded to the demands of the job, many had "developed delusions of grandeur."[65]

The disenchantment of the Viennese Nazis, it should be emphasized, coincided with a general sobering of overall opinion strikingly similar to that engulfing Hanover after 1866 and East Germany after 1989. In all three cases popular expectations exceeded official promises, especially in the economic realm. The changes initiated after the Anschluss actually paid dividends, both in liquidating unemployment and in stimulating a period of spectacular economic growth. But there was also a painful period of readjustment, marked by a crisis in agriculture, new taxes, and soaring living costs. By early June, Viennese housewives were protesting shortages of fresh fruit, vegetables, eggs, and meat; their demonstrations were largely spontaneous outbursts of frustration, but in several instances hostile catcalls and graffiti provoked the intervention of the police.[66]

The discontent enveloping Vienna during the summer of 1938 was accompanied by lawlessness and violence, perpetrated by marauding Nazi malcontents. Brutality and theft in Jewish neighborhoods became so rampant that Bürckel ordered patrols of uniformed SS to restore order. There was no intention of protecting the Jews, of course, but of expropriating already confiscated assets from individual Nazi looters and putting an end to "wild Aryanization." There was also the need to crack down on storm trooper gangs and impose discipline on the municipal party apparatus.[67] Surviving records indicate that a majority of those persons taken into custody by the Gestapo between April and July 1938 were Viennese Nazis. Indeed, one-fifth of all arrests in the nine months following the Anschluss were of party activists.[68]

THE SORROWS OF THE VIENNESE NSDAP

On 19 August 1938 Donald St. Clair Gainer, the British consul general in Vienna, filed his weekly report to Whitehall. In characteristically lucid prose he described the sense of alienation prevailing in the metropolis, exacerbated, he believed, by fear of war, interference in church affairs, and increasing regimentation of economic life. After several paragraphs he concluded: "In Austria there is a small privileged clique of National Socialists, most of them quite unknown, with strange antecedents, who seem not to belong to the Austrian people. These persons are rarely seen, eschew foreigners and are very difficult of access, yet they wield great powers."[69]

In pointing to the tightening control of the Carinthian Nazis, St. Clair Gainer put his finger on a major source of anger and humiliation shared by nearly all Viennese Nazis. Within the arena of Nazi politics their grievances were not altogether misplaced. For many years internal squabbling had been so intense that Hitler himself intervened on more than one occasion to restore order.[70] In 1938 the political position of the Viennese NSDAP was so fragile that despite a large following, no local leader had been able to take charge. On the evening of 11 March SA leader Franz Lahr did manage to move into the city hall as lord mayor, but within forty-eight hours he was sacked by Hermann Neubacher, an associate of Seyss-Inquart. Several days later émigré Gauleiter Alfred Frauenfeld, popular among the party faithful, returned to a hero's welcome, but he was quickly hustled out of town. At this point the dilemma of finding a Gauleiter acceptable to both Hitler and his Viennese retainers became acute; it was a problem never really solved.[71]

Christian Opdenhoff, the senior personnel manager of the Nazi Party, weighed the various nominations with characteristic sagacity. Because Hitler intended to reduce Vienna to the status of a provincial city, expunging it as a center of Austrian culture and consciousness, Opdenhoff recognized the necessity of selecting a figure strong enough to impose the Führer's will without alienating the Viennese, especially the Nazi rank and file. Because the new Reichsgau was also expanding its boundaries to become the second largest city in Greater Germany, Opdenhoff further realized that the designated Gauleiter would inevitably wield enormous power, preserving the sense of separateness Hitler and his provincial lieutenants sought to destroy.[72]

Opdenhoff had no doubt that Frauenfeld was the best Austrian candidate, but thought that a Reich German might be better suited for the job. In suggesting Albert Forster, Gauleiter of Danzig, the personnel chief made an astute nomination.[73] Although a free city of the League of Nations, Danzig was administered by a Nazi government. For that reason Forster might have performed his duties according to Hitler's orders while preserving the fiction of home rule. The problem was that Bürckel had other ideas. The Reich commissioner wanted a man strong enough to contain Seyss-Inquart but sufficiently malleable to control. When Odilo Globocnik insinuated himself into the contest, Bürckel jumped at the chance.[74] On 23 May Hitler appointed the Carinthian adventurer Gauleiter of Greater Vienna. It was a disastrous mistake.

Venal and corrupt, the thirty-four-year-old Globocnik lacked the patience and skill to administer the metropolitan organization. He saw no reason to assuage the Nazi membership. Like so many other provincial Nazis (including Hitler), he loathed the Viennese. In fact, he made no secret of his disdain, remarking to an audience of 2,200 local functionaries gathered in the chambers of the Rathaus, "There is only one center of political authority of the German people and for that reason it is a matter of life and death to destroy forever the second center of power once embodied in Vienna."[75] As if to underline the point, Globocnik regularly bypassed the party organization, awarding political plums to émigré SS officers or Carinthian cronies.[76]

The reaction of the party faithful to the new Gauleiter was intensely hostile from the beginning. Within weeks Nazi accountants discovered that

Globocnik was lining his own pockets from party coffers. There was also hearsay that he was soliciting fees to alter or fabricate membership records. As a number of activists resented the imposition of party dues in the first place,[77] any word of corruption could not help but incense them. By autumn even Bürckel was expressing alarm. On 25 October, while he escorted Hitler through the Museum of Fine Arts and the Hofburg, he bluntly asked for Globocnik's dismissal. The Führer listened to what Bürckel had to say but brushed aside his proposal, explaining that he "would recall a Gauleiter only in the most extreme cases."[78]

Although the evidence is sketchy, Bürckel was not altogether insensitive to the complaints of the Viennese NSDAP.[79] Himself an Old Fighter, he recognized the necessity of cultivating a hardy movement rooted in the city. He was certainly aware of the resentment of those German Kreisleiter who had been posted to the Ostmark as temporary advisors but who were spending most of their time grabbing office space or huddling with interior decorators. That nearly all of them were ordered home on 1 August was surely more than a coincidence. He also saw to it that those Nazis receiving permanent appointments as Kreisleiter in the Viennese Gauleitung were, with one exception, native Austrians. Bürckel also instructed private businesses and firms to provide preferential treatment in the hiring and promotion of local Nazis. In deciding the composition of the Viennese city council, however, the Reich commissioner initially had little influence. Here the pie was cut into several slices, with each of the contending Nazi groups receiving a proportionate serving: the office of lord mayor went to the Seyss-Inquart faction, that of vice-mayor (traditionally three in number) to deputies of the party organization, the SA, and the SS.[80]

Whatever the Reich commissioner's intentions, most Viennese, whether party members or not, resented his high-handed ways and gruff behavior. Nearly all Bürckel's appointments were native Austrians, but because he continued to rely on highly visible cronies from the Saar-Palatinate, he fostered the image of Reich German domination. This made it possible for the losers in the Nazi power struggle to claim that Austria had become an "occupied" country, an accusation that was "technically correct" but hardly representative of the actual distribution of spoils. And there was more to the imputation than a misperception of the facts. The charge of foreign occupation was a canard deliberately circulated by Seyss-Inquart and Glaise-Horstenau, a fiction that gained such widespread acceptance that it was eventually endorsed by politicians of the Second Austrian Republic.[81]

That said, the arrival of German managerial personnel in the police, the civil administration, and industry—not to mention a flood of abrasive tourists—certainly lent some substance to the charge. While the actual number of Berlin officials remained relatively low in Austria, the imposition of Prusso-German rules added another degree of alienation.[82] Still, what most annoyed the Nazi rank and file, especially in Vienna, was their continued exclusion from the positions of power they felt they deserved. The ascendancy of Bürckel and Globocnik provided the most egregious demonstration of acid in the face. Almost as painful was the regime's decision to keep Austrian civil servants at their desks and the Gestapo's crackdown on the unlicensed theft of Jewish property.

Had the Viennese stalwarts known—as some of them surely suspected—that officials of the Christian Corporative regime still controlled the police, even taking charge of the branch office of the Gestapo, their wrath might have escalated beyond control. In one of the best-kept secrets of the Third Reich, the Viennese police president, Dr. Otto Steinhäusl, had conspired with two higher leaders of the Austrian SS, Fridolin Glass and Josef Fitzthum, to retain the existing force structure of the Austrian police. Hoping to preempt a massive reorganization that might place their own careers in jeopardy, they persuaded the chief of the German Order Police, Karl Daluege, to refrain from a purge, claiming that most of the detectives, traffic cops, and even neighborhood patrolmen had been Illegal Nazi activists. Daluege was skeptical, but agreed to wait until evidence could be gathered and scrutinized. The response was the concoction of fraudulent documents that included backdated membership cards, forged dossiers, fabricated reports, and a host of other laundered or counterfeit items. By September 1938 nearly 1,000 policemen were officially certified Illegal fighters, of whom 700 were also admitted to the SS. Simultaneously, a number of high-ranking police officials moved to Gestapo headquarters, assuming positions of great importance and eventually supplanting their German colleagues.[83]

There is no way of knowing how many Viennese Nazis were aware of the pseudometamorphosis of the Viennese police, but a number of activists must have encountered their former tormentors, the lawmen of the hated Schuschnigg regime, now jangling silver Gestapo warrants or wearing the black gabardine of the SS. Hitler's municipal followers had many other reasons, as we have seen, to feel betrayed and abandoned. Their rage ebbed and flowed over the summer months, but by September the British consul general was describing the overall atmosphere as "horrible," emphasizing that "even people entitled to wear the party badge have suffered a great feeling of revulsion."[84] This was a perception shared by the Gestapo, whose agents stepped up arrests of dissident Nazis on charges ranging from belonging to Otto Strasser's Black Front to slandering the Führer.[85]

The molten fury of the Viennese Nazis that erupted in the late summer of 1938 should not be viewed entirely in isolation. Even though the surge of indignation was "restricted largely to the party cadres,"[86] it had a major influence on the attitudes of the general populace. While it would be both glib and perverse to credit the Viennese Nazis with founding the much-vaunted (and overrated) Austrian resistance movement, there can be no doubt that their disillusionment lay at the root of the anti-German mood coming to prevail in the Danubian metropolis during the Anschluss years. Fueled by economic grievances, traditional Viennese xenophobia, and the arrogant, often tactless behavior of a handful of Reich German officials, resentment of the "Piefkes" (Krauts) spread so rapidly from the ranks of the municipal Nazis and their families to all classes of society that by 1939, according to the Gestapo, "Germans from the Reich under any pretext are annoyed and heckled."[87]

The angry mood coincided with the Munich crisis and the growing belli-cosity of the regime. In the explosive atmosphere of the times the *enragés* and their fellow travelers served as useful rabble to be "unleashed" against Hit-ler's enemies, especially the church and the Jews. As we shall see, the anti-Catholic rioting that broke out in Vienna on 8 October was quite unlike anything experienced elsewhere in Greater Germany. This was true also of the savagery of Crystal Night that occurred four weeks later. In this respect, Hitler could not have been displeased by the witches' cauldron still bubbling in Vienna.[88]

NAZI OPINION IN THE PROVINCES

Much like their Führer, the provincial National Socialists relished their triumph over both Vienna and the Viennese. For them the Anschluss meant much more than the sudden release of tribal emotion or the belated realiza-tion of Woodrow Wilson's promise of national self-determination. It also meant the opportunity to lance the "hydrocele on the Danube"; to disman-tle its parasitic bureaucracy; to square accounts with a "Jew-ridden" metrop-olis; to settle up with those who could not resist condescending to outsiders, especially to countrymen from small cities and towns of Austria itself.

Hitler's decision to detach Vienna from its provinces thus met the gloating approval of his adherents in the hinterland. This is not to say that every stal-wart approved the total liquidation of Austria or the new territorial arrange-ments, or that internal feuding ceased. Nevertheless, there was much less of the raucous factionalism that divided and weakened the Viennese NSDAP. While the Social Darwinian structure of the Nazi movement guaranteed the perpetuation of personal feuds and rivalries, the provincial cadres remained, for the most part, in the hands of the Illegals, the underground activists who had opposed the Schuschnigg regime and seized power on 11 March 1938. Tyrol-Vorarlberg constituted a major exception. Here Hofer's pre-1934 Old Fighters held sway, but they owed their ascendancy to Opdenhoff's insistence on a proportional distribution of the Nazi spoils. As for the Leopold loyalists, they could be found scattered throughout the ranks of the movement, even in Carinthia. But outside Lower Austria they no longer constituted an identifiable, let alone threatening, clique. Nor were there significant numbers of Catholic Nationals; aside from a few odd characters, they were not even a fringe group.[89]

While we know less about the attitudes of Hitler's followers in the provinces than in Vienna, recent local studies provide some glimpse of variations of Nazi opinion. In Carinthia and Styria National Socialism had attracted the support of over a third of the populace, enrolling large numbers of peasants and manual workers as well as the usual mix of middle-class elements from the professional and bureaucratic strata of society. Carinthia was a rural land of lakes, castles, and medieval towns; Styria a region of soaring mountains and grim industrial mining communities. Both provinces had fought off foreign invaders for a millennium, both contained large Protestant enclaves, and both shared a dislike of Vienna that stretched back centuries before the Reformation. German Nationalist sentiment was thus deeply rooted in the two frontier territories, and in 1934 the Nazis had come close to winning them in the rising against Dollfuss.[90]

That the Carinthian faction prevailed in the struggle for power within the Austrian NSDAP was due primarily to the foresight and ruthlessness of Rainer and Globocnik, as we have already seen. Although their provincial machine was not altogether free of factionalism, it was a well-organized instrument, based on family connections, internal consensus, and popular support. During the Anschluss the Illegal cadre seized power in Klagenfurt in a swift, well-disciplined operation. There was virtually no violence.[91] In the weeks that followed, the mass euphoria was so tremendous that no less than a quarter of the provincial population turned out to welcome Hitler to Klagenfurt and Villach. On 16 March waving crowds even appeared to cheer a small group of Gestapo agents from Berlin.[92]

Among the rank and file of the Nazis there was concern that the glory and material benefits of victory might have to be shared with the returning heroes of the 1934 rising. As we have already mentioned, the party organization did attempt to accommodate the exiled militants by providing jobs in the party apparatus and even in the private sector. Of the seven provincial Kreisleiter appointed to office, for example, four were Old Fighters, including Sepp Türk, a founding member of the pre-Hitlerite Austrian Nazi Party. Even so, most of the Austrian Legionnaires wound up taking menial jobs or occupying minor posts in the provincial social welfare agency. As for the Illegals, some succeeded in landing positions in the provincial school system or private industry, but most lacked the administrative experience to take over desks in the civil service.[93]

Where a great many Carinthian Nazis did succeed was within the ranks of the SS. Even before the Anschluss, a coterie of exiled insurgents had distinguished themselves in the Adolf Hitler Life Guards; youthful and dedicated, they added a conspicuous Carinthian presence to Himmler's armed formations that expanded steadily until the end of World War II. Further, the network of personal alliances that had been built up between the provincial party organization and the SS made it possible for Deputy Gauleiter Kutschera to lobby successfully in Berlin on behalf of provincial interests. The result was the construction of a Waffen-SS post at Lendorf near Klagenfurt, a complex that evolved into the largest SS training facility in Europe, creating jobs and boosting morale within the party and the general populace.[94]

In Styria the Nazi rank and file had every reason to feel pleased by the outcome of the Anschluss. Although primarily a middle-class movement, the party had attracted miners, laborers, and agricultural workers, many of them out of work. Within the movement there were also many former Heimwehr men. Under these circumstances, the SA was numerous and strong; three brigades with 7,700 storm troopers were stationed in Graz alone. It is more difficult to determine who constituted the rank and file. At the time of the Anschluss "at least 70 per cent of the civil servants of all categories" considered themselves Nazis as did roughly 80 percent of the provincial population.[95]

In selecting a Gauleiter for Styria, Christian Opdenhoff could not overlook the strength and popularity of the SA. Hitler's brown battalions had led a successful rebellion on their own; they had won official patronage for Graz as "Capital of the People's Rising"; they had prevailed in the intrafactional struggle within the local Nazi movement. Although Opdenhoff considered several other candidates, he nominated Dr. Siegfried Uiberreither, the provincial storm troop commander. From the Nazi point of view this was an excellent choice that assuaged the SA and enhanced the autonomy of the new Reichsgau.[96] Unlike his other Austrian colleagues, Uiberreither was neither an emigrant, nor an Illegal, nor a member of the Carinthian faction. He had a robust interest in strengthening his fiefdom, especially against Vienna, a metropolis he loathed with demonstrable envy, hatred, and malice.[97]

Within Styria substantial grass-roots support existed for Hitler's devolutionary policies, especially those reorienting the local economy toward Berlin. A major reason was the already strong German presence in the province, notably at the vast Alpine Montan mining and smelting complex, a subsidiary since 1926 of the Düsseldorf-based Vereinigte Stahlwerke. Within days of the Anschluss orders began to pour in from the Four-Year Plan, making it possible for the conglomerate to reopen closed pits and shuttered factories and to rehire miners and foundrymen long on the dole. The multiplier effect of the new contracts and various government job-creation programs was to snuff out unemployment by midsummer. How many Nazis benefited from the spectacular economic recovery is uncertain. As elsewhere, many activists had their hopes dashed by failing to secure a civil service position, but with so many posts already in the hands of (putative) party members, there was less reason to feel disabused.[98]

Nor was there any evident resentment of the few Germans in the administration or the police. Most Styrians admired their kinsmen from the Reich for their ability and self-confidence. On 3 August 1938 a Munich functionary reported that Gauleiter Uiberreither "spurns every measure and directive from Vienna. He intends to do what he damn well pleases and won't let anyone change his mind, even at the risk of being called a rebel and sent to Dachau."[99] Although the incorporation of the southern Burgenland required a massive reorganization of the provincial civil service, the Gauleiter refused to accept the transfer of eighty ministerial officials from Vienna, forcing Bürckel to back down and retaining control of the provincial administration himself. In August 1939 Sepp Helfrich, the onetime Illegal Gauleiter, filed a formal complaint about hiring and promotion practices in the public sector; he claimed that professional civil servants regularly received preference over proven party members. There was substance to his charge, but the scanty evidence available suggests that the men wielding power in Styria still enjoyed widespread support.[100]

In contrast to the eastern and southern regions of Austria, the Nazi movement in the provinces abutting the former German frontier—Upper Austria, Salzburg, and Tyrol—remained surprisingly modest, even stunted. One may surmise that police surveillance had been tighter in these border districts than elsewhere. In the case of the Tyrol both the religious hostility of the Catholic population and Hitler's well-known refusal to reclaim South Tyrol limited the appeal of Nazi doctrine, at least beyond the city limits of Innsbruck and Kitzbühel.[101] Nevertheless, Anschluss enthusiasm in all three provinces had been so great that the British diplomat Sir Alexander Cardogan later wrote, "I can't help thinking that we were very badly informed about feeling in that country."[102]

Given the paucity of information, it is difficult to assess the sentiments of the Nazi rank and file in Upper Austria and Salzburg, although less so in Tyrol. The underground movement had comprised primarily youthful, middle-class activists supported by plebeian elements in Linz, Steyr, Hallein, and other industrial enclaves. In Upper Austria veteran German Nationalists such as Franz Langoth and Anton Reinthaller wielded some influence, though after some internal bickering they had relinquished formal leadership to the Illegal Gauleiter, August Eigruber, an automobile worker. There were also close ties to Ernst Kaltenbrunner and the SS. Whatever the reasons, Hitler's followers in Upper Austria appear to have been less divided than other provincial cohorts. After the Anschluss, they also enjoyed the special patronage of Hitler who took a liking to Eigruber and expended millions of marks to transform Linz into a major cultural and manufacturing center.[103]

As a small cadre, Upper Austrian Nazis faced comparatively few difficulties providing jobs and benefits for party members. While some of Eigruber's close associates lacked the qualifications to take civil service assignments, most of them assumed lucrative positions in the apparatus of the party or its affiliates; others relied on Kaltenbrunner to find a career in the SS.[104] In the weeks following the Anschluss there was considerable fear of forfeiting the spoils of victory to returning émigrés, especially to figures such as Theo Habicht, Andreas Bolek, or Alfred Proksch who had once dominated the Nazi movement in the region and (briefly) in Austria itself. We have already seen, however, that nearly all of the Old Fighters met a chilly reception or remained in the Altreich. Of the thirty-six members initially appointed to the Linz City Council, only one, the veteran SA commander Gustav Nohel, had distinguished himself as a Nazi militant before Hitler's rise to power in Germany.[105]

In neighboring Salzburg aversion to the Old Guard was so intense that party activists were willing to settle for a Reich German as Gauleiter. Because Hitler wanted a strong leader to check the influence of the commanding generals of the Eighteenth Military District (headquartered in the Alpine city), he appointed Friedrich Rainer, the most intelligent, polished, and capable member of the Carinthian faction. The new Gauleiter moved to consolidate his position by swearing in the provincial civil servants, calculating that he could exploit their devotion to duty and state for his own ends; at the same time, he purged the local police and gendarmerie. Decades later the Austrian historian Ernst Hanisch discovered a notable residue of bitterness among those party members who had lost out in the competition for jobs and benefits. On the other hand, Rainer pleased a great many party comrades by swelling the civil service with younger Nazi attorneys and by securing restitution payments for those activists who had suffered at the hands of the Christian Corporative dictatorship.[106]

The situation in Tyrol-Vorarlberg took much longer to sort out. Here the NSDAP consisted of only a few thousand registered members, bitterly divided over tactics and turf. Before 1932 Hitler's movement had made little progress in the Alpine region. Then in April 1933 Gauleiter Franz Hofer, a radio salesman, mobilized the slender resources of the party to capture 41 percent of the vote in municipal elections in Innsbruck. Arrested soon afterward by the federal government, he staged a sensational escape from prison that won him special recognition at the September Party Congress in Nuremberg. Alone among the Austrian Nazis fleeing to the Reich, Hofer managed to carve out a position of influence and power. Ingratiating himself with Hess, Bormann, and other party bosses (including Bürckel), he established a Refugees' Assistance Board for his fellow countrymen in Berlin that enabled him to dispense bribes and payoffs to followers in Tyrol and retain considerable leverage over the situation in his native province.[107]

During the Anschluss, however, Hofer remained at his desk in the Reich capital, unable to prevent the takeover of Innsbruck by a rival group of Illegal Nazis led by Edmund Christoph. In some respects, the upstarts merited the spoils of victory: they had mobilized an estimated 40,000 activists and fellow travelers; they seized control of Tyrol before the arrival of German troops; they then proceeded with notable savagery to purge the provincial government, civil service, and police forces. Nevertheless, the Illegal faction was small and Christoph seemed both irresolute and weak. Although Bürckel allowed him to remain in office until after the April plebiscite, Christoph really stood no chance against Hofer, the man already designated to succeed him as Gauleiter.[108]

How did the Tyrolean rank and file figure in the Nazi power struggle? As we have already seen, eight Illegal Kreisleiter registered their opposition to Hofer's appointment. They constituted a distinct minority. In contrast to other localities, the Nazi movement in Tyrol remained an aggregation of small-town tradesmen, professionals, and other middle-class elements with little influence outside Innsbruck, Kitzbühel, and several other communities. The evidence suggests that many party members supported Hofer as one of their own. While it is true that the new Gauleiter subsequently went out of his way to put his Illegal predecessors on ice, the most recent scholarly investigation reveals that neither he nor his henchmen regarded them as a numerical threat.[109]

Hofer certainly understood Hitler's polycratic system as well as the other

Austrian Gauleiter. With much of the Tyrolean populace distrustful of National Socialism (although not of the Anschluss), he considered it essential to replace officials of the Old Regime with reliable Nazis as soon as possible. At the same time he knew that he could not purge the civil service of the trained personnel required to stabilize his own control. In achieving his aims he exploited the "excesses" of the Illegals, who had dismissed or pensioned scores of civil servants—including one-third of the senior officials—and replaced them with party hacks. Hofer immediately sacked most of the interim magistrates. This enabled him to masquerade as a judicious governor, a pragmatic moderate interested more in professional competence than ideological zeal. Thus, while he awarded the top posts to his own retainers, he also rehired a substantial number of professional civil servants—albeit at salaries usually 25 to 50 percent lower than their former earnings. In addition, he created a large number of entry-level positions in both the provincial administration and the party bureaucracy, which he staffed with jurists and legal clerks, all ardent Nazis, newly graduated from the University of Innsbruck.[110]

In the months following his return to power Hofer made considerable progress overcoming the factionalism of the Tyrolean NSDAP. There remained malcontents in annexed Vorarlberg, but most stalwarts, especially the large number of youngsters joining the party, approved of his aggressive leadership style and policies, especially those favoring able young men like themselves. As early as June 1938 a British diplomat wrote from Innsbruck: "The principal Austrian Nazis may be disillusioned and discouraged by the appointment of Germans or of radical hooligans (such as the newly-nominated Gauleiter of Tirol) to posts over their heads; but this does not apply to the rank and file and their followers, who have got all they want."[111]

IMPACT OF THE REICH CIVIL SERVICE ACT

By October 1938, Hitler's lieutenants had made considerable progress assuaging and regulating the internal feuds of the Austrian NSDAP. But the Viennese Nazis remained in an ugly mood. Their injured pride was fueled by resentment of both Bürckel and Globocnik as well as by developments affecting the entire population, most notably the soaring cost of living and the general fear of war. It was also stoked by the growing financial debt of the party itself, whose expenditures outstripped both resources and revenue. This was due primarily to a reduction in subsidies from the Reich Treasury, but also to the refusal of the rank and file to pay membership dues. Since party leaders including Kreisleiter continued to receive only minimal salaries, there was ample incitement to seek revenue elsewhere. In practical terms, this meant renewed anti-Semitic violence and the seizure of religious and charitable institutions.[112]

Another measure affecting the pocketbooks of a good many party members was the introduction of the Reich Civil Service Act on 1 October 1938 which consolidated the administrative structure of Greater Germany. The extension of the German salary scale to Austria tended to favor senior civil servants and teachers, to limit promotion, and to impose heavy demands on the existing bureaucracy. It also extended the workweek from forty-one to fifty-one hours, ended overtime pay, and curtailed vacations. Since the Nazis had long promised dramatic improvements for those employed in the public sector, especially for party members, the new regulations aroused widespread indignation. The large number of public officials and employees living in Vienna, many of whom were at least nominal members of the NSDAP or its affiliates, felt particularly incensed; their disappointment affected the already sour mood of the party faithful and added another grudge to a growing list of complaints.[113]

Over the following months and years Austrian dignitaries petitioned Berlin to modify the more onerous features of the Civil Service Act, winning, however, only the most trivial of concessions. The regulations remained a major irritant throughout the entire period of German rule; they alienated so many Viennese Nazis that the security organs felt compelled to ignore Hess's ban on reporting party morale.[114] On 13 December 1939 the SD filed a long paper on the "extremely bad morale" of the Old Fighters (which meant in this case anyone belonging to the pre-March NSDAP). It explained that in "state and municipal offices" veteran militants were "being passed over, not promoted, and denied influence." The Old Fighters were incensed because the "politically indifferent Austrian civil service [had] closed ranks against them."[115]

THE GAULEITER CRISIS AND ITS CONSEQUENCES

The pent-up frustrations of the Viennese Nazis found release in two outbursts of savagery: the first a violent assault on the archiepiscopal palace that occurred on 8 October 1938, the second a rapid acceleration of anti-Jewish terror that culminated in the atrocities of Crystal Night four weeks later. Since both events are described in detail later, they need not detain us here. What is significant about the twin orgies of theft, vandalism, and murder is that they yielded only brief psychological fulfillment. The material grievances of the Viennese rank and file remained unresolved.

On 30 January 1939 Hitler unexpectedly sacked Globocnik as Gauleiter of Vienna. Had the Führer appointed the still-popular Frauenfeld or a well-known national figure (as he did the following year), the raucous discontent of the Nazi rank and file might have been contained. Instead, he entrusted Bürckel with the job, presumably assuming that the Reich commissioner would use his enhanced authority to liquidate the last vestiges of Austrian autonomy. There was also logic in bolstering the position of one of the most ruthless and loyal of the Old Guard.[116]

The problem was that conditions in Vienna had changed since the Anschluss. Within less than a year Bürckel had alienated both the party rank and file and and the general populace. While it is true that he was carrying out Hitler's mandate, his behavior won him many enemies. He had upset groups of blue-collar workers by seeking to unseat their champion, Hermann Neubacher, the imaginative and popular lord mayor appointed by Seyss-Inquart. Second, through his primitive manners and ill-tempered behavior the Reich commissioner had earned the disdain of both the bourgeoisie and the cultural elite, the social set so important in shaping attitudes in Vienna.[117] Third, by spending so much time away from his desk,[118] he had left the day-to-day work to his small staff of Saar-Palatinal cronies, thus intensifying the rising tide of Teutophobia; in addition, he paid too little attention to detail, was arbitrary, and, at times, slothful.[119] Finally, Bürckel was bound to clash with the other Austrian Gauleiter once his charge as Reich commissioner expired: no longer primus inter pares, he was still "far too dominant a personality to accept being placed on an equal basis with the other six."[120]

During the last months of peace, the struggle between Bürckel and the Seyss-Inquart faction reached a climax as the Reich commissioner, acting under the Ostmark Law of 14 April 1939, liquidated the last of the Austrian federal ministries and their staffs.[121] Bürckel dismissed Seyss's influential cultural manager, Kajetan Mühlmann, took the steps to drive Hermann Neubacher from City Hall, and filed trumped-up charges against the police president, Josef Fitzthum. On 14 August, Fitzthum wrote to Himmler: "It has gradually become almost customary in Vienna that the Reich commissioner puts old party members into jail without consideration for their rank and name and without waiting for the result of orderly judicial proceedings in the competent court."[122]

Bürckel's ruthless and slipshod political offensive offended so many individuals and groups that it ignited concern at Nazi Party headquarters in Munich. On 3 June Opdenhoff warned that the Reich commissioner was "about to lose his best chances in Vienna" and that one might have "to look for a new man."[123] This was a view shared by the British consul general; he wrote that while Hitler's popularity continued to soar, there was "a considerable recrudescence of the anti-German feeling in Vienna, especially among the Austrian National Socialists." Bürckel's "importations of Germans to assist him in his new tasks," the diplomat continued, "have called forth great opposition from both the radical and more moderate Nazi elements."[124]

The intraparty feud was not without impact on the general populace. During a gala Theatrical Week in June 1939, there were anti-German outbursts in playhouses, cinemas, and the opera. The British consul general reported that "every time an Austrian actor or singer appeared on stage he or she was greeted with applause, while the appearance of Germans was passed over in silence." Dr. Goebbels was so incensed that he "had a pink slip inserted in the programs forbidding applause while the curtain was up."[125]

Here it becomes difficult for the historian to distinguish the sentiments of the Nazi rank and file from those of the general populace, especially between November 1938 and June 1940 when the number of Viennese dues-paying members more than doubled. By the end of July 1939 there were rumors that Bürckel was about to be replaced, but a British observer regarded the hearsay as wishful thinking, adding that much of the prevailing anti-German sentiment was little more than grumbling about foreign holiday makers.[126]

Even so, the menace of war loomed large. In his last report to Whitehall on 15 August, Donald St. Clair Gainer wrote that "the feeling among the intelligent public is one of impending catastrophe hardly to be averted by anything short of a miracle. Perhaps the only optimists in Austria are those members of the party who have not suffered disillusionment and believe, as they are required to believe, that the problem of Danzig will be solved soon and without a major war."[127]

ON THE EVE OF WAR

The Austrian Nazis had always promised to transcend the conflicts of modern society within the framework of a Greater German Reich, an organic National Community not unlike the "Empire of Seventy Millions" adumbrated by Karl Ludwig von Bruck in 1850.[128] Eighteen months after the Anschluss, they remained, as they had been before March 1938, a "factious and discordant" group—divided, disillusioned, and dissatisfied. The reasons for the continued rancor were diverse and various, as this chapter has tried to make clear. At the root of the problem was the fissiparous nature of the German nationalist movement itself, a movement that embraced such a wide range of occupations and interests that from its founding in the Habsburg monarchy up to the present it has rarely been able to resolve the conflicts of its major constituents. During the 1930s the Austrian Nazis provided an organizational framework and a program of populist goals that went a long way in overcoming these schisms, but the party's blind devotion to Hitler, the leader of a foreign country, meant that internal rivalries and feuding both persisted and intensified.

After the Anschluss, the competition for booty and state power exacerbated the intraparty turmoil. Since the Social Darwinian ideology of National Socialism encouraged struggle as an end in itself, friction and strife became institutionalized. In theory, the toughest and most aggressive were supposed to prevail, but the actual settlement of the spoils in Austria left the entrenched forces of the bureaucracy shaken but still in office. This meant that only so many plums were available for the picking. While many Austrian Nazis landed lucrative positions in the public sector, they tended to be newcomers or careerists. The Old Guard thus felt betrayed and embittered.

Vienna was the vortex of division and discontent. In addition to the struggle between Bürckel and Seyss-Inquart, there were confrontations involving the SA and the SS, the Catholic Nationals, and the Frauenfeld faction. The party faithful were caught in conflicts crossing class, sectional, and generational lines. Among the most embittered were unsuccessful office seekers and those who had lost out in the rush to plunder Jewish homes and assets. At the same time, there was disillusionment with Vienna's diminished status in the new order, a sense of indignation that gave credence to fears of spiritual colonization by Prussia. The problem was highlighted by Bürckel's harsh policies and tactless behavior; it was also compounded by the limitations of the Viennese economy, whose outmoded industrial plant, high production costs, and antiquated infrastructure restricted opportunities in the private sector. This was a predicament quite different from that in the provinces where massive investment by the Four-Year Plan in mining and new industrial enterprises provided immediate benefits and jobs.

For all the sorrows of the Viennese Nazis, it would be a mistake to conclude that Hitler's Austrian compatriots were left holding the bag. Many Nazis received posts in the government or civil service; others established careers in the party organization, the military, or the SS. With the outbreak of the Second World War, still others received appointments in occupied Europe—notably in Poland, Holland, the Balkans, and the Soviet Union—where they distinguished themselves deporting and slaughtering Jews.[129] Nor is there any reason to assume that the Austrian Nazis lost their ideological zeal for Hitler's goals. Morale outside Vienna appears to have stayed high, and even within the metropolis the party faithful expressed strong support of the regime's anti-Semitic measures. Moreover, once economic recovery began in earnest, there was confidence that the industrial working classes could be won completely for the National Community.

4
THE WORKING CLASS
Acceptance and Apathy

Nazism always aspired to win the working class to its cause. Despite the party's middle-class composition, it retained a strong anticapitalist flavor, most notably in its self-image but also in its rhetoric and ideology. Hitler himself admired the courage, tenacity, and fighting spirit of the industrial proletariat. He made no secret of his contempt for the self-seeking bankers and businessmen with whom he had made so many deals. While bitterly hostile to Marxism, he never lost sight of his goal of transforming the labor movement into the backbone of the NSDAP.[1] In his drive to power in Germany Hitler had met stiff resistance from both the Social Democrats and the Communists. Hence it was not surprising that he proceeded brutally against the left-wing parties that stood in his way. After seizing control in Berlin, he outlawed the KPD, arrested thousands of party leaders and functionaries, and dissolved the trade unions. In May 1933 he suppressed the Social Democratic Party. Thereafter the Gestapo kept the working population under constant surveillance. "More than any other group," Kershaw has written, "they felt the pressure of the police state."[2]

In Austria the Nazis had little need to discipline industrial labor. This was a task accomplished in February 1934 by the Dollfuss-Schuschnigg dictatorship. Thereafter, most wage earners were so embittered by their defeat that they withdrew from politics, adopting a wait-and-see attitude. Of those who joined underground resistance groups, roughly a third went over to the Nazis. While most remained vaguely loyal to Austro-Marxist traditions, there was a legacy of enmity and hatred so intense that few shed any tears when the regime collapsed in 1938.[3]

In addition to political persecution, Austrian labor suffered economic hardship during the Depression. Official statistics do not reveal how many of the 400,000 Austrians receiving public assistance in 1938 were manual workers, but as we have seen, 44.5 percent of all industrial wage earners had lost their jobs. Unemployment was most acute among construction workers, day laborers, miners, foundrymen, and skilled workers, especially machinists. Of those still employed, nearly all suffered wage cuts, assaults on "double-dippers," and some form of government interference or harassment. As the Depression deepened, only 15 to 20 percent of youngsters leaving school were able to find work. With average family income reduced to 52 percent of 1929 levels, there was a precipitous drop in food consumption accompanied by an increase of infectious disease and suicide. There was also an escalation of violence and xenophobic hostility directed against minorities, women, and marginal fringe groups.[4]

When the Nazis seized power in Vienna, they moved immediately to relieve social distress and to revitalize the economy. Even before Hitler's entourage reached the former imperial capital, officials of both the party and the DAF—the German Labor Front—had acted to protect onetime Socialist activists from overzealous Gestapo agents.[5] In elaborate, well-staged ceremonies Lord Mayor Hermann Neubacher rehired thousands of February Fighters dismissed by the Dollfuss-Schuschnigg regime. Both he and Gauleiter Bürckel emphasized what they called the Socialism of Action, producing 18,000 jobs for the city's unemployed within a week of the Anschluss. On 26 March 1938 the National Labor Law was extended to the Ostmark. It guaranteed basic rights at the workplace and afforded protection from arbitrary dismissal. Shortly thereafter, the Reich's comprehensive social security system also went into effect. It provided relief to over 200,000 desperately poor who had been ineligible for public assistance and extended the Bismarckian system of health care benefits to the working class.[6]

The major goal of Nazi social policy was to solidify the home front before the outbreak of military hostilities. In the Ostmark this meant mobilizing the labor and talent of the Austrian people for the upcoming war effort.[7] To tackle the seemingly intractable problem of unemployment, the Nazis proceeded on four fronts. First, German industry hired away some 100,000 skilled workers, including 10,000 engineers, providing lucrative jobs in the throbbing manufacturing plants of the Reich. Second, the government awarded defense contracts to Austrian enterprises. Third, both the armed forces and the Reich Labor Service began conscripting the young and able into their ranks. Fourth, the regime invested 60 million marks in a comprehensive program to develop the country's mineral resources and to restructure its industrial base. As part of this massive effort, it also undertook ambitious public works projects that involved constructing bridges and motorways, bases and airfields, and homes and apartments. By July 1938, some 71,000 persons were at work on these projects; by August the number had risen to 90,000, of whom 25,000 were employed by the Wehrmacht.[8]

The results of Hitler's package of employment stimulants were not long

TABLE 5. *Unemployed in Austria, 1938–1939 (in thousands)*

	Austria	Vienna	Lower Austria	Upper Austria	Styria	Salzburg	Carinthia	Vorarlberg	Burgenland
1938									
Jan.	401	183	73	37	45	13	16	7	10
Feb.	396	182							
Mar.	365	173							
Apr.	404	204							
May	351	180							
June	275	152							
July	151	103							
Aug.	114	88							
Sept.	100	74		3					
Oct.	107	79		3					
Nov.	113	78		4					
Dec.	151	88		11					
1939									
Jan.	156	85	24	11	8	3	8	1	7
Feb.		78		6					
Mar.		63		3					
Apr.	95	55							
May		45							
June		32							
July		23							
Aug.		19							
Sept.	33	25							
Oct.		29							
Nov.		30							
Dec.		31							

Sources: Botz, *Nationalsozialismus in Wien*, 301; Josef Moser, "Der Wandel der Wirtschafts- und Beschäftigungsstruktur einer Region," 202.

in coming (see Table 5). In one of the most remarkable economic achieve-ments in modern history the National Socialists reduced the number of unemployed in Austria from 401,001 in January 1938 to 99,865 in Septem-ber; in Vienna from 183,271 to 74,162. The effects were most dramatic in the provinces. In Upper Austria the number of jobless fell from 37,120 in Janu-ary 1938 to 2,756 in September. In Salzburg, Tyrol, and Vorarlberg virtually no one was without work. By Christmas, 27 percent more jobs existed in

Austria than before the Anschluss. As seasonal demand accounted for some of the decline, unemployment climbed again at the end of the year. Within a few months, however, the development of a labor shortage revealed that the ravages of the Depression were at last over. Viewed in another context, the annually adjusted official rate of unemployment in the Ostmark fell from 21.7 percent in 1937 to 12.9 percent in 1938; the following year it dropped to 3.2 percent, in 1940 to 1.2 percent.[9]

The new regime's liquidation of unemployment stimulated a sharp increase in demand. Hitler's insistence on a currency conversion rate of 3:2 also gave a boost to consumer purchasing power, since it revalued the Austrian schilling upward by 36 percent. Investment in munitions plants, infrastructure, and natural resources reinforced expansion and contributed to an immediate rise in the standard of living. Despite official wage restraints, the demand for labor was so acute that between June and December 1938 the weekly income of industrial workers rose 9 percent. In other branches, there were increases of 50 to 65 percent, making for an aggregate rise for the year of between 25 and 30 percent. It is true that not everyone benefited in equal measure: Viennese wage earners took home fatter paychecks than those in the provinces; workingmen in defense plants did better than those in enterprises producing consumer goods; textile and paper workers received only modest increases; women earned less than two-thirds of nonskilled male laborers. Nevertheless, economic growth was spectacular. As Felix Butschek has demonstrated, there was also a regional multiplier effect with substantial growth in the production of steel, electricity, and even consumer goods. All in all, the Austrian GNP rose 12.8 percent in 1938 and 13.3 percent in 1939; without the agricultural sector, the rates were 15 and 16.3 percent.[10]

Although Nazi social and economic policy brought forth real benefits, there were disturbing trade-offs. The regime's efforts at regulating inflationary pressures were inconsistent and unsuccessful. Between April 1938 and April 1939 the Reich Office of Price Control kept the cost of housing at pre-Anschluss levels in cities like Vienna and Linz while reducing the costs of heating and electricity by nearly 10 percent. During the same period, however, the price of meat, poultry, eggs, fruits, and vegetables trebled. By the end of 1938 consumers found themselves paying 22 percent more for overall expenses than before the Anschluss. This was because the sharp rise in income was offset by social security deductions, new taxes, and mounting living costs. By New Year a Viennese family of four spent 30 percent more to live than the year before. On the other hand, overtime pay, marriage loans, and children's subsidies made it possible to make ends meet.[11]

The most vexatious economic problem confronting the Austrian people in the months following the Anschluss was the inability of the Nazi regime to match popular expectations.[12] Between March and December 1938, for example, the government built some 6,778 housing units, a considerable achievement in comparison with the 34,000 dwellings erected between 1921 and 1937. Having also targeted 70,000 Jewish domiciles for expropriation, there seemed every reason to believe that Austria's housing shortage would be addressed in short order. Instead, an influx of Reich German managers, functionaries, police, and military personnel inflated the real-estate market and reduced the number of available dwellings.[13] Even worse, the combination of rural flight, currency revaluation, and accelerating military mobilization made it impossible to align the Austrian economy with that of the Altreich. By 1939 the cost of living in Vienna even surpassed that of Berlin.[14] Despite ongoing efforts by local Nazi officials to improve the material conditions of everyday life, the standard of living in the Ostmark continued to lag behind that of the Altreich. Gradual awareness of that disparity played a major role in shaping popular attitudes, particularly those of the working class.

THE RESPONSE OF VIENNESE LABOR

In 1934 some 55 percent of the population of Vienna belonged to the *Arbeiterschaft*—the working class. As in other great cities of Europe, the workers tended to live and work in grim industrial neighborhoods such as Ottakring, Simmering, and Floridsdorf; there were also large concentrations of working-class families in every one of the town's twenty-one administrative districts. Blue-collar residents thus composed 50 to 70 percent of twelve boroughs, 40 to 49 percent of five others, and 37 to 39 percent of the remaining four. Of those fortunate enough to be employed most worked in large factories, municipal enterprises, or in small-scale workshops run by independent craftsmen. Although not every worker had belonged to the Social Democratic Party, subcultural solidarity remained strong and an "unquestioned majority" still sympathized with the defeated labor movement.[15]

Nevertheless, there was considerable ideological confusion and disarray. There was also widespread disaffection with the (largely Jewish) leadership of the SDAP. After the twin civil wars of 1934 a number of February Fighters had forged bonds of solidarity and friendship with underground Nazi leaders with whom they had shared prison cells at Wöllersdorf in Lower Austria.[16] When the Anschluss actually occurred, outside observers reported that blue-collar workers composed a relatively small proportion of the cheering crowds.[17] According to Botz, comparatively few workingmen joined the jeering mobs tormenting the Jews.[18] Nevertheless, most of the working population felt a rush of malicious glee at the overthrow of the Christian

Corporative dictatorship. There was also positive response to Karl Renner's endorsement of the Anschluss. From his exile in Czechoslovakia even Otto Bauer conceded that the proletariat was not immune to the "monstrous suggestive power of Nazi propaganda."[19] What Hanisch has written about the reaction of provincial labor may apply more to Vienna than to the backwoods: "Class-conscious workers did not align themselves with the National Socialist party, but they also did not protest."[20]

In courting the working class the Nazis called for national unity within the National Community. They appealed to widespread anticlerical and anti-Semitic sentiment by assailing the Christian Corporative system, the Roman Catholic Church, and the "non-German" leaders of Social Democracy who had allegedly led the labor movement to disaster in 1934. As the Gestapo and the Security Service were charged with detecting and rooting out Marxist and Communist influence, the Nazis had to "walk a tightrope between their attacks on Marxism and their anxiety not to estrange the Social Democratic workers by attacking the tenets of democratic socialism outright."[21] Particular attention was paid to wooing the young, a group relatively "untainted" by Austro-Marxist ideology. In retrospect, Nazism's doctrinaire hostility to Marxism hobbled its efforts to win the emotional loyalty of Viennese working people. Even so, the success of Hitler's minions was considerable.

One of the first attempts to assess working-class response to the New Order was made by underground agents of the Sopade, the exiled leadership of the German Social Democratic Party. In a brief but discursive survey they placed emphasis on the deeply rooted Austro-Marxist yearning for union with Germany; at the same time, the observers claimed that blue-collar sentiment had moved so far to the left since 1934 that most workers would bridle under "Prussian discipline."[22] According to the first soundings by the Nazis—specifically by Odilo Globocnik, the Carinthian activist then angling to become Gauleiter of Vienna—labor was responding affirmatively to government attention. Admitting that Hitler posters and swastika streamers had been torn down in the Seventeenth District, he contended that Communist morale was in a state of "panic." Nazi "work creation schemes and the incorporation of those ineligible for public assistance on the welfare rolls have been exceptionally well received," he wrote. "A number of Communist leaders are voluntarily turning in forbidden literature."[23]

Toward the end of May, Nazi authorities learned of serious unrest at the Rannersdorf Brewery. Always sensitive to the danger of residual Marxist influence, the Gestapo undertook an extensive inquiry that did indeed reveal widespread discontent. The disaffection was rooted, however, in personal rivalry and factionalism, not political ideology.[24] The following month a comprehensive investigation of Communist activity in Vienna concluded that the KPÖ had largely suspended operations and that the rank and file were joining the NSDAP. While it was admitted that a handful of activists were spreading rumors of food shortages or trying to incite disturbances at the Central Market (Naschmarkt), their activities were reported to have had little impact on working-class sentiment.[25] All in all, there was little evidence to contradict the claim appearing in the Nazi press that "today we Reds are for the Führer."[26]

This is not to say that Anschluss enthusiasm continued to prevail in Vienna. At the end of May an American correspondent wrote that the metropolis had become a city of "whispers and furtive glances over the shoulder."[27] A month later the British consul general indicated growing disgust with the "vileness of the anti-Jewish campaign now raging in Vienna, the constant rise in prices and the lack of respect for constitutional law."[28] So palpable was the spreading disquiet that even the Nazi leadership acknowledged that measures had to be taken to assuage popular sentiment.[29]

That it was the Viennese Nazis who were the first to feel disillusioned with the reality of the Anschluss is an irony that has been discussed in the previous chapter. As their complaints about "Prussians" and "Piefkes" found their way into everyday conversation, the authorities became worried about the impact of the growing anti-German sentiment on the general population. Bürckel was particularly concerned about the effect of sky-rocketing prices and tried to counter inflationary pressure by what today would be called "jawboning." He appealed to merchants to maintain pre-Anschluss charges for clothing, shoes, leather goods, furniture, and basic necessities. He blamed "Jewish swindlers" for soaring living costs and threatened to send price gougers to concentration camps. But despite intimidation and blandishment, grocery prices rose steeply. By July there were scarcities of fruits, vegetables, and bread. There were also protests and sporadic demonstrations by angry housewives.[30]

To what extent Viennese workers made a class-conscious contribution to the overall discontent is difficult to ascertain. Available evidence is scant and contradictory. The *Rote Fahne*, organ of the underground Communist Party, claimed that by mid-June some 40,000 wage earners had staged demonstrations for higher wages. Disturbances were also reported at the Floridsdorf locomotive works, the Siemens-Schuckert plant, and the Vienna airport.[31] More reliably, the SD indicated considerable unhappiness among those taking jobs in the Altreich. Far from leaving voluntarily, many were being arbitrarily conscripted as "lazy rabble" by the Labor Office; there were tearful "incidents" at the West Train Station as well as complaints about a "climate of fear."[32]

On the other hand, these were also the months that saw nearly 28 percent of the entire Viennese population join the DAF, an association whose membership rose from 89,179 in June to 582,724 at the end of the year.[33] While it is indisputable that many workers succumbed to intimidation and pressure in signing up, it is also true that a considerable number joined of their own volition. One German organizer even expressed astonishment at the "unprecedented attractiveness" of the front.[34] Whatever individual motives or intentions, there was a consensus that the DAF represented something more than a political front organization. Indeed, many workers reported (and later fondly recalled) that Nazi shop stewards were generally receptive to their concerns; they also found that foremen and managers were much more accommodating than under the Christian Corporative system.[35] Toward the middle of July one DAF official wrote to Bürckel that working-class circles were indeed alarmed by the soaring cost of living, but that most people were so grateful to be working again that hardly anyone was muttering against the NSDAP.[36]

Scrupulous examination of the evidence by Gerhard Botz has led to the conclusion that in the euphoric months following the Anschluss both Nazis and Social Democrats felt a genuine sense of solidarity and mutual reconciliation. At the same time, each side remained wary of the other, especially the Nazis who continued to distrust anyone who had once been a Marxist.[37] Whether a less suspicious approach would have gone further to integrate the working class into Hitler's National Community is unlikely, although impossible to say with certainty. The underground Social Democratic network remained largely intact. Despite outward signs of conformity, veteran unionists were actually penetrating the DAF, hoping to protect industrial workers. Since it was known that the Gestapo possessed the names of 5,000 Revolutionary Socialists—underground activists who had opposed the Christian Corporative system—outright resistance appeared both counterproductive and suicidal.[38] To a large extent the Social Democratic strategy of limited cooperation succeeded in preserving the subcultural unity of the Viennese working class. At the same time, there can be little doubt that the policy of accommodation exacted a moral price. After World War II, especially after 1947, the resurrected SPÖ repeatedly appealed to former Nazis. It not only granted them concessions; in 1971 it also awarded them four portfolios in the government of Bruno Kreisky and quashed the judicial investigation of 800 Austrian war criminals.[39]

The Sudeten crisis, as mentioned before, triggered the first mass disenchantment with the Anschluss regime. It also lent credence to longtime Marxist warnings about Hitler's aggressive intentions.[40] By mid-August both the call-up of reservists and the cancellation of Strength through Joy holiday excursions were causing consternation in Viennese communities.[41] There were also incidents involving German soldiers stationed in the city.[42] Gestapo informants reported that blue-collar neighborhoods were seething with discontent. So alarmed were the authorities that Reinhard Heydrich, head of the both the SD and the Sipo, ordered the Viennese Gestapo to "take into protective custody all former SPÖ and KPÖ officials" suspected of subversive activities.[43] Although the Gestapo disregarded the directive as inopportune, it did pick up a number of persons for hostile, slanderous, or insulting remarks.[44]

The reaction of Viennese labor to Hitler's spectacular diplomatic victory in the Munich Agreement of 30 September 1938 can not be divined from the surviving documentation. There seems little reason to believe that the working classes did not share the relief and enthusiasm of the general population. Karl Renner, the semiofficial spokesman of Social Democracy, even published a pamphlet exalting the "unparalleled strength and determination of the leadership of the German Reich."[45] On the other hand, the turbulent weeks following the sack of Innitzer's archiepiscopal palace aroused uneasiness, worry, and anti-Nazi outbursts. Among those picked up by the Gestapo were a good many blue-collar workers, including a man overheard responding to the greeting "Heil Hitler" with the words "I shit on Hitler."[46]

Shortly before the end of the year the Security Service of the SS filed a comprehensive paper on working-class morale. Based on extensive interviews with five shop stewards from the Tenth District, the report indicated that, for the most part, the DAF was winning the confidence of Viennese labor. At the same time, it noted growing criticism of Nazi bigwigs, primarily Reich German functionaries who showed little understanding of Austrian conditions and tended to dismiss constructive criticism as querulousness or disloyalty. There were also instances of local corruption, most notably that of Party Comrade Adler, a DAF official in the Steyr Works, who had managed to wreck three company automobiles while cruising the wine bars of Grinzing.[47]

With regard to political affairs, the SD wrote that "the workers speak with great satisfaction about the strength of the German army and the cause of rearmament." Reservists returning from retraining exercises were even said to be pleased by their treatment, although also wary of being called to active duty. In viewing the Jewish Question, the SD explained that the working classes endorsed the elimination of Jews from the workplace, but expressed qualms about the actual handling of the problem on Crystal Night. In contrast, there was no remorse about the Nazi assault on the church: the workers despised Cardinal Innitzer and recommended even harsher measures against both his clergy and flock.[48]

Whatever their true feelings, Viennese wage earners received a shock when they returned to work after the holiday season: German income taxes that went into force on 1 January 1939 had reduced their take-home pay by as much as 30 percent. Despite official appeals for understanding, there followed spontaneous strikes and collective demands for higher pay. On 16 January the afternoon shift of the Pottendorfer Spinning Mills refused to start the machinery in the sorting and cleaning division; at the Görz Optical Institute in Favoriten, an enterprise essential to the armaments effort, workers scrawled slogans on factory grindstones thanking "our Führer for the new taxes"; at the Siemens Schuckert plant in Floridsdorf sixty lathe operators downed tools to protest the dismissal of an angry cutter for hurling a working part at a foreman.[49]

On 1 February a Viennese SA leader wrote to a colleague in Offenbach that the working population was "extremely agitated." A major cause was incompetent management. At the Anker Bakery an inexperienced team of young Berliners had replaced the Jewish directors. "Aside from awarding themselves immense salaries, they have done nothing." The workforce of 1,600 had been gravitating toward National Socialism, he concluded, but "since the preposterous developments in the main office, they are showing their true colors."[50]

The malaise gripping Vienna in early 1939 was not confined solely to the working class or to the workplace. A substantial part of the discontent, stemmed from renewed factional strife within the Nazi Party as we have already seen.[51] Another factor contributing to overall dissatisfaction was a continued rise in the cost of living. Instead of a gradual stabilization of prices as promised by the regime, the new year saw over-the-counter charges accelerate. There were also shortages of merchandise and food staples. To be sure, elegant sweaters, petit point, and leather goods could still be seen in shop windows on the Graben and the Kärntnerstrasse, but most fine woolens and high-quality shoes had disappeared from the shelves. Coffee was available only in rationed quantities of 100 grams per week; rice, nuts, pears, and oranges could not be had anywhere. The skyrocketing price of vegetables, fruits, and other staples aroused the ire of large numbers of Viennese, especially housewives. One Nazi informant reported that women were constantly asking: "Have you found any onions? How much did they cost today? What about fruit? Any potatoes?"[52]

Working-class disaffection thus constituted only one tessera in a fairly large mosaic of unhappiness and discontent. In two remarkably astute articles appearing in the pages of the *New York Times*, the American correspondent Anne O'Hare McCormick captured the fluctuating and contradictory mood prevailing in Vienna. After explaining the discord raging within the Austrian Nazi Party, she characterized the Viennese as "provincial," "self-absorbed," but "more secure to be with Germany." Walking through the streets of the metropolis, she found cafés "more crowded than they were last year, . . . [offering] coffee, whipped cream, white bread and plenty of butter." Viewed in perspective, "visitors from other parts of Germany are amazed at the contrast between German and Austrian fare."

In the courtyards of the Karl Marx Hof, the public-housing complex bombarded by Dollfuss's howitzers in 1934, she observed residents strolling serenely "in the pale February sunshine, . . . dressed like Sunday crowds in other quarters. For years there had been little elegance in Vienna. Now the population is as proletarian as the rest of Germany. Beggars have disappeared; there is no more unemployment."[53]

Shrewdly piercing the mask of Viennese self-pity and sentimentality, McCormick concluded: "You observe that practically all Austrians complain, and those who complain are of three categories: first, the old Nazis and pan-Germans who expected most from the Anschluss; second, the employers and businessmen generally; and third, intellectuals. But those who complain least are the very young and the lowest level of society—barbers, carpenters, butchers, pinched-faced mothers of poor families. These are the people who testify that they are better off than before."[54]

Assessing working-class attitudes on the first anniversary of the Anschluss, one could safely say that, while shop-floor militancy was increasing, most disaffection was economic, not political. Unlike their German counterparts, Viennese workers had generally avoided the full repression of the Nazi regime or, more precisely, they had experienced a milder degree of it. Further, there were many people who were still grateful to be working again, especially the poor and destitute. As a young waiter told McCormick, the atmosphere in his neighborhood had completely changed. "I look at the the shoes of the people in the streets," he added, "and I know times are better for the poor."[55]

Still, it is hard to take issue with the view of the British consul general, Donald St. Clair Gainer, that the first year of German rule had been "in almost every respect one of uneasiness, discontent, and confusion."[56] Blue-collar families clearly resented the soaring prices, "the tightening of tax regulations, and the very numerous deductions for Party purposes."[57] They also objected to piece-rate pay.[58] What is less clear is whether the disaffection of Viennese labor can be considered distinctive or significantly different from the mobilization exhaustion or *Reichsmüdigkeit* felt by other individuals and groups. While there is certainly evidence of Austrian patriotism in the occasional anti-German outbursts reported by the Gestapo,[59] there is no real reason to conclude that the industrial working population had broken with the Anschluss.

Furthermore, economic conditions continued to improve. In the nine months before the German invasion of Poland some 147,000 new jobs opened up in Austria, and although wages remained officially frozen, personal income rose by 4 percent. During the same period there was a slight decline in public investment, but the slack was more than made up by defense spending. As we have already seen, the nonagricultural gross national product rose by a substantial 16.3 percent.[60] In Vienna, on the other hand, some unemployment persisted and the cost of living spiraled upward. Given the regime's tightening control of agricultural production, there were also spot shortages of meat, potatoes, and other food staples. Around butcher shops and market stalls it was not uncommon to hear crowds of housewives muttering their frustration and displeasure.[61]

In many ways, the attitudes of trolley and transport workers represented the views of Viennese labor. Hostile to the Dollfuss-Schuschnigg regime, the politically conscious trolleymen had generally welcomed the Anschluss. They remained loyal to Social Democratic values, but they did not hesitate to join the German Labor Front. According to a DAF report of 22 May 1939, the municipal conductors, motormen, and switchmen felt shortchanged by a much-touted October wage hike that was supposed to bring municipal earnings in line with those in the Reich but went primarily to management. Instead of receiving equitable compensation in the National Community, a conductor with twenty years service found himself drawing the same pay as a new employee in a managerial position. The introduction of the German income tax further undermined both purchasing power and morale, not just at New Year but on an ongoing basis. Between April and May 1939, for example, deductions for taxes, social security, health insurance, and the German Labor Front rose from RM 41.25 to RM 49.31. That the Vienna Tramway System subsequently became a hotbed of anti-Nazi sentiment and indiscipline should come as no surprise, especially as the municipal workers lacked the market leverage of their brethren in construction or defense industries.[62]

Just how confused and incongruous working-class sentiment appeared to an outsider can be seen in the report of a DAF functionary, a Strength through Joy tour guide, who in early June conducted a holiday excursion to Vienna from the Kulmbach Spinning Mills in Bavaria. According to the account, the tourists were both stunned and outraged by the prevalence of "Marxist elements" in the metropolis. While admiring the neo-Gothic city hall, they had to put up with caustic remarks about "alien Nazis" from Viennese bystanders. One individual, a man wearing a party badge, claimed to be the leader of both the SA and the Communist cadre in his neighborhood. Other Viennese workers also maintained that the SA was "on their side." While the tourists were said to have reacted with shock and exasperation, they readily grasped the root cause of the discontent: the soaring cost of living. Finding prices some 20 to 30 percent higher than in Bavaria, most of the tourists returned home without purchasing a souvenir or memento of their visit.[63]

In summer 1939 the Viennese mood became even uglier. In working-class neighborhoods little attempt was made to conceal open disaffection and anger. Groups of workingmen were even reported going through the streets of Meidling raising clenched fists in the Marxist salute. According to the Gestapo, an "army of complainers" was exploiting the dissatisfaction to ridicule Reich Germans and spread rumors of war.[64] The dissatisfaction was, however, by no means confined to proletarian elements. The British consul general described a "considerable recrudescence of anti-German feeling in Vienna, especially among the Austrian National Socialists."[65]

Despite enormous confidence in Hitler's leadership and overwhelming support for Nazi racial and social policies, anti-German sentiment intensified sharply throughout July and August. According to the Security Service, resentment of Prussian carpetbaggers was so pervasive that at "Heurigen parties Germans from the Reich under any pretext are annoyed and heckled."[66] The threat of war also loomed large. Much more than in rural areas, or for that matter, in other cities of Greater Germany, the Viennese populace grasped the gravity of the Polish crisis.[67] The British consul general wrote: "The menace of war underlies everyone's thoughts as it did a year ago, in spite of the absence of viable military preparations. Those who think that war is inevitable (and there are few educated Austrians who do not) base their forecasts on the logic of events and are unwilling to recognize any redeeming feature in the present situation. Even a peaceful settlement of the Danzig question, they argue, would merely postpone the time."[68]

By late August 1939, then, Vienna had become a city churning with "bitter discontent," "tension and nervousness"; everywhere people felt a sense of "impending catastrophe hardly to be averted by anything short of a miracle."[69] When news arrived of the signing of the Molotov-Ribbentrop

Pact, the miraculous appeared to have occurred. According to one observer, there was an "indescribable" rush of euphoria, a brief effervescence of good feeling shared by Nazis and Austro-Marxists alike. Forty-eight hours later it became known that the British government refused to alter its commitment to Polish independence, plunging the metropolis again into stygian gloom.[70] Throughout the summer dissatisfaction had been particularly rife in factories and in working-class communities. In contrast to the Altreich, Communist activists were still expanding underground operations, circulating clandestine literature, and undertaking acts of industrial sabotage. While their appeal remained limited, they had established cells in Ottakring, Favoriten, and Stadlau; they had also won adherents in the Vienna Fire Department and the Tramway System.[71] Still, it is difficult to distinguish working-class discontent from the overall malaise gripping the metropolis. Besides, as SD documentation makes clear, the main thrust of antiwar propaganda was coming from Catholic conservatives and pro-Austrian monarchists.[72] While working-class cohesion persisted, it was confined primarily to bread-and-butter issues.

REACTION IN THE PROVINCES

Away from Vienna, in the provinces, the working classes lived in scattered industrial enclaves, each isolated from the other, each surrounded by intensely hostile neighbors. Industrial manufacturing had developed randomly in Austria, originating in remote mining areas, along transportation intersections, or in preindustrial commercial centers. Aside from Wiener Neustadt in Lower Austria, there were no towns with the usual mix of mills, foundries, and collieries. Even in Linz, a city with a population of 111,545, production was largely small-scale with well over 60 percent of the workforce employed in handicrafts. In Upper Styria, at the opposite extreme, smoke-stack industries dominated a cluster of mining and steel towns, not unlike those in West Virginia or other parts of rural Appalachia in the United States. Elsewhere, there were scores of villages containing a single combine or factory.[73] For the provincial working class the shop floor was an "island of proletarian existence surrounded by an agrarian world."[74]

In the two decades following the collapse of the Habsburg monarchy, the Social Democratic population outside Vienna had endured a drumfire of intimidation, abuse, and persecution at the hands of employers, the Heimwehr, and the Roman Catholic Church. Particularly demoralizing were the many sermons and pastoral letters demonizing the Socialists as the "Evil Ones." After the civil war of 1934, the workers bore the indignities of defeat, unemployment, and marginalization. As victims of a reverse Kulturkampf they also suffered severe ostracism. While some supported the underground Revolutionary Socialists, others joined the Nazis.[75]

Of these, many looked favorably on Hitler's assurances of new job opportunities, better living conditions, and improved status within the Germanic National Community. In factory towns such as Steyr Social Democratic solidarity remained largely intact. But in smaller communities industrial workers did not hesitate to rub shoulders with Nazi activists, many of whom they had known since childhood and still regarded as personal friends. As one Alpine worker recalled decades later, the local Nazis "were also mountain people; even if they were our opponents, we still stuck together."[76]

When the Anschluss occurred, the reaction of provincial labor ranged from indifference to enthusiasm. While Tyrolean wage earners were said to be "hidden opponents of the [Nazi] movement,"[77] those in Upper Austria eagerly embraced the new order. In Linz, the Gestapo recorded that "an enthusiasm existed among the workers for National Socialism as no other government before had been able to sustain in this layer of the population."[78] Blue-collar opinion clearly depended on specific geographical and historical circumstances, but it appears to have been nearly unanimous in endorsing union with the German Reich. With regard to Nazi rule, attitudes were more ambivalent. A worker in Hallein explained: "We all cheered as they came, all together . . . ; we suddenly had a lot of new jobs." On the other hand, "one had to adapt. You could not say a thing. As a matter of fact, you profited most if you did not say anything. If you protested, then they would fire you right away."[79]

It is thus an exaggeration to conclude that the "National Socialists succeeded in winning over the overwhelming majority of the working class."[80] Still, there can be no doubt that in the provinces Hitler's movement gained considerable blue-collar support. Besides providing jobs and meting out vengeance to the Old Regime, the Nazis appealed to strong local prejudices and resentments. The Führer himself made no secret of his intention of cutting Vienna down to size, both by entrusting the administration of the provincial Reichsgaue to indigenous Nazis and by inaugurating an ambitious program of regional modernization that included the exploitation of natural resources, the expansion of existing production, and the establishment of a vast new manufacturing complex in Upper Danube.[81] For local workingmen the results were swift in coming. Not only did unemployment disappear almost overnight, but thousands of new jobs also appeared suddenly in mining, construction, and industry, a development that provided greater leverage in wage contracts than in Vienna. In some border plants such as the

Dornbirn textile mills, in Vorarlberg, wage levels even reached those in the Altreich.[82]

Furthermore, proletarian attitudes in factory towns and villages tended to be more attuned to Nazi values than in Vienna. Imbued with a strong work ethic, village workers frequently identified as much with region as with class. They looked askance at collective institutions; they took considerable pride in private ownership. Marxist orthodoxy notwithstanding, they were certainly no more immune to xenophobic nationalism than were other groups of society. Nazi social policy had a great deal to offer. As an added inducement, the Strength through Joy scheme made it possible to escape the benighted world of small-town Austria on excursion trips to the thriving cities of Greater Germany or even on cruises to Norway or Italy. For many working men and women these were breathtaking holidays never to be forgotten—or repeated.[83]

Most of all, village workers dreamed of owning their own home, a dream that the German Labor Front managed to exploit and partially to fulfill. Ever since the First World War thousands of destitute families had been crowded together in ramshackle barracks on the outskirts of Linz and Steyr and in the Iron Mountain region of Styria. These whirlpools of filth and squalor were targeted immediately by the Nazis for demolition to be replaced by model communities of single-family homes and semidetached houses. Within weeks of the Anschluss, building began on the new housing projects, with the Gauleiter of Upper Austria, August Eigruber, himself a former automobile worker, overseeing the construction of a village-style complex of 4,500 homes adjacent to the Münichholz Ball Bearing Works in Steyr. Simultaneously, an even larger residential community started to take shape at Linz, in a greenbelt area near the Hermann Göring Iron and Steel Works, a housing project whose completion was expedited by Hitler himself.[84]

Between 1938 and 1944 at least 15,000 working-class homes were built in Upper Danube, some 6,648 others in the industrial towns of Styria. Although these residential projects did not alleviate the severe housing shortage in Austria, they were well built and aesthetically pleasing. They were also hammered together in part by foreign and slave labor. Since the Nazis assigned priority in occupancy to local families, they were able to consolidate and strengthen the support of regional blue-collar elements. A half century later local people would still regard *Hitlersiedlungen* as a positive legacy of the Anschluss regime.[85]

The Nazis did not annex Austria to shower benefactions on its inhabitants. We have already seen that Göring proclaimed the "most strenuous efforts" would be applied to make sure that Austrians solved their own problems.[86] On the shop floor that meant intensified surveillance, harsh discipline, and the constant threat of arrest for sloth or insubordination. The German invaders were determined to root out Austro-Marxist influence, even in the smallest communities, and ordered the police to register or take into custody "all persons of Marxist persuasion—Communists, Revolutionary Socialists and so forth—who might be suspected of undermining the leadership of the National Socialist state."[87] For all that, provincial workers flocked to the swastika banner, especially in remote factory villages and mining towns. From the pits of the Sonnberg coalfields near Guttaring, in Carinthia, for example, at least two-thirds of the miners were reported working for the party; at Niklasdorf in neighboring Styria all but four of the town's six hundred workers were said to support the new order.[88] Even more surprisingly, the police wrote from Upper Danube, a region long unsympathetic to the Nazi movement, that the laboring population in Linz and Steyr as well as in small villages like Kleinraming, Gleink, and Reichraming greeted the Anschluss with considerable enthusiasm.[89]

As in Vienna, the Nazis moved with great dispatch to mobilize provincial workingmen. In ceremonies held in Linz and Steyr, Upper Austrian Gauleiter Eigruber solemnly rehired a number of February Fighters; he also elicited declarations of support from prominent Social Democrats such as Ludwig Bernaschek, brother of the provincial militia commander, and Franz Sichlrader, former mayor of Steyr.[90] Some months later Gauleiter Uiberreither of Styria scored an even bigger propaganda coup by offering a comfortable job to Paula Wallisch, widow of Koloman Wallisch—the onetime head of Styrian labor who had fought with Bela Kun, served in the provincial diet at Graz, and after the February Civil War had gone to the gallows.[91] By all accounts, blue-collar reaction exceeded expectations. From Kirchdorf came word that the "working class is exceptionally satisfied," from Kleinraming that the village's "nine Marxists are showing real enthusiasm for the present system." In Wartberg three persons had to be taken into protective custody for "Marxist views," but in Reichraming the workforce was said to be "entirely for Hitler."[92]

After the April plebiscite, working-class morale remained favorable, despite substantial grumbling about rising living costs. The Gestapo, always fearful of Marxist influence, investigated reports of "Communist agitation" but usually found them exaggerated or misleading. At the Steyr Works, for example, Himmler's agents picked up copies of the underground *Rote Fahne*, but characterized shop-floor discontent as a reaction to unexpected pay deductions and insensitive management. By September the security organs indicated that the Steyr workforce had largely gone over to the NSDAP or was at least sympathetic to the movement. Elsewhere the police claimed that Marxism had "ceased to exist" or was as "good as extinct."[93]

In the meantime, the German Labor Front was expanding into the hinterland. The Front, as mentioned earlier, was the principal instrument of Nazi social policy, a mass organization devised to mobilize labor, to ameliorate working conditions, and, through a combination of compulsory arbitration and force, to keep wages in check. In the Ostmark its leaders were also charged with improving industrial efficiency, overcoming class conflict, and adjusting the pace of labor to the demands of the German military-industrial complex.[94] According to a comprehensive report submitted to Reich commissioner Bürckel on 25 July 1938, the initial response of labor in the Reichsgau of Lower Danube was generally positive: plant workers had cheered DAF chief Dr. Robert Ley on a recent inspection trip through the province; they had turned out in substantial numbers to attend Labor Front assemblies. The paper acknowledged the persistence of small pockets of Marxist and Czech malcontents but dismissed them as nonthreatening. For the most part, it argued, "the workers are marching with us."[95]

In surveying working conditions in Lower Austria, the DAF document provides a glimpse of blue-collar attitudes. It reveals that workingmen were beginning to worry about rising living costs, but felt fortunate to have jobs again. Nearly all complaints involved pocketbook issues, not political concerns. In Amstetten DAF officials reported understandable unhappiness among sawmill workers who were taking home pay checks smaller than other wage earners; in Bruck an der Leitha they encountered disillusionment with the slow pace of economic change, fanned, it was thought, by a handful of Communists. In Eisenstadt, shorn of its status as a provincial capital, there was "great discontent," the result not of Marxist influence but of insufficient wages and appalling working conditions. Elsewhere, especially in impoverished areas of the former Burgenland, the DAF men expressed alarm at the depressed state of the economy and the plight of working-class families forced to sleep on straw mattresses in dirt-floor homes. In St. Pölten, Korneuburg, and Wiener Neustadt, on the other hand, business was observed to be picking up and morale improving perceptibly.[96]

Since industrial and farm wages continued to lag behind living costs, blue-collar grumbling persisted in the provinces of the Ostmark, although at a much lower level than in Vienna. There was a brief miners' strike in Upper Styria, for example, but it was an isolated event.[97] By late summer stations in Upper Danube were nearly unanimous in reporting working-class backing of the National Community.[98] Even in Kirchdorf, where the laboring population had taken a wait-and-see attitude, the authorities now indicated strong support.[99] The security organs also emphasized the virtual disappearance of Marxist agitation, even though they conceded that the Gestapo was still picking up suspects and periodically arresting drunken workers for shouting "Hail Moscow!" At the time of the Munich crisis lively discussion was recorded among most small-town workingmen. At Waldneukirchen, in Upper Danube, the wage earners were said to be counting on Hitler to pull off a diplomatic victory. By contrast, workers in the nearby Steyr Works were reported to be pessimistic and querulous. Once the danger of war had passed, those "Marxist" and "Communist" elements that had supposedly tried to exploit the crisis for their own ends were placed under arrest.[100] In Linz they amounted to forty-seven former Social Democratic functionaries.[101]

During the Christmas season 1938 provincial working-class identification with the Anschluss system appears to have peaked. The authorities stressed both the lack of dissent and the virtual disappearance of Marxist influence. Although the SD in Steyr opined that "subversive elements" were simply keeping out of sight, the police in outlying communities such as Grünburg, Kremsmünster, and Kirchdorf contended that the Nazi system had given the laboring population tremendous confidence and self-esteem. The good feeling was not just a matter of being back on the job. It was also the malicious glee of seeing peasant neighbors groveling in humiliation. Workers were reported picking barroom fights with farmboys, in one case taunting the rustics by boasting, "We're now the masters!"[102]

All the same, this general sense of well-being was not universal. From factory towns of Lower Danube came word of working-class disquiet, the result, it was claimed, of pay deductions and soaring living costs. At the Hemp Jute and Textile Factory, in Neufeld an der Leitha, there was a brief strike; in other workshops there were slowdowns and absenteeism. After the first of the year, village workers were overheard complaining loudly about new withholding taxes. While their grievances remained confined largely to economic issues, the authorities began to worry about what they called a "distemper."[103] Furthermore, since workers lacked the collective means of protecting their interests, many of them retreated *faute de mieux* into their own milieu, seeking refuge in collective grumbling or in remote Alpine retreats.[104] Despite the relative success of the Nazi regime in penetrating the proletarian subculture of small-town Austria, Social Democratic values remained relatively intact, albeit in shaken and disoriented form. Sensing this, an exasperated county executive wrote from Zell am See: "Despite every effort, Marxist and Communist ideas continue to prevail among the working classes just beneath the surface."[105]

The extension of the Reich income tax to the Ostmark on 1 January 1939, therefore, upset and irritated provincial wage earners. For the first time since the Anschluss, Communist resistance groups made some headway establishing underground cells at the Steyr-Daimler-Puch Works in Graz and in plants near Leoben, Knittelfeld, and Bruck an der Mur. Their appeal remained extremely limited, but their clandestine literature shrewdly focused on the inequities caused by frozen wages and skyrocketing living costs. Elsewhere, bands of Socialist railwaymen solicited contributions, set up safe houses, and established contacts with like-minded groups in Bavaria. Given their mobility and long commitment to social democracy, they were a critical group in maintaining links to the outside world; they were also one of the few Austrian resistance groups to cooperate with underground elements in the Altreich. In Salzburg alone 250 of them would fall prey to the Gestapo.[106]

To what extent provincial workingmen reconsidered their generally positive view of the Anschluss is difficult to ascertain. The surviving documentation is scant. It indicates that during the last months of peace industrial workers felt increasingly frustrated by rising prices and growing scarcities; it also suggests that they were acutely sensitive to the thought of losing the pay race to workers at nearby plants or construction sites.[107] Between January and March 1939 the Gestapo broke up a Communist network in Styria. Its agents also reported a resurgence of Communist agitation in the Steyr Works and among road workers near Linz. To the west, near Salzburg, crews laying pavement on the new autobahn were said to be succumbing to the complaints of co-workers from Vienna. By June the economic officer of the Seventeenth Military District was writing that in a number of "individual concerns the mood of the working classes is less than satisfactory."[108]

As the summer wore on, SD agents in Tyrol, Salzburg, Upper Danube, and Lower Danube registered growing labor anxiety about the threat of war. In St. Pölten factory hands were said to be whispering against the DAF; in Graz workmen were alleged to be singing the Marseillaise. There was also near ubiquitous grumbling about low wages. Near Kirchdorf, road workers staged a protest against new withholding taxes; in numerous inns and restaurants in Lower Danube waiters and waitresses objected to a new 10 percent tax on tips. Overall, however, working-class dissatisfaction was regarded as neither substantial nor threatening. It remained primarily economic in nature. There were still reports of good feeling and support. When news of the Molotov-Ribbentrop Pact arrived, it brought the same sense of relief that it did to other Austrians. In short, there was little reason for the Nazis to doubt the support of provincial labor for the upcoming conflict.[109]

CONCLUSION

In the eighteen months following the Anschluss the Nazis achieved considerable success mobilizing Austrian labor. Even Marxist historians have conceded that "for many employment became the measure of all things; lost rights were tolerated and compensated by the feeling of having at last found work again."[110] All the same, working-class attitudes remained complex, multifaceted, and ambivalent: many wage earners embraced Hitler's cause; others opposed it or stood aside. From the outset the level of grumbling in Vienna was so pervasive that both the German authorities and a later generation of historians regarded it as a form of "silent resistance."[111] Given the city's Social Democratic traditions, this may frequently have been the case. Nevertheless, it should not be forgotten that chronic complaining is endemic to Vienna and that much of it emanated from disenchanted Nazis. In the provinces blue-collar support for Hitler's regime was more pervasive, but labor-management relations remained uneasy and outbursts of dissent were not uncommon.

For all their rhetoric, the Nazis were no more successful in overcoming class divisions in Austria than they were in Germany. While most workers were better off than before the Anschluss, they retained a sense of subcultural cohesion. Increasingly subject to regimentation and longer working hours, they demonstrated solidarity in a variety of ways including strikes, slowdowns, and indiscipline. Even though the security organs reported considerable support for the National Community, a majority of workers appear to have remained cynical and indifferent.

To leave the matter at that, however, would be misleading. Timothy Kirk has indeed made a strong case that the Austrian working class remained largely impervious to Nazism during the eighteen months between the Anschluss and the war, "accepting the incidental material benefits and rejecting the ideological principles."[112] The problem with his assessment is that it overlooks the extent of Social Democratic collaboration with the Anschluss system. It also underrates the material and psychological benefits of Nazi social policy, especially in the provinces. Finally, it fails to take into account the enormous emotional appeal of Hitler's anticlerical campaign.[113]

National Socialism, in other words, did fulfill a significant number of working-class aspirations that included the destruction of the Dollfuss-Schuschnigg dictatorship, union with the German Reich, economic recovery and full employment, separation of church and state, and solution of the

Jewish Question. The new regime also gave workingmen a new sense of self-confidence, rewarding performance and encouraging pride in workmanship. While fewer workers joined the NSDAP than any other group of Austrian society, including the peasants, the percentage of those signing up rose from 3.7 in 1938 to 14.6 in 1941.[114] In short, the working classes may have felt only marginally committed to Nazism, but they were by no means opposed to the Anschluss regime.

5

AUSTRIAN CATHOLICISM
Antipathy and Accommodation

The Roman Catholic Church had long enjoyed a privileged position in Austria. Ever since the Counter-Reformation it had played an important role in shaping official policy. It never experienced a serious challenge to its authority, certainly nothing resembling the Bismarckian Kulturkampf of the 1870s. Even after the collapse of the Habsburg monarchy, the Austrian church remained an established faith, a state religion that continued to receive government subsidies, to exert a near monopoly over schooling, and through the Christian Social Party to wield considerable political influence—most notably under Ignaz Seipel, the prelate who twice occupied the chancellor's office in the 1920s.[1]

The leaders of Austrian Catholicism believed in the indivisibility of religion and politics. They regarded the disintegration of the monarchy as a calamity and longed for the restoration of the dynasty. Throughout the interwar period they incessantly warned of the dangers of materialism, liberalism, and, above all, socialism. Their fear of an Austro-Marxist dictatorship became so acute that several bishops threw their support to the Heimwehr, even likening the threat of the "enemy within" to that of the Turks in 1683.[2]

The fears of the Catholic establishment were exaggerated and unwarranted. However much the anticlerical rhetoric of the Social Democrats may have gotten under the skin of the faithful, both bishops and clergy matched their Austro-Marxist opponents in vitriolic abuse, marginalizing them as evildoers and commending them to eternal perdition. Although legislation passed in 1919 prohibited school authorities from pressuring pupils to attend Sunday mass, the position of the church in the Austrian state remained otherwise intact. Nevertheless, the Catholic hierarchy concluded that only the restoration of an authoritarian order could reverse the secular trends of the age and restore the baroque ideal of the unity of the church and the people.[3]

It was hardly surprising that the Austrian episcopate hailed the establishment of the Christian Corporative dictatorship. Although the bishops played only a small role in the founding of the regime, they became one of its principal pillars, showering praise on Dollfuss for crushing the Social Democrats and for reaffirming the Catholic character of the Austrian state. For its part, the government accorded the church an elevated status it had not enjoyed for decades. The regime, having ratified a concordat with the Holy See, reasserted the supremacy of canon matrimonial law, reinstated catechism instruction in schools, and instituted religious conformity as a means test for the selection (and dismissal) of civil servants and teachers. The regime also made a number of symbolic gestures including the placing of crucifixes in military barracks and the adoption of the cross potent (*Kruckenkreuz*) as the official symbol of state.[4]

The Catholic Church could also rely on both its own ecclesiastical apparatus and a vast network of religious orders, clubs, and associations. In 1938 there were two archdioceses (Vienna and Salzburg); four dioceses (St. Pölten, Linz, Gurk, and Seckau); two apostolic administratorships (Eisenstadt and Tyrol-Vorarlberg), and a general vicarate (Feldkirch). The clergy consisted of 8,000 diocesan and ordered priests, many of whom had played an active role in Christian Social politics during both the monarchy and First Republic. Banned from public service by the episcopate in 1933, they were expected to devote their primary attention to pastoral care. As a practical matter, they increasingly found themselves enforcing the ordinances of Christian Corporative officials or policing the behavior of their parishioners.[5]

Supporting the institutional life of the Austrian Catholic Church was an active laity of half a million members. While most belonged to two mass organizations—Catholic Action or the Confederation of Austrian Catholics— it was through 219 denominational associations that the faithful most effectively demonstrated their solidarity and influenced public life. In addition to youth groups, welfare societies, and women's auxiliaries, these included professional clubs, farmers cooperatives, and labor groups. There were also reading societies, sewing circles, and informal parish clubs. The most prestigious and powerful of the Catholic associations was the Alliance of Catholic Students, the Cartellverband (CV), an organization whose alumni dominated provincial political life, controlled official appointments and carefully monitored civic discourse. To the extent that open discussion persisted under the Dollfuss-Schuschnigg regime, public issues were aired and debated in the pages of the Catholic press, an agglomeration of newspapers, magazines, and other publications that in 1931 included an official organ, the *Reichspost*, nine dailies, and over a hundred more specialized journals.[6]

As the Dollfuss-Schuschnigg regime solidified its power, the luminaries of Austrian Catholicism looked to the future with renewed confidence and optimism. Here was an opportunity to go on the offensive against the evils of the modern world, to overcome the ideas of 1789, to take up the torch of a triumphal Counter-Reformation.[7] In fact, the position of the church was less secure and more fragile than it appeared, since the ecclesiastical establishment hardly represented the political views of a majority of Austrian Catholics. While 90.5 percent of the population belonged officially to the Roman Church, only 36 to 45 percent of the electorate before 1933 had regularly voted for candidates of the Christian Social Party; by contrast, nearly two-thirds of German Catholics during the Weimar era had normally cast their ballots for the Center Party, the political arm of the church in the Reich. Since both the Social Democratic and German Nationalist Lager demanded a separation of church and state, it may be assumed that a majority of Austrians supported such a change.[8]

Although the dense structure of Catholic associations provided the semblance of strong subcultural support for church policy, most lay organizations lacked the resilience and independence of their German counterparts. Instead of emerging in response to official persecution, most Austrian groups had been organized from above. As a result, they lacked spontaneity and displayed the sort of bovine passivity characteristic of bureaucratic committees. Furthermore, since only a fraction of professing Catholics outside the rural milieu were active churchgoers,[9] the coercive pronouncements of the hierarchy tended to provoke widespread resentment, ironically undercutting the church's moral position and strengthening the arguments of the anticlericals, especially the National Socialists.[10]

Both the hierarchy and the active laity were increasingly divided in their view of the Nazi menace. Authoritarian and corporatist in outlook, they were so concerned with the Marxist threat that they tended to regard National Socialism as a secondary danger or to look for some kind of modus vivendi with Hitler's movement.[11]

At first, there had been no ambiguity. Meeting in November 1932, the Austrian hierarchy reviled Nazism as incompatible with Christian doctrine; two months later the metropolitan of Linz, Johannes Maria Gföllner, published a fiery pastoral letter that assailed Judaism but condemned racial anti-Semitism, stating bluntly that it was impossible to be a "good Catholic and a sincere National Socialist." As the Nazis stepped up their campaign of terror in Austria, other bishops spoke out against the "wolf in sheep's clothing." Even after the Vatican had signed a concordat with Hitler's government on 20 July 1933, the Austrian church kept up its criticism.[12]

The bishops, however, did not speak with one voice. While most Austrian churchmen recoiled in understandable horror at the assassination of Dollfuss on 25 July 1934, the archbishop of Vienna, Theodor Cardinal Innitzer, joined Bishop Adam Hefter of Klagenfurt-Gurk in calling for a day of reconciliation and prayer. Both men were German nationalists and, like so many other Catholics in Central Europe, were impressed by what they considered to be "positive" elements in Nazi ideology. Still, when Hitler's emissary, Franz von Papen, arrived in Vienna proposing a rapprochement between Austria and the Reich, neither Innitzer nor the papal nuncio, Enrico Siblia, gave him the time of day.[13]

Papen's subsequent success in negotiating the July Agreement with Schuschnigg in 1936 thus came as a shock to the Austrian church, dividing the ecclesiastical establishment into distinctive factions. While traditionalists such as Gföllner and the archbishop of Salzburg, Sigismund Waitz, made no secret of their dismay, Innitzer naively hailed the settlement as an end to a "civil war." Even more remarkably, a third group led by an Austrian based in the Vatican, Bishop Alois Hudal, called for a Catholic-Nazi covenant as the most effective means of fighting Jewry, Marxism, and Protestantism. While few churchmen endorsed Hudal's proposals, his arguments received widespread support in Catholic National circles, especially among Viennese laymen close to Papen and the German embassy.[14]

Although the leaders of Austrian Catholicism never wavered in their support of the Christian Corporative regime, they failed to devise a common strategy to meet the Nazi threat. Deeply disturbed by Hitler's anticlerical campaign in the Reich, especially in neighboring Bavaria, they could not decide after the July Agreement whether to continue resisting Nazism at home or to try to come to terms with it.[15] While the higher clergy could draw on years of political experience, they were reluctant to oppose a movement that was both anti-Semitic and anti-Marxist. It is true that both Pope Pius XI and papal secretary Eugenio Cardinal Pacelli counseled stiffer resistance, but their advice tended to be ambiguous or elliptical.[16] The Austrian bishops never considered a collective response to the possibility of a German invasion.

THE AUSTRIAN CLERGY AND ANSCHLUSS

The Anschluss took the Catholic establishment by surprise. The pace of events was so rapid that the higher clergy had little time to react except on a local basis. Ironically, the Nazis also found themselves scrambling to formulate a coherent policy. On the one hand, they had every intention of settling scores with a hated foe. Hoping to strengthen Hitler's mass support, they planned to fulfill long-standing demands for separation of church and state, especially calls to restrict religious instruction in schools and to permit divorced men and women to remarry. Beyond that, they aimed at seizing clerical assets, neutralizing the church's role in society, and eventually supplanting Christianity with their own pagan ideology. On the other hand, neither Hitler nor his retinue saw any point in dampening popular enthusiasm for the Anschluss. Instead of launching an assault on the church, they decided to woo the bishops, exploiting their clerical authority for Nazi propaganda purposes.[17]

At first there was no clear-cut policy or uniform reaction. Shortly before dawn on 12 March Nazi supporters shattered the windows of the archiepiscopal palace in Salzburg, threw a cordon around the building, and placed Archbishop Waitz under house arrest. In Graz storm troopers broke into the residence of Bishop Ferdinand Pawlikowski, marched him through jeering crowds to the municipal jail, and locked him up. In Vienna Hitler's followers left Cardinal Innitzer undisturbed. Shortly after Schuschnigg's resignation was broadcast, the primate released a statement to the *Reichspost* urging the faithful to support the Anschluss regime. Like the unfortunate chancellor, Innitzer was concerned primarily with avoiding bloodshed. Nevertheless, the wording of his declaration suggested a volte-face, a change of policy that would produce great confusion and lead to a humiliating settlement with the Nazi dictatorship.[18]

Innitzer, like most other Austrians, was swept up by the enthusiasm of the moment. Impressed by Seyss-Inquart's appointment of a cabinet of largely Catholic Nationals, the cardinal agreed that the ringing of bells should accompany Hitler's triumphal entry into Vienna. Innitzer also paid a courtesy call on the Führer. In the course of a fifteen-minute conversation, the dictator evaded the issue of Catholic rights by suggesting that the Austrian episcopate might help him settle the church struggle in Germany. Scarcely realizing what had been said, the cardinal emerged from the meeting both captivated by Hitler and convinced that he had struck a bargain: in return for a declaration of support for the new regime, the government would agree to an accommodation with the church.[19]

Innitzer prepared a rough draft of a pastoral letter and summoned the higher clergy to discuss it with him on Friday, 18 March. The other bishops—notably Waitz, Gföllner, and Pawlikowski—were skeptical and suspicious, but at the Friday conference found themselves unable to air their views. This was because two Nazi officials interrupted the meeting with an alternate document drafted by Reich commissioner Joseph Bürckel; it acclaimed the racial, social, and economic achievements of National Socialism and called on the faithful to vote yes in the referendum ordered by Hitler for 10 April.[20]

In the negotiations that followed, Bürckel's representatives listened patiently to complaints of Nazi abuse. They rejected Waitz's proposal for a more explicit document containing a clause on the pastoral care of the young, but they assured the churchmen that after the plebiscite Bürckel would be more than willing to discuss specific issues. Naively accepting this verbal commitment, the bishops signed the manifesto and agreed to read it from the pulpit on Sunday, 27 March.[21]

Almost immediately there were second thoughts. Waitz confided to his diary that the "matter was handled in haste"; Innitzer thought of a textual emendation. That evening papal nuncio Gaetano Cicognani upbraided both bishops, insisting on the addition of a codicil or conditional preamble. Perhaps Cicognani should have kept his counsel. By complying, Innitzer and Waitz started down a road of bungled negotiations that ended in gestures of even greater subservience.[22]

For his part, Bürckel appeared to be accommodating. He ordered an end to the seizure of ecclesiastical property and banned the removal of crucifixes from public places.[23] He reminded the bishops of his success in dealing with ecclesiastical authorities in the Saar[24] and repeated his promise to adjudicate specific disputes after the April plebiscite. When Innitzer proposed a preamble to the episcopal declaration scheduled for reading on 27 March, the Reich commissioner readily agreed; in fact, he produced a draft of his own. It appealed to Catholics to support the new order with the words "render under Caesar that which is Caesar's and unto God that which is God's." Innitzer and Waitz showed no hesitation in signing. Later in the day the cardinal submitted an accompanying letter with the words "Heil Hitler!"[25]

On Monday, 28 March, thousands of posters appeared on the walls and kiosks of Greater Germany highlighting reproductions of all three documents; there were also millions of copies available in the streets. As might be expected, the reaction of the Catholic world was one of astonishment and disbelief. On 1 April the Holy See broadcast a blistering attack on the Austrian episcopate for violating its teaching role. Immediately thereafter, Pius XI summoned Innitzer to Rome where he and Pacelli chastised the primate for his poor judgment and wishful thinking. Deeply depressed, the archbishop sheepishly signed a new manifesto on behalf of the Austrian episcopate. The document (drafted by Pacelli) demanded retention of the Concordat of 1933, protection of Catholic schools, and an end to government attacks on the church.[26] Just as Innitzer feared, however, the revised declaration also played into the hands of the Nazis. When Hitler received the archbishop on the evening of 9 April, he kept his distance, coldly claiming that the new document jeopardized a definitive settlement with the Austrian church.[27]

THE CATHOLIC RESPONSE

How did the Catholic clergy and churchgoing public react to the declarations of their bishops? The contemporaneous testimony is scant, but at least two conclusions can be drawn. First, nearly everyone obeyed the call to endorse the Anschluss. While a tiny handful of dissenters including the now famous peasant-pacifist Franz Jägerstätter refused to oblige, most of the Catholic population trooped to the polls to vote yes in the April plebiscite. Second, a great many priests and active laymen both in Austria and Germany bitterly resented Innitzer's overconfident and obsequious behavior. This is not to say that they disapproved the Anschluss.[28] The British consul general reported that "Cardinal Innitzer is credited with being both vain and ambitious and prepared to make very far-reaching concessions for the sake of his personal position."[29]

In some cases members of the clergy had difficulty concealing their disgust, especially in Vorarlberg, Tyrol, and Salzburg. It is true that none followed the daring example of the bishop of Rottenburg, Johannes Baptista Sproll, a German dignitary who refused to vote for a regime "hostile to Christianity."[30] Nevertheless, at least one native Austrian bishop, Johannes Maria Gföllner, continued to keep his distance from the Nazis, ordering a strict separation of church and state and declining to receive governmental officials—including Hitler himself. According to a survey undertaken decades later, Innitzer's servile behavior aroused the dismay of most of the clergy and active laity. Looking back in 1979, a majority of the elderly clergymen recalled sensations of surprise and amazement, followed by feelings of anger, indignation, and confusion. Some defended the March Declaration as a realistic attempt to come to terms with the Anschluss regime, but most regarded it as an astonishing sellout. Nearly all felt a deep sense of shame.[31]

There is no way of knowing to what extent the remembrances of those questioned in 1979 corresponded to their actual feelings in 1938. It is hard to imagine that their Anschluss memories were not colored in some way by the searing experience of subsequent persecution. (During the period of Nazi rule some 15 priests were sentenced to death and executed; 110 were dispatched to concentration camps, where 20 died; 724 were jailed, of whom 7 died; 208 were banished from their parishes; and over 1,500 were forbidden to preach or teach.)[32] All the same, the available evidence leaves little doubt that most of the lower clergy, especially in the countryside, felt a sense of confusion and betrayal.[33] While they obliged their bishops by voting yes in the April referendum, many subsequently resisted Nazi attacks on the church. That the overwhelming majority of churchmen destined to suffer abuse at the hands of the Gestapo were diocesan priests provides some indication of the gulf dividing the Austrian hierarchy from the lower clergy. While the rift was of long standing, Innitzer's ill-founded attempt to seek a settlement with Hitler widened it considerably further.[34]

THE SEARCH FOR A MODUS VIVENDI

During the spring and summer of 1938 the Austrian bishops continued their search for a settlement with the Nazi regime. There is no reason to regard their attempt as anything other than imprudent. Still, several mitigating factors deserve consideration. First, Innitzer sincerely believed that he had established a solid working relationship with Bürckel, a notion not entirely misplaced. While the Reich commissioner confided that the cardinal had "offered us his assistance and abandoned his friends,"[35] Bürckel was more than willing to offer an olive branch, or at least several sprigs, to expedite Austria's integration into the Third Reich. Second, despite reservations in the Vatican, there was some hope that a prompt agreement might preclude the spread of anticlerical violence from Germany to Austria. Since radical Nazi activists were already seizing ecclesiastical property and periodically mugging priests, even Cardinal Pacelli endorsed the effort. Finally, there was pressure from a small clique of (largely academic) malcontents, who advocated a confessional peace as the best means of realizing their goal of a "magnificent synthesis" of Christianity and National Socialism.[36]

Generally speaking, the Austrian bishops were willing to forfeit their position of political privilege in return for guarantees of freedom of worship and pastoral care; they also sought the right to circulate pastoral literature and to maintain their system of parochial schools. For his part, Bürckel was inclined to compromise, but he was driven into a more radical posture by officials in both Berlin and Vienna.[37] There was also strong popular pressure within Austria to settle accounts with the Catholic Church, especially among the Nazi rank and file and the Social Democratic working classes.

Details of the negotiations between Innitzer and the Reich commissioner need not detain us here.[38] Despite rising violence and an increasing number of attacks on church property, the cardinal stubbornly refused to believe that anything other than hooliganism was involved. While marauding bands of storm troopers and Hitler Youth were in fact frequently at fault, Innitzer failed to grasp the nature of an antireligious drive being orchestrated by the Führer himself. Indeed, even before formal conversations could get under way, Hitler had secretly decided to abrogate the Austrian Concordat of 1933 as the best way of placing the Catholic Church at the mercy of the NSDAP. Only when Bürckel brutally boasted that he had not needed the bishops' declaration to win the April plebiscite did something of the truth begin to dawn on the credulous cardinal.[39]

Since the Reich commissioner wanted to preserve at least a semblance of legality, negotiations continued throughout the summer. At one point a preliminary understanding was reached under which the Catholic Church agreed to withdraw from politics in return for guarantees of spiritual freedom; there was also to be an ombudsman (*Treuhänder*) for "religious-cultural affairs." Whatever the merits of this settlement, it was never signed or put into effect. To see why requires little imagination: on the one hand, the Vatican condemned it as vague and superfluous; on the other, the Nazis regarded it as window dressing.[40]

Even as the discussions were proceeding, the regime opened a massive onslaught on the church. On 6 July legislation was introduced mandating civil matrimony and reforming divorce. This was followed by a Führer decree revoking the Austrian Concordat of 1933. As the pronouncement also contained a clause exempting the Ostmark from the protection of the Reich concordat, the church was effectively stripped of the last vestiges of its diplomatic status and corporate liberties. With that in mind Hitler sanctioned the retroactive expropriation of ecclesiastical assets. He stipulated that the measure be applied with care, but his Austrian myrmidons seized the opportunity to close 1,417 parochial schools, to dissolve most provincial boards of education, and to launch an unprecedented attack on Catholic symbols and holidays.[41] By mid-August, the church found itself bearing the brunt of an assault unknown since the days of Joseph II.

Nevertheless, both Bürckel and Innitzer still held out hope of reaching a settlement. During the Sudeten crisis the Reich commissioner even issued a personal invitation to resume negotiations. While it was obvious that Bürckel was interested primarily in averting civil strife in the face of an impending war, the cardinal and his bishops agreed to accept. Before the scheduled meeting could take place, however, the semiofficial *Wiener Zeitung* announced the dissolution of the Order of Teutonic Knights and the Association of Catholic Journeymen. For the churchmen this was the last straw; after a brief executive conference they resolved to call it quits.[42]

The decision of the Austrian episcopate to break off negotiations with Bürckel did not mean an end to their policy of appeasement. Like British prime minister Chamberlain, the church dignitaries decided to approach Hitler himself. On 28 September, the eve of the Munich conference, Waitz and Innitzer dispatched a thirteen-page letter of remonstrance to the Führer, a document drafted as a traditional *cahiers de doléance* seeking redress from a paternal ruler. In it the archbishops protested the closing of theological faculties in Innsbruck and Salzburg, the sequestration of ecclesiastical assets in Salzburg, and the suppression of various Catholic associations. They also objected to restrictions placed on the Catholic press, the introduction of compulsory civil marriage, and the secularization of schooling. To conclude, the prelates reaffirmed their commitment to Christian values, but also emphasized their desire to "contribute to the welfare of the German people and fatherland."[43]

Although Waitz and Innitzer regarded themselves as spokesmen of a universal faith, they made no reference in their petition to the repellent violence being perpetuated daily against the Jews of Austria. Nor did they express concern about the plight of the tens of thousands of Czech Catholics cowering in the streets of Vienna. Their letter of protest to Hitler represented the culmination of an effort to find common ground with a regime fiercely opposed to Christian values. In the months to come the princes of the Austrian church would gradually reassess their myopic stance, but even after learning (from Bürckel) of the rejection of their gravamina, they were reluctant to abandon their policy of appeasement.[44] Judging from the behavior of Innitzer, moreover, they were hardly unaffected by the virus of "religious nationalism."[45] On the other hand, it must be acknowledged that the cardinal did have enough sense to proscribe the Association for Religious Peace, an organization of 525 clergymen, primarily of former "bridge builders," who sought to synthesize the principles of Christianity and Nazism.[46]

THE ROSARY FESTIVAL OF OCTOBER 1938

Despite the failure of the Austrian hierarchy to provide meaningful guidance to the faithful, the Catholic Church nonetheless became a center of opposition to the Anschluss regime. By mid-September 1938 the Nazi assault on Catholic institutions and customs had gained such momentum that individual clergymen and parishioners increasingly stood up to the authorities in acts of spontaneous defiance. While the situation in Vienna had remained relatively calm throughout the summer, sporadic protests by rural villagers were already commonplace.[47] Groups of Catholic young people—seminarians, student militants, parish activists—were among the first to consider systematic demonstrations of dissent. Even before the regime's crackdown on Catholic youth organizations, a number of Viennese youngsters had organized small resistance cells or taken to gathering informally in out-of-the-way rectories, chapels, and places of worship.[48] Among the most active of the neighborhood groups was a loose association of former Bündists, Marianists, and Boy Scouts, meeting clandestinely at Breitenfeld, a small parish located between Josefsstadt and Ottakring. Aware of the existence of other like-minded cliques scattered throughout the metropolis, the Breitenfeld activists sought to reach out to them by persuading the archdiocese to convoke a special Rosary Mass on 7 October 1938 at St. Stephen's Cathedral.[49]

The planners hoped that as many as 2,000 worshipers would turn out for the divine service, but when the great doors of the Gothic basilica swung open in the early evening hours of 7 October, some 6,000 to 8,000 enthusiastic youngsters thronged into the sanctuary. Seized by emotional excitement, the youthful celebrants joined in singing the powerful processional hymn "Behold a House of Glory," their voices nearly drowning out the organ. The cathedral chaplain tried to calm the congregation through prayer, but once Cardinal Innitzer delivered a sermon reaffirming his faith in Christ the King and appealing to Catholic youth for understanding, the listeners poured out onto the square chanting "We want to see our Bishop!" They spontaneously mocked Nazi slogans and ritual shouting "We are grateful to our Bishop!"; "Christ is our Führer!"; "Archbishop command, we follow Thee!"[50]

Innitzer hesitated to appear before what was now an enormous anti-Nazi rally. His delay only fed the frenzy of the demonstrators, emboldening several activists to rough up a patrol of Hitler Youth. Not until the cardinal at last acknowledged the ovation by appearing at the window of his archiepiscopal palace did the crowd disperse. As the youngsters made their way home through the darkened streets of the city, they had good reason to feel euphoric. Though unaware of the scale of their achievement, they had taken part in the largest anti-Nazi demonstration ever staged in the history of the Third Reich.[51]

There can be no doubt that the Catholic youth expressed the outraged feelings of many devout Viennese Christians, but just how pervasive or, for that matter, political anti-Nazi sentiment was among the city's Catholics is not revealed in the records—at least to the extent that it is for the provinces, where religious dissent was closely linked to agricultural grievances and hence regarded as more dangerous to the regime.

For their part, the Nazis were not long in striking back. Even before the "Rosary Festival" had come to an end, several hundred party militants converged on St. Stephen's Square shouting "Innitzer to Dachau!" The following evening, Saturday, 8 October, gangs of Hitler Youth stormed the cardinal's archiepiscopal palace, smashing crucifixes, breaking furniture, and slashing paintings. With uniformed police standing by, the brownshirts also shattered some 1,200 windowpanes, manhandled the cardinal's secretary, and hurled the cathedral curate from a third-story casement, severely fracturing both his thighs. Although the authorities eventually intervened to restore order, anticlerical rioting continued throughout the week, culminating on 13 October in a monster rally of 200,000 people on Heroes Square. Here Bürckel accused the church of betrayal and charged the clergy with attempting to exploit the Sudeten crisis to recover their preponderant power in the state.[52]

Exactly how the Catholic population reacted to the initial stages of the Nazi assault on the church is difficult to gauge, at least in Vienna where a significant segment of the Christian Social camp had long embraced Hitler's movement. On the one hand, the available evidence makes it clear that most people were appalled by the outbreak of violence. The British consul general wrote that "these events have revived the latent uneasiness among the people and the reluctant admiration for Herr Hitler, which I stated . . . was growing, has been considerably tempered by the alarm and disgust felt in wide circles at the recent actions of the local party adherents."[53] As the antichurch measures continued and intensified—including a ban on school prayer announced on 26 October—outside observers noticed a dramatic surge in church attendance. "In the dark, unheated aisles of [St. Stephen's] Cathedral," one American correspondent reported, "great congregations stand shivering every afternoon while a young preacher speaks of the rights of conscience and the freedom of the human soul."[54]

On the other hand, it is equally clear that not every Catholic disapproved of all aspects of Hitler's program of secularization, especially those measures separating church and state or liberalizing divorce. The SD frequently chortled about the popularity of anticlericalism in Austria. While we may assume that it was those groups traditionally hostile to the church who were the most supportive, the drop in religious marriages in 1938–39 to less than a third of the weddings annually performed in Vienna suggests greater ambiguity and ambivalence among the Catholic population than might otherwise be expected. Nor should it be overlooked that the continued dithering of the Austrian episcopate compounded the general sense of anguish for individual believers.[55]

AUSTRIAN CATHOLICISM AND THE JEWISH QUESTION

Before the Austrian bishops could protest the pillaging of Innitzer's palace or formulate a coherent response to Bürckel's bloodcurdling tirade, the Nazis shifted the target of their abuse from the church to the Jews. During the Sudeten crisis party activists ranging from Hitler to neighborhood block wardens had been enraged by the pacifism of the masses, concluding that popular timidity and fear of war were the work of "international Jewry." On 14 October Viennese functionaries thus changed the axis of their attack. The result was an unprecedented campaign of violence that temporarily relieved the pressure on the Austrian church and culminated some weeks later in the savagery of Crystal Night. In the view of the British consul general, the renewed Judeophobic outbursts constituted "a sort of safety valve for the passions accumulated but not entirely discharged during the anti-Catholic rioting."[56]

What was the response of Austrian Catholicism to the persecution of the Jews and to the brutality of Crystal Night? In addressing this question some consideration must be given to the Christian roots of anti-Semitism, especially to the scriptural teaching that the Jews bear the responsibility for rejecting the Messiah and crucifying the Son of God. While the Roman Catholic Church firmly rejected racial or biological anti-Semitism, it did hold the Jewish people accountable for the evils of the modern world. In late imperial Vienna, moreover, significant elements of the lower clergy had made a substantial contribution to the rise of modern anti-Semitism through their support of Karl Lueger's Christian Social movement.[57]

During the interwar period Catholic hostility toward both Judaism and Jewry did not abate. Anti-Semitic articles appeared regularly in the Catholic press and Christian Social politicians demanded a radical solution of the Jewish Question. One of them, Leopold Kunschak, an associate of Lueger and head of the Catholic Workers' Association, even called for the expulsion of Jewish immigrants or their incarceration in concentration camps. While the official position of the Catholic establishment was more benign, luminaries such as Sigismund Waitz, archbishop of Salzburg, and Georg Bichlmair, the Jesuit director of the Pauline Missionary Society, publicly referred to the Jews as an "alien people." Even after Hitler had come to power in Berlin, scarcely a soul spoke out against Nazi anti-Semitism. This does not mean that the Austrian episcopate condoned storm trooper violence. Most members of the higher clergy and Catholic elite did, however, demand restrictive legislation or some form of social segregation. "The compromising attitude toward Nazism, which characterized the Catholic church after the Anschluss," Pauley reminds us, "had its origins long before 1938."[58]

Despite the intense anti-Jewish sentiment prevailing within the Austrian church, Cardinal Innitzer had long maintained cordial relations with the Viennese Jewish community. As rector of the University of Vienna, he took concrete steps to protect Jewish students from assault and provided financial assistance to some of them. After his elevation to the archdiocese in 1931 he supported the Zionist movement and joined the pro-Palestine committee. No doubt hoping to solve the Jewish Question through conversion or emigration, the Sudeten-born German nationalist even made attempts to promote understanding between Christians and Jews; in 1936, for example, he spoke out against Nazi racism and pointedly referred to Christ's "brothers in Judaism."[59]

Whether the cardinal gave much thought to the plight of the 169,978 Jews of his diocese during the tumultuous days following the Anschluss seems unlikely. What the record does indicate is that while he and the higher clergy scrambled to cut a deal with Hitler, other ecclesiastical officials labored behind the scenes to protect non-Aryan Catholics. On 19 May, Father Georg Bichlmair, whose Pauline Missionary Society was charged with converting Jews to Christianity, recommended the establishment of a special agency to aid baptized Jews. We have already seen that Bichlmair regarded Jews as an alien race, but as a missionary he felt a concern for all (Catholic) Brethren in Christ. With the support of Innitzer—who contributed a monthly allowance of 3,000 marks—and that of a wealthy aristocrat, Countess Manuela Kielmannsegg, he organized a small group that supported baptized Jews and helped a number of them find refuge abroad. He also redoubled his efforts to accelerate the conversion of Jews to Christianity, an endeavor that clearly met the needs of the church but may also have provided temporary solace for several thousand desperate people.[60]

The concern and sympathy expressed by the Austrian church for Jewish Catholics was not unique. The Fulda Bishops' Conference in Germany had always felt a special obligation to protect non-Aryan Catholics.[61] What deserves emphasis is that the Roman Catholic Church itself showed little Christian compassion for nonbaptized Jews. There were many reasons for this exclusivist approach, some of them stemming from a long tradition of ambiguity toward both Judaism and Jews. The more immediate and fundamental explanation can be discerned, however, in Roman Catholicism's imperiled position in interwar Europe. Besieged by pagan forces on both the right and the left, the Vatican simply hunkered down to look after its own. Official policy thus became "unduly narrow," restricted "to the interests of Catholics, often excluding almost any other consideration."[62]

At no time during the Anschluss era, therefore, did the Austrian church speak out against the Nazi persecution of the Jews, not even after the devastation of Crystal Night. As in Germany, there was a handful of individual priests who made elliptical remonstrations from the pulpit, forged baptismal certificates, or sheltered refugees from the Gestapo.[63] They were solitary individuals. Whatever Innitzer and his Viennese colleagues may have thought of the theft and the violence occurring before their very eyes, they kept their counsel. Their silence and that of other Austrian and German bishops in the face of the monstrous brutalities of Crystal Night was particularly deafening.[64]

THE IMPOSITION OF VOLUNTARY TITHING

The ruthless attacks directed against both Catholics and Jews in the autumn of 1938 were more interconnected than might be surmised. While Hitler's campaign against the Christian churches cannot be compared with his subsequent attempt to exterminate an entire people, we should not forget, as Gerhard Weinberg reminds us, that the Nazis ultimately sought to extirpate the two religions that had arrived in Central Europe at the time of the Romans, "to be replaced first by the worship of Moloch, the idol of blood, and thereafter by Mammon, the idol of gold."[65] The mobs that applauded the storming of the archbishop's palace in October or the burning of the synagogues in November may not have hated Christianity and Judaism in equal measure, but they had pledged their troth to a pagan cause. What the Austrian Nazis soon discovered was that their zeal was insufficient to overcome the cult of respectability.

Ordinary Austrians (and Germans) simply did not share Hitler's sense of impatience and bellicosity. Popular aversion to scenes of disorder and chaos thus induced the regime to revert to legal and bureaucratic means to achieve its goals.[66] In the Ostmark, that meant formal legislation aimed at disestablishing the Roman Catholic Church and marginalizing the Christian religion. During the winter months of 1938–39 Bürckel's office moved on a broad front, issuing decrees that closed parochial schools, banned school prayer, and prohibited obligatory religious instruction. There were also measures directed against individual priests, a number of whom were apprehended by the Gestapo on trumped-up charges of currency violation, immorality, or "malicious practices." By New Year, some sixty-three clerics were imprisoned in Styria alone.[67] The centerpiece of the new assault, however, was a Führer decree eliminating state subsidies to the church. Promulgated on 28 April 1939, it compelled the church to rely on voluntary tithing, thus providing a strong financial incentive for individual parishioners to give up their membership.[68]

That the Nazi assault on the church had already stirred up a hornet's nest of discontent in the countryside has already been mentioned. Nevertheless, nothing comparable with the attack on Innitzer's archiepiscopal palace occurred outside Vienna. There were two notable exceptions: in Salzburg, on 17 October, Nazi gangs again vandalized Archbishop Waitz's residence, hurling insults and chanting "We want to see our bishop in Dachau!" And in Amstetten the Hitler Youth, on 12 October and on 19 November, smashed the windows of the municipal rectory.[69]

Whatever calm that may have existed in church-state relations during the winter months of 1938–39 was broken by enforcement of the Nazi ban on school prayer. In many villages throughout the Ostmark there were petition drives and angry demonstrations; parish priests stepped up house calls to provide spiritual assistance, to comfort the sick and aged, to pray for the bereaved. In the developing conflict for the allegiance of the Austrian people, renewed pastoral care was being sharpened into a potent weapon.[70]

TABLE 6. *Church Resignations in Austria (All Faiths), 1938–1945*

	Vienna	Lower Danube	Upper Danube	Salzburg	Styria	Tyrol
1938	90,835	14,324	5,340	43,912	1,503	
1939	111,027	30,121	16,026	5,775		2,672
1940		5,126	5,472	3,367		3,541
1941		3,049		2,318		1,489
1942			1,346			792
1943			1,636			333
1944						188
1945						44

Sources: Botz, *Nationalsozialismus in Wien*, 390; Stadler, *Österreich*, 97; *WVOÖ*, 167; *WVS*, 2:134; *WVT*, 2:136.

In the meantime, the Austrian episcopate struggled to come to terms with the abrupt discontinuation of state financial support, an entitlement that had poured 16 million schillings into church coffers between 1929 and 1937.[71] Having secured clandestine lines of communications to the Vatican, the Austrian bishops were now in a better position to protest their plight to the outside world.[72] In true Josephinian fashion they composed a formal remonstrance challenging the Führer decree of 28 April. In it they invoked the protection of the Concordat of 1933, cited law and tradition dating from the days of the Holy Roman Empire, and repeated Hitler's own words of reassurance delivered in a dramatic speech to the Reichstag on 30 January 1939.[73]

How did ordinary Catholics react to the regime's decree on voluntary tithing? The available evidence indicates little discussion or articulated response. Aside from pleas by parish priests to keep the faith, most people appear to have remained quiet. On the other hand, between 1938 and 1941 some 303,106 members left the Roman Catholic Church.[74] To what extent they were motivated by ideology, political pressure, or pocketbook concerns is impossible to say. While there can be little doubt that financial advantage played a role in many decisions to renounce the Catholic faith, surviving statistical data suggest that anticlerical sentiment was more significant. The figures in Tables 6 and 7, although incomplete, make it unmistakably clear that church resignations were most numerous in localities traditionally hostile to the Catholic cause: Styria, Carinthia, and Vienna. Conversely, popular allegiance remained firm in areas historically resistant to Protestant or Marxist appeals.

TABLE 7. *Withdrawals from Religious Instruction in Austrian Elementary Schools, 1938–1945 (in percentages)*

Carinthia	44.17
Vienna	43.28
Styria	27.04
Salzburg	13.77
Tyrol	11.55
Lower Danube	6.35
Vorarlberg	5.21
Upper Danube	0.57

Source: Hanisch, "Austrian Catholicism," 174.

The explosive surge of church resignations in 1939 gave the Nazis every reason to boast that their anti-Christian assault had gone "considerably beyond similar measures taken in the Old Reich."[75] Hitler himself must have been pleased, all the more as he dreamed of constructing an observatory in Linz to refute the "superstitions maintained by the church."[76] What neither he nor the Austrian hierarchy could foresee was that the introduction of voluntary tithing would succumb to the law of opposite intent: far from crippling the Catholic cause, the measure ultimately reinvigorated it, freeing the episcopate from government blackmail and allowing the clergy to pursue its spiritual mission unencumbered by the distractions of power.

This was not obvious at the time. The Catholic populace, by all accounts, felt defeated, demoralized, and dispirited. As in Bavaria, the Catholics' sense of alienation grew in direct response to the school question and renewed attacks by party activists; in Tyrol teams of Hitler Youth and the League of German Girls even taunted churchgoers on Good Friday.[77] On the other hand, passive resistance began to spread. On 1 July the SD reported "intense counteraction, . . . particularly in the regions where religion is respected—Tyrol, Salzburg, and Upper Danube."[78] The situation was so alarming, according to the security men, that churchgoers were boycotting party activities.[79] While there is no evidence that organized resistance cells stood behind the growing number of protest demonstrations, a clandestine network of Catholic activists began to take shape. Composed of former youth group leaders, dissident priests, monarchists, and various individuals hostile to the Anschluss regime, the movement was already engaged in recruiting sympathizers, in distributing illegal fly sheets, and in establishing contacts in Bavaria.[80] Whether it would be able to appeal to a Catholic populace soon seething with discontent was a question that belonged to the future.

CONCLUSION

In the Ostmark Hitler always regarded the Roman Catholic Church as his principal ideological opponent. Although frequently distracted by other priorities and issues, he aimed at curtailing its rights and privileges as a means of realizing his ultimate goal of liquidating Christianity altogether. For their part, the leaders of Austrian Catholicism readily recognized the gravity of the issues at stake, but like so many others in interwar Europe, they could not agree on a unified response. When the Anschluss actually occurred, they reacted in the worst possible way: transferring their allegiance to the pagan conqueror of a Christian Corporative order they had vowed to protect and defend.

The bishops, despite decades of political experience, were no match for Hitler. Their endorsement of the Anschluss, their refusal to heed the advice of the Vatican, their willingness to seek a settlement with the Nazis, their refusal to speak out against wholesale theft and racial terror—all combined to vitiate their own hierarchical authority. With the execrable exception of Innitzer, the Austrian dignitaries were generally less susceptible to "religious nationalism" than their German colleagues. But by constantly emphasizing Saint Paul's injunction to "obey the powers that be" they unwittingly aligned the church with what before 1938 and again after 1945 was considered a foreign power. The result was "an absurd situation," as Ernst Hanisch has put it, whereby during the Second World War Austrian Catholics in the Ostmark "were praying for the victory of Greater Germany, whereas those in exile were praying for an Allied triumph."[81]

The failure of the Austrian bishops to provide meaningful guidance following the Anschluss left most Catholics confused, bewildered, and groping for direction. Once the Nazis initiated their assault on the church, the faithful found themselves virtually alone, unable to rely on the episcopate or their associational network for succor. In a sense, they were in the position of unwilling Protestants, having no choice but to look to individual clergymen and Holy Scripture for spiritual solace. For those living in the rural environment there was also the possibility of sanctuary in social solidarity.

On the other hand, certain Nazi anticlerical measures met the aspirations of many churchgoing Catholics, particularly those changes permitting divorced men and women to remarry. Since Nazi marital legislation included the introduction of the Nuremberg racial laws, some parishioners and clergy also glimpsed an opportunity to reverse Jewish emancipation. Still, once the sheer scale of the Nazi assault became obvious, passive resistance grew. As in the Altreich it was generally spontaneous, scattered, and disorganized, springing up, for the most part, in reaction to intrusions in the Catholic "way of life." Whether the Nazis might have avoided such incidents by adhering to the Concordat of 1933, instead of suspending it, is conceivable but beside the point.[82] For those truly dedicated to the cause of Christ there could be no other choice than the *via dolorosa*. That so few hazarded to take it was hardly at variance with the long history of Christianity.

6
THE FARMING POPULACE
Anger and Anguish

The rural masses in Austria, unlike in Germany, had not flocked to Hitler's banner. Most farmers admired Dollfuss and bitterly resented his assassination. For nearly two decades they had resisted Nazism both at the ballot box and in the pubs and squares of country villages. It is true that in 1938 a good many rural communities in Carinthia, Styria, and the Salzkammergut embraced National Socialism, but most Austrian farmers and peasants remained aloof and suspicious. For their part, Nazi officials showed little inclination to make concessions to the peasantry. Apart from genuine sentiment to alleviate the plight of upland farmers and herdsmen, Hitler's retainers generally favored cities over the countryside. Many of them recalled the food shortages and black-marketeering of the First World War and, like their Führer, intended to control the prices of food and agricultural produce as tightly as possible. Given Hitler's decision just before the Anschluss to maximize overall output in preparation for war, there was also pressure from Berlin to take command of the agricultural economy without delay.

The rural world the Nazis sought to penetrate and to dominate in the Ostmark bore a certain resemblance to that of nearby Bavaria (see Tables 8 and 9). As on the other side of the Inn River, farming in Austria was generally mixed with some specialization in the wine-growing districts of the Wachau and Burgenland. On the other hand, two-thirds of Austria was also covered by meadows and dense forest. Furthermore, a greater percentage of holdings was small-scale than in Bavaria. According to the Austrian census of 1930, 27 percent of farmsteads were smaller than two hectares, an aggregate, however, of only 1.5 percent of the country's total land area. By contrast, nearly half of the remaining productive acreage, largely timberland, lay in the hands of only 1.5 percent of the landowners.[1]

What Austrian and Bavarian agriculture had most in common was the family farm. In both regions three-quarters of all peasants cultivated their own holdings with the aid of wives, children, or other relatives. Between 1890 and 1930 the number of assisting family members on Austrian farms

TABLE 8. *Size of Agricultural Holdings in Austria, 1930*

	N	%	Percentage of Agricultural Area
Smallholdings (under 2 ha.)	118,783	27.4	1.5
Small farms (2–5 ha.)	98,034	22.6	
Medium-sized farms (5–20 ha.)	149,450	34.6	
Large farms (20–100 ha.)	61,073	14.0	
Large-scale concerns (more than 100 ha.)	6,020	1.4	45.7
Total	433,360	100	

Source: Bruckmüller, "Sozialstruktur und Sozialpolitik," 391.

had risen from 480,000 to 710,000, while during the same period the number of paid laborers had declined from 380,000 to 281,000. Besides kith and kin, both Austrian and Bavarian farmers could rely on indentured hirelings or *Dienstboten*, teenage farmhands, stableboys, and milkmaids normally hired for a year who were paid in room and board.[2]

THE NAZIFICATION OF AGRICULTURE

During the heady months following the Anschluss the Nazis sought to allay the suspicions of the peasantry by making lavish promises to relieve indebtedness, to protect property from speculators, and to expand the marketing of Austrian produce in the Reich. In impoverished regions like Styria, where half of the farming population subsisted on holdings of five hectares or less, the regime went even further by implementing dramatic measures of immediate benefit. Within days of the German occupation, the Reich Food Estate made purchases of hundreds of head of Styrian cattle, stud horses, and breeding mares; it also bought vast quantities of local wine and over 200 railroad carriages of high-quality apples that had been gathering dust in storage bins.[3] On 27 March (Austrian) Minister of Agriculture Anton Reinthaller announced an end to farm foreclosures, six weeks later issuing a Disencumbrance Order, according to which peasants could refinance their debt by signing a fifty-one-year mortgage contract of 4.5 percent repayable to the Reich government at an annual rate of .5 percent. Just how many farmsteads were saved from the auctioneer's hammer in 1938 is not clear

TABLE 9. *Size of Agricultural Holdings in Bavaria, 1933*

	N	%	Percentage of Agricultural Area
Smallholdings (under 2 ha.)	124,701	22.4	3.1
Small farms (2–5 ha.)	160,128	28.8	13.1
Medium-sized farms (5–20 ha.)	234,914	42.3	55.0
Large farms (20–100 ha.)	35,523	6.4	25.9
Large-scale concerns (more than 100 ha.)	656	0.1	2.9
Total	555,922	100	100

Source: Kershaw, *Popular Opinion*, 33.

because many peasants later withdrew from the refinancing scheme. By 1945, however, some 30,331 concerns, or 6.2 percent of all holdings in the Ostmark, still held government mortgages and a total of RM 79,882,875 had been extended as credit.[4]

Some months before the Anschluss, Hitler had ordered his economic managers to increase food output without raising food prices. In response the Four-Year Plan attempted to close the gap between production costs and consumer demand through a combination of subsidies, flattery, and coercion. In May 1937, Göring announced a wide-ranging plan that slashed fertilizer prices, cut rail costs, and provided funds for mechanization, land reclamation, and rural housing.[5] Although only moderately effective in the Altreich with its limited margin for cost cutting, the extension of this program to the less developed Ostmark brought real benefits. With the elimination of most customs barriers and protective tariffs on 26 April 1938, the price of German agricultural machinery and fertilizers in Austria fell 33 to 50 percent. Between 1930 and 1945 the number of tractors on Austrian farms rose from 753 to 4,900, electric motors from 50,384 to 142,526, and harvesters from 24,866 to 60,000. There was also a dramatic increase in manure spreaders and artificial fertilizers; the use of potash and nitrates trebled between the Anschluss and 1940. Before the end of the Second World War the Reich government would invest RM 120 million in the modernization of Austrian agriculture.[6]

Whatever the long-term gains of German tutelage, however, there can be no doubt that Nazi organizational measures created hardship for most of the rural population. The introduction of the Entailed Farm Law on 27 July 1938 established compulsory peasant entails of between 7.5 and 125 hectares. Described by Kershaw as the "keystone of Nazi agricultural policy," these were indivisible holdings that sought "to retain the peasantry as the blood-spring of the German people" by limiting rights of inheritance to individual adult males. As in neighboring Bavaria, there was considerable regional variation in the distribution of peasant entails, with Carinthia claiming 24.9 percent of the total, Salzburg 12.2 percent, Upper Austria 6.5 percent, and Tyrol a mere 2.3 percent.

Among coheirs the Entailed Farm Law provoked understandable indignation, but there was also widespread general aversion to the scheme, particularly because it became virtually impossible to pass on holdings to female kin or, for that matter, to provide daughters with dowries. On a more basic level, entailed farmers found it difficult to obtain credit and cash loans for everyday operations. While some funds were made available for debt relief and special courts were established to adjudicate disputes, popular resentment was so intense that in 1940 the law was suspended in Tyrol.[7]

Even more onerous to Austrian peasants was the imposition of the Reich Food Estate, a mass organization of agricultural producers, cooperatives, and retailers involved in all aspects of the cultivation, processing, and marketing of food and food products. Extended to the Ostmark on 18 May 1938, it replaced existing cooperatives and interest groups with a bureaucratic apparatus controlled, in many cases, by Reich German administrators. On the village level its directives were carried out by indigenous Nazis known as the "Local Triangle," a group consisting of the local farm leader, the local party leader, and the mayor. By 1938 the chief function of the Reich Food Estate had become to fulfill production goals set in Berlin.

In incorporated Austria this meant requiring peasants to register their holdings, in return for a manor certificate (*Hofkarte*) and a license. Contracts were then issued for the delivery of specified amounts of fruits, vegetables, grain, meat, eggs, and dairy products. Only after fulfillment of these consignments was payment made and credits extended to obtain additional supplies of seed, fertilizers, and labor. Under these conditions, Austrian farmers confronted severe and serious difficulties, compounded by a sudden and unexpected flight from the land. Compelled to make deliveries at fixed prices, they were hard put to meet expenses. Since they could not balance their own rising costs with prices fixed by the regime, they became ensnared in a de facto inflationary spiral in which overall purchasing power declined 2.8 percent by the end of 1938.[8]

For most Austrian peasants the coercive measures of the Nazi regime confirmed their worst fears and suspicions. While the rural masses were not altogether immune to Anschluss enthusiasm, surviving reports indicate that the principal cause was profound relief that violence and bloodshed had been avoided. In Styria and Carinthia, where Nazi sympathies ran deep, there was also gratitude for the purchase of surplus fruit, grain, and livestock. According to police records from Upper Austria, ordinary people still felt emotionally loyal to the Old Regime; many feared an increase in food prices or simply saw no reason "to hope for an improvement in their livelihood." Others were reported coming to terms with the new order—many even looking forward to improved sales in the Altreich. To the extent that outright discontent could be observed, it was confined primarily to the lower clergy.[9] From Amstetten in Lower Danube the mood appears to have been less sanguine. Here, farmers expressed some hope of an economic upswing, but were deeply offended by Bürckel's campaign of slander against Dollfuss and Schuschnigg. There was also strong disapproval of random muggings of members of the Patriotic Front.[10]

In early May the police reported widespread worry about an alarming "flight from the land," an astonishing exodus of stableboys, milkmaids, and farmworkers that would permanently alter the demographic landscape of Austria.[11] By 1938 the Nazi rearmament boom had created an enormous demand for industrial labor that was already emptying the German countryside, leaving peasant proprietors confused, confounded, and concerned.[12] Even before the Anschluss, Austrian farmboys had been taking jobs in the Reich, so that both farmers and Nazi agricultural officials were acutely aware of the danger of the exodus spreading to the Ostmark. For that reason the Press Chamber issued explicit orders prohibiting German firms from recruiting on the land until the end of June. The demand for skilled labor was so intense, however, that within days employers from business and industry were crisscrossing the countryside, offering work in the Reich. There were also recruiters from the armed forces, the motorized police, and the Reich Labor Service (RAD). By April architects, engineers, and contractors were hiring unskilled labor for massive construction projects starting to get under way in the Ostmark itself. On 2 May the constabulary in Bad Hall reported the first signs of a massive migration of hirelings (*Dienstboten*) from nearby farms and manors.[13]

What was notable about the "flight from the land" in Austria was its sudden appearance and immediate impact on the rural economy. In the two years between 1938 and 1940 nearly a third of the paid workforce abandoned the countryside; in some regions of Styria, Carinthia, Salzburg, and Tyrol two-thirds of the farmhands vanished almost overnight. As Kershaw has shown in the Bavarian setting, the effect on peasant agriculture was calamitous. Most farm families relied on the labor of milkmaids and stableboys, and although some holders managed to raise wages 17 to 45 percent, most were in no position to match offers in construction or industry. Nor were they able to purchase machinery to mechanize operations.

As elsewhere in Greater Germany, peasants were quick to blame industry for enticing agricultural workers away from the land, but Nazi officials responded that hirelings and farmhands were only fleeing an outmoded and unconscionable form of rural servitude: no longer forced to sleep in stables or barns, at last free to marry without the consent of the master, and finally released from the threat of summary dismissal, thousands of youngsters streamed to cities in search of both a paying job and a better life in the National Community.[14]

During the summer of 1938 the Austrian peasantry appear to have become more "passive," "reserved," or simply indifferent to political affairs.[15] In the view of the police even the hard core of the Patriotic Front was coming to terms with the new order. At the same time, there were complaints about the disappearance of the workforce, skyrocketing labor costs, and the imposition of price controls on farm produce. From Reichraming, near Steyr, the constabulary reported a surge in the turnover of commodities, accompanied by cautious hope for an increase in cattle prices; according to the same report, there was also dismay that a summer camp for Jewish children remained open in the village, partly because it was placing an undue burden on the facilities of an impoverished community, partly because upland peasants and lumberjacks took offense that their favorite inns and guest houses were still "overrun by Jews." At the other end of the spectrum, hotelkeepers in Bad Hall, a holiday resort traditionally favored by Viennese Jews and Czechs, were said to be complaining about a slack tourist season; they went so far as to suggest that the Nazi ban on Jews was "premature."[16]

Stoking the growing disaffection in the towns and villages of rural Austria was Hitler's unprecedented assault on the Catholic Church.[17] Here traditional peasant society was deeply rooted, dominated by dense social relationships, and profoundly suspicious of outsiders. It was a culture "based on typical parochial piety which might be transgressed by neither the wealthy nor the poor."[18] After the Anschluss, the local party leader—usually a resident physician, attorney, or teacher—and the mayor, normally a farmer or village tradesman, would launch a frontal assault on Catholic symbols, ordering the removal of crucifixes from schools and public places, canceling significant holidays, or interfering with religious processionals. As in rural Bavaria, villagers sought solace from the parish priest, who responded by providing comfort or even by denouncing the Nazis from the pulpit—although often elliptically and only for a specific transgression.[19] Regarded by the authorities as hostile or subversive, the "religious obstinacy" of the rural populace should not be interpreted as political in character or intent but rather "tenacious adherence to what was seen as traditional and customary."[20]

The first major anticlerical foray into the Austrian countryside occurred in June 1938 when Nazi authorities imposed severe restrictions on Corpus Christi processions. Party leaders banned the wearing of uniforms by firemen, prohibited participation by middle-school children, and forbade the display of church regalia from public buildings and private homes. In Pettenbach, near Kirchdorf, the local SA leader went house to house to enforce the ban. Popular reaction to the limitations imposed on this important Catholic celebration was irate and bitter. In Aschbach enraged firemen were charged with making "subversive remarks"; in Bad Hall the traditionally joyous procession was said to "resemble an enormous funeral cortege rather than a festive celebration"; in Steinbach the parish priest, Father Cassian Kitzwankl, lost his temper and attacked the local party leader with his bare fists.[21]

Despite widespread anger, the Nazi regime further tightened the screws. On 12 July Hitler abrogated the Austrian Concordat of 1933.[22] For the rural populace the official restrictions were much less offensive than random, feckless attacks by party activists on sacred holidays, statues, and crucifixes. The cancellation of Saints Peter and Paul Day, for example, provoked an uproar that led to sporadic protests throughout the Ostmark, fueling in Tyrol what the Security Service considered a dangerous opposition movement. According to one official report, scores of Catholic activists were strewing Christian Corporative crosses in the streets of Innsbruck, distributing subversive leaflets, and slapping "malicious posters" on vacant walls.[23] By August there were acts of public protest. The desecration of a wayside crucifix near the Tyrolean village of Karres even prompted the parish priest, Dr. Josef Steinkelderer, to incite several dozen villagers to storm the home of the Nazi mayor. Hurling insults and promising to "flail the SA alive," the crowd demanded the drafting of a formal petition expressing the community's indignation and disgust. In a letter to Reich commissioner Bürckel in Vienna, Gauleiter Hofer contended that the incident was a "classic example" of the sort of unrest spreading throughout his province.[24]

Adding to the general sense of unease and discontent in the Austrian countryside was a growing apprehension of war. The surviving evidence suggests that the rural populace recognized the combustibility of the Sudeten crisis earlier than most city dwellers.[25] By mid-July the security organs were reporting a groundswell of anxiety in the villages of Upper and Lower Danube. As the war of nerves continued into August and September the call up of reservists, the requisitioning of workhorses, and the massive movement of troops toward the Czech frontier combined to drive home the gravity of the crisis to ordinary people, especially those living in border districts. The "war psychosis," as in Bavaria, tended to be most acute in frontier regions and among the older generation who had experienced the Great War. In the village of Pettenbach farmers were also reported retreating deep into the private sphere: they refused to use the "German greeting" and spoke only with great caution. Deliberately contrasting the mood with that in 1914, the police described overall morale as "unenthusiastic" or "depressed."[26] Nor was there much positive response to Nazi efforts to provide reassurance. At a party gathering in the village of Pöttsching in Burgenland, for example, "the majority of participants listened to the speaker's comments with indifference, only now and then applauding or making angry remarks."[27]

News that war had been averted by Hitler's triumph at Munich brought immense relief and satisfaction. In Carinthia and Styria there were torchlight parades to demonstrate support for the Nazi regime. As elsewhere in Greater Germany the authorities stressed a surge in popular confidence and trust in the Führer's leadership. Attempts to exploit the euphoria by staging hundreds of rallies and pep talks met, however, only limited success. Within a week of the Munich Agreement word arrived of the Nazi attack on Cardinal Innitzer's archiepiscopal palace in Vienna. Once details grew more widely known, rural sentiment became more apprehensive and concerned.[28]

THE NEW AGRICULTURAL CRISIS

In addition to spiritual woes, many peasants continued to express grave concern about the crisis in agriculture. There were some, however, who derived benefits from Nazi economic policies. Among them were smallholders who had been saved from bankruptcy, lumbermen who saw wages rising 10 to 40 percent, and village masons and carpenters who were bringing home paychecks 15 percent higher than before the Anschluss. Moreover, as unemployment declined and jobs expanded, consumer demand for merchandise began to grow, a trend obviously advantageous to small-town merchants and businessmen. According to the security organs, regime approval remained firm among these groups.[29]

Still, for most of the rural population the agrarian crisis remained acute and painful. Despite a slight elevation of morale in the weeks following

TABLE 10. *Crop Yields in Austria, 1938–1944 (in hundreds of kilograms)*

	Wheat	Rye	Barley	Potatoes	Fodder Beets
1938	5,174	5,489	3,016	31,008	20,327
1939	4,473	4,493	2,855	27,648	19,374
1940	2,849	3,131	2,798	26,033	17,248
1941	3,417	3,884	2,338	26,021	19,950
1942	2,760	2,701	2,218	22,515	20,156
1943	3,434	3,557	2,147	17,728	18,084
1944	2,938	2,790	1,808	17,509	17,456

Source: Mooslechner and Stadler, "Landwirtschaft und Agrarpolitik," 88.

Munich, there was anxiety about the dwindling labor supply and seething anger at tightening price regulations. Upland herdsmen bringing their stock to market at Windischgarsten were able to sell only 28 of their 133 head of cattle, at Vorderstoder a mere 5 out of 103. From Pettenbach the constabulary reported that some 250 to 300 farmers had to be issued citations for selling pigs at one mark per kilogram (*Lebendgewicht*) instead of the 80–83 pfennig stipulated by the Reich Food Estate. Compounding the general sense of disquiet was the spread of hoof-and-mouth disease from Bavaria, an epidemic that afflicted 9,680 Austrian farmsteads by the end of 1938. Not without reason, the county councillor in Kirchdorf portrayed his jurisdiction as a "disaster area" (*Notstandsgebiet*).[30]

By New Year 1939, overall expenditures on fertilizers and machinery had declined by 18 percent on Austrian farms, but these gains were more than offset by soaring labor costs of 35 percent. In Upper Danube, where between 1938 and 1941 agricultural wages rose 133 percent for men and 176 for women, the burden was even more staggering. Since farm prices were fixed by the Reich Food Estate, peasant purchasing power fell 2.8 percent in 1938, a trend that continued throughout the entire period of Nazi rule. Between 1937 and 1939, it dropped from 96 percent of pre-Depression levels to 91 percent, for mountain peasants from 81 to 70 percent.[31]

Nazi agrarian officials were not altogether unsympathetic to the plight of the farming populace. Shortly before the Anschluss, Herbert Backe, chief of the agricultural division of the Four-Year Plan, had submitted a long memorandum, recommending substantial price increases as the best means of boosting food production. Both Hitler and his deputy, Rudolf Hess, rejected this proposal. Obsessed with maintaining price stability during the coming war, they felt it hazardous to alienate the urban masses, especially the industrial workers who in their view had brought down the imperial German

TABLE 11. *Domestic Livestock in Austria, 1938–1944*

	Horses	Cattle	Pigs	Rabbits
1938	246,555	2,578,804	2,868,148	541,010
1939	230,581	2,619,508	2,830,126	—
1940	225,767	2,582,830	2,189,642	589,481
1941	226,351	2,493,504	2,043,468	—
1942	220,593	2,505,386	1,772,815	1,233,203
1943	223,641	2,530,302	1,842,364	1,491,168
1944	239,689	2,536,337	1,697,261	1,062,455

Source: Mooslechner and Stadler, "Landwirtschaft und Agrarpolitik," 89.

government in 1918. With that in mind the Nazi leadership insisted on staying the course until new agricultural resources had been conquered in the East. As a consequence, overall yields continued to decline, especially in Bavaria and Austria where farming remained labor-intensive and largely unmechanized[32] (see Tables 10 and 11).

The ever tightening regimen of the Reich Food Estate was accompanied by intensified pressure on the church. For the rural faithful the most iniquitous of the new measures was a ban on school prayer, a regulation that went into effect on 1 February and led to the eventual removal of some 1,500 priests from the classroom. Popular reaction was angry and hostile. In Strengberg an enraged crowd broke up a meeting of the Nazi Women's Association; in Weistrach there was an attack on the mayor. In other villages mothers drew up protest petitions, gathering scores of signatures. Despite pleas by Nazi speakers and officials, peasant opinion was nearly unanimous in condemning the regime as "hostile to religion."[33]

Taking stock of rural sentiment on the first anniversary of the Anschluss, the police characterized the mood as "varying from place to place," but concluded that most of the farming population was "irritable," "suspicious," and "not especially friendly." In the tiny hamlet of Spital am Pyhrn members of the local cooperative had attacked and beaten the party leader during the course of a stormy meeting in mid-February. Although Nazi agricultural officials still held out hope of winning over the peasants, they were frustrated by their obstinate disinterest in "ideological problems and discussion." Party leaders were also hard put to explain shortages of sugar, lard, soap, and matches.[34] One security agent wrote discouragingly that "the behavior of most of the farming populace clearly shows it has no interest in National Socialism and regards the movement with deep inner hostility."[35] For most people, in other words, Nazism was "experienced as a kind of elemental force, like floods or avalanches: to survive, one had to protect oneself as best one could until the disaster had passed."[36]

On the other hand, surviving documentation indicates that Catholic villagers did not mourn the disappearance of unemployment and panhandling from their midst.[37] It also reveals that for the young and able National Socialism offered glittering, unparalleled opportunity to escape the backbreaking drudgery of rural life. By early 1939 tens of thousands of hirelings were fleeing remote and far-flung Alpine valleys to take jobs in industry and construction. According to the security organs, teenage boys were chafing at the bit to join the Reich Labor Service or the armed forces. Air force recruiting offices were reported overrun by underage applicants; boys as young as fourteen or fifteen were said to be going to work on the railroad. Nor were the opportunities limited to male adolescents. Milkmaids were also described deserting farms in droves, often marrying former workmates who had landed relatively high-paying jobs in road or housing construction.[38] Perhaps the most tangible evidence of the massive internal migration unleashed by the Nazi revolution was a subsequent surge in the already soaring birthrate.[39]

On 15 March 1939 word arrived of Hitler's stunning seizure of Prague; it was followed a week later by triumphal announcement of the annexation of Memel. Despite the somber and suspicious mood prevailing in the Austrian countryside, popular reaction appears to have been both favorable and enthusiastic. According to reports from Kirchdorf, Kremsmünster, Ried, Grünburg, and Windischgarsten, the fait accompli both raised morale and aroused profound admiration for Hitler. Though most of the farming population still remained "aloof and skeptical," there were also numerous expressions of approbation, "even among those circles otherwise neutral or hostile to National Socialism." In a number of small villages there were spontaneous displays of flags or bunting from windowsills. Even on the land, veterans of the Great War voiced satisfaction with Germany's daring diplomacy and dramatic recovery of power.[40]

To what extent Hitler's occupation of Bohemia and Moravia enabled him to win over the Austrian peasantry is difficult to gauge. As elsewhere in Greater Germany, the dominant feeling appears to have been one of profound relief that war and bloodshed had again been avoided. In a number of localities there was hope that territorial gain might alleviate the agricultural crisis. If one considers the ground swell of support for Hitler, it may be inferred that the Führer cult was making a dent in traditional village culture. Whatever the actual attitudinal climate, police analysts went out of their way to emphasize the persistence of rural dissatisfaction and discontent, especially among housewives and "chronic complainers."[41]

Even so, overall morale clearly picked up in the following weeks. In their official summaries for April and May, the authorities characterized the mood as "calm," "satisfactory," "again favorable," "moderately good," or in a number of instances "reliable." Popular turnout for ceremonies honoring Hitler's fiftieth birthday on 20 April 1939, they reported, was fairly substantial, even in remote towns and villages where it might be unexpected. While some of the farming population had deliberately ignored the birthday celebrations, for example, in the fields surrounding Windischgarsten and Pettenbach, party officials were nearly unanimous in feeling that rural opinion was slowly moving in their direction.[42] From remote and secluded Steinbach am Ziehberge the police wrote that "aside from a few incorrigibles, it appears that persons previously aloof are bit-by-bit declaring their loyalty to the NSDAP, even though they may not participate in formal ceremonies."[43]

Local authorities tried to exploit the improving mood to their own advantage. As it was an article of faith that even the most intractable economic problems could be overcome by a mixture of coercion and persuasion, Nazi speakers fanned out through the countryside to explain the government's position on agricultural policy. Their words fell on deaf ears. In Nussbach, in the Innviertel, the county farm leader spent three hours addressing sixty local stockmen and growers on the agricultural crisis. He urged patience and cooperation, pushed the use of artificial fertilizers, and advised raising wages for hired help. The audience responded to his remarks by stalking out of the room in stony silence.[44]

POSITIVE REACTIONS AND THE IMPACT OF TOURISM

That the attitudes of the Austrian farming population remained more constant and unbending than envisaged by the Nazis is fairly well known. That rural sentiment accepted or endorsed certain aspects of the regime is less well known, though hardly less significant. Among the policies winning popular support were vigorous measures against price gouging, the liquidation of both unemployment and begging, and the roundup of gypsies, vagrants, and other marginal groups traditionally despised by farmers and peasants. In a report characterizing the local mood as otherwise "wretched," the constabulary in Euratsfeld wrote, for example, that "the Gypsy razzia of 26 June 1939 was hailed by the populace. People simply cannot grasp the fact that numerous sievemakers, cutters, and basketmakers etc. are gadding about. The populace regards them as Gypsies too and wonders why in the face of a rampant labor shortage such asocial elements are still on the loose."[45]

Despite resentment of the disruptions caused by fluctuating call-ups, the

Austrian farming population also endorsed service in Hitler's Wehrmacht. It is true that in the months following the Anschluss reservists had returned home from retraining exercises bellyaching about maltreatment by "Prussian" drill instructors. Notwithstanding far-fetched claims of "resistance" by postwar historians,[46] most of the complaining was little more than good-natured grousing. The truth was that Austrian soldiers experienced little if any discrimination in the German armed forces. "The highest and most sensitive positions were open to them."[47] By May 1939, moreover, conscripts were returning to their villages burning with enthusiasm.[48] This was hardly astonishing. Ever since the days of Hector and Achilles, military service has appealed to the cult of masculinity. In rural Austria "a true man was always obliged to prove his masculinity, be it at work, while trading livestock, while fighting in the local pub, in bed or even at war. The ideal masculine model in the village was the avid hunter, the keen soldier."[49]

Finally, it should not be overlooked that by the summer of 1939 a number of enterprising villagers and peasants were beginning to reap rewards from an upturn in the tourist trade, a boom that both revitalized traditional holiday resorts and brought paying sightseers to scenic communities, often in impoverished mountain regions. As we have already seen, a number of hotels and restaurants normally dependent on wealthy foreigners or Viennese Jews had been hurt by the Anschluss. They were, however, the exception. During the first Anschluss summer there was a massive influx of visitors from the Reich. Guesthouses in Tyrol, Salzburg, and the Salzkammergut were filled to overflowing. Nearly 100,000 motorists navigated the Grossglockner highway to the summit of "Germany's loftiest peak." In Gau Salzburg alone, overnight stays shot up from 1,856,300 in 1936–37 to 2,988,286 in 1938–39. It is true, of course, that the many visitors on package tours brought less to spend than wealthy British or American tourists and that some expensive hotels reported a poor season. All the same, the endless busloads of Hitler Youth and Strength through Joy vacationers poured more money into the rural economy and benefited many more ordinary people than the traditional tourist trade in a peak year.[50]

To what extent the advent of mass tourism molded or shaped political attitudes in the rural Ostmark is unclear. Fragmentary documentation from Zell am See, St. Johann, and Hallein in Salzburg and Oberdrauburg in Carinthia suggests considerable ambivalence. On the one hand, there was indisputable excitement and gratitude, especially for the 140,000 marks spent by skiers on the slopes of the Pinzgau in the winter season 1938–39. The following summer the "metal avalanche" of tourists in Carinthia was so enormous that hotels and inns were booked by noon, compelling thousands of motorists to spend cramped and uncomfortable nights in their cars or in makeshift campsites along roadside meadows. The presence of so many prosperous visitors from the Altreich, especially in backward Carinthia, lent credence to the Nazi promise of better economic times. For millions of Austrians the prospect of owning an automobile, especially the much-touted Volkswagen, a vehicle designed in part by the Führer himself, no longer seemed far-fetched. While the number of privately owned cars actually declined under Nazi rule, the hundreds of thousands of Austrians who enrolled in the Labor Front's Volkswagen savings scheme provides evidence of the optimism kindled by the new regime.[51]

On the other hand, there was also jealousy and disaffection. The surge of mass tourism put an enormous strain on outmoded roads, bridges, and hotel facilities. Villagers complained about noise, litter, and the stench of motor fumes; bicyclists and pedestrians sometimes feared for their lives. There was also resentment of well-heeled city dwellers taking advantage of the social and economic crisis gripping the countryside. In the heady days following the Anschluss, thousands of Germans had gone on a shopping spree, buying up stocks of woolens, leather goods, and other merchandise unavailable in the Reich. The following summer thousands more returned on "foraging" expeditions, this time to villages and farms to purchase black-market quantities of coffee, flour, lard, butter, eggs, and even meat. The authorities reported that most of the "scroungers" were Bavarians, especially housewives from Munich; others were minor party dignitaries. A few were major racketeers. Regardless of their origins or intentions, the "tactless behavior of Germans from the Old Reich" was said to have triggered considerable anxiety and dismay. There was also widespread muttering against "Prussian" outsiders.[52]

THE RESURGENCE OF DISCONTENT

From the Nazi perspective, rural morale remained generally "favorable" or "acceptable" throughout the spring of 1939. On 19 May the constable in Ried went so far as to argue that his district, the Innviertel, had become a "people's community."[53] At the end of June there was a sharp drop in the mood. The complaints were not new. They focused on the dwindling labor supply, the decline of farm income, and the tightening regimentation of agricultural production—all consequences of Hitler's policy of favoring guns over butter. In a number of localities peasants were reported relying on elderly parents or teenage daughters to do the work of two to three farmhands. Without recognizing the inconsistencies of their views, they and their neighbors demanded police intervention to stanch the hemorrhage of agricultural labor. A new wave of call-ups only worsened the situation.[54]

There were also renewed reports of scarcities. Onions disappeared from markets. Binders, smiths, and cobblers found raw materials in short supply. Village butchers accused farmers of marketing their best livestock in cities, leaving them stew meat and unhappy customers. For their part, the peasants raised a new howl of complaints against the Reich Food Estate, bitterly objecting to an order of 1 June 1939 mandating the delivery of virtually their entire output of milk, cream, lard, and eggs to government cooperatives. Transcending the divisions in rural society, there was also near universal condemnation of Sunday closing laws that went into effect between April and June 1939. Farmers long accustomed to shopping for supplies and necessities after Mass found themselves stymied. As one and a half hours were normally required to get to town by horse-drawn wagon, there was no other real opportunity to purchase staples or, as many complained, to have their hair cut. Some shopkeepers expressed satisfaction with the new regulations, but not all were happy. Even local Nazi officials had second thoughts.[55]

Still, it was not the agricultural crisis that was mainly responsible for the latest outburst of discontent and ill feeling. Just as decisive was another crackdown by Nazi firebrands on Catholic holidays traditionally celebrated in the weeks following Easter. As National Socialism regarded Christianity as its main ideological enemy in Austria, the police reported at great length on the sizable turnout for rogation ceremonies, the solemn days of chanting and prayer preceding Ascension Day. From Kirchdorf the county executive wrote that the participation of 800 persons in a procession from Pettenbach to Magdalenaberg provided incontrovertible evidence of a "distinctly hostile attitude."[56]

Given such a cast of mind, anticlerical zealots moved aggressively against Corpus Christi parades. Their interference provoked nearly unanimous "annoyance," "indignation," and "ill feeling." In Ried the otherwise optimistic security agent wrote embarrassingly that more villagers had showed up than the year before. Confronted with a ban on musical instruments, many of the participants responded with insults and "subversive remarks," leaving the authorities no choice but to take selected troublemakers into custody. Even then, the crowd did not hesitate to take up a collection for the musicians or to offer them beer and cigarettes. In Opponitz the diversion of the procession into back streets and alleys provoked "great indignation." In the tiny community of Oed the exclusion of teachers, schoolchildren, and church groups elicited "severe criticism." In Euratsfeld villagers were said to have put up with the new restrictions but flown into a rage upon hearing that their neighbors in Scheibbs had experienced no obstruction; within days many of them resigned in protest from the Nazi Women's Aid Society and the Reich Veterans' Association.[57]

In other localities restrictions were ignored or evaded. In Steinbach am Ziehberge the local farm leader, the SA, and some three dozen party members marched in the procession. In Pettenbach and Nussbach over 1,000 parishioners paraded unimpeded in traditional regalia accompanied by local ensembles. Probably hoping to save face without alienating the population, the Kreisleiter waited for several days to issue a retroactive directive dissolving the village bands and confiscating their instruments—too late for Corpus Christi Day but just in time for a visit by Hitler to nearby Fischlham and Lambach. According to the police, popular reaction was one of bemusement rather than rage. On the other hand, nearly everyone condemned an order dismissing nuns from nursery schools and kindergartens.[58] In Carinthia there were also demonstrations protesting the sporadic removal of crucifixes from village classrooms.[59]

At the end of June, the SD in Vienna tried to assess the impact of Hitler's campaign of de-Christianization. It concluded that the most unyielding rural areas were Tyrol, Salzburg, and Upper Danube, "regions where religion is respected." Despite the best efforts of the party, "the population counters every measure against the church."[60] This was a perceptive observation. While there was no organized "counteraction," as the SD contended, people did close ranks behind the church against sacrilegious vandalism, restrictions on religious holidays, and attacks on the clergy.

There was also an unanticipated reaction to the separation of church and state. As mentioned earlier, a Führer decree of 28 April 1939 had terminated all state financial assistance, compelling the church to depend on voluntary contributions and inducing members to give up their faith.[61] Although opposition by the bishops was confused and feeble, the lower clergy sought to galvanize the countryside by resuming an active ministry. On Ascension Day 1939 a special mass was staged at Maria Scharten in support of Christian values, an occasion that attracted the participation of nearly 1,000 boys and girls from Upper Danube.[62] Such large celebrations were both rare and risky. More often than not, parish priests would deliver ambiguously constructed homilies and sermons, "metaphorically inspired by the biblical motto enjoining the Church to be as clever as snakes, but meant to depict the concrete state of affairs in which the Third Reich found itself."[63] On Mothers Day 1939, for example, Dr. Maurus Morhardt presented a disquisition at the rural vicarage in Steyrling on the marriage of Mary and Joseph. Illustrating his remarks with lantern slides of the Holy Family, he pointedly reminded his parishioners that matrimony outside the Roman Catholic Church was unacceptable. Similarly, Father Simon Bischof at nearby Wartberg preached a Sunday sermon some months later on Napoleon. In less than Aesopian language he contrasted the ephemeral achievements and disastrous fate of the French emperor to those of the Prince of Peace, implying that Nazi aggression could lead to disaster and damnation.[64]

That these remarks alarmed the Gestapo should come as no surprise. Over the summer months the development of the Polish crisis revived deep-seated anxiety and fear of war. Farmers, villagers, and tourists were observed hoarding food and supplies. Rumors swirled that "in six weeks there might be war."[65] And yet, nerves appear to have been less frayed than during the Sudeten emergency. There was also less awareness of the gravity of the threat than in Vienna, no doubt because farmers were toiling fifteen to sixteen hours daily in the fields. Furthermore, the springtime assault on the church had left many people numb; the rural populace simply turned inward and hunkered down.[66] For their part, the Nazis seemed amazed that so many villagers remained sullen, indifferent, or in some locations downright hostile. In Ried the police refused to characterize the mood as oppositional but did admit to "undeniable dissatisfaction."[67] Elsewhere, there were reports of continuing "ill temper," "depression," and "tension." Farmers were reported boycotting party meetings, declining to contribute to Nazi charities, or refusing to make the slightest sacrifice to the regime. Almost as an afterthought, it was added that the Hitler salute had virtually disappeared from use—perhaps out of sheer boredom.[68]

Economically, conditions improved slightly during the last summer of peace. Although some farmers near Behamberg and Seitenstetten in Lower Danube suffered severe hail damage to their fields, the overall harvest was bountiful. Furthermore, teams of youngsters from the League of German Girls, the Hitler Youth, and the Reich Labor Service provided short-term assistance getting in the crops. The peasants regarded the help with feelings running from mistrust to indifference to reluctant gratitude; the boys and girls viewed the experience with exhaustion and exhilaration, or so the authorities claimed. By the end of July overall morale was said to have become more favorable or at least "somewhat improved."[69] Soon thereafter it tumbled. Ominous headlines and radio bulletins aroused tremendous apprehension and fear; the arrival of draft notices, the acceleration of call-ups, and the requisitioning of workhorses all added to the sense of dread. Rural stations described the mood as "depressed," "apathetic," "somewhat uneasy," "agitated," "tense," and, above all, "worried."[70]

On 24 August the crisis seemed to pass; villagers awoke to learn that Foreign Minister Joachim von Ribbentrop had signed a nonaggression treaty in the Kremlin with Soviet Russia. In a spasm of collective credulity rare even in Nazi Germany the rural populace hailed the Molotov-Ribbentrop Pact as a breakthrough for peace. There were even euphoric tributes to Hitler. A new wave of call-ups, however, exposed the chimera of the moment; on 28 August wartime rationing went into effect. Once again, nerves became taut. Security officers indicated that although a good many people were counting on the Führer to pull another rabbit out of the hat, most were resigned to war. When news arrived of the outbreak of hostilities with Poland, the reaction in the Austrian countryside was anything but enthusiastic.[71]

CONCLUSION

In the eighteen months between the Anschluss and the outbreak of World War II the Nazis made little progress penetrating the "social milieu" of the Austrian countryside. In contrast to the Altreich—including bordering Bavaria—the largely Catholic population had battled the brownshirts with ballots and bullets for nearly two decades. While nearly everyone endorsed the Anschluss, few were under any illusions about what to expect. As the Nazis moved immediately to control all aspects of agricultural production, it is hardly surprising that the farming population reacted with resentment and anger. Almost overnight, farmers and peasants found themselves in the midst of a severe agricultural crisis marked by a massive drain of labor and a sharp decline of farm income. Hitler's assault on the church also inflamed rural hostility, both provoking acts of defiance and reawakening the baroque ideal of the unity of Austria and Catholicism.[72] In Tyrol there were even some resistance cells.[73] Despite encouragement and support by the lower clergy, protest was confined primarily to passive disobedience and aloofness. It did not develop into outright resistance.[74]

Still, the rural population was not entirely impervious to the siren song of National Socialism. Hitler's social revolution brought more than distress to the Austrian countryside; it also brought hope and the promise of a better future. Almost overnight farmers were saved from foreclosure, if not indebtedness. They gained access to the enormous market of Greater Germany; they obtained new equipment; they mechanized operations. The major beneficiaries, it is true, were medium-size holders and large landowners, but village craftsmen, innkeepers, and tradesmen profited as well. The biggest winners were, however, the poor and destitute. While a majority of proprietors suffered hardship and material losses, countless numbers of milkmaids, stableboys, and farm laborers gained from Nazi agricultural policies. Suddenly there was a premium on the sweat and toil of the wretched of the earth. In two short years their wages rose at astonishing rates, both in the countryside and at nearby construction sites. Decades later one farm laborer would recall, "Hitler came like a God for the little people"; another remembered that "there was a feeling in the air as though paradise would come." That Nazi membership soared in rural areas was therefore no coincidence. In Tyrol-Vorarlberg, well known for discontent and defiance, some 14.4 percent of the population joined the party, the largest percentage of dues-paying members in the Ostmark and well above the average in the Greater German Reich.[75]

On balance, the rural masses of Austria showed little inclination to support the Anschluss regime, but they were not a monolithic community. Certain individuals and groups approved the Nazi system; others endorsed specific aspects of it. As in Bavaria, the farming population showed indifference to foreign affairs, but remained sedulously alert to the slightest rumor of war. It is true that most peasants were reported favoring Hitler's diplomatic victories, but what garnered popular approbation was the Führer's avoidance of bloodshed, not his territorial triumphs. At the same time, there can be no doubt that his occupation of Prague elicited widespread satisfaction, a clear reflection of deep-rooted animosity toward the Czechs. Thereafter, the development of the "Danzig question" and the growing likelihood of hostilities contributed to a "war psychosis" that was broken only by the outbreak of war itself. In the years ahead the rural masses would grow even more disaffected and disenchanted with the Nazi regime. Nevertheless, they and the Roman Catholic Church would continue to accept it until the collapse of the Third Reich itself.

THE POPULAR ASSAULT
ON THE JEWS

7

Long before the Anschluss, ordinary Austrians had reached consensus on the Jewish Question. Their attitudes were by no means uniform, but most people held the Jews at least partly accountable for the suffering and distress of the past half century. Anti-Semitism had been "the single most pervasive and persistent issue in Austrian politics."[1] It was a multifarious creed, but it provided coherence and cohesion for a confused and divided people. The collective phobia may not have envisaged mass murder, but subsequent events suggest that thousands of Austrians, especially in Vienna, yearned to strip the Jews of their rights and property, to segregate them from society, to eliminate them from their midst. In 1938 the spontaneous anti-Semitic riots accompanying the Anschluss were so violent that they shocked even the Germans.[2]

In retrospect, the predominant position of the Jews in an impoverished country only intensified the fear and loathing of the Austrian masses. As we have already seen, Jewish businesses and financial institutions managed much of the country's economic life. At the time of the Anschluss three-quarters of Vienna's newspapers, banks, and textile firms were in Jewish hands. With 212,000 non-Jewish wage earners employed by Jewish firms, Herbert Rosenkranz has observed that the "destructive influence of Jewish bankruptcies on Christian-Jewish relations can easily be imagined."[3]

The extraordinary success of the Jews in the learned professions also inspired jealousy and spite. Over 50 percent of Austria's attorneys, physicians, and dentists were Jewish. At the world-famous University of Vienna, the achievements of highly competitive Jewish students provoked numerous fistfights and assaults. There was intense pressure to reduce their numbers to correspond to their actual proportion of Austrian society: 2.8 percent of the total population.[4]

In sharp contrast to Germany where Jews resided in both cities and small towns, over 90 percent of the Jews in Austria lived in a single metropolis: Vienna. Their numbers had declined from 176,034 in 1934 to 169,978 in

TABLE 12. *The Jewish Population of Austria, 1934 and 1938*

	1934	1938
Vienna	176,034	169,978
Lower Austria	7,716	8,010
Upper Austria	966	980
Styria	2,195	2,028
Salzburg	239	189
Carinthia	269	257
Tyrol	365	346
Vorarlberg	42	18
Burgenland	3,632	3,220
Total	191,458	185,026

Source: Rosenkranz, *Verfolgung*, 311.

1938 (see Table 12), but with 9.4 percent of the municipal population they constituted the largest Jewish community in German-speaking Europe.[5] Outside the capital some 16,439 of their coreligionists dwelled in scattered communities, usually in provincial capitals where they engaged in retailing or practiced a profession. As in Bavaria, most provincial Jews regarded themselves as assimilated, kept a low profile, and attracted little personal hostility from their neighbors. At the same time, they participated only marginally in community affairs, having to put up with exclusion from local clubs as well as the opprobrium of the church. Only in Burgenland where they had long enjoyed the protection of the Esterhazys, the well-known Hungarian land magnates, did Jews live as members of a relatively well integrated community.[6]

Despite their preeminence in business, finance, and the professions, Austrian Jews scarcely wielded the influence imagined by the rest of the population. It is true that most of them lived a clannish existence in self-segregated Viennese neighborhoods, but they were divided into antagonistic factions mirroring the cleavages of Austrian society along rationalist, atavistic, and religious lines. In addition, there were geographic, social, and religious fissures, fragmenting the community into Western Jews and Ostjuden, believers and nonbelievers, assimilationists and Zionists, and modern and traditional orthodox. Within the Community Council, the Kultusgemeinde, the major fault line ran between Liberals and Jewish Nationalists, the former regarding Jewish identity in purely religious terms, the latter seeking to define it along ethnic lines.[7] All told, there were 444 Jewish organizations in Vienna alone. Of these, only 88 were religious or prayer groups; the rest consisted mainly of welfare associations, Zionist bands, professional societies, student fraternities, and athletic clubs. There also existed affiliations of war veterans, journeymen, and political fringe groups.[8]

Because Jewish society was so divided, its members had difficulty comprehending the rise of anti-Semitism and Nazism. Between 1933 and 1938 the discord separating assimilationists and Jewish Nationalists was so acrimonious that the Zionist directors of the Community Council could neither overcome internal cleavages nor formulate a coherent program for confronting the problems of poverty, dictatorship, and racism. The Jewish community regarded the Dollfuss-Schuschnigg regime as its protector, even though Austrian authorities sought to segregate the Viennese school system and exclude Jews from public service. For most Jews these were minor irritants. In their view the government had crushed the Nazi uprising of 1934, put an end to anti-Semitic violence, and made the streets safe once again for men and women of the Hebrew faith. As a result, nearly all Jews shared a false sense of security as well as a belief that Hitler had already been defeated in Austria. When the Christian Corporative system collapsed, most of them were taken completely by surprise.[9]

THE ANSCHLUSS ONSLAUGHT

Between 1933 and 1938, Jews in Hitler's Reich had been subjected to recurring waves of Nazi terror, haphazardly orchestrated by the state and party. Some "Aryan" civilians had participated in the pogroms, but most ordinary people had generally kept their distance. It is true that individual acts of malicious discrimination and violence were more commonplace than once thought. It is also certain that a majority of Reich Germans harbored feelings of disdain for the Jews. Nevertheless, popular loathing had not spurred Hitler's anti-Semitic depredations; the civilian population shared a degree of complicity, but its members were, for the most part, only marginally involved.[10] Such a generalization is difficult to make about the Austrian people. By 1938 hatred of Jews had become so tightly woven into the fabric of Austrian society that it constituted "a Sorelian political myth, immune to empirical falsification."[11] On Friday, 11 March 1938, tens of thousands of Viennese took to the streets bellowing "Down with the Jews! Heil Hitler! Hang Schuschnigg!"[12] Hour after hour they dragged passengers from taxicabs, plundered homes, and clubbed or beat hundreds of Jews. The British correspondent G. E. R. Gedye estimated that 80,000 to 100,000 Viennese spent the evening rampaging through Leopoldstadt, the Jewish quarter.[13]

In the meantime, Gestapo agents streamed into Austria to manage and coordinate the arrest of Hitler's political opponents. The security forces rounded up some 10,000 to 20,000 persons within days of the Anschluss,[14] as party activists and vigilantes stepped up their campaign of terror and "wild Aryanization." It was a medieval pogrom in "modern dress."[15] For weeks gangs of Nazis roamed the streets of the city, desecrating synagogues, cleaning out department stores, and raiding apartments. Mobile squads of storm troopers robbed, beat, and killed at random. Surrounded by jeering mobs, they dragged Jewish families from their homes, "put scrubbing-brushes in their hands, splashed them with acid, and made them go down on their knees and scrub away for hours at the hopeless task of removing Schuschnigg propaganda."[16]

The humiliations and horrors visited on the Jews also had symbolic and ritualistic overtones: the rebellious masses attacked rich and poor alike.[17] They stole cash, jewelry, furs, clothing, and furniture; they tore Torah rolls from synagogues and prayer halls; they forced Jewish patriarchs to scrub toilet bowls with prayer bands; they sheared the beards of rabbis with scissors and rusty knives. On weekends storm troopers dragged hundreds of Jews to the Prater, the woodland preserve to the east of Leopoldstadt on the Danubian Canal. In the shadow of Vienna's enormous ferris wheel they forced elderly men to submit to beatings, to do endless calisthenics, even to eat grass.[18] Some months later, an SS correspondent wrote admiringly in *Das Schwarze Korps*: "The Viennese have managed to do overnight what we have failed to achieve in the slow-moving, ponderous north up to this day. In Austria, a boycott of the Jews does not need organizing—the people themselves have initiated it."[19]

There was much truth in this unmerciful observation. Before the Anschluss the Jews of Germany had suffered only partial exclusion in the Third Reich. They had lost their civil liberties; they had been barred from both government service and the professions. Nevertheless, they still retained control of their proprietary assets. In late 1937 Göring had formulated plans to expropriate Jewish resources for the armaments industry, if necessary by force. What he did not anticipate was the revolutionary radicalism of the Austrian Nazis and the Viennese mob.[20] Whether the German occupiers were unable to control the mass violence of the March days or deliberately fostered it as a "safety valve" for pent-up social tensions is unclear.[21] The indiscriminate theft of millions of marks earmarked for defense spending certainly alarmed the new masters. Not until the promotion of Josef Bürckel to commissioner for the reunification of Austria with the German Reich on 23 April 1938 did the Nazi government take steps to act.[22]

First, the Gestapo dissolved the Jewish Community Council and arrested its officers. On 2 May, the thirty-two-year-old SS officer, Adolf Eichmann, reopened its offices, summoning Dr. Josef Löwenherz, the former executive director, to his headquarters. Eichmann greeted the dignitary with a slap in the face. He then charged him with the onerous task of expediting the expulsion of the Jewish community by soliciting funds from foreign Jews. The result was the establishment the Central Office for Jewish Emigration, an agency designed to expel Austrian Jews by a conveyor-belt system that also robbed them of their assets. Second, Reich commissioner Bürckel issued the Decree on the Declaration of Jewish Assets, an order requiring the registration of all property in excess of 5,000 marks. His aim was to put an end to private looting and to establish procedures for the expropriation of the estimated Jewish wealth of RM 3 million.[23] A lead article in the *Völkischer Beobachter* appealed to popular sentiment. In exceptionally harsh and prophetic language it explained:

> By the year 1942 the Jewish element in Vienna will have to have been wiped out and made to disappear. No shop, no business will be permitted by that time to be under Jewish management, no Jew may find an opportunity anywhere to earn money, and with the exception of those streets where the old Jews and Jewesses are using up their money—the export of which is prohibited—while they wait for death, there must be no sign of Jews in the city.
>
> No one who knows the Viennese opinion regarding the Jewish Question will be surprised that the four years in which the economic death sentence on the Jews is to be carried out seems much too long a time to them. The Viennese wonders at all the trouble [the authorities] are prepared to take, at the scrupulous care devoted to the protection and maintenance of Jewish property. After all, he thinks, it is all perfectly simple: the Jew must go—and his cash stays here.[24]

With the passage of the Decree on the Declaration of Jewish Assets, a flood of discriminatory measures went into effect. Jews were banned from livestock and meat markets. They were prohibited from working in tourist agencies, real-estate firms, and credit information bureaus. After the extension of the Nuremberg Laws to Austria on 20 May, they were made second-class citizens and dismissed from public service. In the months that followed, they lost the right to practice medicine and law. They were banned from parks and public benches. To spur them to leave the country, the Gestapo issued orders "to arrest disagreeable Jews immediately, especially those with a criminal record," a directive that led within days to the dispatch of some 1,600 to 1,700 intellectuals, engineers, attorneys, and physicians to Dachau. As for the general public, although Bürckel's office put an end to incidents of "wild Aryanization,"[25] anti-Semitic outbursts continued throughout the summer of 1938. They accelerated rapidly in October, finally culminating in the devastation of Crystal Night in early November.[26]

POPULAR ACCLAMATION AND CONSENT

How pervasive was the lynch mood hysteria? Until recently, investigation of the social reality of Hitler's Germany has yielded little information regarding the views of ordinary people on the Jewish issue. The confidential reports of the Gestapo, the SD, the county executives, and other agencies charged with public surveillance provide only occasional glimpses of popular reaction to the persecution of the Jews. Between 1933 and 1938 most Germans considered the Jewish Question a marginal issue, far removed from the cares and sorrows of everyday life. While Hitler and Nazi activists used anti-Semitic arguments to rally the party faithful, the general population remained, for the most part, apathetic. In the view of the security organs their indifference hardly merited mention or discussion.[27]

Given the intensity of Judeophobia in Austria, it is all the more remarkable that surviving Nazi records contain few details about popular attitudes in that country toward the Jews; they disclose little about the suffering of the victims; they provide only limited and intermittent testimony about the feelings and behavior of the majority of the population.[28] Eyewitness accounts by diplomats, foreign correspondents, and Jewish survivors make it unmistakably clear, however, that ordinary Austrians were anything but indifferent to the fate of the Jews. As we have seen, enormous crowds welcomed the Anschluss by joining Nazi gangs to attack, rob, and humiliate Jews.[29]

Is it possible to identify the mobs of jeering bystanders who surrounded Jewish victims, spat in their face, or chased them from parks and public places? Surviving testimony suggests involvement of broad strata of society ranging from well-tailored young women and prosperous businessmen to petty bourgeois shopkeepers, domestics, workers, and prostitutes. The British correspondent G. E. R. Gedye claimed that the crowds were "predominantly middle class, with very few workers apart from those who had been marched in detachments from their places of employment."[30] Most Jews recalled, however, that nearly all Gentiles were hostile, even those long regarded as friends.[31]

Attempting to draw conclusions from photographic evidence, Gerhard Botz has suggested that the leading Jew baiters were predominately middle-aged babbitts or teenage hoodlums. Admitting the presence of proletarian onlookers, he argues that those getting the spoils tended to be veteran party members, long out of work.[32] Another historian, Hans Witek, uses statistical evidence to show that the Viennese who actually seized Jewish firms as "provisional directors" came primarily from the ranks of white-collar employees or small businessmen; others, he reveals, were lawyers, bank tellers, and tradesmen.[33] Whatever their social origins, both contemporaneous and historical evidence make it clear that at least "ten thousand Viennese participated in the spoilation of the Jews or were themselves instigators."[34]

To reconstruct a social profile of the Vienna mob is a futile task; there were simply too many participants. In this regard, it is worth noting that although the viciously anti-Semitic *Stürmer* first appeared in Austrian news stands on 18 March, the regime refrained from a media assault on the Jews until 11 April—exactly a month after the Anschluss and the day following the plebiscite. Thereafter, the party press was merciless. On 2 August Gauleiter Globocnik opened an exhibit at the Northwest Station on "The Eternal Jew." Preceded by a massive advertising campaign, the exposition combined display cases, posters, and film to depict the Jews as the source of societal pestilence and decay. Willingly paying an admission charge, 4,000 visitors showed up in the first hour, 10,000 on the first day. By the time the exhibition closed on 30 September, some 350,000 Viennese had attended with relish.[35]

There is, of course, no accurate way of assessing the impact of "The Eternal Jew" on popular sentiment. The pervasive and lethal Austrian fixation on the Jewish issue is, however, all too apparent in a collection of anonymous letters addressed to the Reich commissioner for the reunification with the German Reich.[36] Examination of the letters reveals complaints about random violence, "excesses" damaging to the NSDAP, or difficulties caused by Aryanization, such as a frozen bank account or the temporary loss of a job. After 1 May, as the regime itself struggled to curb marauding bands of storm troopers and teenage gangs, the epistolary evidence suggests widespread distress with the ongoing lawlessness. There were also protests against the maltreatment of Jewish war veterans, elderly Jews, or individuals such as the neighborhood grocer. Nevertheless, few of the protest letters question the Nazi goal of removing the Jews from the National Community, and many of the others make accusations against specific Jews—usually for "masquerading" as Aryans.[37]

Among the letter writers a number of embittered women claimed to have been seduced and abandoned by wealthy Jews; others objected to being mistreated by Jewish gynecologists. There was also notable abuse directed against Jewish attorneys, bank managers, and landlords. By midsummer many of the anonymous complaints focused on the legal exemptions granted

Jewish-Gentile *Mischlinge* under the Nuremberg Laws, a group regarded as exceptionally dangerous and perfidious. As details of the Nuremberg legislation became better known, there were calls for harsher measures ranging from immediate expulsion to outright extermination of what one writer called the "bloodsuckers of the German people." In short, although large segments of the Viennese public clearly objected to acts of random violence, a strong consensus appeared for ridding the metropolis of Jews in a legal and orderly manner.[38]

PROVINCIAL RESPONSES

Since the Anschluss was to a great extent a backwoods uprising against cosmopolitan Vienna, a metropolis perceived as overrun by foreigners and Jews, it was only logical that the Austrian Nazis would also target the 16,439 Jews living outside the capital. Even before German troops crossed the frontier, brownshirts in Graz, Linz, and Salzburg were beating up Jews, seizing their businesses, and desecrating their prayer halls. In the weeks that followed local authorities proceeded even more ruthlessly, placing Jews under arrest, expropriating their assets, and forcing them to pack their bags. To be sure, circumstances varied from place to place: in Innsbruck, party functionaries expropriated property but refrained from violence; in Graz, there were summary arrests and evictions but no "scrubbing actions"; in Carinthia, mistreatment was limited to random house searches, cottage seizures, and verbal abuse—an approach reflecting not so much indifference as the grim determination of local Nazis to settle accounts first with the Dollfuss-Schuschnigg regime and the church. Overall, while some Jewish people suffered only petty indignities, none had reason to view the future with optimism.[39]

Indeed, it should be emphasized that the first systematic effort to expel Jews by force from Nazi Germany took place in the Burgenland. Here the Gestapo started rounding up Jewish families on Saturday, 26 March, driving them from their homes and villages, herding them into stables, clubbing or murdering them on the spot. Although the mass arrests did not completely "cleanse" the Burgenland, the Gestapo was able to boast by 11 August that 1,200 men, women, and children had been forced to emigrate. Elsewhere, it was the party that took the initiative.[40] On 18 September the Kreisleitung in Horn, in Lower Danube, gave the town's Jews twenty-four hours' notice to clear out, authorizing the local notary to dispose of their assets. "The operation proceeded smoothly," the SD recorded, "aside from theatrical outcries, 'more amusing than tragic' in character, by several women. The populace regarded the affair with understanding, notwithstanding a tiny minority of red sympathizers and installment-buyers."[41]

The savagery of the anti-Jewish terror in the provinces differed from that in Vienna in one respect: it was organized and executed primarily by party activists, the Gestapo, or the SS. There was relatively little mass violence or active participation by the civilian population.[42] This does not mean that ordinary people disapproved what was going on. Nor were they always simply onlookers. As we have just seen, most residents of Horn endorsed the expulsion of their Jewish neighbors. Furthermore, although the evidence is exiguous, few Austrians appear to have sympathized with local Jews: unlike in Germany few people made distinctions between Jewish acquaintances and the rest of those slated for deportation.[43] Villagers in Reichraming, a hamlet in Upper Danube, reportedly even took the initiative in evicting an elderly Jewish widow and her son, two longtime residents who had transformed their home into a summer camp for Jewish children. According to police records, local people were so fed up with the "aliens" that they welcomed their extradition.[44] Nor was this an isolated instance. When Father Alois Hanig baptized eight Jews in the tiny community of Stillfried, he was said to have "deeply offended" his parishioners.[45]

Hitler's anti-Jewish policies therefore elicited considerable support in the Austrian provinces, particularly in the cities and small towns. As one paradigmatic police report put it, "The measures against the Jews are especially welcome."[46] Still, there were exceptions. When Dr. Mandl, an Arbesbach physician, died some months after losing his home to the Nazis, hundreds of farmers and villagers attended his funeral to express their devotion and grief.[47] The large turnout suggests that most country people were disinterested in the Jewish Question as such; they no doubt shared the Roman Church's vehement aversion of Judaism, but like their Bavarian kin disapproved the persecution of neighbors or respected acquaintances.[48] On 23 September a rural constable in Waldneukirchen wrote, for example, that "Jewish influence has never manifested itself here and is virtually unknown. It must be noted that the populace is still in the dark about this issue and needs to be enlightened about the noxious influence of Jewry."[49]

THE JEWISH RESPONSE

How did the Jewish populace react to the violence perpetrated by the Austrian Nazis and their accomplices? This is a difficult question to address. There is little contemporaneous evidence and only a handful of memoirs by refugees.[50] Even a recent collection of "oral histories" of Viennese survivors provides little information on their recollections of the Anschluss.[51] Politically conscious Jews had always recognized that their survival depended on the continued independence of Austria.[52] To be sure, many of them lionized

German culture and admired Prussian virtues; some even respected Hitler for his achievements. Nonetheless, an overwhelming majority believed in Austrian independence and counted on Chancellor Kurt von Schuschnigg to preserve it. "We did not close our eyes to what was going on in the Third Reich," George Clare wrote decades later, "but we didn't open them too wide either."[53] He was not exaggerating. In November 1937 Stefan Zweig journeyed from London to Vienna to warn his friends of the "ever-closer catastrophe." Their reaction was one of mocking disbelief.[54]

It was not until Schuschnigg's fateful meeting with Hitler at Berchtesgaden that the Jewish community took serious notice of the impending danger. Word of the conference shocked and perturbed a great many individuals.[55] German ambassador Papen chortled that Vienna "resembled an ant hill. Quite a few Jews were preparing to emigrate."[56] Soon thereafter, the Jewish Telegraph Agency indicated that the Jewish Question had not been discussed at the Austro-German summit, an accurate but misleading report that restored the prevailing sense of complacency. Subsequent articles in the Orthodox press even assured readers that those pro-Nazis entering the Austrian government could be trusted. According to George Clare, most people fell prey to "self-deception," believing that the situation had become more serious, but not hopeless. Another survivor, Robert Adler, ruefully recalled that both he and his coreligionists had been "utterly naive."[57]

What did concern many Viennese Jews was the sudden upsurge of Nazi agitation following Hitler's threatening radio speech of 20 February. Schuschnigg's rousing response four days later allayed fears, however, and restored a false sense of confidence. "We thought we had all Europe behind us," Alfred Kessler recalled six decades afterward.[58] Furthermore, an increasing number of progovernment demonstrations seemed to keep the brownshirts in check. "The hectic days did not produce in us excessive tension," Clare later wrote. "There was excitement and fear, but we also had hope and expected life to go on in its firmly established way."[59]

Even after Hitler's followers had assumed virtual control of Graz and other provincial localities, most Viennese Jews continued to discount the danger of a Nazi takeover. When Schuschnigg proposed his plebiscite on 9 March, they united in support; Dr. Desider Friedmann, the president of the Community Council even contributed 800,000 schillings to the Patriotic Front.[60] Within two days rumors of an electoral cancellation started to circulate, but few Jews appear to have taken them seriously. "People went about their business," Gertrude Schneider laconically recalled.[61] As evening shadows fell on the metropolis, thousands of Jewish families prepared to observe sabbath; most were unaware of the crowds of Nazis converging on the city center.

Schuschnigg's resignation, broadcast shortly before eight o'clock, left Jewish listeners thunderstruck. "My family and I heard the speech in stunned silence," Henry Grunwald recalled. "My father said, 'I didn't believe it would come to this. I still can't believe it.' "[62] George Clare remembered that before any one had a chance to utter a word, "the sounds of hundreds of men shouting at the top of their voices could be heard."[63] Rushing to the window of his home on the Nussdorferstrasse, he looked down on a crowd of thousands of Nazis alternately chanting "Death to the Jews!" and "One Reich, One People, One Leader!" Another émigré, Estra Perl, heard the commotion only after leaving evening services at a synagogue near the Wallensteinstrasse. Although she and her father returned home safely, many others did not. Heinrich Berger emerged from his carpet shop on the Maria-hilferstrasse to fall prey to a squad of drunken storm troopers; they hurled epithets in his face, draped a "Sow Jew!" placard on his shoulders, and abruptly disappeared into the night.[64]

For the next week Vienna experienced a wave of anti-Semitic savagery unmatched since the Middle Ages. The Austrian Jews learned to their horror that there was more to the cruel, wanton, violent language of Austrian anti-Semitism than empty rhetoric. Each reacted differently, of course, but most immediately realized that their world belonged to the past. No one expressed the sense of terror better than George Clare, then a seventeen-year-old boy. Quite by accident he caught sight of the neighborhood patrolman beating a helpless victim. "Within minutes of Schuschnigg's farewell," he later wrote, "that policeman, yesterday's protector, had been transformed into tomorrow's persecutor."[65]

Given both the deep divisions within the Jewish community and the lack of contemporaneous evidence, it is impossible to talk about a unified response to the wave of Nazi persecution. The one common denominator was a sense of dread and disbelief.[66] Many of Austria's most prominent Jewish writers and artists had already moved abroad, seeking refuge from the stuffy intolerance of the Christian Corporative system. Others managed to flee on foreign passports within days of the Anschluss.[67] Those who remained faced a terrible fate, partly because of their prominence, partly because the Nazis preferred to target the educated classes—especially intellectuals, physicians, and attorneys. According to G. E. R. Gedye, they were the ones singled out "to scrub, polish, and beat carpets in the flat where the tragedy had taken place, insisting the while that the non-Jewish maid should sit at ease in a chair and look on."[68] They were also the ones, he observed, to be thrown out on the street "grey faced, with trembling limbs, eyes staring with horror and mouths that could not keep still."[69]

For a number of distinguished Jews the only way out of this hopeless situation was suicide. Within days of the Anschluss Egon Friedell, author of the popular *Cultural History of the Modern Age*, leaped to his death from the third-floor window of his home. His fate was shared by other luminaries.[70] In 1940 the *Jewish Morning Journal* indicated that 3,741 Austrian Jews had committed suicide during the first year of the Anschluss.[71] While recent scholarship has determined that these figures are inflated, it has confirmed Gedye's eyewitness report that those taking their lives came predominately from the Jewish cultural elite: artists, journalists, physicians, lawyers, civil servants, and executives.[72]

What about ordinary people? Judging from the experience of the Clare family, many men fell apart, realizing both the destruction of their world and the end of their careers.[73] They talked of emigration but prattled mostly about "past mistakes" or the loss of worldly possessions. In contrast, the women mustered both the strength and courage to comfort their husbands and plan for the future: "Neither mother nor Klara were in the least concerned about the past, about what happened yesterday or last year," Clare recalled. "They were only thinking of the future. . . . They took over from the men."[74] There were also generational differences. According to Gertrude Schneider, the younger generation saw no alternative to emigration, whereas the middle-aged and elderly thought that they might weather the storm.[75]

At first, the older generation appeared the better meteorologists. Within a fortnight attacks on Jews petered out. And, as the German authorities scrambled to solidify their control, they ordered an end to "wild Aryanization." But while some Jews may have felt a sense of relief, their persecution had just begun.[76] On 18 March the Nazis closed the Jewish Community Council and moved into the central synagogue on the Seitenstettengasse. Eight days later Göring promised a cheering audience in the Northwest Train Station to rid Vienna of Jews within four years. Bürckel and Goebbels, as mentioned earlier, made similar pledges. Meanwhile, random house searches resumed, and on 1 April some 60 Jews were deported to Dachau— roughly a quarter of an initial 154 political prisoners shipped to the Bavarian concentration camp.[77]

The first three weeks of April passed with deceptive calm. We know little about the feelings of the Jewish community during this brief interval. There is evidence that a number of individuals hoped that Bürckel might protect them from the envious wrath of the Viennese Nazis;[78] on the other hand, many others besieged foreign consulates seeking resident permits. Only a handful ventured to join underground resistance cells. The few who dared chose the Österreichische Kampffront—a monarchist group rapidly wiped out by the Gestapo.[79] Whatever faith Austrian Jews may have placed in the Germans to restore the rule of law was shattered by two official acts: the Decree on the Declaration of Jewish Assets and the opening of Adolf Eichmann's Central Office for Jewish Emigration.[80]

George Clare has written powerfully about the response of his family to the Anschluss onslaught. His experience may not have been typical of the entire Jewish community, a fragmented and diverse subculture of 200,000 persons, several thousand of whom were Christian converts. Other assimilated families, for example, harbored incurable optimists, Habsburg loyalists, or Austrian sentimentalists.[81] In addition, there were thousands of Orthodox who remained more concerned with their religious life-style than the immediate future. About the attitudes of impoverished Eastern Jews we know next to nothing.[82]

Nevertheless, Clare is surely right in claiming that "the paradox of Vienna's volcanic outburst of popular anti-Semitism was that it saved thousands of lives. The 'lousy' anti-Semitism of the Germans led many German Jews to believe that they could go on living in their beloved Germany, while the 'first-class' anti-Semitism of the Austrians left no Jew in doubt that he had to get out of the country as quickly as possible."[83] During the summer of 1938 roughly 50,000 Jews fled Austria; by May 1939 another 50,000 had found refuge abroad. They were followed by an additional 25,000 within the next two years. Of those who remained behind or were later rounded up in German-occupied Europe, 65,000 would perish in the Holocaust.[84]

CRYSTAL NIGHT

If there was a single event that convinced Jews in Austria and Germany that they stood in deadly peril, it was the massive assault of 10 November 1938, the pogrom known as Crystal Night. Throughout the summer state and party officials had been pushing for an accelerated program of Aryanization. "It is not by chance," the Foreign Ministry recorded, "that the fateful year 1938 has not only brought about the realization of a Greater Germany, but at the same time has brought nearer the solution to the Jewish Question."[85]

During the Sudeten crisis, party activists exploited the widespread fear of war to expand their campaign of indiscriminate terror from Vienna to Berlin and other cities of the Reich.[86] Not to be outdone, the Viennese NSDAP staged a series of vicious raids designed to drive as many Jews as possible from the city. On the eve of the Day of Atonement gangs of storm troopers hauled hundreds of Jews out of bed, stripped them of their belongings, and dragged them to the banks of the Danube Canal. Although the victims were permitted to return home two days later, the violence continued. During the week of 14–21 October SA and Hitler Youth invaded Jewish homes, looted businesses, and clubbed or beat hundreds of people. By the end of the month, at least 2,000 people had been manhandled or imprisoned, perhaps as many as twenty synagogues torched or vandalized.[87]

Still, it was not until the night of 9–10 November 1938—Crystal Night—that German and Austrian Jews experienced the unbridled frenzy of the Nazi regime. On that evening Propaganda Minister Goebbels ordered a nationwide pogrom, a massive orgy of violence contrived secretly by Hitler to mete out vengeance for the shooting of a German diplomat in Paris by a desperate Jewish youngster. In the hours that followed Nazi gangs destroyed 267 synagogues, devastated 7,500 businesses and homes, and murdered 91 people; they also rounded up 26,000 other Jews, beating many senseless and dispatching the rest to concentration camps.[88] It should come as no surprise that, aside from Middle Franconia, the level of violence and bloodshed in Vienna exceeded that of any other locality of Greater Germany. Here alone 40 to 50 synagogues were burned, 4,038 Jewish shops were looted, and over 6,000 people were taken into custody, of whom at least 27 were murdered, 88 were severely injured and hundreds committed suicide. Outside the city so little Jewish property remained to pillage or expropriate that the pogrom was limited by the success of previous purges. Nevertheless, local Nazis raped and plundered, tortured and maimed, and in Innsbruck beat or stabbed to death four distinguished Jews.[89]

In contrast to the anti-Semitic rioting of the spring and early summer, the atrocities of Crystal Night were neither spontaneous nor unpremeditated. They were carried out under strict orders from Berlin by party functionaries and by gangs of SA, SS, and Hitler Youth. While motorized detachments of the Eleventh and Eighty-ninth SS burned and blasted all but one of Vienna's forty-three synagogues, squads of storm troopers shattered shop windows and emptied stores of their merchandise. Simultaneously, teams of Gestapo and brownshirts routed Jews from their homes, herded them into cellars or holding cells, and, for the first time, undertook mass arrests of Jewish women, forcing at least two hundred of them to strip and join in humiliating lesbian acts. Of the 6,000 persons placed under arrest, at least 3,000 were dispatched immediately to Dachau.[90]

For the Viennese public the appalling savagery of Crystal Night was hardly a onetime event. Occurring within weeks of extensive anti-Catholic riots, the November pogrom constituted "an organic continuation of preceding developments."[91] While few Germans in the Altreich had ever experienced Nazi outrages on such a massive scale, thousands of Austrians had already witnessed or participated in some form of mob violence against Jews. In Vienna the carnage took place in broad daylight. It began shortly after eight in the morning, within minutes attracting enormous crowds of spectators, including housewives and schoolchildren. For those unable to venture out into the streets, it was possible to get some sense of the excitement by simply reaching for the radio dial. With Eldon Walli, a native New Yorker, reporting from the scene of a burning synagogue, the local network provided live coverage.[92]

Although the November atrocities were planned and executed by the Nazi Party, the general reaction of the Viennese populace was approval, encouragement, and, in some cases, active participation. Some people, to be sure, were appalled by the terror, especially by the ferocity of violence, a fury that according to one SS report met with "condemnation and shock"[93] or to another "had a depressing effect on the general mood whereby the initial favorable reception of the entire operation turned to sympathy."[94] However, those who rejected the disorder frequently did so because of the unnecessary destruction of property or because they felt cheated of the spoils. Most surviving records indicate "great satisfaction" with Crystal Night, an operation "not only approved by the entire populace and SS, but embraced with enthusiasm."[95]

From Leopoldstadt the Security Service reported that "we could scarcely hold back the crowds from mishandling the Jews. A great many people, usually workers, frequently broke through the barriers and beat the Jews. There were multiple cries such as, 'Beat them to death, the dogs,' and 'Teach them to work in Dachau!' "[96] According to another official account, a comprehensive report prepared by SS Hauptsturmführer Trittner, bystanders cheered the arsonists, shouted encouragement, and "began to take an active part in the action." Recalling the "presumptuous gall with which the Jews had infected the body of the Viennese people," the consensus held that justice was at last being served. "There was hardly a sign of sympathy for the Jews, and where it awkwardly came to the surface, it was immediately and energetically rejected by the crowds; some obvious philosemites were arrested." As the day proceeded, "Jews were not dealt with lightly; mistreatment eventuated primarily in Leopoldstadt." When orders arrived at 5:00 P.M. to end the purge, "voices were raised regretting that the operation could not continue, since the present day was the opportunity to solve the Viennese Jewish problem once and for all."[97]

In surveying the devastation of Crystal Night, Nazi leaders in both Berlin and Vienna were outraged by the magnitude of the material and financial damage. On 12 November, Göring flew into a rage. It would have been better, he bellowed to a special task force meeting on the Jewish Question, to have "killed 200 Jews and not to have destroyed so much of value."[98] This was a sentiment shared by party functionaries of the Viennese Economic Office. Objecting to "scandalous scenes that have damaged the reputation of the party and the Reich," they concluded at a meeting on the same day that "pogroms and vandalism are not the means to solve the Jewish Question and that the destruction, theft, and looting have provoked disgust among the populace and among wide circles of the party."[99] So far as the Gestapo was concerned, the "unleashing of the lowest instincts" had been counterproductive.[100]

The reservations expressed by Nazi bigwigs in the days after Crystal Night appear in later documents describing popular reaction to the pogrom. Whether the views portrayed in these records accurately mirrored prevailing sentiment or were tailored for Göring's office in Berlin is difficult to say. On 21 November, SS Hauptsturmführer Trittner, author of the previously cited report, wrote that the "confiscations and senseless destruction aroused the strongest indignation of the populace."[101] Gauleiter Globocnik echoed these words, admitting that "a series of events occurred that alienated the public."[102] Reich commissioner Bürckel may have come closest to the truth: "Anyone familiar with the mentality in Austria I have described during the months March, April, and May knows that such destructive operations cannot be stopped on the minute. What is allowed one hour cannot be treated as a crime the next."[103]

In general, Viennese reaction to Crystal Night resembled that elsewhere in Greater Germany: ordinary people criticized the pogrom, but primarily because of its random violence and wanton destruction of property.[104] As a former Social Democratic shop steward explained, "National Socialism doesn't need this sort of thing. If the Jews are to be done away with, then it should be done officially and legally, not by individuals who make a witch-hunt [*Hetze*] out of it."[105] On the other hand, the sheer magnitude of anti-Semitic violence appears to have been much greater in Vienna than in any other city of the Reich. In no other municipality did crowds of ordinary people eagerly join in the savagery; in no other locality did attacks on Jews persist into December—and beyond. Unlike in Hamburg, Berlin, or Munich, few onlookers were "horrified." Furthermore, although a considerable number of people gradually developed a sense of revulsion, virtually none went out of their way to comfort Jews or to express remorse.[106] Given the many cases of kindness, compassion, and sympathy shown by Reich Germans to their Jewish neighbors, particularly in Hamburg, one is tempted to agree with Joachim Fest that Crystal Night "was only successful in Vienna."[107]

The reaction of the provincial population was little different from that of the Viennese, although few individuals witnessed spectacles of massive violence. Nearly half of Jews living in the provinces had already moved to Vienna or left the country. Local Nazis in Salzburg, Linz, Graz, Klagenfurt, and Baden burned or demolished synagogues almost as a routine matter. They also invaded Jewish homes, seizing cash, jewelry, silverware, furniture, carpets, and other belongings; in Klagenfurt they wielded "axes, table legs and the like, threw furniture out the windows, and rendered clothing, carpets, armchairs and similar objects unfit for use."[108] Simultaneously, the SS and Gestapo rounded up most of the remaining provincial Jews, beating or torturing them, and dispatching hundreds to Dachau. In Innsbruck they mistakenly stormed the Italian Consulate, threw an elderly couple into the Sil River, and brutally murdered four prominent Jews, including Dr. Richard Berger, president of the local congregation. According to the Tyrolean SD, "If there is any Jew who did not suffer harm through this operation, he must have been overlooked by the population."[109]

In contrast to Vienna, most of the devastation in the provinces was carried out before daybreak by formations of the SA and SS; the populace was generally unaware of what had happened until after the fact. Ordinary people surveying the shattered shops and smoldering synagogues found themselves confused and bewildered; some openly expressed a sense of outrage or shame. Few, however, went out of their way to say a kind word to a Jewish acquaintance or to reconsider the anti-Semitic goals of the Nazi regime. Only in Innsbruck was there a sign of personal remorse: a handful of women who called on the local rabbi to convey their sympathy and regret.[110] Otherwise, the SD wrote, most residents of the Tyrolean capital did not know what to make of the carnage: some considered it the work of provocateurs, others thought Communists were to blame. While there was some criticism in "liberal and clerical circles," the "full details of the operation are not yet known."[111]

Popular knowledge in Linz, on the other hand, appears to have been more widespread. A surviving victim recalled a crowd of onlookers applauding a storm trooper as he pranced up and down of the steps of the burning synagogue, brandishing a torah and mimicking Jewish ritual prayer. To what degree the spectators mirrored the views of the larger municipal population is impossible to say, but the SD claimed that town dwellers "welcomed the protest action . . . as absolutely necessary."[112] There was also acclamation in outlying areas. From neighboring Steyr came word that "the entire population approves the measures of the government against Jewry without exception and without reservations"; from Kirchdorf that "the harsh measures against the Jews are both understood and welcome"; from Hinterstoder that "the operations against the Jews were welcomed by the populace with real satisfaction."[113]

To the east, in Lower Danube, popular responses were more various. The demolition of synagogues in Eisenstadt, Berndorf, Vöslau, and Baden reportedly proceeded without incident, but in Lilienfeld, there were "excesses." While looting had been kept to a minimum, the Security Service admitted that the violence in Lilienfeld "affected the mood of the populace in a negative way."[114] In Amstetten, Waidhofen an der Ybbs, and Kematen, on the other hand, an "embittered populace" was said to have endorsed the roundup of Jews and the destruction of their property.[115] From Baden, the elegant holiday resort south of Vienna, an SD man bubbled over the telephone: "This day's operations have aroused real enthusiasm, especially among the poor. A first-class propaganda achievement. Nowhere has any sympathy for the Jews been detected, not even among the so-called better bourgeois circles."[116]

Paradoxically, the loudest outcry against the violence of Crystal Night came from SD officials stationed in Styria, a province with exceptionally strong grass-roots support for the Nazi system. The security agents were enraged because the pogrom had upset their own timetable for resolving the Jewish Question by the end of the year. This was because gangs of storm troopers in Graz had unwittingly destroyed official emigration documents, thus preventing Eichmann's deportation orders from being carried out on schedule.[117] The SD did write, however, that "legal measures against the Jews would have found a better resonance than vandalism."[118]

Austrians living outside Vienna, then, responded to the anti-Jewish terror of 10 November 1938 with a mixture of shock, confusion, and indifference. Since relatively few persons experienced scenes of "expiatory retribution," there was little collective horror or shame. A few prominent individuals did object to the reckless disregard for law. Dr. Johannes Ude, a Graz professor of dogmatics, wrote to both Seyss-Inquart and Gauleiter Uiberreither protesting what he called "lynch justice." The Nazis, as might be expected, replied to the letter by exiling its author from Styria, but even within the party there were reservations. One Carinthian official, Dr. Wladimir von Pawlowski, actually bellowed that Goebbels should be "stood up against the wall."[119]

To what extent others shared this view is not revealed in the sources. Postwar accounts suggest that the savagery of Crystal Night provoked widespread reflection and shame.[120] Contemporary documents reveal, however, that the central issue of concern was the Nazi assault on the church, especially the October ransacking of Cardinal Innitzer's archiepiscopal palace.[121] They also reveal that on 12 November Heydrich boasted to Göring that since the Anschluss 31,000 more Jews had been driven from Austria than from all of Greater Germany.[122] Whatever the real attitudinal climate, feelings of remorse were less intense in the Ostmark than in the Altreich. When it came to the Jewish Question, few Austrians were disposed toward compassion, understanding, or magnanimity.

BETWEEN CRYSTAL NIGHT AND WAR

In one respect, Crystal Night illuminated popular thinking in both Austria and Germany: it revealed a broad consensus of support for Hitler's goal of putting an end to the so-called Jewish Question. Ordinary people made it clear that while they condemned lawlessness, violence, and the senseless destruction of property, they did not object to Nazi anti-Semitic measures. So long as Aryanization was carried out in an orderly, legal, and constitutional manner, the general population would not object.[123] That the Nazi leadership immediately grasped this reality is evident by the discontinuation of pogroms and spontaneous violence. Thereafter, the authorities used legal and bureaucratic means to segregate, marginalize, and eliminate the Jews. Despite inconsistencies, bottlenecks, and overlapping measures, they pursued this approach relentlessly until the last days of the Second World War.[124]

On 12 November 1938 two orders—the Decree on an Atonement Fine for Jews with German Citizenship and the Decree on the Exclusion of Jews from Economic Life—unleashed a new torrent of anti-Semitic legislation. The Nazis fined the Jews 1 billion marks for the damage of Crystal Night, confiscated their insurance policies, and transferred all indemnification payments to the government. They also banned Jews from managerial positions in retailing, crafts, and the mail-order business. Other ordinances ousted Jews from the universities and the professions; stripped them of property rights, tax exemptions, and welfare benefits; and excluded them from cinemas, concerts, exhibitions, athletic contests, and bathing facilities. In 1939 Nazi legislation obliged Jews to adopt the middle names of "Sarah" and "Israel," to register all foreign equities and assets, and to surrender all jewelry and precious possessions. On top of these cruel measures, Reinhard Heydrich established a Central Office for Jewish Emigration in Berlin, thus extending Eichmann's "conveyor-belt system" of deportation throughout Greater Germany. By 14 May 1939 the number of Jews living in the Altreich had declined in the five years since 1934 from 502,799 to 213,930; in the Ostmark from 191,481 to 81,943.[125]

Although ordinary Germans and Austrians appear to have lost interest in the Jewish Question after Crystal Night, there is no reason to assume that they disapproved the newer policy of statutory segregation. In Vienna popular pressure to drive the Jews from the city remained acute. Throngs of teenagers continued to make forays into Jewish neighborhoods, routinely mugging pedestrians, smashing shop windows, and looting homes and businesses.[126] The City Council, in an evident attempt to placate the masses, accelerated the expropriation of Jewish housing, managing to transfer 5,572 dwellings to "Aryan" tenants between March and September 1939. Since roughly 4,000 other homes fell to private individuals during the same period, the municipal administration next found itself confronting the problem of dealing with the thousands of Jews still huddling together in the metropolis.[127]

From the first day of the Anschluss the process of "Aryanization" had been carried out in the Ostmark "without orders from above and without following rules."[128] Having concentrated the surviving Jews in a "semi-ghetto" on the shores of the Danube Canal, the Austrian Nazis had no choice but to continue improvising. Throughout the summer of 1939 there was intense discussion of how to get rid of the remaining Jewish population. On 8 July it was decided to relocate them to work camps in Gänserndorf, a village in Lower Danube, not far from Vienna. Although each camp had room for only 6,000 prisoners, the City Council intended to move the 50,000 Jews still living in Vienna to the facility. That most of the inmates would be worked to death or die from disease was a fact seemingly taken for granted.[129]

Although ordinary Viennese had no knowledge of these dreadful plans, there is little reason to suppose that a large number would have disapproved. This is not to suggest that the silent majority would have countenanced mass murder; most Viennese simply wanted the Jews to disappear. Nevertheless, it would be foolish to presume that many of them imagined the Jews would escape harsh treatment. Given the magnitude and intensity of popular anti-Semitism, massive expulsion was simply the next logical step.[130]

That the Nazi policy of deportation was "a reaction to pressure from the 'Aryan' Viennese, proletarian as well as lower middle class"[131] is all too apparent in a paradigmatic document published by Botz in one of his most important studies. According to the record, an opinion survey of a Viennese neighborhood taken shortly after Hitler's invasion of Poland, "The extent of anti-Jewish feeling in the population is beyond measure. It is entirely thanks to the exertion of all our energy that in no case have riots occurred. . . . People cannot understand why Jews receive the same quantities of food-stuffs as Aryans. They fail to understand why Jews are not conscripted for forced labor and are left to pursue their dark schemes. . . . People feel severely disadvantaged as long as Aryans have to live in damp cellars while Jews are permitted to live in their filth in beautiful apartments."[132]

ASSESSMENT AND CONSEQUENCES

From the moment Hitler ordered the German Eighth Army to move into his Austrian homeland, he could count on the native population to support his anti-Jewish measures or at least not to oppose them. Having imbibed anti-Semitic sentiment as a boy in Linz, he had come to understand the Judeophobic loathing of the Viennese masses, cutting and polishing it into the "granite foundation" of his thought. The Führer's followers could not have come to power on their own in Austria, but German intervention enabled them and the Viennese mob to concentrate the full fury of decades of pent-up rage against the Jews. For weeks the streets of the Danubian city resounded to the noise of jeering crowds convulsed in a frenzy of exhilarating terror. On 26 March 1938 Göring promised to expel the Jews from Vienna within four years. His pledge represented more than an idle boast. It was a solemn guarantee to the Austrian people: a mandate to be carried out both in response to their demands and with their cooperation.

In Austria, much more than in Germany, anti-Semitism functioned as an integrating element for the Nazi system. It was the irresistible chord that attracted millions of ordinary people otherwise immune to the siren song of Hitlerism. Elimination of the Jews bolstered the regime's popularity because it satisfied the social, economic, and psychological needs of broad strata of the population. The process made housing available to both speculators and the poor; it opened up opportunities in the professions and business; it reinforced self-esteem and ethnic identity within Hitler's National Community.

At the same time, Austrian society remained highly segmented. Even on the Jewish Question diversity of opinion continued to exist. Since most of the provincial population had never even seen a Jew, their sentiments ranged from traditional Catholic animosity to indifference. In Vienna attitudes were indisputably more virulent, comprising a mixture of avarice, detestation, and what Arthur Schnitzler once called "disinterested meanness." Yet even in the Danubian city there were individuals willing to help or hide Jewish victims.[133]

On balance, however, Austrians shared a broad anti-Semitic consensus. Popular support for the Anschluss system rested as much on Hitler's promise to tackle the Jewish Question as it did on the hope for economic recovery and emotional loyalty to the idea of Greater Germany. In the view of many people Christian anti-Judaism and racial anti-Semitism remained separate phenomena, but whether the two coexisted or merged in the popular mind is beside the point. While historians have written that the "twisted road to Auschwitz" was "built on hate and paved with indifference,"[134] they have paid little attention to the route running through the Ostmark. Should they take a closer look, they would find a branch surveyed, engineered, and graded to meet the demands of a critical mass of the Austrian people.

III

The Austrian People and Hitler's War

8 A DISTANT CONFLICT, 1939-1943

During the Second World War the sentiments of the Austrian people generally coincided with those of their German brethren. There were distinctive fluctuations in the barometer of opinion as well as notable regional, social, and psychological variations. There were also significant attitudinal discrepancies between Vienna and the rest of the Ostmark, especially in the modernizing West and South. On farms in Upper and Lower Danube and in the high mountains of Tyrol many people still retained a strong sense of Austrian patriotism; in the factories and assembly lines of big cities numerous blue-collar workers remained aloof and suspicious. All the same, most residents of the Ostmark supported Hitler's war to the end.[1]

POPULAR SENTIMENT AND THE BEGINNING OF THE WAR

This is not to say that the Austrian people welcomed the outbreak of World War II; like most civilians in Greater Germany they were flabbergasted by the news.[2] A diary entry by the once-and-future Austrian diplomat Josef Schöner offers a somber snapshot: "Adolf Hitler's speech, first announced at 8:30, brought the expected declaration. I heard it at the Carlton, the club packed with 'listening guests.' Everybody with grave expressions. No applause. A small crowd of people on St. Stephen's Square. Those near the loudspeakers raised their arms during the national anthem. Those standing further away not at all. Everywhere depressed spirits. Vague hopes of a short local war. Not one trace of enthusiasm."[3] In rural areas some farmers were reported to be indignant, but Schöner recorded ruefully: "The broad masses have been convinced by well-executed propaganda that the war has been foisted on us by England."[4]

A week later the mood started to pick up. The stunning success of the Wehrmacht dissipated fears and unleashed both admiration and rejoicing. By the end of September, police stations were reporting "confidence" and "enthusiasm" at the triumph of German arms. In Kirchdorf, there were some negative comments, but also a resurgence of reliance and trust in

Hitler. From Ried came word that the war was strengthening the National Community. In Vienna, the outbreak of war brought angry calls for new restrictions on the Jews, followed by a collective sigh of relief at the end of the Polish campaign. Within days returning troops were showered with flowers, cigarettes, and food.[5] "In the euphoria of reunion," one official salaciously chortled, "no one is offended that formerly prevailing bourgeois morals are no longer observed."[6]

Throughout the period of the "phony war," most Austrians shared with Reich Germans a common belief in Hitler's desire for peace. Though Catholic dissatisfaction persisted and Communist activity in Vienna reportedly exceeded that of any city in Greater Germany—including Berlin and Hamburg—there was shock, indignation, and anger, followed by relief at its outcome, of the unsuccessful assassination attempt on Hitler in the Bürgerbräukeller in Munich on 9 November 1939.[7] In Pettenbach the authorities indicated that while many remained reticent, "the deed was generally condemned, especially as the Führer is beloved by the populace."[8] Only a tiny minority disagreed. In the Steyr Works several workers openly approved the attempt; in Wiener Neustadt a mechanic remarked that the perpetrator deserved the Iron Cross.[9]

THE ECONOMIC IMPACT

Once the Polish campaign drew to a close, most Austrians became increasingly preoccupied with bread-and-butter issues. At the start of the conflict they had been in the midst of an economic boom, but wartime wage and price controls froze their standard of living at a level about 10 percent below that in the Altreich. In 1940 industrial production fell 2.1 percent; agricultural yields declined 16.1 percent. The real income of Viennese workers even dwindled by 20 percent.[10]

At first, rationing and controls proceeded smoothly despite shortages of milk, flour, and coffee; in Vienna there were occasional lines at grocery stores and butcher shops. In the countryside peasants objected to regulations requiring daily deliveries of cream. For most consumers allotments of food, clothing, and basic commodities remained both ample and adequate.[11]

More serious was the impact of the war on the industrial workforce, the group most feared as potential opponents by the Nazi regime. As elsewhere in Europe, the outbreak of hostilities dealt a serious blow to consumer production, especially to textile manufacturing. In the Ostmark alone some twenty-two cotton mills shut their doors between September and November. The impact on factory villages such as Gross-Sieghardt in Lower Danube was calamitous. Elsewhere, managers tried to avoid dismissals by cutting working hours, but these and other stopgap measures only reduced the income of already poorly paid wage earners. All told, the industrial workforce in Austria shrank by 10,000 during the first year of the war. The effect on morale was devastating.[12]

For those employed in munitions plants or other enterprises essential to the war effort, the outbreak of hostilities brought few benefits. The War Economy Decree of 4 September 1939 put an end to overtime pay, wage bonuses, and statutory holidays. That meant a 10 percent cut in earnings and the perpetuation of the wage gap between Austrian and German labor. Almost immediately there were loud and angry protests. They became so intense that Bürckel wrote a personal letter to Hitler, pleading for a restoration of the bonuses. Whether the Führer replied to his man in Vienna is unknown. At the end of October the Gestapo reported a sharp rise in insubordination, absenteeism, and seditious remarks. There were also signs of sabotage and intense Communist agitation. As the regime saw no point in alienating the working population, it backed down. On 10 November the Reich minister of labor ordered the restoration of bonuses; one week later it agreed to the reintroduction of paid holidays.[13]

Modification of the War Economy Decree brought immediate dividends. Within days the SD reported a significant rise in morale, several weeks later claiming that the spirits of the working class had reached a level of "general satisfaction." By Christmas the situation was so much better that the SD made a point of contrasting the "good" and "positive" mood prevailing in blue-collar Floridsdorf with the pessimistic climate of working-class areas of Bavaria.[14]

During the winter of 1939–40 a massive coal shortage that developed in Greater Germany hit Vienna especially hard—although no more severely than it did Berlin, Kiel, and other large cities. Accompanied by bottlenecks in food rationing, shortages of shoes and clothing, a war surtax, cuts in social security benefits, and another rise in the cost of living, the coal crisis in an unseasonably cold winter unleashed a new wave of anti-German sentiment in the metropolis. There were even public outbursts at the Technische Hochschule and the Volkstheater. In the first instance, scores of flyers circulated calling for "Austria to the Austrians"; in the second, cheers and hand-clapping interrupted a performance of Franz Grillparzer's *König Ottokars Glück und Ende* following a famous soliloquy emphasizing differences between Austrians and Germans.[15] The general malaise was exacerbated by the introduction of the German salary schedule, which in practice meant substantial raises for administrators and senior physicians but cuts of roughly 100 marks for interns and residents.[16]

Ironically, Reich planners had long been trying to meet local economic grievances by awarding defense contracts to Viennese industry but were finding that obsolete equipment, high transportation costs, and outmoded production techniques limited orders for advanced military weapons. Instead of opening up jobs, the war had the reverse effect of accelerating an exodus of skilled labor for better-paying positions in the Altreich, a trend that not only retarded modernization but aggravated tensions by separating large numbers of families.[17] What gave the deteriorating public mood its distinctive anti-German tone, however, were the many complaints and grievances expressed by Viennese Nazis. Still excluded from top party offices, their anger came to a boil in early 1940 when Reich commissioner Bürckel dismissed one of their own (Josef Fitzthum) as metropolitan vice police president and, on 1 April, announced the final dissolution of Austria as a territorial unit.[18]

Meanwhile, people in other regions of the Ostmark were enduring similar hardships and deprivations, although not to the same degree as many Viennese. Rising taxes produced predictably loud and angry complaints, especially in working-class families. There was concern about shortages of coffee, sugar, spices, and wearing apparel—especially footwear. There was also open resentment of seemingly endless Nazi collection drives for the party welfare organization (NSV), Winter Aid, or the Red Cross. On the land farmers were reported worried about fodder shortages and requisitions of their draft horses by the Wehrmacht; in high mountain areas families without electricity deplored the near disappearance of kerosene needed for lighting. Among country villagers there was renewed criticism of local Nazi authorities for their constant intrusions into everyday life. On the whole, however, food allotments remained adequate, the war appeared remote, and daily life continued much as normal. From the Mühlviertel the security organs even reported that family farmers, largely self-sufficient and not dependent on hired help, were beginning to enjoy a small measure of prosperity.[19]

ATTITUDES TOWARD FOREIGN WORKERS

Even so, there was a new issue that provoked intense discussion and rancorous criticism of the party: the official treatment of foreign workers, now arriving in ever increasing numbers to toil in the fields, workshops, and factories of Greater Germany. As a depressed area, the Austrian lands had long suffered from chronic unemployment, but, as we have already seen, the combination of Nazi economic policy and military conscription had largely emptied the countryside. In late 1939, a labor shortage suddenly developed, a lack of manpower subsequently filled by prisoners of war, foreign laborers, and, after 1943, concentration camp inmates. In the eleven months between February and December 1940 the number of prisoners of war in the Ostmark rose from 10,957 to 87,768, of whom roughly half worked in agriculture and the other half on construction projects.[20]

The attitudes of the Austrian people toward the imported aliens varied considerably. In Styria the farming population regarded Poles with disdain and contempt, preferring Italians and Yugoslavs. In Tyrol there was ill will toward Italians, in Upper Austria toward Czechs. Many indigenous farmhands in all regions simply resented the cheap competition.[21] On the other hand, innumerable Catholic families greeted Polish prisoners of war with open arms, treating them as welcome agricultural laborers, even providing them with extra provisions of food and clothing. "In many farmhouses," the SD wrote with exasperation, "Poles are treated the same as German help, indeed even favored."[22] That such acts of solicitude and charity were encouraged by the church, at least for the Catholic Polish and French prisoners of war, was particularly galling.[23]

As more and more Poles flooded into Greater Germany, the Nazi regime formulated a sheaf of regulations to supervise and control their every move. Himmler, who took a keen and prurient interest in such things, ordered the instantaneous punishment of Poles and Germans caught in sexual liaisons: the former to be strung up on the spot, the latter to be publicly pilloried. Writing to Rudolf Hess on 8 March 1940, the Reichsführer SS approved the practice of the local NSDAP meting out lynch justice.[24]

Across the Ostmark, as throughout all of Greater Germany, the party took harsh measures against those apprehended for "racial defilement."[25] On the morning of 11 February 1940 storm troopers seized Katharina Schnell, an Upper Austrian maidservant accused of sleeping with a Polish laborer. Escorting her to the town of Sierning, the brownshirts clipped her hair, draped her with a placard highlighting the "betrayal" of her "German blood," and paraded her around the village square. The following day the SA men drove her seven kilometers to neighboring Steyr, where she was again put on public display, spit on by howling teenagers, and forced to stand at the factory gate of the Steyr munitions works. Schnell was reported to be "completely broken," but she had survived her ordeal. To the east, in the tiny hamlet of Behamberg in Lower Danube, another young woman was not so fortunate: shaved, publicly defamed, and paraded through slushy streets by local storm troopers, she died from exposure and frostbite.[26]

Judging from the available evidence, popular reaction to Nazi lynch justice was by no means acclamatory, although in one locality villagers endorsed the defamation of an adulterous farmwife.[27] There were also cases of sexual jealousy. In Salzburg five youngsters were taken into custody after an eighteen-year-old had scribbled on the wall of a firehouse:

> Brothers and friends in the field,
> get killed and maimed.
> Girls at home
> with Serbs get laid.
> The greatest insult to stand
> for our beloved fatherland.[28]

In most communities, however, anger ran high, especially in villages like Behamberg or Euratsfeld in Lower Danube where 90 percent of the population viewed the Nazi regime with unmistakable hostility. On the factory floor in Steyr workers even yelled out catcalls and insults, openly leveling charges of "medieval" torture. Although there are gaps in the documentation, the level of outrage and anger in both Austria and Germany appears to have been so high that in late 1941 Hitler ordered an end to pillorying practices—though not, of course, to the summary execution of alien paramours.[29]

BLITZKRIEG IN THE WEST

Meanwhile, Hitler's spectacular victories in the West in the spring of 1940 temporarily eased tensions in the Ostmark, leaving much of the public "breathless" and brimming with admiration of the Führer. Throughout the crowded streets of Vienna enormous throngs gathered before loudspeakers and sound trucks to cheer the latest news from the front; in movie theaters, packed houses viewed newsreels "with enthusiasm and pride," especially during footage depicting Austrian mountain troops in action in Norway. People felt profoundly moved by the official line attributing General Eduard Dietl's daring capture of Narvik to "men from the soil of Carinthia and Steiermark." The media stressed that the "blood flowing through their veins also flows through the veins of the Führer." Although the Security Service reported that small groups of moviegoers regarded the bombing of Rotterdam as "gratuitously brutal," the conquest of the Low Countries and France both dampened opposition—especially in Catholic conservative circles—and won new converts for the National Community.[30]

Outside Vienna the exuberance appears to have been even greater. Throughout Lower Austria the authorities reported a dramatic surge of morale, even in towns and villages normally wary of the regime. In Rosenau there was "general rejoicing," in St. Pantaleon "tremendous joy," in Oed "beaming confidence." According to one report, it was industrial workers who were most caught up in the excitement of the moment. In the Böhler

Works at Waidhofen an der Ybbs the entire workforce listened spellbound to the radio broadcast of the French surrender at Compiègne, jumping spontaneously to their feet at the conclusion to give the Hitler salute.[31]

VIENNA BLUES

Although an overwhelming majority of the Austrian people endorsed the triumph of German arms, particularist feeling, class division, and diversity of opinion persisted, especially in Vienna. Even during the halcyon days of spring and early summer, the SD lamented the continuation of "offensive and tasteless attacks on Germans from the Reich," mainly in taverns, cabarets, and theaters. According to the security agents, "anti-Prussian" sentiment was fueled primarily by traditional opponents such as the Communists, who were still managing to circulate underground fly sheets in the First District, and the Catholic clergy. In the outlying communities of Hacking, Purkersdorf, Stadlau, and Altmannsdorf, priests warned residents against leaving the church by flashing pictures of skulls or skeletons to passersby with the words "abandonment of the church means death at home." Discontent was also nourished by a bewildering array of new German tax regulations, a hike in trolley fares, and a severe shortage of fresh fruits and vegetables that lasted from Pentecost well into the summer; Viennese housewives even charged that, while their cupboards stood bare, vast quantities of Austrian produce were readily available in market stalls in Berlin and Munich.[32]

Still, it was the self-pitying Viennese Nazis who felt most abused, particularly after party headquarters in Munich issued new party books dating their membership from only 1 May 1938. Charging that no distinction had been made between Old Fighters and "March Violets," many of them refused to accept the books or threw them away in disgust. Among Nazi neighborhood groups, there was also an outburst of disenchantment when yet another Reich German—this time from Düsseldorf—was awarded the much-coveted plum of the Department of Health. Hitler's municipal followers still derived great satisfaction from his triumphs and supported his national policies without question. All the same, many felt that the national leadership was soft on the Jewish Question and that anti-Semitic restrictions needed to be stepped up, particularly after local shopkeepers started showing sympathy for Jewish customers by claiming that "Jews are also human." In Türkenschanze party militants demanded that Jewish homes post identity plates, in Kettenbrücke that Jews wear identification badges.[33]

The war enthusiasm of 1940 did not last very long. By autumn, the SD was reporting complaints about high prices and low wages still out of line with those in the Altreich, quarrels in markets over scarcities of food, clothing, and shoes, and apprehension of another winter of war. Due to the persistence of Nazi anticlerical measures and to growing manpower shortages on the farm there was also unrest in the countryside.[34]

Although shortages and sagging morale prevailed throughout the entire Reich in the autumn of 1940, dissatisfaction in the Ostmark focused, as usual, on the German element in Vienna, especially after it was announced that Hitler had replaced Bürckel, whom he dismissed on 1 August, not with an Austrian Gauleiter, as in the provinces, but with Reich Youth Leader Baldur von Schirach, born in Berlin.[35] At the end of October a foreign correspondent described the metropolis as "gray and listless, the people, weary and threadbare,"[36] a characterization hardly different from the Security Service, which reported indifference, war-weariness, and "great pessimism." While the security agents prudently credited Schirach with "considerable success," they also indicated pervasive "criticism of all personnel and policies emanating from the Reich." It was a "daily occurrence," they wrote, "that Germans who seek information receive wrong directions. Women from Germany are often refused what Viennese can buy."[37]

In the following weeks there was an upsurge of confrontations in taverns, renewed outbursts in theaters, and a series of soccer riots that culminated in a wild melee on 17 November at a Sunday afternoon match between Admira Wien and the German champion, Schalke 04. As 52,000 Viennese fans cheered on their team, chanting "against the Germans from the Reich," young toughs stoned and pummeled Gauleiter Schirach's limousine, shattering its windows and slashing its tires. More than two hundred fans were arrested, mostly blue-collar workers. That same evening, according to a correspondent of the *New York Times*, Reich Marshal Göring's wife attended the opera wearing an "exaggerated evening dress and an expensive tiara." She was greeted by the audience chanting, "Where did you steal the tiara?" Although twenty operagoers were taken immediately into custody, the police were unable to put an end to the disturbance; Frau Göring had to leave her box in embarrassment once the houselights dimmed. That Hitler regarded Vienna as a "rebellious metropolis at the southeast border of the Reich" was not entirely without reason.[38]

From the Nazi perspective, it is to Schriach's credit that, despite Hitler's later disapproval, he was able to shore up the Anschluss consensus in Vienna for at least a year, if not longer. After moving into the Ballhausplatz with his wife, four children, and seventeen liveried servants, the Gauleiter made a number of public statements reassuring the Nazi rank and file. He openly acknowledged the insensitivity of many "repugnant and ill-mannered Germans," promised to make the opera the leading stage of Greater Germany, and awarded government posts to a number of veteran militants such as Alfred Proksch, who had headed the Austrian NSDAP between 1926 and 1931. In February 1941, Schirach traveled to Obersalzberg, where he persuaded Hitler to consider a carefully drawn-up package for economic development, including subsidies of 150 million marks, allocations of machinery, special import-export agreements, freight reductions, and tax relief. Due to the invasion of Russia four months later, the plan was scarcely implemented, but it did result in the return of some 80,000 skilled workers from the Altreich.

In October, Schirach again met with Hitler, this time pressing him to undertake the construction of new housing units. The dictator responded with anger, however, communicating through Bormann that "you should see your task in Vienna not in the construction of new residential areas" but in the deportation of the Jews, Czechs, and "all other foreigners who have made political indoctrination and education in Vienna extremely difficult." Once the population of the city was reduced to 1.5 or 1.4 million, "the housing crisis will be solved in the best, easiest, and quickest way."[39]

Schirach complied; always a faithful lackey, he cooperated enthusiastically with the SS in deporting the city's remaining 60,000 Jews to the ghettos and gas chambers of Poland. At the time of the liquidation of the Warsaw ghetto he boasted: "If anyone reproaches me with having driven from this city, which was once the European metropolis of Jewry, tens of thousands upon tens of thousands into the ghettos of the East, I feel myself to reply: I see in this an action contributing to European culture."[40]

Overall, Schirach made some headway in mollifying the municipal Nazis, flattering the cultural elite, dampening clerical unrest, and appeasing some blue-collar elements. Owing to Hitler's animosities and to the pressures of war, the Gauleiter did not succeed in closing the economic gap between Vienna and the Altreich, in improving food supplies, or in solving the critical housing situation, despite the fact that 70,000 dwellings were eventually taken from the Jews.

As far as can be ascertained, the Viennese public reacted with considerable ambivalence. On the one hand, there was widespread ridicule of Schirach for his pompous and pretentious ways, continued grumbling about wartime scarcities and "Piefkes," and growing anxiety about the war, especially after the beginning of the Russian campaign, in which substantial numbers of Viennese troops participated. According to the Gestapo, there were also many more acts of sabotage and arrests for political offenses than in the Altreich. On the other hand, Vienna contributed more to Winter Aid

(Winterhilfswerk) in 1941 than any other city in Greater Germany; the upper crust appreciated the town's cultural revival; and the public turned out in great numbers to cheer speeches by Hitler, Goebbels, and other Reich dignitaries.[41] After addressing an enormous rally in March 1941, for example, the propaganda minister confided to his diary, "When I leave the Heldenplatz, I find myself trapped by the enthusiastic crowd. It takes three-quarters of an hour for me to get out. I have rarely seen anything like it."[42]

Above all, there was considerable support for the expulsion of Vienna's remaining "non-Aryans." Ever since the Anschluss, Jews had been regularly beaten in trolley cars, or kicked in the streets by passersby.[43] Once Schirach's deportations got under way the streets of the city were frequently lined by jeering crowds, yelling catcalls and obscenities as SS trucks rumbled by to the Aspang depot with their fearful cargoes bound for Theresienstadt, Treblinka, or Auschwitz. "Jews were taken on open trucks like animals to the slaughter," one onlooker recalled. "The aged who could not walk were put on trucks while seated on their chairs. As to the reactions to the expulsion, most people looked away, ashamed; others laughed and enjoyed the view."[44] Another witness, a Swedish pastor who had headed a mission in Vienna between September 1939 and May 1941, confided to his diary that Judeophobia was not the "hatred of a small clique," but a genuine "popular hatred" (Volkshass). Everywhere in the city of music he had heard, "The Jews must be exterminated. They must be smoked out, the way lice are smoked out of a house." Most of all, he recorded, cultivated, affluent, and otherwise reasonable people could not grasp his concern for the Jews: "You are helping the Jews! That is not true! That is simply not possible!"[45]

To what extent ordinary Viennese were aware of the ultimate fate of the Jews is not altogether clear. As the death camps in Poland did not begin full operations until mid-1942, only a small number could have known that mass murder awaited the proscribed and evicted. At the same time, the many acts of spontaneous insults, robberies, and beatings that had provoked and accompanied the marginalization of Vienna's Jewish community suggest that few Austrians expected, or wanted, better treatment for Jewish neighbors deported to the East. There is also some evidence that word of mass shootings rapidly made its way back to Austria from the eastern front. On 13 November 1941 a twenty-one-year-old architectural student, Maria Czedik, confided to her diary: "Norbert Berger told me yesterday that Russians taken prisoner are divided into three camps: the deserters and those who surrender without resistance, the many Communists, and the Jews. The last two, as well as the Jews we send to Poland, are shot on the spot. Norbert sees nothing wrong with that!!!"[46]

Although anti-German sentiment remained largely confined to Vienna, overall morale in Austria, as in most of Greater Germany, deteriorated perceptively in the winter of 1940–41. Shortly before Christmas, massive call-ups in both Upper and Lower Danube severely cut the native workforce, making it necessary to import thousands of additional foreign laborers. The Reich Food Estate issued orders requiring delivery of enormous quantities of hay, straw, and oats; the shortage of consumer goods showed no signs of abating.[47] And just after New Year, Nazi functionaries unexpectedly resumed their attack on the Catholic Church.

In May 1940 Hitler had issued a directive "to avoid all unnecessary measures during the war that could worsen the relationship of the state and party to the church." But since the same directive also transferred jurisdiction over spiritual affairs in the Ostmark to provincial Gauleiter, the order actually sent a strong signal to the dictator's Austrian retainers to resume their assault on organized religion. Between January and September 1941, Nazi officials seized numerous monasteries, including St. Peter and Michelbeuern in Salzburg; St. Florian, Schlägel, Hohenfürth, Kremsmünster, and Wilhering in Upper Danube; and Klosterneuburg near Vienna. Under direct orders from Hitler they also sequestered a number of teacher-training academies and theological seminaries and expelled several dissident priests from the Ostmark.[48]

Popular reaction to the new wave of persecution was widespread and angry. In the Tyrolean community of Oberhofen a crowd of enraged women stormed into the town hall to protest the seizure of religious statues and processional banners from the village church.[49] Elsewhere, people were exasperated by the curtailment of Catholic holidays and by the petty harassment of the Gestapo. On Palm Sunday trench-coated agents seized consecrated leaves; on Corpus Christi Day they blocked the route of march or directed participants back to parish grounds. As in neighboring Bavaria, both clergy and laity ignored the new guidelines, deliberately doubling the number of worshipers at open masses and processionals or in strongly Catholic areas even enlisting the support of the village Nazi elite.[50] On 1 July 1941 the Austrian bishops submitted a formal remonstrance to the Reich Ministry of the Interior. In it Cardinal Innitzer and his colleagues accused the regime of attacking "the church and religion as such, in order to separate our church from the people and to rob our Catholic people of the church and their Catholic faith." They protested "in the name of the dignity and freedom of mankind" and demanded "that these actions hostile to our church and religion should be stopped."[51]

Adding to the mounting disquiet in the first months of 1941 were disturbing rumors that large numbers of the mentally ill and physically handicapped were being put to death in euthanasia sanitariums. On 1 January 1940 the extension to Austria of the Law for the Protection of Diseased Offspring (in force in Germany since 1933) had enabled medical doctors to begin sterilization of at least 5,000 patients suffering from schizophrenia, manic depression, blindness, or chronic alcoholism. In May 1940 a T4 euthanasia center for the killing of the physically handicapped began operations at Castle Hartheim, near Linz; two months later another clinic, Am Steinhof, in Vienna, became an abattoir for severely handicapped children and adolescents. By the end of the war 20,000 patients and concentration camp inmates would perish in these facilities.[52]

As elsewhere in Hitler's Reich, word of the killings spread rapidly through the population, provoking considerable unrest and isolated protests. In Vienna, reports came that "the most impassioned scenes were played out for weeks before and during the transport of the invalids";[53] in Salzburg crowds of distraught relatives were observed besieging the clinic of Dr. Leo Wolfer, the psychiatrist responsible for dispatching several hundred women and children to their death.[54] In the vicinity of Castle Hartheim, SS authorities warned local residents to ignore the constant smell of burning flesh from the crematorium, even when "tufts of hair flew through the chimney onto the street." They also reportedly threatened that "everyone who further spread these absurd rumors would have to reckon with the death penalty or, at least, with being sent to a concentration camp."[55]

For almost a year the German clergy, both Protestant and Roman Catholic, had been speaking out against the murder of innocents. While there was not the same public outcry in Austria, a number of nuns, parish priests, and higher clergy, including the vicar-general of Carinthia, Andreas Rohracher, did correspond with Nazi functionaries or file formal letters of protest.[56] Concerned initially with the loss of institutional control of the retarded and disabled, the German Catholic bishops joined a rising chorus of popular outrage that reached a crescendo on 3 August 1941 when Bishop Clemens August von Galen denounced the euthanasia program from his pulpit in the North German city of Münster. To placate Catholic opinion Hitler on 28 August ordered a "stop order."[57] Thereafter, the killing centers switched to the gassing of concentration camp inmates. At Hartheim the physicians and nurses continued to kill prisoners from nearby Mauthausen and Gusen until the end of the war. They gassed the inmates, Henry Friedlander writes, "as a kind of professional courtesy to a neighboring institution."[58]

During the second winter of war, popular sentiment in Austria remained extremely downcast. Struggling daily to make ends meet, ordinary people were alarmed both by the new wave of attacks on the church and by the duration of the conflict. In the countryside they were vexed by the worsening agricultural crisis, now evident in severe shortages of agricultural machinery, farm implements, and spare parts. The peasants also had to contend with skyrocketing lumber and iron prices, a declining number of repairmen, and new mandatory deductions for taxes and health insurance. Also annoying to the rural population was the arrival of increasing numbers of women and children from bombed-out and imperiled cities in western and northern Germany. Although given free room and board in Austrian homes, they were exempt from family chores. As most of the refugees received dependent allowances or supplements, or both, from the party welfare organization, they were seen as living high on the hog while their hosts toiled long hours in the fields.[59]

On the other hand, membership in the Nazi Party continued to remain stable, or in the case of Upper Danube to increase substantially.[60] In anticlerical bastions like Carinthia and Vienna there was strong support for the latest attacks on the church.[61] More significantly, these were the months in which Hitler's "Marshall Plan" of economic modernization began to bear fruit in provincial cities like Linz. In March 1941 the Hermann Göring Steel Works started producing steel and armor plate for armaments factories in Steyr and St. Valentin. At the same time, aircraft firms in the Altreich began relocating or constructing branch plants in Dornbirn, Bregenz, Kematen, Wels, and Wiener Neustadt. Despite severe shortages of labor, the Austrian GNP shot up 7.2 percent in 1941. By the end of the war, the country's plants were producing 10 percent of Greater Germany's small arms, 20 percent of its locomotives, 30 percent of its Me 109 fighters, and 55 percent of its Pz Mk IV tanks.[62]

Personal appearances by Hitler and Goebbels at ceremonies commemorating both the Anschluss and the beginning of production by the Hermann Göring Steel Works aroused wild enthusiasm.[63] In his diary, the propaganda minister described the scene:[64]

> To the meeting in the evening. Between huge crowds. The cheering never stops. Meeting overflowing. Fantastic atmosphere. I speak on the war situation. Each sentence is punctuated by storms of applause. I am on good form. Then the Gauleiter makes a short speech. And now, completely unexpected so far as the meeting is concerned, the Führer arrives. The storm of applause is quite indescribable. The Führer is lively and

buoyant. He speaks for thirty minutes with the greatest elan. Total confidence in victory. The crowd goes wild.

By 1941, in other words, wartime mobilization was bringing palpable improvements in the material conditions of everyday life to many Austrians in the West and in Styria. Ordinary people benefited from the development or expansion of heavy industry, military bases, and vacation resorts. At Linz some 2,700 buildings with 11,000 apartments were constructed by 1943–44; in the Styrian towns of Bruck, Judenburg, Leoben, and Mürzzuschlag the number of dwellings rose from 62,487 in 1939 to 82,675 in 1945. Financed both by private industry and the state, the new homes were usually up-to-date structures with indoor plumbing that included a bath or shower.[65] Other welfare state measures also kept pace in the first years of the war. In 1940 German pronatalist benefits were extended to the Ostmark, bringing relief to working mothers by restricting overtime hours, raising weekly wages, and, above all, mandating maternity leaves. Not surprisingly, the already high birthrate continued to hold steady so that as late as 1943 there were 40,000 more live births in Austria than in 1937.[66]

During these years the cultural and social measures introduced in 1938 continued to expand. The Nazi regime made enormous sums available for the promotion of music, the fine arts, and literature: it poured money into the Salzburg Festival, the Vienna opera, and the Graz theater; it proceeded with the renovation of Hitler's favorite city, Linz. Despite a ban on ballroom dancing, people flocked to movie houses and music halls. Cafés remained open; the tourist trade boomed; soccer matches attracted large crowds. Even in the countryside troupes of artists and musicians provided live entertainment for remote villages and farms. For many Austrians everyday life either improved or remained unaffected by what was still a distant conflict.[67]

With regard to military developments, most Austrians shared a common German fear that extension of fighting to the Balkans would needlessly prolong the war. Reaction to the British-sponsored coup in Yugoslavia in the spring of 1941 was thus one of "uncertainty" and "impatience." Hitler's lightning conquest of Yugoslavia and Greece in less than three weeks, however, unleashed a wave of exultation that was particularly strong in the borderlands of Carinthia and Styria and no doubt more intense than in the Altreich. Thereafter, the annexation of Upper Carniola and Lower Styria and the uprooting of the Slovenian population also met with general approval.[68]

REACTION TO BARBAROSSA

The Austrian people, like their German kin, were strikingly unprepared for Hitler's attack on Soviet Russia.[69] According to the SD, announcement of

Operation Barbarossa triggered "great dismay," particularly among house-wives with husbands or sons stationed in Poland. Many Austrians consid-ered the Soviet Union a formidable opponent, and people feared, as in the past, that expanding the theater of combat would not bring a successful end to the war.[70]

In Vienna, Josef Schöner wrote that word of the new offensive touched off intense discussion. Strolling through the streets and parks of the sun-drenched city, he observed groups of individuals engaged in fierce debate. Nearly everyone anticipated a victorious campaign, he recorded, but several Austrian patriots dared to hope that Hitler might come to grief before Leningrad or Moscow. Most Nazis, however, welcomed the campaign with considerable satisfaction, convinced that Bolshevism at last faced extinc-tion; at the same time, some of them feared renewed domestic unrest or sabotage.[71]

According to the security organs, underground Communist activity rose sharply during the summer, though mainly in the form of rumormongering or, as judicial authorities reported from Salzburg, occasional shouts of "Hail Moscow!" Among pious Catholics there was ambivalence: while some cler-gymen and laymen were heard to mutter that the outcome of the war hardly mattered, others expressed satisfaction with what they regarded as a final settling of accounts with atheistic Bolshevism.[72]

By late summer 1941, therefore, few ordinary Austrians—or Germans—shared the ebullience of their Führer. Instead of an end to the war, they faced a myriad of hardships and worries, accentuated by a sharp deteriora-tion in the quality and availability of food and basic services. On the pave-ments of Vienna and other great cities, including the Reich capital, people clad in shoddy clothes were overheard "grumbling openly," their tempers "perceptibly short." Harry E. Carlson, who closed the doors of the Ameri-can consulate in early August, wrote that "there are not more than 20 per cent of the Vienna population who are in full accord with the present regime." A majority of individuals regarded the war as a "Prussian enter-prise" and looked upon the conflict with "apathy," "indifference," and "leth-argy." One man was even heard to exclaim: "I do not care how the war ends. All I want is to be able to get my motor car back again."[73]

In the countryside there was resentment of tightening agricultural regi-mentation and, as we have seen, strong opposition to the new wave of attacks on the church. In early September announcement of spectacular victories in the East broke the overall atmosphere of worried indifference, restoring so much confidence in victory that even skeptics expressed pangs of guilt for doubting Hitler's ability to break Soviet power. Nonetheless, feelings of disappointment, bewilderment, and apprehension underlay the official mood of "calm and composure." The unease was accompanied by an upsurge of Communist violence in Salzburg and in railway yards in Styria and Carinthia. There was also an increase of arrests for "malicious practices," though primarily for economic offenses such as hoarding or "illicit sexual intercourse" between "women of German blood" and foreign workers. Underlying the discontent and pent-up tension were fears of heavy casualties, especially once lists of those killed in action began to appear in newspapers and public places.[74]

Nonetheless, an extraordinary emotional attachment to Hitler transcended the sense of alienation and gloom gripping Greater Germany that autumn. In the face of disaffection, worry, and grief, millions of Austrians and Germans continued to place their faith in the leader whose very name mentioned in the presence of skeptics, as an Innsbruck official put it, "works wonders."[75] Toward the end of September special radio bulletins trumpeted the investment of both Leningrad and Kiev and the capture of an astonishing 1.8 million Russian prisoners of war. With victory seemingly in sight, the public yearned to be reassured by the Führer, if for no other reason than to allay reports from frontline soldiers of "increasing difficulty with provisioning" and "incredibly great Soviet Army reserves in manpower and material."[76] On 3 October Hitler obliged. In a stem-winding speech he defended his decision to attack Soviet Russia and boasted that the enemy was as good as beaten. Several days later the Reich press chief, Otto Dietrich, announced that the "last remnants" of the Red Army were being annihilated.[77]

Owing to a significant gap in the documentation, the Austrian response to these dramatic events is not known. That it was much different from elsewhere in the Reich is unlikely. One may assume that there was a release of tension, rising euphoria, perhaps even "excessive optimism." After several weeks of heavy fighting, however, public confidence began to flag, slowly giving way to bemusement and disquiet. By November, people were wondering "how an end to the war against Russia is even possible." A month later there were rumors of mass murders and heavy losses. In Catholic areas, especially in the Ostmark, the morale was further depressed by continuing attacks on the church.[78]

Hitler, as we have already seen, had reacted to the intense Christian opposition to "mercy killings" by issuing a stop order. Faced with what threatened to become public resistance in wartime, he also declared an armistice in his anticlerical campaign, deciding to postpone further incursions until after the war. Given the dictator's mafialike technique of communicating only indirectly with subordinates, it took some time for word of the cease-fire to reach grass-roots functionaries. For that reason a number of local activists kept up the witch-hunt. The campaign was most rabid in neighboring Bavaria where Gauleiter Adolf Wagner's "crucifix decree" provoked protests, petitions, school strikes, demonstrations, and even threats of violence. Once word of the uproar made its way to the Ostmark, it had a predictably unsettling effect.[79]

In actual fact, few crucifixes appear to have been taken from Austrian classrooms. Nevertheless, popular reaction was negative, even hostile. Just before Christmas, the local group leader at Ardagger in Lower Danube tried to calm a throng of protesters gathering in the village square. Before he could open his mouth, the demonstrators shouted him down and demanded the return of the crosses. The crowd then proceeded to the school building, invaded the principal's office, and retrieved a crucifix from the supply room. After returning it to its rightful place, the group dispersed and went home.[80] In the neighboring communities of Euratsfeld and St. Pantaleon, similar crucifix removals ignited "restlessness and bad blood." As had happened in Bavaria, the regime was accused of Bolshevik behavior at a moment local boys were locked in mortal combat on the eastern front.[81] In another case, near Salzburg, nine soldiers' mothers made the same point in a formal petition to Gauleiter Gustav Scheel.[82]

Despite harassment and persecution, the Austrian episcopate concluded that further accommodation was the best means of protecting both its flock and the institutional integrity of the church. On 27 November the bishops ordered the reading of a pastoral letter reiterating their support of Hitler's war against Soviet Russia. In it they solemnly declared that Germany was conducting a crusade against a monstrous "threat to Western civilization." Rather than "keep silent," they urged the faithful to "recognize the danger for all Europe should Bolshevism prevail."[83]

There can be no doubt that Hitler's campaign in Russia stabilized Nazi rule in the Ostmark by neutralizing potential opposition from that segment of the population with the strongest sense of Austrian identity: the Catholic peasantry. Though individual clergymen and churchgoers continued to protest religious restrictions including the conscription of seminarians, the removal of church bells, and the expropriation of clerical property, they could not be expected to turn against the regime so long as the church hierarchy supported Hitler's anti-Communist crusade.[84] In the Diocese of Linz, for example, Bishop Josef Calasanctius Fliesser established a cordial working relationship with Gauleiter Eigruber and endorsed the German war effort.[85] Even if the bishops had taken an ambiguous stand on Hitler's war, it is still difficult to see how the rural population would have behaved much differently, particularly in the face of Nazi ideals that appealed to deeply ingrained Alpine Catholic values: manly prowess, fierce wartime allegiance to the state, anti-Semitism, fear of Asiatic barbarism. Overall, then, attitudes still paralleled those in the Altreich, but due to the expansion of industry and continued immunity from Allied air raids, morale fluctuated less and, until the surrender of the Sixth Army at Stalingrad, may have remained higher—especially in the booming West—than in many parts of Greater Germany.[86]

MOSCOW AND PEARL HARBOR

Confidence in victory, according to the security organs, stood high in late 1941. Despite grumbling about manpower shortages, particularly those caused by the ongoing call-up of desperately needed physicians, cobblers, blacksmiths, and chimney sweeps, the food distribution system worked both smoothly and efficiently. There were few problems to report. In the countryside peasants made no secret of their resentment of regulations restricting the slaughter of livestock, but political dissent remained minimal.[87] Reaction to the government's sudden appeal for winter clothing for the troops before Moscow—in contrast to the Altreich—was not so much one of shock and anger as of confusion and dismay followed by an outpouring of massive support. In areas of Wiener Neustadt men and women even sacrificed their ration stamps to purchase woolens and furs as their contribution. In Tyrol 18,212 pairs of skis were donated by tourists and locals within just a matter of weeks.[88]

Although rumors of setbacks and retreats circulated, few people comprehended the gravity of the military crisis at Führer headquarters precipitated by the Red Army's counteroffensive against the Wehrmacht's freezing and exhausted forces. When questions began to be raised regarding inadequate military provisions or withdrawals from the gates of Moscow, they were directed to the Army High Command, not to Hitler or the Nazi leadership. As elsewhere in Greater Germany people inclined to accept the Führer's version of the emergency, holding Field Marshal Walther von Brauchitsch accountable for the failure to take the Soviet capital before the onset of winter.[89] In the confusion of the moment there was also little grasp or understanding of the significance of Hitler's declaration of war on the United States. As throughout most of Greater Germany, a majority of the Austrian populace welcomed Japan's attack on Pearl Harbor as a way of shortening the war, though in Tulln, Wiener Neustadt, and Amstetten certain groups, most notably farmers and veterans of World War I, were reported fearful of a protracted conflict. The Japanese Imperial Navy's near destruction of the U.S. Pacific Fleet on 7 December, followed within a few days by its sinking of

the British *Repulse* and *Prince of Wales* off the coast of Malaya, further oc-
cluded the situation, diverting attention from the eastern front, boosting
confidence in a welcome new ally, and restoring overall morale. As the
otherwise perceptive county executive in Eisenstadt wrote, "Japan's entry
into the war has been hailed everywhere with a sense that in this case a
worthy ally has appeared to achieve final victory according to plan. The
decisive blows against the American battle fleet have served to relieve the
anxiety stemming from the world war of a conflict with the United States."[90]
On 12 January the SD in Innsbruck reported that some Tyroleans were even
predicting the withdrawal of enemy forces from both Africa and Russia to
the Far East.[91]

During the third winter of war Goebbels's propaganda machine subjected the German and Austrian people to a barrage of stirring broadcasts,
striking phrases, and slick articles designed to shore up their morale. By mid-
February 1942 it became possible to present the news more "calmly and
factually" as Rommel's Afrika Korps drove the British Eighth Army from
Libya and the Japanese captured Singapore. There were also sensational
"special bulletins" trumpeting U-boat successes in the Atlantic.

Most Austrians responded to the latest military news with relief and
slightly numbed confidence. There was tremendous enthusiasm for Rommel's exploits, but also war-weariness and concern for the future. When
Hitler delivered his annual address on 30 January, recalling the ninth anniversary of his "seizure of power" and repeating his warning that the war would
"end in the destruction of Jewry," the reaction in the Ostmark was positive.
In Innsbruck the security organs made no mention of the Führer's Judeo-
cidal threats, but indicated that his "lively and fresh" delivery both raised
spirits and reinforced morale, thus "silencing fears of an unfavorable outcome of operations on the eastern front." While there was still worry about
the duration of the conflict, most people believed that renewed offensive
operations in the spring would lead to victory. In a unique regional twist, the
SD added that a number of locals, notably from South Tyrol, took exception
to Hitler's words of tribute to Germany's Italian ally; they argued that any
praise of Mussolini's war effort could not help but be misplaced.[92]

With conditions on the battlefronts apparently under control, daily life in
the Ostmark reverted to a relatively "normal" wartime existence; throughout the late winter and early spring of 1942 people again focused their cares
and worries on the deprivations of the home front. As before, there was
much complaining about shortages of normal conveniences and necessities:
clothing, footwear, cosmetics, toothpaste, and mouthwash. There was also
concern about scarcities of fuel and firewood that in some parts of Tyrol

closed schools and public buildings for three weeks.[93] On the other hand, proprietors of Alpine ski lodges reported a successful season. According to the security organs, a number of "fashionable" ladies wintering with their consorts at resorts in St. Anton and Zürs were consuming enormous quantities of champagne, schnapps, and other culinary delights.

As for most everyone else, food was still fairly easy to obtain, although inns and restaurants were required to serve blue-plate specials or stew dishes cooked according to field kitchen recipes; worse, those Austrians normally obliged or accustomed to eating out found themselves entitled to only one unrationed meal per day. On 22 March, a government directive ordered a severe cut in consumer food rations; it reduced weekly allotments of meat from 400 to 300 grams, butter from 150 to 125 grams, margarine from 96.87 to 65.62 grams, and bread from 2,250 to 2,000 grams. With the clothing ration at only half the official allotment since October, the government also announced the introduction of a tobacco ration for smokers.[94]

Not unexpectedly, overall morale plummeted throughout Greater Germany, including the Austrian lands. To be sure, scuffles between smokers in lines at tobacco stands came to an end and special allotments of both eggs and oranges at Easter met an appreciative response, but there was real despair at no longer being able to eat one's fill. By late April unhappiness was reported from nearly all localities in the Ostmark. Housewives felt depressed and flustered by the meager quantities of potatoes, vegetables, cooking oils, and even skimmed milk available at markets; workers groused that bread consumption was insufficient for heavy labor. Single people protested that restaurant food was too expensive, the portions minuscule.[95] As the West German historian Marlis Steinert later concluded, nearly everyone was "beginning to view the whole war, including German endurance, military capacities, and prospects for victory, from the perspective of food requirements."[96]

Within many Austrian communities, growling stomachs aggravated already uncomfortable feelings of discomfort and disaffection. In the squares of towns and villages the relentless posting of lists of fallen and missing soldiers brought inconsolable grief to thousands of wives and mothers, sons and daughters, fathers and brothers, many of whom scarcely understood or condoned Hitler's conflict. The increasing number of military funerals deepened peoples' heartache; they also focused and sustained the antagonism of the Catholic population towards the Nazi system, especially in instances where the Gestapo picked up priests on charges of "manipulating" the emotions of mourners for the cause of Christ. The regime's ongoing removal of bells from country churches as well its sporadic detachment of

complained constantly about inadequate supplies of meat, potatoes, bread, and cooking fats. Frazzled mothers were overheard deploring the minuscule quantities of milk available to their children, workingmen coveting food parcels received from home by French prisoners of war and Italian workers. Nearly everyone expressed disgust with the quality of black bread, the loaves of which were acknowledged even by the authorities to be both unpalatable and a major cause of both gastrointestinal illness and flatulence. To make matters even worse, there were also malfunctions in the food distribution system, with towns and cities receiving irregular shipments of fruits and vegetables at a time rural communities were still subsisting on winter staples.[101]

In early May the situation on the battlefronts changed dramatically. In Russia Manstein's Eleventh Army regained the initiative. On 13 June Rommel's Afrika Korps outflanked the Free French in the Gazala–Bir Hacheim position in Libya and drove the British Eighth Army back into Egypt. At sea there were signs that Dönitz's wolf packs might be on the verge of breaking the back of Allied merchant strength. Word of Hitler's latest military triumphs came as a relief to most of the Austrian people, partly because they identified with the cause of German arms, partly—and more fundamentally—because they glimpsed an end to the war before Christmas. That a great many individuals in early June reacted with horror and trepidation to the assassination of Reinhard Heydrich, Himmler's dreaded deputy, can be explained, in part, as a reflection of their "fear for the life of the Führer," the man they were counting on to bring victory. Indeed, when a major offensive in the East did not materialize until 28 June, the SD in Innsbruck reported a "certain impatience" spurred on by fear of another Russian winter.[102]

After the Army High Command at last announced the beginning of Operation Blue, the enormous push to the Volga and Caucasus, fluctuations in Austrian sentiment showed little sign of diverging from those in the Altreich. As elsewhere in Greater Germany, there was an initial sense of release, followed by feelings of cautious, wait-and-see optimism. From Behamberg the constabulary reported that a personal inspection tour by Hitler of the Nibelungen tank works had made a particularly deep impression on blue-collar workers; from Amstetten came word that the normally distrustful farming population again recognized the necessity of victory. According to the SD in Innsbruck, individuals known to keep a close eye on military developments were following the progress of the eastern army with "satisfaction" while tracking the thrusts of the Afrika Korps with truly passionate enthusiasm. Once Tobruk and Marsa Matruk had fallen to the Desert Fox, news junkies and armchair generals speculated that his forces would soon sweep across the Suez Canal into Sinai. There were even revealing rumors that Waffen SS units would be deployed for the drive into Palestine "since no one knows how to clean out Jews better than the SS." As for the eastern front, prevailing wisdom had it that after crushing the Soviets, an eastern wall would be constructed on the right bank of the Volga River.[103]

Although Rommel's victories indisputably fired the collective imagination and lifted overall morale, the available evidence indicates that many Austrians, like their German kith and kin, regarded military affairs with indifference or, after a brief revival of interest, retreated into the private sphere of coping with the cares and frustrations of daily life. Nearly all the July reports characterize the prevailing mood as "calm," yet also "varied," with sentiments ranging from cautious optimism to apathy and depression. Interestingly, it was in the countryside that spirits appear to have risen the most, albeit to a minuscule degree, as the otherwise resentful farming population looked forward to a plentiful harvest of hay, rye, and oats. Sustained by the arrival of Soviet prisoners of war and other "eastern workers," numerous farming families made a point of ignoring Nazi apartheid regulations for their treatment; as in Bavaria, they allowed the new help to eat at the same table, provided clothing for women workers—many of whom had shown up in tatters—and, in some cases, even paid a monthly bonus of twenty marks.

By contrast, in towns and cities where support for both Hitler's war and his ideas tended to be extensive, there was ill feeling, primarily because of the deteriorating food situation.[104] On 10 August the SD wrote from Innsbruck that many townsfolk were exhausted, losing weight, and experiencing difficulty in job performance: "To an increasing degree the discrepancy in the provisioning of town and country is being discussed. Country folk are frequently seen in traffic, the farming youngsters in possession of buttered bread, bacon, and similar items, whereas the children of workers and employees have scarcely a dry crust. By the same token, people simply cannot understand why farmers invariably have adequate quantities of whole milk and seemingly no shortages of butter and fat."[105]

VIENNA AND THE END OF THE JEWISH QUESTION

Due to bottlenecks in the distribution system and to the lack of household refrigeration, the prevailing food shortages were felt most keenly in Vienna. Here the disaffected populace was reported paying little attention to news from either Africa or Soviet Russia. To be sure, there had been an initial upsurge of interest in military operations, but most people regarded the latest victory bulletins with a characteristic mixture of skepticism, self-pity, and disinterest. According to a handful of surviving documents from mid-July, "a considerable number of countrymen doubt the announcements that 'everything is in order' and advancing relentlessly forward," primarily because of the "confusing, unclear, and opaque" official version of events. Terrified of another winter of war, most Viennese sublimated their anguish in chronic complaining about both the scarcities of food and the wearying conditions of everyday life. Housewives, in particular, directed their anger at local distributors, holding them accountable for delivering inadequate or spoiled quantities of fruits, vegetables, milk, white bread, and fish. The homekeepers also vented their rage at neighborhood grocers for restricting shopping hours and at the Nazi Gauleitung for prohibiting direct purchases from producers, particularly for banning trips into the countryside to pick apples, peaches, cherries, or other produce.[106]

Overarching the welter of Viennese complaints and grievances was, as might be expected, a transcendent belief in the guilt of the surviving metropolitan Jews for most wartime hardships. The popular conviction was unshaken even by the weekly sight of transports of doomed men, women, and children passing through ocher-colored neighborhoods in broad daylight to the Aspang Station, where between 12:00 and 4:00 P.M. they were bolted into cattle cars for final journeys to Minsk, Theresienstadt, or Auschwitz. On 20 July the SD wrote that most people felt that "punishment of Jews and friends of Jews can never be too harsh." The populace also held that "any countryman profiteering from selling victuals to Jews deserves an [even] harsher penalty, perhaps even the death sentence."[107]

The sentiments expressed in the SD report reflected the party line, but there is no reason to assume that they misrepresented or distorted basic Viennese attitudes. As Hitler remarked four days later over dinner at the Wolf's Lair in East Prussia, "Elimination of the Jews of Vienna is receiving top priority [sei am vordringlichsten] since in Vienna there is only perfunctory whining."[108]

Outside the Danubian city, reaction to deportation of the few hundred Jews still remaining in the provinces of the Ostmark, mostly in "privileged mixed marriages," was more varied; in one or two known cases it was even hostile. Most non-Viennese, like their blood brothers in the Altreich, generally paid little attention during the war to the Jewish issue. To be sure, those living in the shadow of Mauthausen or its subcamps periodically witnessed unspeakable mistreatment of inmates, many of whom were non-Jewish; but given the threat of arrest for talking, their responses tended to be mute. At the lakeside resort of St. Wolfgang in Upper Danube, however, loud indignation was reported at the behavior of Sara Gertrud Peter, the Jewish wife of a local physician; she was charged with spending the summer of 1942 in luxury at the Weisses Rössl hotel, daring not only to sail on the Wolfgangsee but also to lounge in a reclining chair on the hotel terrace and to socialize in the lobby with a "typical clique friendly to Jews."[109] In May 1943, on the other hand, the SD in Innsbruck registered intense disapproval of the "removal of Jews married to people of German blood." There was shock at the suicides of a retired Colonel Teuber and his Jewish wife. According to an accompanying report, the seizure and deportation of an elderly Jewish cobbler in nearby Schwaz also provoked "ill feeling." The unhappy townspeople, it stated, felt that "it is obvious that there can be no exceptions for Jews, but in the case of a very old man, who was always a diligent worker, this is really an outrage. In view of total wartime mobilization measures, he could surely have been of help to many people through his work."[110]

THE VIEW FROM THE WEST

Aside from occasional references to priests denouncing Nazi racial policy from the pulpit,[111] the surviving documentary evidence reveals few critical comments and virtually no expressions of compassion for nonbaptized Jews. As the war ended its third year, people had their minds on other things. By late August, in fact, sentiment oscillated between cautious hope and despair, in some areas resembling manic-depressive mood swings. Although the German army had slashed its way into the Caucasus and was driving on Stalingrad, people remained confused and worried. In Lower Danube, six stations indicated that morale was "calm" or "satisfactory," but eight others emphasized that it was extremely "depressed." In what had long been a remote and distant war, mounting casualty lists increasingly brought grief and heartache to more and more families. At Behamberg the conviction prevailed that the war would be over by the end of the year; from Haag came word, however, that most people had given up hope of immediate victory. The population was also annoyed by metastasizing wartime ordinances and restrictions, especially new regulations prohibiting the slaughter of pigs for family consumption, a measure that had a serious impact on numerous households sustaining one or two animals on table scraps. On the other hand, despite a good deal of complaining about black bread still leavened with indigestible chemical preservatives, both a bountiful harvest and an abundance of fresh fruits and vegetables offered the prospect of enough to eat in coming days. The unexpected announcement in mid-August of an increase of potato rations also raised spirits.[112]

It is not without interest that wartime morale, particularly during the summer of 1942, was more positive and optimistic in the West than in Vienna and Lower Danube. The security organs indicated many of the same worries and complaints as in eastern Austria, but examination of the surviving documentation suggests that in rapidly modernizing industrial centers a real sense of well-being prevailed. In Laakirchen for example, the authorities took pains to emphasize that nearly all the 950 workers in the Schuppler and Steyrmühl paper mills, almost to a man former Social Democrats, identified with both the regime and the war effort.[113]

The documentation reveals, too, that large numbers of ordinary people were buoyed by triumphal bulletins from the front. When mountain troops raised the swastika banner over Mount Elbrus on 21 August, tremendous enthusiasm was reported in the streets of Innsbruck. With elements of the Sixth Army already on the high banks of the Volga north of Stalingrad, Tyroleans glued their ears to radio receivers, listening for news of the fall of the city, to be followed, they speculated, by announcement of Turkey's entry into the war as an Axis ally. When regular broadcasting continued without interruption, there was a sudden urge to be reassured by the words of the Führer.[114] Instead of a Hitler speech, the airwaves crackled with word of a significant raise in the food ration, "proving," as Goebbels put it in a morning conference, "that we are not just chasing after bloodless ideals, but are waging the war in the East for very real reasons."[115]

As might be imagined, the effect was electric. From Innsbruck the SD wrote that "announcement of the hike in the meat and bread ration unleashed tremendous surprise and elation." People considered it more important than a special bulletin trumpeting a military victory. Many "think that the worst times lie behind us and that economic conditions will steadily improve." In fact, it was "precisely in those circles in which a certain warweariness has been recently noted that the upswing in morale has been most pronounced." For them, the security men concluded, "final victory is no longer in doubt."[116]

Meanwhile, there had also been an enormous boom in the tourist trade of Tyrol and the Salzkammergut. By the end of June the number of guests booked into local hotels and resorts was so great that available cooks and kitchen personnel could no longer meet the demand. As was the case in neighboring Bavaria, the vacationers brought lucrative earnings but also frustration and resentment. Many well-to-do guests arrived with an abundance of cash or valuables which they exchanged with local farmers for eggs, butter, sausage, or other edibles; the behavior of others provoked disapproval, for example, in the Biedermeier resort of Gmunden where German women drew criticism not only for their "masculine" apparel, but also for their habit of smoking cigarettes while strolling along the elegant esplanade beside Lake Traun.[117]

By midsummer a good many Austrians were feeling overcrowded, even claustrophobic. The SD in Innsbruck described the mood: "In tourist areas morale is being unfavorably influenced by the numerous visitors. There is much complaining of inconsiderate behavior toward the native population. Autobuses and trains are so overfilled with them that it is frequently impossible for local people to use public transportation to get to work." In Kitzbühel a "severely injured officer" spent an hour trying to stir up a ride from the depot, even though "a number of one- and two-horse rigs were standing idle at the depot," each one already "reserved by ladies to drive them to their hotels." Incidents such as these as well as the "shopping mania of the outsiders" were provoking "indignant remarks by the native populace.[118]

Although relations between hosts and guests were not always so strained, the simultaneous arrival of large numbers of evacuees from bombed-out or imperiled cities, notably Essen, both eroded profits and further accentuated cultural differences between Germans and Austrians. From the regime's perspective the most alarming aspects of the German presence were, first, the obvious and blatant disenchantment with the Nazi system shown by so many of the evacuees, particularly those from the Rhineland and Berlin; and, second, the terrifying personal stories of suffering and loss of life under British bombs that were passed on to the local population. The public prosecutor in Innsbruck wrote that "even the person of the Führer is being dragged through filth by some of these countrymen."[119] Although the Ostmark still remained safe from Air Marshal Harris's Lancasters and Halifaxes, a good many Vorarlberger and Tyroleans were seized by a "psychotic fear" of aerial attack.[120]

ON THE BRINK

By the end of September, therefore, the euphoria of midmonth was again being displaced by feelings of anxiety and apprehension. With widespread discussion of looming aerial bombardment, residents of Innsbruck as well as those of the aircraft manufacturing towns of Jenbach (Heinkel) and Kematen (Messerschmitt) were reported spending sleepless nights reading or taking refuge in country villages or farms. When Hitler delivered an unexpected address at the Berlin Sports Palace on 30 September, his words went a long way to soothe frazzled nerves. Since his address raised the prospect of more to eat in days to come, the response was overwhelmingly positive throughout Greater Germany. Even more effective in raising overall spirits was a striking harangue by Hermann Göring delivered four days later at Harvest Thanksgiving Day. On this most appropriate occasion, the well-fed Reich marshal proclaimed another increase in the food ration as well as a special Christmas allowance.[121]

With restored confidence, the war-weary populace of the Ostmark looked forward to word of the fall of Stalingrad and the conclusion of the Barbarossa campaign. By late October there were even rumors of an armistice, generated by the extension of leave for logistical reasons to soldiers home from Russia. With the Sixth Army actually bogged down in a grim house-to-house struggle for the city on the Volga, the German and Austrian home front continued to receive optimistic assessments from both the Army High Command and the Propaganda Ministry. In Tyrol the constant sight of trains rolling through the Brenner Pass laden with supplies for the Afrika Korps also gave hope for a final push in Egypt. When an erroneous report arrived from the Pacific trumpeting the destruction of four American carriers and a battleship, there was even serious thought of an end to the war itself. According to widely believed hearsay, armistice negotiations were already under way, some said in Stockholm between Ribbentrop and Molotov, others insisted in Ankara between Papen and Stalin himself.[122]

Sudden word of American landings in Morocco and Algeria and Rommel's "disengagement" from El Alamein came as a bombshell to the Austrian people. Startled and confused, their immediate anxieties were allayed by the words of the Führer. In a speech to the Old Guard broadcast from the Löwenbräukeller in Munich, Hitler dispelled the apprehension of the moment by reminding his audience of the fluid nature of desert warfare and by claiming that in Stalingrad only a "few more tiny pockets" remained to be mopped up. For some days thereafter people struggled to get a clearer picture of the fighting in North Africa. Once it became obvious that the Afrika Korps was in full retreat, many became intensely worried and concerned. In the Ostmark, possibly more than in the Altreich, popular anger and recrimination resounded against Austria's traditional "allied enemy," Italy. Ill feeling was particularly intense in Tyrol where ancestral rivalry and frontier grievances reinforced charges of cowardice, incompetence, and looming betrayal. There was also well-founded fear that Allied air operations in northern Italy might soon extend to targets in the Ostmark.[123]

By the end of November eyes turned again to the eastern front. Few people knew that between 19 and 23 November a massive Soviet counteroffensive had thrown a noose around the Sixth Army. But in Linz and Innsbruck rumors of encirclement were already rampant, and many individuals sensed that the situation was clearly "threatening." On 7 December the SD in the Tyrolean capital characterized local morale as "extremely depressed." Elsewhere in the Ostmark there were reports of an upsurge of divorce, of a renewal of Communist activities in both Wiener Neustadt and Eisenstadt, and of the reappearance of extensive war-weariness. And yet, despite growing misgivings about the fate of the Sixth Army at Stalingrad, most people were not as alarmed by the military situation as the year before, when many had been seized by fear of a Russian breakthrough.[124] Indeed, by mid-December the authorities in Linz were reporting a "calmer mood," those in Innsbruck one of confidence in the defensive capabilities of the Wehrmacht.[125]

Much of the reason for the lower anxiety level was the availability of ample quantities of food, including such delicacies as vermouth and coffee. In a successful attempt to divert attention from the deteriorating situation at the front, the regime, as we have seen, had increased rations of bread, fats, and meat, even doubling or nearly doubling those of potatoes. With Christmas fast approaching, shops were overrun by customers looking for presents. In Innsbruck they had little luck, since few of the goods shown in display windows were actually available for purchase; in Linz, on the other hand, shoppers were able to make selections from a variety of used clothes, landscape paintings, and nearly 200,000 brightly colored toys handcrafted by the Hitler Youth. There were also special "Führer packages" for soldiers home on furlough that included 2,500 grams of flour, 1,000 grams each of meat and sugar, and 500 grams of other edibles. Thanks to Goebbels's propaganda machine and a mild winter, the war seemed almost forgotten.[126]

By New Year, however, rumors of encirclement of the Sixth Army at Stalingrad were swirling from house to house, from person to person. Within three weeks the grim truth became generally known. In St. Anton at Arlberg, near the Swiss border, general awareness of the real military situation was astonishingly accurate. Accompanying the worry and concern was a sharp increase in shortages of household articles and necessities such as calendars, combs, toothpaste, and sanitary napkins. At Lambach, near Wels, women were reported lining up before sunrise to buy shoes. The large number of foreign workers riding trolley cars and trains also added to the stress because of their "rude and insolent behavior." According to the SD, there was open criticism of both the war and party bosses. Everywhere women could be seen, their "eyes red with tears," tormented by "growing nervousness, anxiety, and worry."[127]

Once the sepulchral "special bulletin" finally rumbled over the airwaves on 3 February, popular reaction was one of shock, grief, and depression. In Innsbruck the authorities spoke of a "devastating impact"; in Linz they indicated "deepest grief, depression and despondency"; in Eisenstadt there was a sense of "helplessness." Throughout Lower Danube farmers and villagers were reported "staggered," "deeply shaken," "war-weary," and "fearful." In Vienna, the mood was "infinitely depressed"; residents shook their heads in disbelief, mumbling to each other, "Stalingrad, my God!" Nowhere did people express relief or happiness that the tide had turned against Hitler. The truth was that, for all its differences, the Austrian home front still felt bound to the cause of the Greater German Reich. With their backs to the wall, most Austrians still stood behind the Anschluss regime.[128]

FOR THE COMMON CAUSE

During the first half of the Second World War sentiment in Hitler's Ost-mark closely paralleled that prevailing elsewhere in his Reich. While there were constant fluctuations and variations in the mood, nearly everyone longed for an end to the war as soon as possible. Few expressed sympathy for Hitler's enemies or believed that Greater Germany was in any way re-sponsible for the conflict that had broken out in 1939. What ordinary people wanted was a settlement allowing them some largesse of conquest. Beneath the veneer of national determination there was also an astonishing degree of dissent, disaffection, and noncompliance that both postwar Austrian and German historians would mistakenly label "resistance." Although the evi-dence reveals widespread disenchantment with the NSDAP and its func-tionaries, most dissent focused only on specific policies or aspects of Hitler's regime. Even in Catholic areas where protest came close to rebellion in 1941, hardly anyone questioned the legitimacy of the existing system.

Within the general attitudinal climate, Austrian sentiment manifested distinctive particularist and regional strains. After the outbreak of hostilities there was a dampening of Anschluss enthusiasm, especially in Vienna where resentment of "Prussian" carpetbaggers was already running high. Despite food shortages and mounting loss of life, however, there was little sign of disapproval of Nazi domestic values or goals. Substantial numbers of Vien-nese endorsed the regime's policy of expelling the Jews. In a similar though also different way, the beginning of the war saw the emergence of legitimist and Communist groups pledged to the cause of Austrian independence. Spreading crude fly sheets or daubing graffiti in public places, they appealed to scant numbers of individuals; what their efforts did reveal was that not every Austrian stood behind the regime.[129]

On the other hand, few people in Austria considered themselves "Hitler's first victims" or evinced any sense of defeat or humiliation under German rule. Rather, everywhere they continued to apply in large numbers to the NSDAP, so that by May 1943 two-thirds of a million had signed up.[130] As for those who remained politically disinterested or generally indifferent, there was tremendous admiration for Hitler and his achievements. In the rapidly developing regions of the West and in Styria, those who benefited from his program of technocratic and social modernization felt especially appreciative. It is true that by late 1942 civilian morale was waning, especially along the Danube in the East; the security organs also reported heightened anti-German sentiment in Vienna and a number of Alpine vacation resorts. Nevertheless, few were hoping for Hitler's defeat. With 1,286,000 Austrians serving in the Wehrmacht, the Austrian people remained committed to winning the war.

9 BETWEEN STALINGRAD AND THE MOSCOW DECLARATION

For over half a century it has been an article of faith that the shock of Hitler's defeat at Stalingrad broke his spell over the Austrian people. As early as February 1943 a Swedish correspondent reported from Vienna that the city had become "a seething mass of anti-Hitler opposition." The security organs also noted a rise of anti-Nazi outbursts and, here and there, shouts of "Hail Austria!" According to the recollections of the Social Democratic politician Adolf Schärf, by the summer of 1943 most Austrians had been thoroughly "cured of their love for the German Reich."[1] On the basis of this and other evidence, there can be little doubt that the Stalingrad debacle severely depressed morale in the Ostmark and provoked an upsurge of separatist sentiment. Whether Hitler's disaster on the Volga "awakened" widespread Austrian patriotic feeling or kindled a distinctive resistance movement is less clear and rather problematic.[2] As examination of the available documentation reveals, Austrian attitudes remained diverse, but they did not diverge significantly from the general climate of opinion in other parts of Greater Germany.

THE SITUATION IN VIENNA

Shortly after the surrender of the German Sixth Army at Stalingrad, Arvid Fredborg, Berlin correspondent of the *Svenska Dagbladet*, arrived in Vienna on holiday. No stranger to the Danubian metropolis, he was shocked to discover that it had become an enormous complex of military hospitals, overrun by foreign workers, and experiencing a deterioration of public services. "The trains were even more worn and creaking," he wrote, "the taxis were more rattling, and the railway stations were even dirtier than last time. On public buildings the plaster was flaking and the facades of the houses clearly revealed that for years they had not been cleaned."[3]

Even so, Fredborg was pleased to find that the shops offered more than those in Berlin and that most restaurants still offered top-quality cuisine to their guests: " At the old, stately Sacher they still served Palatschinken, the familiar thin pancakes that tasted just as good as in old times; the soups were excellent and were without chemicals; and the bread was considerably better than in the German capital."[4]

What astonished Fredborg was not so much the changes and continuities in urban life as the open animosity of the Viennese to the Germans, a hostility, he wrote, "that extends through Austrian society from top to bottom."[5] He emphasized that "it was not so much National Socialism they disliked as things German in themselves." Nonetheless, he was emphatic in claiming that a majority of Austrians had broken forever with the Anschluss.[6]

Fredborg's portrait of a Vienna seething with discontent is substantiated by reports compiled several months later by the American embassy in Stockholm from the testimony of Allied agents, Austrian exiles, and Nazi informants.[7] According to the accounts, disenchantment with German rule was widespread throughout the middle classes, particularly among the many Viennese Nazis who still resented losing administrative and party posts to Germans from the Reich. Within the business community, there was a similar sense of discrimination accompanied by dissatisfaction with the burden of wartime taxation and, in the case of small producers and merchants, indignation at the forced closing of small businesses and shops. According to one observer, the conscription of women into the workforce also aroused the ire of the upper and upper-middle classes, "as they often see their wives or sisters working at jobs which they ordinarily would consider a disgrace."[8] As a whole, the Viennese bourgeoisie had become fed up with German rule, but were unwilling to resist it. "One cannot yet speak of any resistance on the part of the middle classes," one informant explained. "In March 1938 they all ran over to Nazism as soon as Austria was annexed. In 1943 they began to withdraw from it, since Nazism disappointed them. It meant war, distress, and great losses in human lives as well as what is called 'brown communism.'"[9]

Among industrial workingmen, resentment and opposition prevailed as well. According to Allied sources and postwar testimony, most Viennese workers, especially in older firms and the transport sector, remained ideologically opposed to National Socialism and loyal to trade-union traditions. Nearly all yearned for a return to a more pluralistic order. Forced to work long hours under constant surveillance for frozen wages, they refrained, however, from active resistance. Further, they still remained loyal to the Anschluss, fearing a return of unemployment and even preferring the Nazi term Ostmark to Austria—a name they associated with the Dollfuss-Schuschnigg regime.[10]

Overall, most witnesses concurred in characterizing the Viennese mood in 1943 as one of sagging morale, war-weariness, and apathy. With the loss of so many Austrian soldiers at Stalingrad, thousands of grief-stricken families began tuning in Radio Moscow for word of the fate of relatives or loved ones. Defeat at Stalingrad also unleashed a torrent of criticism of Nazi leaders ranging from Göring (*ein ausgefressenes Schwein*) to local party bosses though not extending to Hitler who, as elsewhere in Greater Germany, was viewed as a solitary father figure engulfed in tragedy. There was also great unhappiness with continued shortages of fats and vegetables, though general agreement that supplies of rationed food remained ample.[11]

Whether the Viennese by 1943 had really been "cured of their love for the German Reich" is debatable. While Fredborg remained adamant that the "vast majority of Austrians desire separation from the rest of Germany and above all North Germany,"[12] the testimony of others is ambivalent, suggesting particularist disgruntlement with Hitler's policy of keeping Vienna under Reich German control rather than a break with the Anschluss system.[13] As for the Nazi authorities, they took no chances as the Gestapo stepped up sweeps of working-class neighborhoods and intensified its campaign of visible terror against dissenters and resistance groups. While the Viennese public prosecutor reported no perceptible rise in subversive activities for the first half of 1943,[14] the People's Court continued to mete out hundreds of death sentences. According to one account, there were "daily executions of from ten to fifteen anti-Nazis" in Josefsstadt. Thereafter, the "bodies and chopped-off heads [were] thrown into a large box and carted to an open mass grave" in the Central Cemetery.[15]

PROVINCIAL CONDITIONS

Outside Vienna, popular attitudes continued to parallel those prevailing elsewhere in Greater Germany. As in the Altreich, the overall response of the population to Hitler's defeat at Stalingrad was one of shock and disbelief, followed by waves of despondency, cynicism, fear for the fate of relatives at the front, and wishful thinking.[16] In both Upper and Lower Danube the security organs reported astonishment "that the Führer has allowed Ostmärker of all people to be driven to their deaths."[17] The collapse in morale was accompanied by a sharp rise in church attendance and intense discussion about the war's duration, especially in the countryside where the conflict was scarcely comprehended and widely resented. Among blue-collar workers the reaction was one of cynical detachment, marked by general belief that conditions under Bolshevism could not be worse than under the existing system.[18]

The Stalingrad debacle also widened the gap between the Nazi Party and the general population. Authorities in Upper Danube recorded instances of bitter criticism and even personal abuse of party functionaries. In Gries-kirchen the grief-stricken mother of a fallen soldier slapped a local group leader for delivering a message of condolence;[19] in Böheim an uncle attacked a cell leader on a similar errand with the words "You with the party badges are to blame for this shitty war!"[20] For the most part, Berlin's efforts to galvanize the home front for total war provoked the same sort of reactions in Austria as in the Altreich. Long before the surrender of the Sixth Army on the Volga, the regime had been preparing measures for drafting an addi-tional million servicemen into the armed forces, conscripting women into the workforce, and closing all nonessential small shops and businesses.[21] As elsewhere in Greater Germany, most Austrians responded to the mobili-zation orders of 13 January with initial enthusiasm, followed by second thoughts and a division of opinion along lines of class and gender.[22] Accord-ing to a substantial number of intelligence reports from Vorarlberg, Tyrol, and both Upper and Lower Danube, there was strong approval for "comb-ing out" shops and offices for malingerers and draft dodgers, especially since it was felt that these last reserves would break the stalemate on the eastern front. The announcement of shop and restaurant closings also elicited gen-eral support, although proprietors and owners greeted the news with some-thing less than enthusiasm.[23]

Even before Goebbels's "total war" speech of 18 February, it was becom-ing clear that the regime's measures appealed primarily to disaffected em-ployees and industrial workers. While the general impact of the address was "unusually great and generally favorable," its real effect, as Marlis Steinert has shown, was to divert "attention from the Reich's increasingly dangerous foreign situation by exploiting widespread working class resentment of con-tinued evidence of class distinctions."[24] The SD reported from Innsbruck that the "intelligentsia" reacted to the propaganda minister's words with scorn and that Catholic "political opponents" regarded the military situation as hopeless; ordinary people, however, took heart that the powerful and well-heeled might at last have to assume the dangers and burdens of all-out warfare. In Linz the reception was almost the opposite: the middle classes were described as jolted from their delusions of preferential treatment by the Allies, the Catholics were again alerted to the perils of Bolshevism. As for the industrial workers, they were said to have gloated that the "better ranks" might be forced to work in ammunition plants.[25]

Just as in the Altreich, therefore, overall reaction to the propaganda min-ister's mobilization promises was by no means uniform. Among working-class men and women feelings of disappointment and resentment did, however, gradually crystallize against the large number of women who continued to evade employment. In the face of the regime's misogynist pronouncements, German and Austrian women, or more precisely those of childbearing age, actually constituted one of the more favored groups of Greater German society. Ever since the beginning of hostilities military and civilian managers had sought to mobilize them for war production, but even in the wake of Stalingrad Hitler refused to go beyond ordering the mandatory registration of females from ages seventeen to forty-five. While it is true that disproportionately more women went to work in Austria than in the Altreich (28.3 versus 24.8 percent), many of them became receptionists, adopted foster children, or even conceived babies to avoid the conveyor belt. In the tourist areas of the Ostmark and Bavaria, moreover, single women and soldiers' wives could be seen relaxing at health spas or congregating near army bases.[26] The SD in Tyrol wrote: "When people see the many women from all parts of the Reich gussied up in all colors of the rainbow hanging around winter sports centers, they have to view with some suspicion all the talk of mobilizing those who are required to work. It's obvious at first glance that these ladies are hardly munitions workers in need of rest and recuperation."[27]

The growing antagonism to winter tourists in the Alpine regions of Greater Germany reflected not only wartime stress and the social prejudices of the local population; it also mirrored the changing position of Austria in the German war economy. Beginning in 1941, as already seen, the heavy industries founded after the Anschluss went into production and rapidly expanded output. Besides the foundries and rolling mills of the Hermann Göring complex, these included the aluminum refineries at Ranshofen and Salzburg, a ball bearing plant in Steyr, a synthetic fibers plant at Lenzing, oil refineries in Lobau, and the massive Messerschmitt works in Wiener Neustadt. By 1943 Austrian factories had become essential to the German war economy, particularly those producing chemicals, explosives, shells, tanks, assault guns, locomotives, and submarine parts. Further, due to intensified Allied bombing of the industrialized cities of northern and western Germany, specialized manufacturing firms relocated or dispersed to new sites in the Ostmark, especially in remote Alpine valleys of Styria. While it is true that a great many Austrian women managed to avoid onerous war work, thousands of others took jobs in the new industrial enterprises or defense plants. Simultaneously, wives and widows toiled from sunrise to sunset in the countryside, milking cows, tending livestock, harvesting grain. That so many locals—both men and women—should vent their rage at "ladies from town" riding ski lifts or cuddling up to fireplaces at winter resorts is not surprising.[28]

Meanwhile, 1,500 kilometers to the east, Field Marshal Manstein launched a series of counterattacks across the Donets that led in early March to the temporary stabilization of the Russian front. At home, word of these developments brought a sense of relief, even a return of confidence; at the same time, there were sharply differing views regarding the military situation, considerable discontent, and grave concern about the future. In a series of well-differentiated reports the SD in Innsbruck tried to make sense of the kaleidoscopic sentiment. The security agents indicated that the party faithful as well as most workers and employees were again exuding "quiet confidence in victory." In contrast, higher civil servants and factory managers were on the brink of despair, some contending that only a miracle could save the Reich from internal collapse. Among pensioners and retirees there was a terrifying fear of renewed inflation. As for the Catholic rural population, few farmers regarded the war as either winnable or worthwhile. Many of them argued that Britain and the United States had deliberately spared the Ostmark from aerial bombardment, even planning, thanks to the efforts of Otto von Habsburg, to restore Austrian independence.[29]

As the lull in the fighting continued, speculation on the future course of the war intensified. While ordinary people strained to comprehend the situation at the front, many daring to tune in Radio Beromünster or the BBC, they could not decide whether the Red Army might finally be subdued in a summer campaign or whether the war in the East might rage on indefinitely. As was so often the case during the Second World War, the arrival of frontline soldiers on leave raised morale, especially when they boasted that poison gas would finish off Stalin's troops within months. News of an upsurge of U-boat triumphs in the North Atlantic also lifted spirits.[30] On the other hand, once the winter skies started to clear over the Alps, dread of imminent bombing again gripped the population. There was also renewed disquiet at the prospect of housing hundreds of thousands of additional refugees streaming into Austria from the shattered cities of the Ruhr. Rumors spread that requisitions would be made of household silverware and even underclothing. In the garrison town of Krumau in Upper Danube several hundred officers refused to allow refugees near their homes.[31]

Whatever misgivings Austrians had about the future in early 1943, their emotional bond of loyalty to Hitler still remained largely intact. As in most parts of Greater Germany, ordinary people tended to exempt the Führer from criticism, blaming their Italian allies for military reverses or holding party bosses accountable for unpopular wartime restrictions. While there was a good deal of worry about Hitler's health, trust in his leadership remained unshaken; even skeptics considered him "too overburdened" to deal with domestic problems or wartime inequities. Indeed, after a rare public appearance by Hitler in Linz on a Sunday in April 1943, morale soared. "If the Führer has time to visit Linz," it was said, "things can no longer be so bad."[32]

THE REVIVAL OF AUSTRIAN PATRIOTISM

What distinguished popular opinion in the Alpine and Danubian Regions of Greater Germany—as Berlin officially referred to the Ostmark after 1942—was a recrudescence of Austrian feeling and sentiment. We have already seen that a strong sense of regional or particularist identity remained among Catholic villagers and farmers, especially in the Tyrol and Lower Danube, that genuine patriotism motivated monarchist and Communist resistance fighters from the outset, and that Teutophobia prevailed among the grouchy and grumbling Viennese ever since the outbreak of war, if not earlier. Nonetheless, Hitler's defeat at Stalingrad gave rise to popular thought of restoring the state that until just a few years before nobody wanted, or, more precisely, it offered the prospect of reestablishing some form of Austrian autonomy.

At first, people approached the problem from the perspective of wishful thinking, hoping that relatives captured by the Russians would receive better treatment than Reich Germans. Rumors circulated in Linz that Austrians had surrendered wearing distinctive badges and armbands, that Austrian prisoners of war in Britain already enjoyed better food and warmer blankets than "Prussians," and that Churchill intended to unite Austria and Bavaria into a postwar state ruled by Otto von Habsburg. Among middle-class circles, word had it that the Allies were deliberately sparing Austrian cities from aerial bombardment.[33]

Besides wishful thinking, there was also a good deal of self-pity, characterized by an intensification of anti-German feeling. Even in Graz it became common to hear people saying: "Berlin does not understand Austrians. They regard us as enemies, and they make no effort to treat us as friends."[34] Elsewhere, officials reported a rash of anti-Nazi graffiti and in Tyrol an alarming groundswell of Austrian patriotism. According to one remarkable document, many Tyrolean Catholics actually hoped for a collapse of the Reich in the coming summer.[35]

There can be little doubt that Hitler's defeat at Stalingrad gave birth to what the British historian Robert Knight has called a "sense of Austrian otherness" that "could and sometimes did provide an inspiration for resistance."[36] Even so, it is difficult to determine to what extent the new sense of Austrian identity was based on daydreams, discontent, anti-German sentiment, rejection of Nazi ideology, opportunism, or authentic patriotism.

The most likely explanation is that for most people the new feeling was a reaction formation or a natural tendency to fall back on regional loyalties in times of crisis. There is also strong evidence of split-mindedness: a tendency to dream of Austrian independence while still supporting the cause of Greater Germany.[37] At the same time, patriotic sentiment was indisputably developing, or reemerging, in Tyrol—the rugged Alpine province where an indigenous uprising would actually liberate Innsbruck at the end of the war. Still, it needs to be kept in mind that strong particularist sentiment was also bubbling up in parts of Swabia and Bavaria, especially in Catholic conservative areas where, in the words of Professor Kershaw, "Nazism had only partially penetrated the subculture."[38]

Many Austrians still continued to exempt Hitler from criticism and to keep faith in his leadership. In Tyrol-Vorarlberg membership in the Nazi Party even kept rising well into May 1943.[39] While it is indisputable that "malicious practices," illegal broadsides, and resistance activities multiplied both in number and scope, these were by no means confined to the Ostmark. Furthermore, as the public prosecutor in Graz took pains to emphasize, much of the upsurge of blue-collar political crime was among foreign workers.[40] Unlike the Altreich there were no overt acts of public courage such as those displayed by the heroic White Rose Society in Munich.[41] Finally, whatever feelings of solidarity Austrians may have felt were not accompanied by pacifist sentiment or by a commitment to democratic ideals. The attitudes of the people in Austria, suggested the American OSS, comprised a blend of nostalgia for the monarchy, a longing for peace, confusion, and "deep distrust regarding the intentions of the Allies."[42]

SPRINGTIME STUPOR

Generally speaking, Austrian sentiment still did not vary much from the German norm, although Hitler's popularity evidently remained stronger in the Ostmark than in other parts of his Reich—especially those crumbling under Allied bombs.[43] For a period of several months the general mood continued in a semistupor, being characterized as "calm," "reliable," "generally confident," but also "war-weary," "depressed and listless." Even when Manstein's troops recaptured Kharkov, there was comparatively little discussion of the fighting in the East. While some Austrians speculated that the Red Army might at last be crushed in one final offensive, others refrained from comment or expressed doubts that the war could be ended at all—let alone won.[44]

Once again, people reverted to worrying about wartime shortages. There was both surprise and outrage at the announcement of a significant cut in the tobacco ration, partly because smokers claimed that cigarettes were indispensable in stilling hunger, partly because European tobacco production remained firmly under German control. With Hitler's failure to secure Europe's Ukrainian "bread basket," a major goal of the Stalingrad campaign, rumors started spreading of a reduction in food allotments. When the meat ration was slashed in mid-May, the reaction was one of "deep depression." There was also criticism of Göring for failure to fulfill blustering promises made some months before at the Harvest Thanksgiving Festival; scarcely a word, however, was reported hostile to the Führer.[45]

Meanwhile, ordinary people focused their attention on the battlefields of North Africa. While announcement of the loss of Tunisia on 13 May was not unexpected, it produced a downward slide in morale, leading to pessimism, apathy, and serious doubts about the outcome of the war. As elsewhere in the Reich, the surrender of the Afrika Korps gave rise to widespread condemnation of Italy, not only because of the lackluster performance of Mussolini's forces and the reemergence of traditional feelings of enmity. Just as fundamental was the sudden realization of the threat to the Reich's borders by an Allied invasion of the peninsula, an Italian surrender, or both. With word of thousands of tons of British bombs again falling on the great cities of western and northern Germany, Bavarians and Austrians grasped that they were no longer immune to attack from the skies. As a sign of the schizophrenic fear and confusion of the moment, the SD in Innsbruck reported that while most Tyroleans spoke positively of the Western Allies, arguing that London and Washington were deliberately sparing Austrian towns from aerial bombardment, many of the same people were applauding proposals to string up captured British and American flyers.[46]

SOCIAL CHANGES

As elsewhere in Greater Germany, the springtime stupor was accompanied by a sharp rise in political offenses such as "malicious practices," defeatism, listening to foreign radio broadcasts, and black-marketeering.[47] While instances of ordinary crime remained low, there were perceptible changes in social and sexual behavior as well. These included a sharp increase in the purchase of birth-control devices, the breakup of innumerable marriages, and an upsurge of "sexual license" between lonely housewives and prisoners of war.[48] On 1 July the public prosecutor in Vienna reported that although morale in his district could not be characterized as "poor," both he and the Gestapo had observed "a certain mood of apathy."[49]

There was also concern with the large number of foreigners in the city, many of whom could be seen night and day congregating in public places, dealing on the black market, and making advances to local women. The authorities were particularly alarmed by a sharp rise of "illicit intercourse" between Viennese women and French POWs: "The culprits are not just girls but primarily women who engage quite frequently in sexual relationships with prisoners of war." Worse, "even wives of active-duty soldiers do not hesitate to cultivate intimate relations with prisoners of war."[50]

Among the young, there was also alienation from the Nazi Party and its associations. As in the cities of western and northern Germany, the SD reported a rise in juvenile crime and—in Vienna and Hollabrunn—a growing number of scuffles between teenage gangs of Schlurfs and the Hitler Youth.[51] Composed largely of working-class boys, the Schlurfs had been meeting in the Prater and hanging around street corners since around the time of the Anschluss. After the beginning of the war, they attracted a number of apprentices, armament workers, and other young men who had been passed over for military service, including some "misfits" and cripples. Like other adolescent groups in Greater Germany, the Schlurfs formed a subculture that opposed the "regimented leisure"[52] of the Hitler Youth and the League of German Girls. Otherwise apolitical in outlook, the Schlurfs sought to imitate the casual elegance of Hollywood, wearing flashy, double-breasted, pin-striped suits, growing manes of neatly combed, slicked-down ducktails, and affecting the sort of cool detachment later associated with the postwar actor James Dean. While some Schlurfs became gamblers, hustled on the black market, or settled down as pimps, most spent their spare time lingering in bars, listening to jazz records, and dancing "hot numbers" with their girlfriends—the "Schlurf Kittens."[53]

Unlike cliques of working-class youth in the Altreich whose members usually spent weekends hitchhiking or tramping through the countryside, the Schlurfs gravitated to the Prater where they kept their distance from underground Socialist or Communist groups, strummed guitars, and aped the manners of Viennese dandies. They directed their hostility against the Hitler Youth, whose formations they ridiculed for compulsory drills, senseless discipline, and mindless conformity.

Until 1941 the Schlurfs managed to stay out of trouble with the authorities. But as wartime conditions became more politicized, they found themselves targets in a crackdown of dissident youth groups ordered by Himmler. In the process, troops of Hitler Youth, sometimes supported by detachments of police, SA, or NSKK, swept into adolescent dives and hangouts, beating up Schlurfs and shearing their curly locks. For their part, the Schlurfs retaliated in kind or deliberately disrupted performances of Nazi folk music by jeering and making noisy remarks. In August 1942 they appeared in large numbers at a Hitler Youth band concert in the famous Sofiensaal in the Third District. After the first numbers, they and their girlfriends raucously made for the doors or remained seated, loudly interrupting choral works with laughter or endless applause.[54]

Over the course of the following year clashes between Schlurfs and Hitler Youth escalated sharply. There were rumbles in Wiener-Atzgerdorf, muggings in the Prater, and stone-throwing attacks on various Hitler Youth neighborhood headquarters. In late summer 1943 the Gestapo reported an assault on the Hitler Youth dormitory in Wiener Neudorf in which drums were smashed and pictures of both Hitler and Schirach torn to ribbons.[55] Not surprisingly, there were also incidents of Schlurfs becoming involved with randy wives and widows. According to one salacious report from the Nazi Local Group in Wienerfeld: "While the husband L.G. is serving on active duty in the field, his wife receives visits of young lads nearly every day. They are usually five or six Schlurfs, who stay through the day and well into the night. They make noise and howl, play the gramophone, dance or play cards until two in the morning. From her window the neighbor, Mrs. R., was able to see Mrs. G. sitting stark naked on the toilet with the door wide open— even though a number of Schlurfs were in her apartment at the time."[56]

REFUGEE PROBLEMS

In the meantime, Hitler's forces were struggling to keep his enemies at bay. While the military situation had stabilized in the months after El Alamein and Stalingrad, the summer of 1943 brought a series of stunning setbacks that included the loss of Sicily, defeat by the Red Army at Kursk, and the overthrow of Mussolini in Italy. On the home front, word of these reverses weighed heavily on morale; even worse, Allied bombers unleashed a rain of incendiaries and explosives over an arc of great cities from the Ruhr to Hamburg, igniting unprecedented firestorms and taking thousands of civilian lives. By all accounts, demoralization was enormous, the prestige of the Nazi regime at an all-time low.[57]

In the Ostmark the currents of sentiment continued to run parallel to those in the Altreich—albeit through different channels and tributaries. During the news blackout following the loss of Tunisia there was renewed speculation about both the war's duration and a Habsburg restoration. At the same time, the SD reported a positive response to radio speeches by Goebbels and Armaments Minister Albert Speer, especially among factory workers. Still, there was a gnawing consensus that the end of the war was nowhere in sight. People appeared war-weary, depressed, and disillusioned: many eagerly embraced rumors of secret Allied-Axis negotiations in Spain;

others expressed confidence that the construction of an eastern wall would put an end to the slaughter in Russia. Toward the end of June, as the weather in the Alps turned warm and pleasant, the rural population streamed to their fields. According to the authorities, they evinced little outward interest in military or political developments. Only here and there were farmers overheard muttering about the "insolent and presumptuous" behavior of their foreign help, most notably after the murder of a cowherd by a Polish farmhand near Schwaz.[58]

Announcement of the Allied capture of the Italian islands of Pantelleria and Lampedusa in mid-June provoked some discussion in Austria, but it was the intensifying air war over western and northern Germany that aroused the most concern. There was little information available in the official media, but people living in Vorarlberg, Tyrol, and other areas overrun by German refugees and tourists were getting daily earfuls of horror stories from their guests. Curiously, the composite reaction to tales of suffering and agony under Allied bombs was not so much one of sympathy—although individual hearts did go out to many—as one of anxiety, dread, and aversion to the Germans themselves. Just as Hitler's insistence on keeping Vienna on a tight leash had aroused indignation in the Danubian metropolis, preserving a strong sense of Austrian consciousness, so did the stream of thousands of desperate refugees into the "air raid shelter of the Reich" stir resentment of "Prussian" carpetbaggers. While there is little evidence of a groundswell of opinion against the Anschluss—except among traditional Catholic conservatives—local resentment focused more and more on kith and kin in the Altreich.[59]

On 5 July the SD in Innsbruck reported that the entire populace of Tyrol and Vorarlberg had been seized by a *grande peur* of imminent air attack, a fear not surprising in light of stepped-up civil defense measures, including the compulsory cleaning of attics, the stockpiling of sandbags and fire extinguishers, and the intensification of blackouts. Popular conviction had it, the security men continued, that while Anglo-American bombers had heretofore spared the Ostmark from assault, the arrival of a critical mass of Reich German refugees now made it a prime target. A week later the population was still on edge: many were outraged that the Cologne Cathedral had been hit by the Royal Air Force; others were both puzzled and frustrated that Hitler had not struck back, some of them even proposing the use of poison gas. With thousands of new refugees streaming into the province from Cologne and Wuppertal, farmers complained that they would soon be eaten out of house and home.[60]

By the end of the month, the refugee problem was becoming acute.

Despite Gauleiter Hofer's official words of welcome, few Tyroleans stood ready to lend a helping hand. Instead, they chided the evacuees for occupying valuable hotel space, for improper behavior, or for petty theft. There was also anger with the Nazi welfare organization (NSV) for organizational failures and improvisatorial shortcomings, especially those connected with seemingly arbitrary requisitions of rooms and housing. A report from Bregenz indicated that local residents refused accommodations for homeless or displaced "Prussians." Another from Scharnitz, near Seefeld, asserted that innkeepers were shunning refugees, leaving beds unmade, or neglecting to provide clean sheets and towels. In Kufstein a hotel manager slammed the door on a bombed-out mother and child despite a previous agreement to provide room and board. There were also reports of misdirected trains and ugly confrontations in NSV offices.[61]

The cultural clashes between evacuees and hosts were by no means one-sided. In Tyrol there were reports of Rhenish housewives making unreasonable demands or insulting remarks, in some cases even denouncing their household proprietors to the Gestapo. Furthermore, squabbles erupted over the use of irons, sewing machines, or other family appliances—not to mention bathing facilities. In Vienna traditional animosities were exacerbated by reports of theft and churlish behavior by German refugees. In one instance, a Rhenish housewife blithely cut up dresses from her landlord's open chests to fashion clothing for her own children; in another, a German couple shouted at their Nazi hosts when admonished to look after the new furniture and rooms put at their disposal. "Who has taken care of my furniture in the Rhineland?" beseeched the wife. "No one did, and everything has been destroyed."[62]

THE OVERTHROW OF MUSSOLINI

In the midst of this high-tension summer of confusion, worry, and recrimination came word of Mussolini's deposition by his own Fascist Grand Council; according to the security organs, the news struck the public "like a thunderbolt."[63] Grass-roots shock and dismay were notably intense in Austria, especially in Tyrol where people feared the imminent spread of fighting to the Alps. According to the local branch of the SD, "In this district the shock effect of the radio announcement of Mussolini's resignation (!) is conspicuous to an unusual degree, since local people still vividly recall Italy's treachery in 1915."[64]

Nevertheless, overall reaction was by no means uniform. In "hostile circles," Mussolini's overthrow "unleashed great rejoicing" as the "beginning of the end," the SD reported. There was "lively agitation" among

Catholic conservatives including calls for Hitler to step down. In a good many shops in Bregenz and Innsbruck customers made "spiteful outbursts against the leadership"; in a railwaymen's neighborhood green-chalked graffiti appeared with the words: "Tyroleans! Look up: 1943 = 1918!" The collapse of Italian fascism also stirred the hopes of both South Tyrolean refugees and local veterans of World War I. Survivors of the fighting in the Dolomites talked loudly of settling scores with their ancient foes; some even blustered of rejoining the colors.[65]

By early August contradictory feelings were swirling at high tide. With trainloads of troops and equipment flowing through the Brenner Pass, ordinary Austrians vented their frustrations and rage on the Italian people, deriding them as *Katzelmacher* or *Tschingeler* and loudly demanding military reprisals. At the same time, traditional conservatives stepped up their claims that the protective hand of Otto von Habsburg was still shielding the Ostmark from aerial bombardment: "Everyone has to realize," the argument ran, "that it is no coincidence that not one bomb has fallen on Austria. Were it not for him (Otto), there would be terrible devastation here just as in Hamburg, Essen and other German cities."[66] Just how effective this sort of reasoning was in appealing to people's sentiments, especially in "awakening" a sense of Austrian patriotism—as postwar historians would later claim—is difficult to say. What the evidence does reveal is that Mussolini's overthrow, much more than Hitler's defeat at Stalingrad, sent a shudder through Austrian hearts precisely because it raised the prospect of being blasted or burned to death by Allied bombs. Caught in a terrifying trap, people blamed everyone but themselves.

Certainly, they did not resist heaping contumely on their German blood brothers. The reason was plain. Visitors from the Reich tended to regard the Ostmark as a Nazi Disneyland, an Alpine paradise of holiday resorts, soothing music, and good food. The problem was that few Austrians thought that they were living in a theme park, especially in wartime. According to the SD, there were numerous accusations of black-marketeering, theft, and arrogant behavior. There were also ugly incidents. In Innsbruck a "lady from the Altreich with lacquered fingernails and a purple mouth" unwittingly provoked a row when she flounced into a shop with a fox terrier to claim that ration stamps were unnecessary for purchases in the Ostmark. Many Austrians even lashed out at German tourists for gathering wild berries in the Alps. Local people also spread rumors that Berlin intended to turn Tyrol into a Prussian province and to resettle the indigenous population in Poland or the Ukraine. According to the security organs, the overwhelming majority of the Tyrolean population wanted the Reich Germans to clear out as soon as possible.[67]

And yet few people seem to have broken with the war effort or the military leadership. To be sure, most Austrians yearned for an end to the conflict; many of them openly expressed disillusionment with certain aspects of the Anschluss system, most notably with the obtrusive behavior of party activists and Reich German carpetbaggers. While the attitudes of specific groups are difficult to discern, the surviving documentation nonetheless suggests strong consensual support for the German armed forces. On 16 August the SD in Innsbruck wrote that civilian morale was once more "assured and composed." There was a renewed sense of popular confidence in the leadership, especially among men in overalls, many of whom looked forward to punitive action against Italy. As one worker put it, "This time the welsher can't toy with us as in 1918; this time he'll have to dance to our tune." The popular mood was also buoyed by the sight of massive German reinforcements passing through western Austria on their way to Italy. From Innsbruck the SD wrote that "the morale of these troops, their appearance, and their outstanding equipment—especially that of numerous contingents of SS—have not failed, according to various reports, to have a positive impact on the indigenous population."[68]

Meanwhile, early in the afternoon of 13 August, sixty-one B-24 Liberators of the U.S. Ninth Air Force suddenly appeared in the skies over Wiener Neustadt, a small manufacturing city south of Vienna that had once forged arms for the Habsburgs and now produced fighter aircraft, locomotives, and rocket engines for Hitler's Reich. In only a few short minutes the American bombers laid down a carpet that destroyed a third of the aircraft assembly line and ended production for a month. Although comparatively few civilians lost their lives, the bombing raid unleashed a general panic that sent hundreds of foreign workers scurrying into the countryside and thereafter led to a general exodus of city dwellers to outlying areas. The demoralization caused by the attack was so great that the municipal police director characterized the mood as "restless and fearful." Worse, he continued, "popular trust and faith in final victory have been deeply shaken."[69]

By the end of August morale in both the Ostmark and the Altreich was again plummeting to new depths. SD opinion surveys throughout Tyrol and Lower Danube indicated "deep depression" and renewed longing for peace. Days before the fourth anniversary of the beginning of the war, a bulletin announcing the loss of Kharkov to the Red Army sent a shock wave through Greater Germany. Those who had been following the news suddenly shifted their attention to the eastern front, where the unreported defeat at Kursk had forced a retreat to the Dnieper River. While few Germans or Austrians had any idea of the magnitude of the disaster sustained by the Wehrmacht, the danger of losing the food and mineral resources of the Ukraine became all too apparent. Particularly demoralizing were the growing streams of Allied bombers in the skies over the Lower Inn Valley. On moonlit nights, the SD reported, the woods and forests surrounding Innsbruck were filled with campers seeking safety from Allied air attack. In the Upper Inn, however, the staunchly Catholic population continued to insist that Austria would be spared attack, most locals arguing that the Wiener Neustadt raid had been a mistake.[70]

In the crisis atmosphere popular disaffection with the Nazi regime began to spread throughout the Ostmark. Surviving opinion surveys suggest that initial criticism may have been more overt among German refugees and tourists than their Austrian hosts, but SD branch offices reported an upsurge of local radio listeners tuning into the Swiss station in Beromünster. There was also a rash of graffiti calling for a "Christian, God-fearing Austria" as well as daubed signs of "Hail Austria!" Indeed, Hitler was no longer immune to reproach: one farmer blurted out that "the Führer should finally put an end to it"; a workingman that "there can be no peace with the Führer; someone else should take over the government, preferably an emperor." Worry and dissatisfaction also prevailed among party activists. As in the Altreich, party badges were seldom worn, the "German greeting" scarcely used. On the first day of the school year in Hohenems, for example, the village principal issued written instructions to his faculty mandating the Hitler salute and prohibiting the traditional greeting of "Grüss Gott!"[71]

THE DESERTION OF ITALY

Early in the evening of 9 September, German radio announced the landing of the American Fifth Army at Salerno, south of Naples. Although long anticipated, the news came as another shock. Twenty-four hours later Hitler broadcast a brief address. In it he paid tribute to Mussolini, castigated the "reactionary elements" around the Duce's successor, Marshal Badoglio, and insinuated that neither the Allied invasion nor Rome's change of sides had come as a surprise. By all accounts, the Führer's speech lifted spirits enormously, especially as it was followed by an army bulletin announcing the disarmament of Italian units in Italy, Albania, Croatia, Greece, and France. Two days later there was even more startling news: SS commandos under Otto Skorzeny had rescued Mussolini in the Apennines.[72]

As usual, Goebbels accurately assessed the popular mood: "The news of our heavy blows against Italy—especially the capture of Rome—as well as the Führer's speech acted like champagne on the people. It was almost as though we were on a great and successful advance comparable to that of

1939 and 1940."[73] The Main Office of the Security Service added: "The way in which the situation, initially regarded as critical, was mastered by the German command is seen as a sign of German resourcefulness and strength and of the Wehrmacht's unimpaired striking force."[74]

The immense sense of relief, not unlike that experienced by the British after the fall of France, was by no means confined to the German people. Indeed, the dramatic upturn of morale seems to have been particularly pronounced in the Ostmark, where detestation of Italy was far more immediate and atavistic. Ordinary Austrians responded to Hitler's speech with "satisfaction, joy, and even enthusiasm"; after listening to the confident voice of their native son, many people were said to be gathering hope of meting out vengeance, first to the Italians for their treachery, and second to the British for their bombing raids. To be sure, some hard-core Catholic conservatives and Communists still looked forward to a Nazi collapse, but even in "hostile circles," the SD wrote, there was strong approval of settling accounts with Italy and recovering South Tyrol for the Germanic family. So intense was popular feeling that in Innsbruck crowds of Italian residents were reported begging protection or seeking sanctuary within the church.[75]

As might be expected, the Nazi authorities were not long in exploiting the upswing in the popular mood, especially the visceral urge for revenge against Italy. The military bulletin disclosing Badoglio's surrender to the Allies, with its emphasis on betrayal and perfidy, closely paralleled the language of Emperor Francis Joseph's somber proclamation of May 1915 that condemned Italy for its desertion of the Triple Alliance and declaration of war on the Central Powers. On 12 September Hitler invited two Austrian Gauleiter to his headquarters, Friedrich Rainer of Carinthia and Franz Hofer of Tyrol. Over luncheon the dictator awarded his satraps large chunks of Italian territory, including South Tyrol. While care was taken to avoid de jure annexation in deference to Mussolini, Hofer's appointment as supreme commissioner of the Alpine Foreland Operational Zone clearly showed that the Reich's frontiers were intended to extend beyond Trent and Bozen.[76]

Renewed confidence in both Hitler and the war effort prevailed, for the most part, throughout the autumn; it was bolstered by Luftwaffe successes over the Reich and increased U-boat victories in the Atlantic. Simultaneously, ordinary people continued to harbor feelings of uncertainty, doubt, and apprehension. On 1 October a haphazard American raid on Feldkirch took the lives of 171 servicemen and civilians, leaving townspeople "moaning, groaning, and wailing" in the streets. Worrisome remarks by soldiers on leave from the eastern front further troubled spirits and stirred trepidation. Over the years frontline troops had played a highly visible role in stabilizing home front morale. Now they spoke of heavy losses, even of a massive retreat stretching from Leningrad to the Crimea. Despite official characterization of the withdrawal as "strategic maneuvering," servicemen convalescing in the Alps did not hesitate to call it a rout. In the Ostmark, especially in Tyrol, these developments provoked distress, even alarm. In the many households with fathers, brothers, or sons stationed in the Crimea or north of Lake Ladoga, the anxiety was acute. According to the SD, there was also fear of losing the foodstuffs of the Ukraine.[77]

Toward the end of October morale again began to flag. Even though Field Marshal Kesselring had brought the Allied advance in Italy to a standstill along the rugged line of the Garigliano and Rapido Rivers, south of Rome, news from the eastern front weighed heavily on people's minds, especially the profusion of notices of local soldiers killed in action.[78] In Linz the SD noted that radio listeners anticipated daily military bulletins with dread and apprehension, expressing relief "if the situation has not deteriorated."[79] No doubt, as Earl R. Beck has observed, "the accounts of the growing brutality of the war in the East tended to add more than propagandist fervor to the fear of Bolshevism."[80] That both casualties and the duration of the conflict already exceeded those of the First World War also did not go unnoticed, especially among veterans of the Habsburg army.[81]

Officials and security agents throughout Tyrol and Lower Danube thus increasingly characterized popular sentiment as "reserved," "depressed," or downright "pessimistic." While Allied air activity had almost ceased, the obvious gaps in the Reich's early warning system, the stepped-up construction of shelters, and the installation of antiaircraft batteries all combined to keep people nervous, jittery, and worried. As in the Altreich, there was widespread desire for vengeance against Britain, but also skepticism that effective retaliation was even possible.[82] From Innsbruck the SD discreetly suggested that even Hitler's credibility was at stake: "There is constant criticism of leading personalities, who for months have promised a counterstrike that has not yet taken place."[83]

As the skies darkened over Central Europe in late 1943, the general sense of pessimism pervading Greater Germany was accentuated by a return of defeatism and a longing for peace almost at any price. In the Ostmark the sense of desperation was accompanied by acute shortages of footwear, clothing, kitchen utensils, stoves, and, for the first time in well over a year, fruits, vegetables, and even potatoes.[84] From Bregenz the SD wrote that the war had so polarized opinion that the Anschluss itself was being called into question: "While only one part of the populace is for immediate peace, the other is uneasy about the future, with the result that we dare not stop waging war, as surrender would mean the end of the German nation."[85] In Neunkirchen, south of Vienna, the county executive put the matter more bluntly: "It must be stated with deep regret that the Greater German idea, the idea of the unity of all tribes of the German people, was much stronger and keener in the years before the Anschluss than today."[86]

It was at this point, on the afternoon of 8 November, that Hitler seized the rostrum of the annual meeting of the Old Guard in Munich to deliver a radio address. In it he reviewed the military situation and devoted considerable attention to the home front, especially to the sacrifices of women and children. Invoking the aid of the Almighty, he anointed the bombed-out victims of Allied air power the "avant-guard of revenge." He also emphasized that with hundreds of thousands of men falling in battle, he would not hesitate "sending several hundred criminals at home to their deaths without further ado."[87]

The effect of this speech, all authorities concur, was electric. Broadcast at 8:15 P.M. to the nation, it resuscitated morale and restored confidence, especially among the party faithful.[88] For the most part, the address had much the same impact in Austria as elsewhere in Greater Germany: it gave heart to the general population and encouraged Hitler's most devoted followers to affirm their support of the Führer. According to surviving opinion surveys, there were few, if any, negative remarks—a reflection, no doubt, of the "extensive fear of denunciation for critical or defeatist comment."[89] Austrians also appear to have responded more favorably in the Alpine West than in the Danubian East.

From Innsbruck the SD wrote that Hitler had "taken the right time to say the right thing," that his words had "fallen on fruitful ground." Tyroleans were said to be impressed by his "courage and dash," by his "witty manner," by his "confidence in victory." Above all, the security agents emphasized, shirkers and opponents had been thoroughly cowed.[90] In contrast, the authorities in Lower Danube were more circumspect. The county executives in Krems, Zwettl, and St. Pölten reported that the dictator's speech had bolstered morale, reinforced the will to hold out, or made people "more confident." Those in Lilienfeld, Korneuburg, Horn, Amstetten, Oberpullendorf, and Scheibbs, however, made only cursory reference to the talk or passed over it in silence, describing the mood as unchanged, indifferent, or apathetic.[91] On the other hand, officials in Tulln recorded that the local populace placed real stock in the Führer's promise of revenge as they had learned that "rocket artillery of enormous range is at our disposal for retaliation" as well as "unmanned, remote-controlled bomber aircraft."[92]

Months before Hitler's speech, the Nazi regime had been tightening the screws of repression and judicial terror. As early as 1942 the People's Court (Volksgerichtshof) in Berlin was handing out twelve times as many death sentences as in the preceding year. Reflecting both the intensification of the war and the Nazification of the judiciary, the number of Germans condemned for treason, high treason, espionage, sabotage, or undermining morale increased from 102 to 1,192; in the year after Stalingrad the figure rose to 1,662. By early 1944 the Ministry of Justice was including defeatist or anti-Nazi remarks as "deserving of the death penalty."[93]

Whether the number of Austrians persecuted for resistance, sabotage, dissent, noncompliance, or defeatism was proportionately higher than that of their kinsmen in the Altreich—as has been frequently claimed—is by no means clear.[94] What is certain is that by 27 April 1943 some 7,713 men and 473 women were behind bars for political crimes and that within nineteen months the figures climbed to 11,146 and 2,109 respectively.[95] In Vienna, as we have already seen, the year 1943 saw a dramatic rise in sweeps by the Gestapo. According to available statistics, the monthly number of arrests soared from 2,097 in February to 2,656 in March of the following year.[96] This increase of 27 percent would have been substantially higher, Reich prosecutor Ernst Lautz noted in an official report, but for "the fact that there exists insufficient space in the prisons for detainees."[97]

Of those persons taken into custody, however, only a small number were engaged in political resistance or sabotage. The overwhelming majority of them faced charges of insubordination, disruptive behavior, or refusal to work (*Arbeitsniederlegungen*). Furthermore, over 80 percent of the arrests consisted of foreign workers, primarily Soviets, Poles, and other Eastern Europeans. In November 1942 only 62 persons arraigned in Vienna and Lower Danube for work stoppages were native Austrians; between February 1943 and March 1944 the monthly numbers ranged between 48 and 68.[98] Even so, between 1938 and 1945 at least 32,600 Austrian dissenters died in Gestapo jails or concentration camps and 2,700 patriots were executed for treason.[99]

In June 1943 there also took place a sudden and highly visible expansion of Himmler's concentration camp system from its Austrian base at Mauthausen to some forty-nine other sites in the Ostmark. Leased to industry as slave laborers, the subcamp inmates could be seen throughout the country working in fields, digging bunkers, pouring concrete, or clearing rubble. At isolated locations near Redl-Zipf, Ebensee, and Melk, tens of thousands of them were forced to excavate underground factories for Hitler's rocket program. The sight of prisoners marching through towns and villages, as

Gordon J. Horwitz has shown, left an indelible mark on the civilian population. With so many victims dying of accidents, beatings, or sheer exhaustion, nearby residents were literally frightened into silence. A schoolgirl witness recalled decades later, there was "an unwritten law: do not talk, do not ask."[100]

Nazi opinion surveys make little reference to the impact of the intensification of repressive measures on the home front, but there can be no doubt that Gestapo terror both muffled criticism of the regime and contributed to the somber mood engulfing the German and Austrian people in the last third of the Second World War.[101] In the case of Austria, the jarring foreign and domestic developments in the months after Stalingrad produced a confusing intersection of conflicting and contradictory sentiments that cut through communities, families, and even individuals. On the one hand, there were uncontrollable feelings of shock, dismay, and grave anxiety caused, first, by Hitler's defeat on the Volga and, second, by the extension of massive British bombing to the Ruhr and northwest Germany. Gravely concerned about the situation on the eastern front, Austrians shared with their German brethren an intense desire to end the war as soon as possible. For a handful of genuine patriots—almost exclusively Habsburg legitimists and Communists—that meant the destruction of Greater Germany and the resurrection of Austria, either as a small republic or as part of a federation with neighboring Bavaria, a price they were willing to pay. On the other hand, for most people the vision of a settlement was nebulous, vague, or not well thought out. The surviving documentation indicates, for example, that most Austrians wanted to call it quits in Russia but felt it essential to retain control of the Ukraine. Since the Western Allies still remained far away, there was also wishful thinking that the Ostmark might somehow be spared the ravages of aerial bombardment.[102]

Under these conditions of extreme worry and stress, reinforced by awareness of Austria's long history as a great power, it was probably inevitable that many persons vented their frustrations on Reich German outsiders, much as Bavarians had railed against "Prussian pigs" after German unification and East Germans would fume about "Wessies" after Bonn's annexation of the German Democratic Republic. In the case of the Ostmark, strong devolutionary sentiment bubbled to the surface in 1943, especially in Vienna but also in the provinces where traditional xenophobia focused on Reich German tourists or refugees, many of whom were Protestants from big cities. While growing numbers of Austrians wanted the "Piefkes" to clear out, some of them even turning against what they regarded as foreign domination, there is little evidence that a majority desired an end to the Anschluss or, for that matter, to Nazi rule. Even after Stalingrad, the prevailing view (undergirded by official propaganda) was that the breakup of Greater Germany would mean a return to poverty and misery. Besides, as Professor Parkinson has pointed out, traditional Austrian attitudes toward Germans have always been "an amalgam of envy, admiration, subservience, and mild amusement."[103] Just how devoted most Austrians remained to the cause of Greater Germany in late 1943 was revealed by their reaction to the surrender of Italy to the Allies. Instead of welcoming the defeat of Hitler's closest ally, they threw their full support behind their Führer, seeking to mete out vengeance to a hereditary enemy for betraying the Axis cause.

REACTION TO THE MOSCOW DECLARATION

It is not without irony that the Allies drew completely different conclusions about the impact of the Italian surrender on the Austrian people. Aware of growing friction in the Ostmark between Austrians and Germans and believing expatriate tales of widespread resistance and sabotage to the Nazi war effort, Anglo-American intelligence analysts rashly concluded that an Austrian revolt was at hand. In late summer 1943 they formulated a propaganda declaration designed to incite such an insurrection. Emended and approved by London, Washington, and Moscow, the document emerged as the Moscow Declaration of 1 November 1943. In it, the Allies called Austria "the first free country to fall victim to Hitlerite aggression" and promised to reestablish "a free and independent Austria" after the war. Simultaneously, they admonished the country "that she has a responsibility for participation in the war on the side of Hitlerite Germany, and that in the final settlement account will be taken of her contribution to her liberation."[104]

Whether a more forceful call would have inspired Austrians to take up arms against German rule is doubtful. Just three weeks after the publication of the Moscow Declaration, Allied analysts concluded that the "Austrians had apparently failed to take notice of it."[105] This time their assessment of the situation in the Ostmark was more to the point. Simultaneously, a comprehensive report prepared by the SD for Berlin indicated that word of the declaration did touch off some discussion:

> The fact that an independent Austrian state is supposed to be set up again has aroused "old memories" among countrymen. Tied to this is the hope in Vienna, for example, that the city will be spared enemy air attacks, since according to the Moscow interpretation, "Austria" is an occupied country. The impact of the editorial "We Austrian Balkanese" in the *Oberdonauer Zeitung* of 6 November has been propitious in that it has made

clear to readers that only [we in] the Ostmark itself can put an end to the enemy's notion of a restored "Austria."[106]

Whatever the concern of the authorities, there is little evidence to suggest that the Moscow Declaration stimulated Austrian patriotism or indigenous opposition, although it undeniably gave heart to those already engaged in active resistance.[107] From Innsbruck the SD wrote that most Tyroleans regarded the document as an Allied promise to keep their bombers from Austrian skies because of its allusion to Austria as "occupied territory."[108] As early as 17 January 1944, the OSS in Switzerland concluded that "our declaration with regard to an independent Austria has not had any profound effect within the country." The Social Democrats were "not quite certain that they would not prefer to be part of a larger, left-oriented Germany," the Christian Socials "not particularly interested in reverting to an Austria within its post-1919 boundaries."[109]

Several months later an Austrian prisoner of war explained that "the Moscow Declaration was well known insofar as it contained a promise for Austrian independence," but, expressing what may have been a common view, he added, "The fact that the declaration was associated with 'Moscow' stands in the mind of people . . . for Bolshevism, despite the participation of the governments of the United States and Great Britain."[110]

Overall, the impact of the Moscow Declaration was to resuscitate a view that Austria might escape the ravages of war, especially an intensification of Anglo-American bombing. During the winter of 1943–44 what appeared to be a suspension of air attacks was accompanied by a rise of anti-Nazi propaganda, emanating from both the Allies and native resistance groups. By spring, virtually everywhere thousands of pamphlets addressed "To the Austrian People!" were raining down from Allied aircraft.[111]

The response of the Austrian population to the flood of new propaganda appears to have been indifference. Most people showed little inclination to follow the Communist lead and usually approved the execution of Communist "traitors" by Nazi courts;[112] there was also widespread hostility to partisan bands beginning to operate on the borderlands of Carinthia and Styria, though one participant recalled after the war that attitudes actually ranged from "passive to denunciatory."[113] Nor was there much positive response to the appeals of monarchists or Catholic conservatives, for although expressions of sympathy for Otto von Habsburg were reported here and there, the continued support of the church for Hitler's war on the eastern front helped keep the anti-Communist faithful from breaking with the regime.[114]

It does seem that some segments of the population placed stock in Western Allied appeals "To the Austrian People," but the resumption of bombing in late spring 1944 dashed their hopes and aroused deep anger.[115] On 5 June the public prosecutor in Linz wrote that the Allied air attacks came as a "cleansing thunderstorm for 'Austrian-infected minds.' Despite all the pamphlets, the stupid-minded talk that the Ostmark will receive preferential treatment from the enemies of the German people is believed by no one anymore."[116]

Meanwhile, in faraway London, an analyst of the Political Warfare Executive of Special Operations tried to appraise the tepid response of the Austrian people to the Moscow Declaration. Despite limited information on conditions within the Ostmark, he prepared a report that came astonishingly close to penetrating the ambivalent attitudes of the populace.

He began by emphasizing that Nazism was "a native Austrian growth— its most characteristic features, such as anti-Semitism, [with] antecedents in Austrian rather than in German politics." Austrian "local patriotism" was indisputably stronger than Bavarian particularism, but did not constitute "real national feeling." While the Anschluss had lost its popularity, even among the Nazis, "many intelligent Austrians do not believe Austria is capable of independent existence." For that reason the Social Democrats still favored "attachment to a democratic Germany," the Christian Socials union with Bavaria or a Danubian Confederation. Hence "active opposition to the Nazi regime in Austria" was "largely ineffective" and "divided."

"A notable change in the situation since the beginning of 1943," he went on to say, was "an increased volume of evidence of pro-Habsburg feeling. It seems to be widely believed that the Allied policy of distinguishing Austria from Germany and sparing Austria punishment is due to the influence of 'Otto.' " Monarchist sentiment, however, was confined primarily to the rural population of the provinces. The working classes, he concluded, were "almost certainly still bitterly opposed to any Habsburg or Clerical regime."[117]

10 CONQUEST AND COLLAPSE, 1944–1945

Whatever individual Austrians may have thought of the Moscow Declaration, most of the population remained preoccupied with wartime concerns. On 15 December 1943 an American formation of 48 B-17s dropped 126 tons of bombs on Innsbruck, leaving 269 dead, 500 injured, and 1,627 homeless.[1] As the raid occurred without warning, the survivors remained in a state of shock for days. The SD reported fear, nervousness, and anxiety combined with hatred and loathing of the Anglo-Americans, even among "clerical circles." (A parish priest noted, however, that it was the Nazis who were the most nervous.) The party and its auxiliaries, notably the Hitler Youth, were said to have gained recognition for their relief efforts immediately following the attack, but there was also official concern that many clergymen had provided succor to the dying and wounded, even offering unauthorized requiem services for the dead. In contrast, the behavior of foreign workers was considered exemplary: "There were only seven known cases of looting, [each] expiated by immediate hanging." (Also sentenced to death for pilfering was a thirty-four-year-old housewife.) By Christmas, local sentiment had crystallized into an oxymoronic conviction that, although the Germans were to blame for the devastation, Hitler's Luftwaffe should mete out punishment to the British.[2]

WINTER OF GROWING DISCONTENT

On 19 December there was a second air strike against Innsbruck. This time German fighters were up and waiting. In an enormous aerial battle that raged over most of Tyrol and northern Italy, American bombers scored direct hits on the provincial capital's central train station, killing 70 persons. The Allied formations were then diverted to Schwaz, where their bombs caused relatively little damage.[3] In the course of the subsequent winter months there were raids on Klagenfurt (16, 31 January) and Steyr (24 February) as well as tactical strikes against Zell am See (25 February), Graz (25 February, 19 March), and the outskirts of Vienna (17 March). Nevertheless, the notion persisted that Austria was still off limits to Allied bombers. The few raids that did occur tended to be explained away as "mistakes." Nevertheless, the constant drone of B-24s on their way to and from targets in Bavaria undermined both morale and confidence in the leadership of the Reich.[4]

The strongest backing of Hitler and the war effort probably persisted among the three overlapping groups identified by Kershaw in his studies of Bavaria and the Altreich: the younger generation, frontline soldiers, and Nazi activists.[5] As for the rest of the populace, the New Year found a majority of them demoralized and apathetic. The security organs even reported lukewarm response to radio speeches by Hitler. Although ordinary people were reported to have listened carefully to the Führer's words, they expressed disappointment in their lack of substance. The SD in Salzburg, however, recorded alarm at his bloodcurdling declaration that "in this struggle there can be only one victor, and this will be either Germany or Soviet Russia." In raising the specter of defeat, Hitler's "either-or" allusion "deeply disturbed" the populace.[6]

More than dismay attended the dictator's words. Throughout the Austrian lands the authorities reported a growth of defeatist and anti-Hitler outbursts.[7] From Zwettl a Nazi official indicated that residents were susceptible to the arguments of "outside agitators." In Baden leaflets appeared carrying such slogans as "Down with Germany!" "Down with the Lying Big Mouths!" and "Down with Hitler!"[8] From Eisenstadt the county executive wrote that although the populace remained "calm," the loss of Rovno and Luzk to the Red Army had precipitated a sharp decline in morale. "These places are not simply hollow names to veterans of the Great War but battlefields whose distance from major hubs is well known. People are openly saying that the war against Soviet Russia could have been avoided and through misjudgment of military and economic conditions has been frivolously waged."[9]

On 2 April 1944 Allied bombers resumed and intensified their attacks on Austrian targets.[10] The major effect on civilian morale was an abrupt end to wishful thinking about both the Moscow Declaration and the "protective hand" of Otto von Habsburg. As in other parts of Greater Germany, the escalating rain of fire and explosives enabled the Nazis to divert attention from criticism of the regime to renewed hopes of revenge and retaliation. By the spring of 1944, the security organs in Tulln, Gänserndorf, Lilienfeld, Wiener Neustadt, Baden, and Linz were reporting that the public welcomed news of retaliatory raids over Britain, no matter how small. Popular morale was, therefore, higher than the year before. Many people looked forward to the summer with the hope that secret weapons and determined resistance would bring a favorable end to the war.[11]

D-DAY AND "RETALIATION"

Word of the Anglo-American landings in Normandy on D-Day, 6 June 1944, brought a sense of relief that the moment of decision had at last arrived. Announcement ten days later of the first V-1 attacks on London elevated the mood to a level unparalleled in years. Throughout the towns and villages of both Upper and Lower Danube there was a return of confidence, a feeling that the "leadership has done the right thing."[12] The county executive in St. Pölten wrote that "the use of reprisal weapons has fulfilled a pent-up wish. All countrymen are hoping that with these engagements a decisive stage of the war has been reached and that they can count on a speedy conclusion to it."[13]

But not everyone was sanguine. In Vienna and Wiener Neustadt, where air raids were more frequent, people remained "anxious and nervous." Many speculated openly about the duration of the war, even counting on an end to it by September. In Mistelbach, Gänserndorf, and Scheibbs there was fear of the awesome material superiority of the enemy forces.[14] In Eisenstadt, the county executive wrote that the populace was "behaving quietly and earnestly, but is quite unhappy." Depressed by setbacks in France and Soviet Russia, people were "caught up in daily cares and sorrows, quite indifferent to good and bad news. Even the use of V-1 reprisal weapons has not evoked the anticipated response."[15]

The nervous, fluctuating mood in the weeks after D-Day was accompanied by deteriorating material conditions and physical exhaustion. In the countryside, many farmers found themselves in the anomalous position of suddenly having enough cash to pay off long-standing mortgages and debts but being unable to keep up cultivation due to shortages of labor, motor fuels, lubricating oils, and agricultural implements—including scythes and sickles.[16] While rationed food supplies were generally adequate, some wage earners showed signs of malnutrition. From Lilienfeld, near St. Pölten, the county executive reported that workers in heavy industry were approaching the point of exhaustion.[17] In Wiener Neustadt collective stress was so great "that it takes only the slightest incident for men as well as women to lose their nerve" and "burst into tears."[18] Adding to the atmosphere of worry and fear was news of the fall of Cherbourg and the collapse of Army Group Center in the Ukraine.

By mid-July, public spirits had tumbled to a new low. The stygian mood was exacerbated by sight of endless formations of Allied bombers passing overhead through crystalline skies. The Alpine and Danubian branch of the Security Service recorded: "The fact that terrorist fliers can make their way to industrial targets critical to the war effort without interception by German fighters has had an adverse impact on morale and strengthened the feeling that we are exposed to the arbitrary will of the enemy."[19]

Nevertheless, few Austrians showed significant signs of breaking with the Nazi regime. There was no evidence of a "solidarity of opposition,"[20] no indication of "a new national consciousness among a great number of Austrians."[21] Indeed, popular reaction to the brief "liberation" of Vienna in the wake of Count Stauffenberg's unsuccessful attempt to assassinate Hitler on 20 July 1944 revealed that, despite great unhappiness, most Austrians remained loyal to the Greater German Reich.

NIGHT OF THE GENERALS IN THE OSTMARK

By the fifth year of the Second World War well over a million Austrians had served in Hitler's armed forces, 326 of them winning the Knight's Cross and many others rising to command positions, most notably in the SS. While none became a field marshal, 227 earned the crimson stripes of general officers: 147 in the army, 27 in the air force, 9 in the Waffen SS, 20 in Himmler's police, 1 in the Gendarmerie, and 22 in the medical corps or other support branches. There was also a rear admiral. During the conflict Austrian soldiers served in every major theater of operations, particularly in the Balkans. Here the largely Austrian 717th Infantry Division took part in hundreds of antipartisan operations, including the notorious massacres at Kraljevo, Kragujevac, and Kávrita. This was no mere coincidence. Hitler considered Ostmärker the best-qualified soldiers to pacify his southern frontiers and he appointed them to do the job.[22]

That not one Austrian general became involved in the plot to kill Hitler is not without significance. Only one officer of Austrian origin, Lieutenant Colonel Robert Bernardis, himself a disillusioned Nazi, was apprehended and executed for his role in the conspiracy. Nevertheless, the generals' coup came ironically close to success in Vienna. On 20 July officers in the headquarters of the Seventeenth Military District responded to Stauffenberg's orders by arresting the chiefs of the Viennese Gestapo, the SS, and the NSDAP. Some hours later a telephone call from Berlin countermanded the orders and put an end to the putsch. In Salzburg officers on duty at the headquarters of the Eighteenth Military District ignored the conspirators' directives and placed no troops on alert. The next morning the Gestapo began massive arrests of the—largely unwitting—Viennese putschists as well as hundreds of suspected opponents, including former members of parliament, party leaders, ministers, mayors, and civil servants of the First Austrian Republic.[23]

As elsewhere in Greater Germany, most people in Austria reacted to news of the assassination attempt with shock, anger, and dismay. Among all classes of society in Lower Danube there was a feeling of initial horror followed by relief and joy at the Führer's "miraculous" escape.[24] In Vienna, a young army officer was struck by both the oppressive weather and the sense of emotional loyalty to Hitler. "There was much complaining in Vienna," he recalled, "but the belief in the omnipotence, genius, and foresight of the Führer was still at hand."[25] As details of the plot became known, people expressed bewilderment, outrage, and indignation at the betrayal by so many high army officers at a time of military crisis in both West and East. The public prosecutor in Linz wrote that "the perpetrators elicited not the slightest sympathy and were everywhere detested. Remarks that might have approved the assassination attempt were absolutely unknown to me."[26] In Vienna, the prosecutor later noted "the populace expressed its horror at the crimes of 20 July. Until now, citations for approving these events have been issued only rarely."[27]

Generally speaking, the July bomb plot, like the Allied landings in Normandy, had the effect of briefly solidifying popular opinion behind the Nazi regime. On 28 July SS security chief Ernst Kaltenbrunner claimed in a preliminary assessment that the attempt had deepened devotion to Hitler, especially in Innsbruck; despite obvious damage to Germany's international prestige, he wrote, there was also hope that such a "cleansing thunderstorm" would turn the tide on the eastern front.[28] On 22 July some 40,000 Upper Austrians had crowded onto the main square in Linz to demonstrate their loyalty to the Führer; in neighboring Salzburg the turnout was estimated at 20,000. There were also rallies in Innsbruck, on the Schwarzenberg Square in Vienna, and in Gmünd, Amstetten, Oberpullendorf, Melk, and many other towns. According to surviving records, attendance was heavy in all cases.[29]

Morale, however, remained low. Nazi officials reported that "the will to resist can still be found in most circles, but not the slightest doubt exists that it will really be of much use."[30] The once bumptious Maria Czedik recorded that everyone was "so overwhelmed by events that nothing much makes an impression. The radio plays light music, and everything is as it once was— one, three, or ten years ago. And yet, people are sitting on a powder keg, not knowing if at this time tomorrow they'll have a roof over their heads.[31]

With the introduction of the seventy-two-hour workweek, the intensification of Gestapo terror, the acceleration of Allied bombing, and the ominous approach of the Red Army, there was little talk of victory or re-

sistance. The county executive in Eisenstadt wrote that while nearly everyone reacted to "news of the attempt on the Führer and his deliverance with
immense excitement and relief," only 2 percent of the population could be
considered loyal National Socialists. "Faith in the superiority of the highest
military and diplomatic leadership has [largely] vanished," he continued;
"only negative impulses such as fear of disorder and Bolshevism are holding
people together."[32]

UNREST IN VIENNA

Although the events of 20 July 1944 did little to inspire a sense of Austrian
patriotism among ordinary people, the Reich leadership was so alarmed by
reports of deteriorating morale that Ernst Kaltenbrunner made a special
inspection trip in early September to Vienna, Lower and Upper Danube,
and Salzburg. In Vienna he found the mood extremely dejected and "the
bearing of nearly every level of the populace in need of immediate attention." The defeatist attitude in the city, he reported, was "susceptible to all
the news from the Southeast, to all kinds of atrocity propaganda, to certain
'Austrian tendencies,' and naturally to every type of Communist propaganda. Personal impressions in working-class and suburban districts especially at the beginning of work, during shift changes, and at first-aid stations
and similar places are exceedingly unfriendly."[33]

To restore morale Kaltenbrunner recommended ending Reich German
control of the metropolis and entrusting its administration to the Viennese
NSDAP, whose discontent was, after all, responsible for much of the prevailing anti-German sentiment. He found the mood much better in Lower
Danube, though easily "infected" by Vienna, and a "fresh, positive breeze"
blowing in Upper Danube. Best of all was the situation in Salzburg.[34]

Stunned by Kaltenbrunner's account, Hitler's deputy, Martin Bormann,
sent an aid, Helmut Friedrichs, to see for himself. After conferring with
Viennese functionaries and the Gauleiter of Lower Danube, Hugo Jury,
Friedrichs reported that Kaltenbrunner's fears were exaggerated. According
to Jury, the mood was "typically Viennese," mirroring the city's diverse
population and 140,000 foreign workers. While admitting a certain danger
from Slavic elements, he emphasized that the general reaction to recent
bombing raids indicated that the population stood behind the party. To the
extent that dissatisfaction existed, he attributed it to the outcome of the
Aryanization program that had left too many Austrians without sufficient
spoils. Overall, the Gauleiter argued, the Viennese would hold up as other
Germans, especially if the front should draw near to Vienna from the South.
In that event, "the Viennese, workers as well as middle class, will summon

their full strength . . . against Bolshevik troops."[35] In a separate report, the prominent Viennese Nazi Alfred Eduard Frauenfeld conceded that National Socialism had indeed lost much of its popular appeal but added perceptively: "None of these people want to lose the war; they simply see no logical way out of the present situation."[36] Maria Czedik scrawled in her diary: "Desperate mood in Vienna. Pervasive question: When will the Russians be here?"[37]

Although Berlin refused to replace Schirach with an Austrian Nazi, some effort was made to mollify popular opinion by broadening the Viennese City Council in favor of local interests. After his appointment as lord mayor in January 1944, the veteran party militant Hans Blaschke proposed returning a greater share of the municipal government to "native Viennese." He even paid tribute to the Social Democratic achievements of the 1920s. Until the late summer his pleas fell on deaf ears. In the wake of Kaltenbrunner's visit to Vienna, Blaschke was able to purge the City Council of all but two German councillors. Although popular reaction to his reforms is not known, it seems likely that they were perceived as too little, too late.[38]

UNDER THE BOMBS

Meanwhile, American bombers expanded their targets from outlying airfields, railyards, and oil depots to city centers in Vienna, Wiener Neustadt (already severely damaged), Linz, Steyr, Innsbruck, Graz, and Villach. On a single day, 16 October, the Fifteenth Air Force attacked fifteen locations in the Ostmark; thereafter the Allies escalated their raids, destroying hundreds of kilometers of track, blasting whole city blocks, incinerating thousands of civilians. As in the Altreich many months before, the initial reaction was one of shock, defiance, and solidarity—followed by rapid demoralization.[39]

The first attack on Vienna on 10 September took the civilian populace completely by surprise. According to Josef Schöner, those who emerged from shelters and cellars to survey the damage appeared more astonished than dismayed. A few cursed the British; a few broke into tears. Most expressed astonishment that the "capital of a restored Austria" had been subjected to a "terrorist strike." Within days the general sense of confusion gave way to feelings of jittery nervousness and dread. There were rumors of a new assassination attempt against Hitler, apprehensive chatter about the advance of the Red Army, and frightened talk of another raid. Aside from a small clutch of the party faithful, few believed in victory.[40]

By mid-October the popular mood had become even more apathetic and resigned. There were constant air-raid alerts, a deterioration of basic services, and interruptions of every imaginable kind. There were also perceptible changes in dress and behavior: fashionable women abandoned frocks and gowns for jogging clothes or make-shift slacks; men began carrying shaving gear, tobacco, and a change of underwear in their briefcases. As goods disappeared from the shelves of bombed-out stores, a thriving black market developed in the carnival district of the Prater, an illicit operation that persisted well into the postwar period to be filmed as part of the famous movie, *The Third Man*. Indeed, long before the end of the year cigarettes were already replacing Reichsmark as the medium of exchange.[41]

In Salzburg, the author Thomas Bernhard recalled the eerie sensation of dreading aerial bombardment while secretly longing "for the actual experience of an air attack." After the first raid, on 16 October, he and his schoolmates "ran to the station and turned into the Fanny-von-Lehnert Strasse. Here the Co-operative Building had been bombed and many of the employees killed. When we saw the rows of bodies covered by sheets, their bare feet visible on the dusty grass behind the iron railings of the so-called Co-op; and when for the first time we saw the trucks arriving in the Fanny-von-Lehnert-Strasse with enormous consignments of coffins, the sensation suddenly lost all its fascination, forever."[42]

GROWTH OF RESISTANCE

By November 1944, the security organs were reporting near universal defeatism and despair throughout Austria. There was also a striking upsurge of anonymous letters threatening Nazi bosses and, for the first time, real concern about organized resistance, particularly the activities of the Catholic Austrian Freedom Movement.[43]

What sort of active resistance efforts were challenging Nazi rule in Austria? To what extent did they appeal to popular sentiment? In the years following the Anschluss, legitimist and Catholic conservative groups were the most successful in establishing networks for distributing pro-Austrian, anti-Nazi literature, as we have already seen. While appealing to the emotions of disgruntled traditionalists, primarily in Vienna and Tyrol, they failed to develop a unified chain of command and were penetrated by the Gestapo. After the outbreak of war, their leaders were imprisoned or executed, their activists drafted into the armed forces. On the left, the Social Democrats chose to stay out of the fray. Under these circumstances, it was the Communists who provided the most stubborn and consistent resistance to National Socialism: their cadres organized cells in factories and municipal enterprises, printed and distributed illegal leaflets, and undertook acts of sabotage. Contained and nearly crushed by the Gestapo in late 1942–43, the Communists continued the struggle to the bitter end; their appeals, however, generally fell on deaf and hostile ears.[44]

Meanwhile, in the turbulent and confusing months after Stalingrad, a number of older politicians of the First Republic established a bare-bones network dedicated to the reestablishment of Austrian independence. Having exchanged views while hiding or passing through concentration camps, Christian Social and Social Democrat elites buried enough of their differences to agree on future cooperation without, however, organizing a central leadership. Like the members of the Kreisau Circle in Germany, they were interested primarily in postwar planning, specifically an end to the Anschluss and Nazi rule. In the enormous wave of arrests following 20 July 1944 many of them fell prey once again to the Gestapo. At the same time, Hans Sidonious Becker, a former official of the Patriotic Front, succeeded in bringing other disparate groups, including the Communists, into an alliance called O5, standing for Österreich. On 12 December a Provisional Austrian National Committee was founded in Vienna, whose members both coordinated resistance activities with the American OSS and planned to assume portfolios in a postwar Austrian government.[45]

According to surviving documentation from Vienna and Lower Austria, the Nazi power structure reacted to individual acts of sabotage and mushrooming threats to party bosses with considerable foreboding. Still, despite Hitler's fear of domestic unrest or revolt, his Austrian satraps worried more about the impact of oppositional activities on the 320,000 foreign workers in the city than on the Viennese.[46] Did the Nazis also have cause to worry about the Austrian workforce? For half a century it has been left-wing doctrine that they did. According to the prevailing view, Austrian men in overalls were the most steadfast and stubborn opponents of Hitler's regime; even in cases of unintentional hostile activity, their noncompliant behavior has been seen as constituting a form of "functional resistance" to the Anschluss system.[47]

The record of working-class discontent in Austria is certainly well documented, but recent scrutiny of the evidence has called into question the notion of massive opposition. Timothy Kirk, as mentioned earlier, has shown that labor indiscipline did indeed grow exponentially after 1943, but that it was generally random and sporadic. There were many incidents of negligence, insubordination, and sabotage, but they did not represent a threat to the regime. He has also affirmed that while the Communists provided the most stubborn and consistent resistance to Nazism, most of the laboring population remained indifferent or hostile to their activities. Finally, after examining lists of thousands of workers taken into custody by the Gestapo, he has discovered that "the proportion of cases involving native Austrians was very small"—at most only 10 percent of the labor offenses, normally less than 5 percent. In other words, most of those arrested continued to be Poles, Russians, and other Eastern Europeans.[48]

Meanwhile, Allied intelligence analysts on the other side of the lines were trying to determine the success of resistance fighters in appealing to the general population. Based on the interrogations of Austrian prisoners of war and the reports of underground agents, their conclusions tended to be sketchy, imprecise, and, in some instances, wrongheaded. Nonetheless, they constitute the only real contemporaneous evidence available.

The picture that emerges from the fragmentary sources is of a people suffering severe physical and nervous strain but only marginally aware of underground resistance. One captured Viennese student claimed to be conscious of an organization of Social Democrats and Communists "with a membership of no less than 70,000, and with definite plans for seizing power at the appropriate moment,"[49] but another prisoner contended that he "knew nothing about underground movements beyond the point that some existed."[50] Given the increasing hardships imposed by Allied bombing, escalating Gestapo terror, and the full mobilization of the civilian population, most people experienced great difficulty "simply in keeping in touch with each other."[51]

The evidence also suggests confusion distinguishing Allied admonitions from the appeals of indigenous resistance groups. A Swedish observer argued in late October 1944 that if only Moscow and Washington refrained from propaganda a "bloc of Revolutionary Socialists and certain groups of democratic bourgeois would probably gain support among the broad masses and be able to establish a democratic regime."[52]

While this view obviously represented a good deal of wishful thinking, it also reflected something of the turbulence of popular sentiment in late 1944, buffeted as it was by powerful and contradictory emotions of war-weariness, anti-German rage, residual allegiance to Hitler, dread of Russian conquest, and apprehension of the future. By the end of the war, more than 100,000 Austrians would join the ranks of active resisters, in Vienna and Tyrol some of them even taking up arms. Without gainsaying their political and moral achievements, especially for the postwar world, it is important to recall Radomir Luza's observation that after 1943 "the Resistance moved much faster than general public opinion, which still refused to espouse the Resistance's aspirations."[53]

LAST WARTIME WINTER

Whatever dreams or nightmares individual Austrians had about the future of their country, by late 1944 scarcely anyone believed in a German victory. The evidence indicates extreme despondency and despair, especially on the Styrian and Carinthian borderlands where residents were becoming alarmed by escalating partisan raids.[54] Adding to the sense of hopelessness were news of Field Marshal Rommel's death, fear of a Hungarian surrender, and the conscription of all remaining able-bodied men and boys either to fight in the Volkssturm or to begin construction of the so-called southeast wall. According to the SD in Vienna, most women seemed eager for peace at any price, but the great fear of communism was still keeping the population as a whole loyal to the war effort.[55] At mid-December the Viennese SD logged a further decline of morale, indicating that "expressions of war-weariness are becoming louder and louder."[56]

Severely depressed spirits were also reported in Upper Austria. The provincial Court of Appeals in Linz wrote that although the launching of V-2 rockets had elevated morale slightly, "the conviction prevails in wide circles that the war cannot be carried on to the end."[57] With regard to the future, American OSS agents shrewdly guessed that "most of the people in Austria have the fatalistic feeling that it makes very little difference what they themselves do, and that their action will not influence in any way the future status of Austria."[58]

Nevertheless, the Wehrmacht's spectacular Christmas attack in the Ardennes temporarily raised morale along the Danube—just as elsewhere in Greater Germany. According to an SD report of 2 [or 22] January 1945, Hitler's New Year's address aroused popular hope, especially in Vienna where it relieved anxiety about his health—a reaction suggesting that in the face of Soviet invasion many Austrians were still reluctant to end their long affair with the Führer. With the collapse of the German western offensive at the end of January, morale plunged once again to a new low. Nearly all reports indicate that the populace was worried and frightened by the penetration of the Reich's frontiers, by the success of the awesome Soviet offensive toward the Oder, and by the stepped-up bombing of Vienna. News that Breslau, Liegnitz, and the coalfields of Silesia were under threat by the Red Army was especially unnerving.[59]

And yet while opinion prevailed that the war was lost, there was resolve to resist Soviet invasion, especially in the Catholic farming population among many ordinary people who had never favored Hitler or his war. Conditioned by years of anti-Communist propaganda and more recent horror stories from East Prussia, they were terrified by what the Salzburg historian Ernst Hanisch has called a *grande peur* of the East, a dread extending back in historical memory through the Turkish wars to the Hungarian invasions of the Middle Ages.[60]

On 2 February 1945 residents of the wooded Mühlviertel, north of Linz, reacted with fear and trembling to the spectacular escape of 419 Russian officers from nearby Mauthausen. The escapees had hoped to find refuge among locals believed hostile to the Nazi system, but in fanning into the cold and icy countryside they encountered fright, morbid curiosity, or downright hostility. While it is true that three Austrian families living close to the camp took in four escapees, courageously providing shelter until the end of the war, most of the civilian populace looked on in stunned silence as the SS rounded up and shot hundreds of the fugitives. With the mobilization of the Volkssturm and Hitler Youth, local farmers and foresters rushed to join what they called the "Mühlviertel rabbit hunt," behaving with frenzied brutality as they stabbed, shot, or skewered all but a dozen of their prey.[61] Trying after the war to explain the popular response, an Austrian witness recalled, "Many rejoiced in the continuous shooting. A part of the population was scared, and another part was incensed over the criminals who had broken out."[62]

Even as the Allied armies drove further into Greater Germany, sweeping across frozen rivers, obliterating great cities by air or artillery, choking the roads with refugees, the economic distribution system in the Ostmark continued to function remarkably well. Despite severe shortages of fruits, vegetables, salt, and, above all, coal, people still found enough to eat and factories managed to continue production—in the case of the Nibelungen Works in St. Valentin, even manufacturing Panther tanks until the last days of the war. In some localities firewood was sufficient to keep essential enterprises functioning, though in larger towns such as St. Valentin and Amstetten the fuel shortage made it impossible to pasteurize milk. Thanks largely to adequate supplies of rationed food, the mood deteriorated only slightly in February. At the same time, serious criticism of the regime began to build: in Korneuburg the population blamed National Socialism for the war and its disastrous outcome; in Stockerau broadsheets circulated calling for a Free Austria.[63]

In Vienna the coal shortage, escalating bombing, and the ominous approach of the Red Army from the Hungarian plain all severely depressed and worried the population. As late as 22 January, however, SD agents were still claiming that the overall "bearing" was "relatively satisfactory" and that most people remained on the job doing their duty. Word-of-mouth propaganda by a team of fifty soldiers also had some impact countering defeatism.[64] By the end of February the material conditions of everyday life had deteriorated to the point of despair. Streets were choked with dust, debris, and broken glass; public and private toilets were stopped up; gas and electricity barely functioned. Josef Schöner recorded that a good many of his educated friends were hoping for a mass uprising, but glumly added that he detected no willingness whatsoever to take action: "The fear of the state police, SD, and SS is simply too great; people are less actively hostile than tired and resigned."[65]

The White Russian princess Marie Vassiltchikov, who spent the period from 3 January to 1 April in the city as a Red Cross volunteer, found that "the trams (which are the only public transport inside the town that still functions) run apparently only at midday."[66] On 10 February she noted that over 80,000 people were daily crowding into the railroad tunnel below the Türkenschanz Park to escape the bombs: "They start queuing up at 9:00 A.M. and by the time the sirens sound, there is a seething mass milling around the entrance trying to force their way in."[67]

Two weeks later after Sunday mass at St. Stephen's Cathedral, the princess wrote that "the streets are filled with people. Nowadays thousands of Viennese from the suburbs crowd into the center of the town because the ancient catacombs are, reputedly, the safest shelters of all."[68] On 7 March she accepted a dinner invitation in a private dining room in the Hotel Sacher. Amid the rubble and carnage she found "the atmosphere was still antediluvian—waiters in white gloves, pheasants shot personally by our host, champagne in a bucket."[69]

THE COLLAPSE OF NAZI AUSTRIA

By all accounts, it was in February and March that morale in Vienna began to crack as Allied bombers brought entire working-class neighborhoods to the point of insurrection.[70] On 6 March an official of the Seventeenth Military District wrote that "after heavy air raids auxiliary groups of the Wehrmacht and party have been publicly abused and even physically threatened," that "the campaign of antagonism and slander of Reich Germans is constantly increasing," and that among the upper classes and artists "hostile agitation for the 'Free Austria Movement' is particularly active and dangerous."[71] Four days later, the SD reported "real fermentation" among the working classes; in Favoriten, the Ortsgruppenleiter in Kudlichgasse declared that after an air raid he could enter his precinct "only with pistol ready to shoot"; in Absberg, where "there would be shooting if people had weapons," political leaders risked being beaten to death; in Anstalten an enormous crowd of women prevented a Kreisleiter with a drawn pistol from making an arrest; in Erdberg, the scene of massive anti-Semitic riots in 1938, outraged residents hurled epithets at party functionaries calling them "brown dogs," "bloodsuckers," and "shits."[72] Everywhere people said that "they ought to be hanged! These Nazi bandits brought upon us the death of so many men, women, and children. If the Nazis had not come to power, we would still be living in deep peace."[73]

While large numbers of blue-collar workers had broken with the regime, other Austrians—though disillusioned and scared—remained equivocal. As the historian Radomir Luza writes:

> The population was still plagued by fear of the Red Army and the Bolsheviks and of the many unpredictable consequences of foreign occupation and the future of their country. It was a natural reaction of many who at some point had thrown in their lot with the Reich. Thus at the end of February many Viennese still watched hopefully as the fresh well-equipped divisions rolled through the city on their way to the Hungarian front.[74]

Nevertheless, the unrelenting hail of bombs drove even the hopeful into dumb resignation. Every day thousands of women and children streamed to the city's massive flak towers and air-raid shelters, shivering for hours in the cold. At the first sound of the wailing sirens, usually around noon, they and countless others pushed and shoved to gain entry. According to Josef Schöner, the general outlook was completely selfish and mean-spirited: no one bothered to look after the other, each scrambled to save his own skin. Within the unheated bunkers people frequently snapped at each other or speculated about the future. Word of the American seizure of the Rhine bridge at Remagen on 7 March touched off endless discussion. There was also loud and angry condemnation of Guido Schmidt, Schuschnigg's foolhardy state secretary, a figure widely despised as the "Judas of Austria," even by unrepentant Nazis.[75]

On 20 March the Red Army smashed across the Austrian frontier at Koszeg and began driving on Vienna. With defeated SS units streaming through Lower Danube, Heinrich Himmler rushed to the city in an armored train to coordinate its defense with party leaders and military commanders. On Easter Monday, 2 April, Gauleiter Schirach plastered the town with posters, urging women and children to get out; he then proclaimed Vienna a fortress to be defended by four SS divisions, the Volkssturm, and the Hitler Youth. Just before the beginning of the Russian assault, one of his subordinates filed a final report on morale. In it he complained about the disintegrating situation, writing: "I have been deeply shaken by the lack of leadership. If there is no quick change, Vienna will be taken by the Bolsheviks."[76]

Within the beleaguered metropolis Josef Schöner recorded that the populace seemed either apathetic or terrified. There was a widespread wishful thinking that the city might somehow escape the terrible fate of house-to-house combat, that Vienna would not become a "second Breslau" (the Silesian capital ordered to fight to the last man). In contrast to Berlin, the morale of the defending troops appeared slack and dispirited. Schirach's bravado notwithstanding, the population knew that little had been done to prepare the town's defenses. When would the Russians arrive? That was the question on everyone's lips.[77]

The truth was that Soviet troops had already encircled Vienna. On 6 April they reached the municipal outskirts where they met stiff resistance from elements of the Waffen SS. The fighting lasted for nearly a week. On 10 April Russian guardsmen marched the into the heart of the Habsburg capital, an area that had suffered devastation from artillery fire but no hand-to-hand combat. They encountered groups of Viennese gathered in doorways or converging in the streets. As in Budapest the initial contacts were polite, even friendly. As Josef Schöner made his way from the Ringstrasse to the Stiftskasserne, he sensed immense relief; even local Nazis told him that the worst was over.[78]

They were mistaken. By late morning a crowd of Viennese housewives had broken into Herzmansky and Gerngross, two department stores on the Mariahilferstrasse. Joined by foreign workers, they ransacked the shelves and storerooms to make off with stocks of food, shoes, and wearing apparel of every kind; they also took bolts of satin and other fabrics. The following day the local crowds were joined by bands of Russian soldiers. There were also incidents of rape and violence. In Vienna the Anschluss ended as it had begun: in an orgy of spontaneous looting and random theft.[79]

Meanwhile, SS detachments were marching thousands of concentration camp inmates and Hungarian Jews over the backroads of the Salzkammergut and Styria from outlying camps or the Hungarian border to the main SS complex at Mauthausen-Gusen. For a period of four to five weeks ordinary people bore witness to the random slaughter and mass murder of parents and children, clubbed or shot to death before their very eyes. Most of the Austrian bystanders stared in fright and disbelief at the sight of living skeletons moving through their towns and villages. Unable to grasp the horror of the indiscriminate beatings and shootings, many of them reacted with compassion, some even providing bread, potatoes, or water. One young woman even cursed the SS with the words that "Hitler knows nothing about it. He would do away with it immediately."[80]

As the hastily organized retreat moved into the interior, the diminishing SS detachments were reinforced or replaced by local Volkssturm, Hitler Youth, gendarmes, firemen, and Wehrmacht stragglers. Instead of leniency, the new guards kept up the pace of haphazard slaughter, even inviting civilian onlookers to join in the bloodshed. Near Wiener Neudorf, a giggling girlfriend persuaded her beau, an SS Blockführer, to let her pull the trigger, chortling "Bubi, you have already made boom-boom so often, now let girly make boom-boom for once."[81] At Eisenerz, party officials recruited an "alarm detachment" of vigilantes, who on 8 April machine-gunned a column of 200 Jews outside the town. According to postwar testimony, "It was for the men of the company seemingly a truly special joy to be able to seize the weapons."[82]

Although only a minuscule number of Austrian civilians rushed to kill Jews in the last days of the war, there is scant evidence to suggest that popular attitudes toward the "racial enemy" had in any way softened. In 1946, despite the disappearance of Jews from the country and growing awareness of the full details of the Holocaust, at least half of those persons surveyed in the American zone of occupation believed that although "the Nazis had gone too far in the way they dealt with the Jews, something had to be done to place limits on them."[83] In other words, while Austrians may have broken forever with the Anschluss, few of them expressed regrets that the Jews had disappeared from their midst.

In the absence of opinion surveys for the last weeks of the war it is impossible to gauge popular reaction to the violence, bloodshed, and indescribable confusion accompanying the Russian capture of Vienna, the anti-German uprisings in Tyrol and Upper Austria, and the Franco-American conquest of the West. Nor is it clear how people responded to the founding of the Second Austrian Republic. Many still hated the Anglo-Americans; on 4 March a mob of Styrians chased down four American fliers and shot them to death. In Salzburg, some diehards continued to believe in the Führer to the bitter end; as late as 13 March the mother of four children confided to her diary that "the Führer will know in any case what is to be done."[84] Most other people were less sure. In mid-April Dr. Robert Ley, head of the German Labor Front tried to rally the tired and weary men of the Salzburg Volkssturm; although a man of considerable forensic skill, he found his words falling on deaf and despondent ears. Two weeks later Gauleiter Scheel announced Hitler's death. In nearby Schwarzbach a parish chronicler noted, "people don't talk much about it. In light of the Führer cult, who would have thought that possible?"[85]

Meanwhile, Ernst Kaltenbrunner had sent a bizarre telegram to Berlin, providing a last glimpse of attitudes in what was left of the Ostmark. In it, he called attention to the "outstanding cooperation" of the Austrian Gauleiter with the local military commanders. He described the inner resolve or "bearing" of the population near the Czech border as "satisfactory," but he characterized the area south of Mank-Mariazell as "Catholic (schwarz) to hostile," filled with deserters, and in the rugged country near the Styrian frontier threatened by partisans. The clergy he found aloof. In Styria, he continued, the atmosphere was "hardworking and active," even in the face of "somewhat shaky" political and security considerations; in Carinthia the situation was "better"; in Salzburg there was "stable leadership." In Tyrol, however, the mood was simply "wretched."[86]

EPILOGUE

Between 1938 and 1945 the Austrian people experienced a breathtaking period of industrial and social modernization that kindled opportunity, loosened family ties, and weakened the authority of traditional elites. As a laboratory for Hitler's pagan and pseudoscientific theories, Nazi Austria became a site for the realization of visionary projects that ranged from the separation of church and state, to the extermination of social and racial undesirables and the mass production of rocket engines. For those who profited from the redistribution of resources or the new high-performance economy or both, it was an exhilarating experience. For others the Anschluss left a legacy of unbearable emotional and physical suffering: 247,000 soldiers killed or missing in the Second World War; 24,300 civilians destroyed in air raids; 24,203 buildings left in ruins. Even more catastrophic were the losses sustained by the shunned and persecuted: 128,000 Jews banished from their home and country; 32,000 outcasts and dissenters driven to death in Gestapo jails or concentration camps; 65,459 remaining Jews slaughtered in the Holocaust, 2,700 patriots executed for resistance. Overall, more than 372,000 Austrians or 5.6 percent of the population lost their lives under Nazi rule. Nonetheless, a majority of the populace supported the Anschluss system and the German war effort to the end.[1]

On 27 April 1945 a coalition of Socialist, Catholic, and Communist politicians met in Soviet-occupied Vienna to proclaim the Second Austrian Republic. In a brief document they abrogated Nazi Germany's "political, economic, and cultural annexation" and promised to reconstruct society on the basis of liberal democracy and traditional patriotism. Several days later the provisional president, Karl Renner, spoke to the Viennese civil service. The crusty politician defended his support of the Anschluss, regretting only the course it had taken and ruefully adding that "for us nothing remains than to give up the idea of the Anschluss, [though] for many that may be difficult."[2]

Renner's words no doubt reflected the sentiments of many Austrians, who in defeat perceived the Second Republic as the only way to appease the victors and to escape retribution for the crimes of the Nazi era. In September the four-power Allied Control Council met in Vienna and reaffirmed the provisions of the Moscow Declaration. Although no reference was made to the provisional Austrian government, the Viennese cabinet instantly accepted the Allied declaration that Austria was "the first free country to fall victim to Hitlerite aggression." It also agreed on a program of de-Nazification, democratization, and economic reconstruction.[3]

In seeking a judicial confrontation with crimes of the Nazi era the founders of the Second Republic proceeded with real conviction. Numerous atrocities committed in the last days of the war had created a climate of opinion that did not oppose a policy of punishing high-ranking Nazis and extending the hand of conciliation to nominal party members. Between 1945 and 1948 Austrian tribunals tried and convicted 10,694 persons for war crimes (usually committed on Austrian soil) and sentenced 43 to death. During the same period the government also passed legislation imposing penalties that ranged from loss of voting rights to job dismissals, fines, and compulsory labor.[4]

As in occupied Germany, however, it did not take long for de-Nazification measures to arouse resentment, especially in the American zone of occupation in Salzburg and Upper Austria. Here the attempt of the U.S. military government to compile dossiers on every member of the Nazi Party and its affiliated associations created a bureaucratic nightmare that permitted major offenders to escape prosecution and led to the conviction of fellow travelers. The result was a wave of sympathy for nominal party members, even among non-Nazis. Where there had once been a "community of fate" there now stood a "community of suffering."[5]

Even without American bungling, it is difficult to see how the Austrian government could have made a more successful effort to confront the horrors of the Nazi past. Stunned by the realization that 600,000 registered Nazis and their dependents made up one-third of the population, the founders of the Second Republic changed course. The "vast majority" of Hitler's followers, they now argued, were victims, "victims of economic, social, or even personal coercion."[6] Renner and his associates clearly wanted to eradicate Nazism in Austria, but like Konrad Adenauer in West Germany they were forced to conclude that economic reconstruction and social integration required the support of "harmless followers and soldiers who believed that they were doing their duty."[7] Haunted by the memory of the civil strife that had destroyed the First Republic, the Viennese leaders had no choice but to "create a fiction of history that bore little relation to the historical truth."[8]

That a majority of Austrians were ready to accept this official version of the recent past became evident within a matter of months. On 1 June 1945

Gertrude Schneider arrived in Vienna with her mother and sister from Auschwitz to find the local populace consumed by self-pity and amnesia. "There was no joy in those who saw us once again," she later recalled.[9] Within two years, however, returning refugees were astonished to discover that the Alpine Republic had suddenly become chic. "Having mentally mislaid the Hitler years," George Clare observed in 1947, most people had "filled the void with Austrian patriotism."[10]

This dichotomous memory of the Nazi past did not diverge along political lines, as it did in divided Germany. Instead, the Austrian government reinforced the myth of collective suffering by publishing the *Red-White-Red Book*, a collection of carefully selected documents designed to convince the Allies of patriotic hostility to the Anschluss regime. The thrust of the collation was that Germany had annexed Austria against the will of its people, exploited the land as a colonial territory, and provoked massive resistance and sabotage. A later publication went so far as to contend that 70 percent of the populace was imbued with a "fanatical will to resist."[11]

In the frigid winter of 1947 few observers would be prepared to dispute the official view of Austria as a "nation of victims." Numbed by shortages of food and fuel, a currency crisis, and the failure of the Allies to agree on a state treaty, most people saw no end to their tribulations. In response, the Austrian government formulated a package of multiple strategies that proved remarkably successful both in restoring public confidence and in overcoming the domestic and foreign hazards of the early cold war.

At the heart of the package was the decision to participate in the Marshall Plan. The guarantee of American capital made it possible to stave off economic collapse, to stabilize the currency, and to expand the Nazi program of industrial modernization. It also provided the impetus for the coalition government to purge the cabinet of Communist ministers and to accelerate the reintegration of Hitler's former followers into society. In practical terms this meant extending the penumbra of "victimization" to civilian bystanders, to returning war veterans, and to rank-and-file party members. Once a general amnesty in June 1948 restored voting rights to all but a handful of autochthonous Nazis, the leaders of the two major political parties, the ÖVP and the SPÖ, launched an all out campaign to win their support.[12]

Ultimately, the odd confluence of the Moscow Declaration and the cold war enabled the founders of the Second Republic to lay the groundwork for a thriving economy, to expand the social safety network, and through difficult bargaining to gain the support of the country's political, economic, and social groups. The same nexus also gave the Austrian government the leverage to detach the country from the fate of defeated Germany and through tenacious diplomacy to bring the Allies to sign the State Treaty of 1955. This was an achievement that inspired broad patriotic feeling and contributed significantly to a strong sense of Austrian identity.[13]

Yet, in dissociating the Austrian people from any sense of guilt or responsibility for the crimes of the Hitler era, the founders of the Second Republic left authoritarian and anti-Semitic attitudes largely intact. In March 1948 a public opinion poll conducted in Linz revealed that 55.2 percent of the municipal population thought that National Socialism had been a good idea badly carried out. Of those questioned, one-third looked back favorably to the social policies of the Nazi regime, another third to its job creation schemes, and a quarter to its success in provisioning the general populace. Only 2 percent of the respondents endorsed the idea of a union of the Germanic peoples.[14]

After 1949, the recruitment of former Nazis by the two major political parties neutralized or modified the views of many of Hitler's constituents, giving them a real stake in the development of democratic institutions. The process of absorption also succeeded in limiting the appeal of the revived German Nationalist movement, founded in 1949 as the League of Independents (VdU) and reorganized in 1955 as the Freedom Party (FPÖ). On the other hand, the largely successful integration of the Nazi elements into state and society hindered any meaningful discussion of the Anschluss years. It also encouraged politicians to laud the heroes of the German Wehrmacht and to ignore or tolerate anti-Semitic discourse.[15]

When the last Allied soldier left Austrian soil on 25 October 1955 most citizens rejoiced that "seventeen years of occupation" had at last come to an end. Thereafter, a triad of diplomatic neutrality, political stability, and steady economic growth enabled the Alpine republic to develop into one of the world's wealthiest democracies. The question of what it meant to be Austrian continued to be debated, but popular pride in the Second Republic eventually swelled to what an American political scientist considered "conceit and self-satisfaction."[16] In 1985, however, a sophisticated opinion survey indicated that aside from voting in elections, a vast majority of Austrians still eschewed political participation in civil society or the workplace. Other data from the same period revealed that although only 13 percent of the population considered themselves members of a Germanic nation, 74 percent believed that they were on the losing side in World War II. In addition, roughly 50 percent thought that the Nazi experience had been "good as well as bad."[17]

More disturbing than the persistence of authoritarian thoughts, habits, and opinions was the survival of widespread anti-Semitism. In 1945, few of the 4,500 Jewish concentration camp survivors who resurfaced or returned to Austria received a sympathetic homecoming. The Renner cabinet, washing its hands of responsibility for the deeds of a "foreign tyranny," refused to restore émigré assets or to provide restitution. Instead, it compelled the returnees to depend on the assistance of the American Jewish Joint Distribution Committee. Nor did the government act to discourage popular agitation against the 170,000 Eastern European Jews who passed through Austria between 1945 and 1953.[18]

There was, in other words, little incentive for ordinary Austrians in the immediate postwar era to reexamine their prejudices, especially after blame for their own suffering and for the Holocaust had been projected onto the shoulders of the Germans. As mentioned earlier, an American public opinion poll revealed in 1946 that roughly half of the populace thought that it had been necessary "to place limits" on the Jews.[19] Another prevailing view held that "today many are of the opinion that the Jews are the winners of the present situation, and that after victory over the Hitler regime they are having a pleasant time."[20] In subsequent months, crowds staged anti-Semitic disturbances, most notably near displaced person's camps in Graz and in Bad Ischl.[21]

Government authorities, fearful of Allied reaction to outbursts of Judeophobia, confronted the problem either by denying it or promising to curb it. What became an official line was formulated by Theodor Körner, lord mayor of Vienna and later federal president. It was that Austrians were "too cosmopolitan to be prejudiced against Jews." In 1955, the Austrian government accepted an obligation to provide "assistance" to victims of "political persecution," but thereafter either stonewalled or paid nonresident claimants a fraction of the original fair market value of their assets. By 1961, 5,483 applicants had received 51,340,252 schillings ($22 million) in compensation.[22]

There can be little doubt that the unwillingness of Austrian authorities to confront the legacy of anti-Semitism contributed to its persistence. While it is indisputable that right-wing extremism virtually disappeared from public life, anti-Jewish attitudes remained tightly woven into the fabric of popular discourse. Under the chancellorship of Bruno Kreisky, himself a Jew, they even regained a measure of respectability. On the other hand, it is unlikely that anyone of Jewish descent could have been resoundingly elected to high office in the monarchy or the First Republic.[23]

In 1986, the election of Kurt Waldheim as federal president ignited an international firestorm that at long last forced the Austrian people to come to grips with their "compartmentalized past." The furor arose because Waldheim lied about his wartime service in the Balkans as a lieutenant in German

Army Group E, a deception that called into question Austria's collective memory of the Anschluss years and focused worldwide attention on the embarrassing problem of collaboration. Initial public reaction to the Waldheim affair was to condemn the World Jewish Congress, but from the beginning opinions were sharply divided. Assuming office in the midst of a highly charged atmosphere, Chancellor Franz Vranitzky chose to take the painful steps to make his fellow citizens aware of the skeletons in their closet.[24]

Vranitzky, who had made a career in the international world of finance, moved rapidly on a number of fronts. He dissolved his Socialist coalition with the right-wing Freedom Party, called for new elections, and on 14 January 1987 joined the opposition ÖVP in a Grand Coalition. When in April the United States Department of Justice placed Waldheim on its "watch list" as an undesirable alien, Vranitzky responded to the "unjust accusations" by paying a visit to a Jewish Historical Museum in Holland. He also made an official trip to Washington and in June spoke out against anti-Semitism.

In 1988, the fiftieth anniversary of the Anschluss deepened public awareness of the Nazi past. Millions of television viewers witnessed solemn ceremonies in which both Waldheim and Vranitzky acknowledged Austrian complicity in the Holocaust. There were also public debates, scholarly conferences, and publications devoted to resistance and collaboration. On the anniversary of Crystal Night, Vranitzky reminded his countrymen of the long history of Austrian anti-Semitism.[25]

The following year, the collapse of the Iron Curtain simultaneously diminished Austria's status as a neutral power and opened up economic opportunities in the Danubian basin. Even as Austrian firms scrambled to negotiate 7,500 joint-venture agreements in Eastern Europe, Vranitzky reminded his countrymen that they could not distance themselves from the burdens of the past. In 1990 his government allocated $195 million in financial restitution to Jewish victims of Nazi persecution, both at home and abroad. Furthermore, he continued to lend his support the "moral and material claims" of those who had been overlooked, most notably in July 1993 at the Hebrew University in Jerusalem.[26]

Exactly how ordinary Austrians reacted to the disputes of the Waldheim years is not altogether clear, most likely because contemporary concerns outweighed reflection on the architecture of memory. One examination of the media coverage of the commemorative year 1988 contends that the overall response was one of skepticism. Another suggests that many people became more anti-Semitic. A Gallup poll taken in 1991, for example, revealed that over half of those questioned disapproved the prosecution of Nazi war criminals and desired an end to further discussion of the Holocaust. The same poll indicated, however, that only a third still thought that Austria had been Hitler's first victim.[27]

Disconcerting as these attitudes may appear, they need to be seen in context. If the founders of the Second Republic left a legacy of selective amnesia, they also established a liberal order that made it possible to debate the neuroses and conflicts of the past. When the Waldheim affair erupted in 1986, a new generation of scholars, literary writers, and opinion makers were prepared to challenge the taboos of public and popular memory. At their side stood influential members of the Church of Rome, most notably Francis Cardinal König of Vienna, who had long spoken out in support of the declaration of the Second Vatican Council absolving the Jews of blame for the death of Jesus.[28]

This is not to say that the Waldheim affair magically transformed Austrian society. At the end of the of the twentieth century, corruption in high places and anti-immigrant sentiment remains as much a part of the political landscape as in Britain, France, Germany, and the United States. Nor can it be overlooked that the flamboyant Jörg Haider, head of the FPÖ, rarely shies from courting veteran groups or using prejudicial slogans to mobilize voters against the establishment. Nevertheless, educators, clergymen, and political elites seem determined to confront the facts and myths of a difficult past. If this study of the attitudinal climate of Hitler's Austria assists them in their quest, it will have achieved one of its aims.

NOTES

ABBREVIATIONS

In addition to the abbreviations used in the text, the following abbreviations are used in the notes.

AVA   Allgemeines Verwaltungsarchiv (General Administrative Archives, Vienna)

BH   Bundeshauptmannschaft

Boberach, *Meldungen* *Meldungen aus dem Reich: Die Geheimen Lageberichte des Sicherheitsdienstes der SS 1938–1945*. 17 vols. Edited by Heinz Boberach. Herrsching: Pawlak Verlag, 1984.

DNSAP   Deutsche Nationalsozialistische Arbeiterpartei (German National Socialist Workers' Party; Austrian Nazi Party before 1926)

doc.   document

Domarus, *Hitler* *Hitler: Reden und Proklamationen 1932–1945: Kommentiert von einem deutschen Zeitgenossen*. 4 vols. Edited by Max Domarus. Wiesbaden: R. Löwit, 1973.

DÖW, *"Anschluss"* *"Anschluss 1938": Eine Dokumentation*. Edited by the Dokumentationsarchiv des österreichischen Widerstandes. Vienna: Österreichischer Bundesverlag, 1988.

DÖW, *Erzählte Geschichte* *Erzählte Geschichte: Jüdische Schicksale: Berichte von Verfolgten*. 3 vols. Edited by the Dokumentationsarchiv des österreichischen Widerstandes. Vienna: Österreichischer Bundesverlag, 1993.

F   frame

FO   Foreign Office

G   Gendarmerie

GstA   Generalstaatsanwalt (public prosecutor)

LR   Landrat (county executive)

M   microcopy

NA   National Archives, Washington, D.C.

NÖLA   Niederösterreichishes Landesarchiv (Lower Austrian Provincial Archives, Vienna; now St. Pölten)

OLG   Oberlandesgericht (higher regional court)

OÖ   Oberösterreich (Upper Austria)

OÖLA   Oberösterreichisches Landesarchiv (Upper Austrian Provincial Archives, Linz)

Pol. Akten   Politische Akten (political records)

PRO	Public Record Office, London
R	roll
Red-White-Red Book	*Justice for Austria! Red-White-Red Book: Description, Documents and Proofs to the Antecedents and History of the Occupation of Austria (from Official Sources)*. Part 1. Vienna: Austrian State Print House, 1947.
RfSS	Reichsführer SS
RG	Record group
Rk	Reichskommissar für die Wiedervereinigung Österreichs mit dem Deutschen Reich
RSHA	Reichssicherheitshauptamt (Central Office for Reich Security)
RStH	Reichsstatthalter
Sch.	Schachtel (box)
WVB	*Widerstand und Verfolgung in Burgenland 1934–1945: Eine Dokumentation*. Edited by the Dokumentationsarchiv des österreichischen Widerstandes. Vienna: Österreichischer Bundesverlag, 1979.
WVNÖ	*Widerstand und Verfolgung in Niederösterreich 1934–1945: Eine Dokumentation*. 3 vols. Edited by the Dokumentationsarchiv des österreichischen Widerstandes. Vienna: Österreichischer Bundesverlag, 1987.
WVOÖ	*Widerstand und Verfolgung in Oberösterreich 1934–1945: Eine Dokumentation*. 2 vols. Edited by the Dokumentationsarchiv des österreichischen Widerstandes. Vienna: Österreichischer Bundesverlag, 1982.
WVS	*Widerstand und Verfolgung in Salzburg 1934–1945: Eine Dokumentation*. 2 vols. Edited by the Dokumentationsarchiv des österreichischen Widerstandes. Vienna: Österreichischer Bundesverlag, 1991.
WVT	*Widerstand und Verfolgung in Tirol 1934–1945: Eine Dokumentation*. 3 vols. Edited by the Dokumentationsarchiv des österreichischen Widerstandes. Vienna: Österreichischer Bundesverlag, 1984.
WVW	*Widerstand und Verfolgung in Wien 1934–1945: Eine Dokumentation*. 3 vols. Edited by Herbert Steiner, Peter Eppel, and Johann Holzner. Vienna: Österreichischer Bundesverlag, 1975.

PREFACE

1. Pelinka, "The Great Austrian Taboo," 72.
2. On the distinction between public opinion and popular sentiment, see Lukacs, *Historical Consciousness or the Remembered Past*, 75–93. See also Davidson, "Public Opinion," 188–93.
3. Marx, *The Eighteenth Brumaire of Louis Bonaparte*, 146.
4. Burke, *History and Social Theory*, 91.
5. Hutton, "The History of Mentalities: The New Map of Cultural History," 238.
6. Davidson, "Public Opinion," 192–93.
7. Quoted in Sked, *The Decline and Fall of the Habsburg Monarchy, 1815–1918*, 45.
8. Ibid., 44–52; Kann, *Habsburg Empire*, 283–85.

9. Stokes, "SD," 2–19, 101–11, 194.

10. Hagspiel, *Ostmark*, 122–23.

11. Gellately, *The Gestapo and German Society*, 72–75. Gellately's latest research on the social history of Nazi Germany emphasizes the magnitude of the denunciations that were made by individuals. Gellately and Fitzpatrick, "Introduction to the Practice of Denunciation in Modern European History," 753. See also Connely, "The Uses of *Volksgemeinschaft*: Letters to the NSDAP Kreisleitung Eisenach, 1939–40," 899–930, and Gellately, "Denunciations in Twentieth Century Germany: Aspects of Self-Policing in the Third Reich and the German Democratic Republic," 931–67.

12. Gellately, *The Gestapo and German Society*, 65–75; Stokes, "SD," 21–195.

13. Unger, "The Public Opinion Reports of the Nazi Party," 565–82; Stadler, *Österreich*, 14–18; Stokes, "SD"; Steinert, *Hitler's War and the Germans*, 1–25; Kershaw, *Popular Opinion*, 1–10; Kershaw, *The Hitler Myth*, 1–10; Kirk, *Nazism and the Working Class in Austria*, 15–18.

14. Kershaw, *Popular Opinion*, 7.

15. That the father of modern social-science research, Paul Lazarsfeld, was an Austrian may be something more than coincidental. In his classic study of unemployment in Marienthal, an impoverished village in Lower Austria, he and his collaborators sought to combine ideological perspectives, American market research techniques, and statistical analysis to understand the consumer choices, attitudes, and general behavior of an entire community. Much like Sedlnitzky's police agents, they sought to use "unobtrusive measures" and other "data deriving from daily life without interference from the investigator." At the same time, they also relied on questionnaires and interviews, tools rarely used in authoritarian or totalitarian societies. See Lazarsfeld, "An Episode in the History of Social Research: A Memoir," 270–337.

16. Kershaw, *Popular Opinion*, 7–8; Stokes, "SD," 7–8.

17. Kershaw, *Popular Opinion*, 8.

18. Cf. ibid., 7–10, and Calder, *The People's War*. See also Bell, *John Bull and the Bear*.

19. Stadler's pioneering study *Österreich 1938–1945 im Spiegel der NS Akten* was constructed primarily on microfilm records of the central office in Berlin, now available in print: Boberach, *Meldungen*, 17 vols.

20. Timothy Kirk writes mistakenly that "relatively few of the SD reports for Austria have survived, and are mainly from Vienna and Upper Austria"; Kirk, *Nazism and the Working Class in Austria*, 17.

21. See *WVW*, *WVB*, *WVOÖ*, *WVT*, *WVNÖ*, and *WVS*.

CHAPTER ONE

1. Ingrao, *Habsburg Monarchy*, 36.

2. Ibid., 34–39; Kann, *Habsburg Empire*, 103–17.

3. Ingrao, *Habsburg Monarchy*, 39.

4. Hanisch, *Der lange Schatten des Staates*, 24–29.

5. Ibid.

6. Quoted in ibid., 28.

7. Kann, *Habsburg Empire*, 116.

8. Ibid., 156–208; Ingrao, *Habsburg Monarchy*, 150–209, especially 159–72, 179–92, 197–209.

9. Ingrao, *Habsburg Monarchy*, 181.

10. Blanning, *Joseph II*, 72–76, 92–101; Ingrao, *Habsburg Monarchy*, 197–209; Kann, *Habsburg Empire*, 187–92.

11. Johnston, *The Austrian Mind*, 18.

12. Hanisch, *Der lange Schatten des Staates*, 28–29; Kann, *Habsburg Empire*, 183–87; Ingrao, *Habsburg Monarchy*, 197–209. The most astute recent assessment of Joseph II and his legacy is Blanning, *Joseph II*, especially 82–84, 198–206.

13. Boyer, *Political Radicalism in Late Imperial Vienna*, 23.

14. There is an enormous literature on Josephinism, almost all of it in German. The best English-language distillation is Kann, *Habsburg Empire*, 183–87. Also insightful is Epstein, *The Genesis of German Conservatism*, 158–63.

15. Blanning, *Joseph II*, 70–72.

16. Kann, *Habsburg Empire*, 183–87.

17. Carsten, *Fascist Movements*, 9–14; Pauley, *From Prejudice to Persecution*, 20–44; Whiteside, *Socialism of Fools*, 9–42, especially 10 for Bauer's quotation.

18. Whiteside, *Socialism of Fools*, especially 43–140; Schorske, *Fin-de-Siècle Vienna*, 116–33; Carsten, *Fascist Movements*, 11–27.

19. For details, see Whiteside, *Socialism of Fools*, 131–88; Carsten, *Fascist Movements*, 19–39.

20. Whiteside, *Socialism of Fools*, 301–25; Carsten, *Fascist Movements*, 21–27; Schorske, *Fin-de-Siècle Vienna*, especially 130–33; Pauley, *Hitler and the Forgotten Nazis*, 18–24.

21. On this point, see Wandruszka, "Österreichs politische Struktur," 369–82, and Tweraser, "Carl Beurle and the Triumph of German Nationalism in Austria," 403–26.

22. The authoritative study of Hitler's formative years in Austria is Hamann, *Hitlers Wien*. See also Bukey, *Hitler's Hometown*.

23. Carsten, *Fascist Movements*, 37–38.

24. There now exists a substantial literature on the etiology and pathogenesis of the National Socialist movement in the Austrian monarchy, but there is still need of comparative analysis and synthesis. See Whiteside, "Nationaler Sozialismus in Österreich vor 1918," 333–59; Whiteside, *Austrian National Socialism before 1918*; Brandstötter, "Dr. Walter Riehl und die Geschichte der DNSAP in Österreich"; Carsten, *Fascist Movements*, 31–39; Pauley, *Hitler and the Forgotten Nazis*, 24–29; Hanisch, "Zur Frühgeschichte des Nationalsozialismus in Salzburg," 371–410; Botz, "Strukturwandlungen des österreichischen Nationalsozialismus (1904–1945)," 195–218.

25. Carsten, *Fascist Movements*, 31–39; Pauley, *Hitler and the Forgotten Nazis*, 24–29.

26. Pauley, *Hitler and the Forgotten Nazis*, 26; Hanisch, "Zur Frühgeschichte des Nationalsozialismus in Salzburg," 373–78.

27. Smelser, "Hitler and the DNSAP: Between Democracy and Gleichschaltung," 139.

28. Carsten, *Revolution in Central Europe, 1918–1919*, 78–126; Klemperer, *Ignaz Seipel*, 94–109; Pauley, *The Habsburg Legacy, 1867–1939*, 60–99; Jelavich, *Modern Austria*, 151–73. For an incisive introductory assessment of the assets and liabilities of the First Republic, see Klem-

perer, "The Habsburg Heritage: Some Pointers for a Study of the First Austrian Republic," 11–20.

29. Quoted in Klemperer, *Ignaz Seipel*, 127.

30. Andics, *Der Staat, den keiner wollte*.

31. Jelavich, *Modern Austria*, 172–73. For a balance sheet of the assets and liabilities, see Pauley, "Social and Economic Background," 21–37.

32. Luza, *Austro-German Relations*, 3–8; Jelavich, *Modern Austria*, 172–77.

33. Luza, *Austro-German Relations*, 5–8; Jelavich, *Modern Austria*, 144–47, 173–91; Carsten, *Fascist Movements*, 87–94.

34. The standard works are Gulick, *Austria from Habsburg to Hitler*; Goldinger, *Geschichte der Republik Österreich*; Mikoletzky, *Österreich im 20. Jahrhundert*; Andics, *Der Staat, den keiner wollte*; Tálos et al., *Handbuch des politischen Systems Österreichs 1918–1933*; Carsten, *The First Austrian Republic, 1918–1938*. See also Steiner, *Politics in Austria*, and Simon, "Democracy in the Shadow of Imposed Sovereignty," 80–121.

35. Gruber, *Red Vienna*.

36. Jelavich, *Modern Austria*, 173–84. The literature on the vicissitudes of Austrian social democracy is immense, but see Rabinbach, *The Crisis of Austrian Socialism*. On the Heimwehr, see Edmondson, *The Heimwehr and Austrian Politics, 1918–1936*, and Wiltschegg, *Die Heimwehr*.

37. Stiefel, *Die grosse Krise in einem kleinen Land*; Hautmann and Kropf, *Die österreichische Arbeiterbewegung*; Hertz, *The Economic Problem of the Danubian States*, 148; Jelavich, *Modern Austria*, 185–91.

38. For a convincing analysis that takes the Social Democrats to task for the failure to reach an accommodation, see Simon, "Democracy in the Shadow of Imposed Sovereignty," 100–107.

39. Jelavich, *Modern Austria*, 188–96.

40. Low, *Anschluss Movement, 1931–1938*, 1–20; Steininger, "Der Anschluss—Stationen auf dem Weg zum März 1938," 9–18.

41. Low, *Anschluss Movement, 1931–1938*, 106.

42. Pauley, *Habsburg Legacy*, 128–29. For details, see Low, *Anschluss Movement, 1931–1938*, 40–47.

43. Pauley, *Hitler and the Forgotten Nazis*, 29–68; Carsten, *Fascist Movements*, 71–83, 141–66.

44. Pauley, *Hitler and the Forgotten Nazis*, 78.

45. Ibid., 69–80; Carsten, *Fascist Movements*, 189–210. For an exhaustive statistical analysis of Nazi electoral fortunes, see Hänisch, *NSDAP-Wähler*.

46. Using bivariate correlations, multiple regressions, and ecological estimates, Hänisch provides convincing evidence to disprove Botz's more precise statistical calculations. Cf. Hänisch, *NSDAP-Wähler*, 170–80; Botz, "The Changing Patterns of Social Support for Austrian National Socialism (1918–1945)," 212–13.

47. Pauley, *Hitler and the Forgotten Nazis*, 79.

48. Falter and Hänisch, "Wahlerfolge und Wählerschaft der NSDAP in Österreich von 1927 bis 1932: Soziale Basis und Parteipolitische Herkunft," 223–44; Hänisch, *NSDAP-Wähler*, 235–37, 271–90, 399–403.

49. For details, see Pauley, *Hitler and the Forgotten Nazis*, 104–9; Carsten, *Fascist Movements*, 204–7, 232–34.

50. Carsten, *Fascist Movements*, 231.

51. Miller, *Engelbert Dollfuss als Agrarfachmann*.

52. The literature on the Austrian civil war is extensive, but for a comprehensive account see Kitchen, *The Coming of Austrian Fascism*. See also the essays in Neck and Jedlicka, *Das Jahr 1934*.

53. Pelinka, "The Great Austrian Taboo."

54. For conflicting assessments of the Dollfuss regime, see Pauley, *Hitler and the Forgotten Nazis*, 155–71; Carsten, *Fascist Movements*, 229–48, 271–92; Rath and Schum, "The Dollfuss-Schuschnigg Regime: Fascist or Authoritarian?," 249–56; Tálos and Neugebauer, *"Austrofaschismus"*; and Kluge, *Der österreichische Ständestaat 1934–1938*. For an admirable historiographical assessment of the Christian Corporative system, see Gellott, "Recent Writings on the Ständestaat, 1934–1938," 207–38.

55. The definitive account of the July putsch is Jagschitz, *Der Putsch*.

56. Jelavich, *Modern Austria*, 207–8; Luza, *Austro-German Relations*, 24–25; Carsten, *Fascist Movements*, 265–66.

57. Mikoletzky, *Österreich im 20. Jahrhundert*, 302–3; Carsten, *Fascist Movements*, 270–92; Jelavich, *Modern Austria*, 208–13; Low, *Anschluss Movement, 1931–1938*, 170–76.

58. Hagspiel, *Ostmark*, 10–16; Brook-Shepherd, *The Austrians*, 296–319.

59. Schuschnigg later claimed that his overture to Berlin was an attempt to buy time "until a different world situation emerged." Low, *Anschluss Movement, 1931–1938*, 183, and Brook-Shepherd, *The Austrians*, 300–306.

60. Low, *Anschluss Movement, 1931–1938*, 183–88; Jelavich, *Modern Austria*, 212–13. See also the essays in Neck and Jedlicka, *Das Juliabkommen von 1936*.

61. Low, *Anschluss Movement, 1931–1938*, 188–219.

62. For a guide to the enormous literature on the Anschluss, see Low, *The Anschluss Movement, 1918–1938*.

63. Pauley, "Social and Economic Background," 24–31; Hertz, *The Economic Problem of the Danubian States*, 118–23, 137–50.

64. Hertz, *The Economic Problem of the Danubian States*, 147–50; Rothschild, *Austria's Economic Development between Two Wars*, 51–65; Kernbauer, März, and Weber, "Die wirtschaftliche Entwicklung," 366–70; Bruckmüller, "Sozialstruktur und Sozialpolitik," 407–13.

65. Hertz, *The Economic Problem of the Danubian States*, 118–23; Mooslechner and Stadler, "Landwirtschaft und Agrarpolitik," 83.

66. Mattl, "Die Finanzdiktatur: Wirtschaftspolitik in Österreich 1933–1938," 133–59; Rothschild, *Austria's Economic Development*, 65–81.

67. The official unemployment figures in 1937 were 464,000 or 21.7 percent of the workforce. At the same time, those employed represented only 67.4 percent of the already low level of 1929. Considering seasonal fluctuations, underemployment, and the large number of people who had despaired of finding a job or, in the case of the young, had never been employed at all, the actual number of unemployed will probably never be determined. Cf. Hertz, *The Economic Problem of the Danubian States*, 59, and Bruckmüller, "Sozialstruktur und Sozialpolitik," 407–13.

68. See the sources cited in the preceding note and Pauley, "Social and Economic Background," 30.

69. Cf. Kershaw, *Popular Opinion*, 11–18, whose scheme I follow here, and *Statistisches Handbuch für die Republik Österreich* (1938), 18:23.

70. The occupational figures for 1934 are misleading to a degree, as they included the unemployed. Bruckmüller, "Sozialstruktur und Sozialpolitik," 385.

71. Ibid., 385–87.

72. Ibid., 408; *Statistisches Handbuch für die Republik Österreich* (1936), 16:12–13.

73. Kershaw, *Popular Opinion*, 15.

74. Bruckmüller, "Sozialstruktur und Sozialpolitik," 383–85.

75. Pelinka, "The Great Austrian Taboo," 71.

76. Carsten's systematic and thorough use of police records is particularly illuminating. See his *Fascist Movements*, 271–92.

77. Ibid., 280–87. Quotations from p. 286.

78. Ibid., 298, 302–4.

79. Botz, "The Changing Patterns of Social Support for Austrian National Socialism (1918–1945)," 215–16.

80. The classic account still remains Buttinger, *In the Twilight of Socialism*.

81. Konrad, "Social Democracy's Drift toward Nazism before 1938," 110–36; Bukey, *Hitler's Hometown*, 136, 147–48, 185; Bukey, "Nazi Rule in Austria," 211.

82. Pauley, *Hitler and the Forgotten Nazis*, 193–215, especially 213–14.

83. Kreissler, *Der Österreicher und seine Nation*, 174–80.

84. Carsten, *Fascist Movements*, 271–314, especially 287–88, 296–300, 308–10.

85. Botz, "Der 'Anschluss' von 1938 als innerösterreiches Problem," 3–19.

86. Pauley, *From Prejudice to Persecution*, 202. For a concise history of Austrian anti-Semitism, see Albrich, "Vom Vorurteil zum Pogrom: Antisemitismus von Schönerer bis Hitler," 309–66.

87. Pauley, *From Prejudice to Persecution*, 45.

88. Ibid., 13–60.

89. Ibid., 61–203. Quotation from p. 190.

90. Ibid., 260–76; Carsten, *Fascist Movements*, 284–88; Parkinson, *Conquering the Past*, 318.

CHAPTER TWO

1. The most comprehensive works, each written from a strikingly different perspective, are Brook-Shepherd, *The Anschluss*; Gehl, *Germany and the Anschluss, 1931–1938*; Schausberger, *Der Griff nach Österreich: Der Anschluss*; Schmidl, *März 38*. For additional bibliographical information, see Low, *The Anschluss Movement, 1918–1938*, and Bukey, "Nazi Rule in Austria," 202–33.

2. Quoted in Carsten, *First Austrian Republic*, 268.

3. Quoted in ibid., 269.

4. Gedye, *Betrayal in Central Europe*, 247.

5. Pauley, *Hitler and the Forgotten Nazis*, 199.

6. Ibid., 207–10; Weinberg, *The Foreign Policy of Hitler's Germany*, 296–99. Although Weinberg emphasizes Hitler's preference for an internal seizure of power "on the Danzig model," he

downplays the dictator's hesitation to send German troops over the border. In contrast, Schmidl makes a convincing case for the Führer's initial reluctance to order a military invasion. See his astute assessment in *März 38*, 109.

7. For an exemplary account of these events, see Wagner and Tomkowitz, *Anschluss*, 80–166.

8. Ibid., 171.

9. As reported by Edmund Glaise-Horstenau, Seyss's war minister and honored guest at Hitler's late evening monologue on 9–10 March 1938. Broucek, *Ein General im Zwielicht*, 245.

10. Pauley makes a forceful case that the German invasion was "directed against the Austrian Nazis themselves whose 'dangerous' autonomist tendencies would have been increased by a takeover of the government in Vienna." Pauley, *Hitler and the Forgotten Nazis*, 213–14.

11. This is the consensus view, first suggested in 1941 by the Austrian Nazi Friedrich Rainer and largely substantiated by the meticulous research of Gerhard Botz. For more historiographical information, see Bukey, "Nazi Rule in Austria," 203–6.

12. Zuckmayer, *A Part of Myself*, 45.

13. Wagner and Tomkowitz, *Anschluss*, 135–37, 143–44, 151–53, 155–61; Gedye, *Betrayal in Central Europe*, 280–88.

14. Shirer, *Berlin Diary*, 100.

15. Ibid.

16. Shirer, *Nightmare Years*, 296.

17. Gedye, *Betrayal in Central Europe*, 284.

18. Zuckmayer, *A Part of Myself*, 50.

19. Ibid.

20. Wagner and Tomkowitz, *Anschluss*, 177, 189; Schmidl, *März 38*, 167–86.

21. Quoted in Schmidl, *März 38*, 164–65.

22. Ibid., 175.

23. Guderian, *Panzer Leader*, 32.

24. Ibid., 32–33; Wagner and Tomkowitz, *Anschluss*, 192–202; Bukey, *Hitler's Hometown*, 162, 167–70.

25. Schmidl, *März 38*, 189–90.

26. Ibid., 200.

27. Schmidl, "Die militärische Situation in Tirol im März 1938," 496.

28. Guderian, *Panzer Leader*, 33.

29. Ibid.

30. Botz, "Hitlers Aufenthalt in Linz in März 1938 und der Anschluss," 185–214.

31. Schmidl, *März 38*, 169; Wagner and Tomkowitz, *Anschluss*, 207–8.

32. Ibid., 189; Karner, *Steiermark*, 53–54.

33. Karner, *Steiermark*, 53–55; Schmidl, *März 38*, 188–96.

34. Walzl, *"Als erster Gau,"* 70–74.

35. Wagner and Tomkowitz, *Anschluss*, 221–22.

36. *Manchester Guardian*, 15 March 1938.

37. Wagner and Tomkowitz, *Anschluss*, 223.

38. Ibid.

39. Gedye, *Betrayal in Central Europe*, 307.

40. Quoted in Wagner and Tomkowitz, *Anschluss*, 225. For the full text, see Domarus, *Hitler*, 2:822–23.

41. Fest, *Hitler*, 549.

42. Wagner and Tomkowitz, *Anschluss*, 226–27.

43. *Manchester Guardian*, 16 March 1938.

44. Wagner and Tomkowitz, *Anschluss*, 227–29.

45. Full text in Domarus, *Hitler*, 2:823–24.

46. Ibid., 824.

47. NA, M 1209, R 6, F 0626: Wiley to State, 16 March 1938.

48. *Manchester Guardian*, 16 March 1938.

49. R. H. Bruce Lockhart, *Guns or Butter: War Countries and Peace Countries of Europe Revisited* (London, 1938), 251, quoted in Luza, *Austro-German Relations*, 57 n. 1.

50. Wagner and Tomkowitz, *Anschluss*, 230.

51. *New York Times*, 16 March 1938.

52. Schmidl, *März 38*, 184–86.

53. Ibid., 193.

54. Ibid., 229.

55. Recollections of Kurt Tweraser, in Hall, *World War II*, 59.

56. Botz, "Eine deutsche Geschichte 1938 bis 1945? Österreichische Geschichte zwischen Exil, Widerstand und Verstrickung," 23. The recently discovered photograph depicts a group of unenthusiastic onlookers at Innsbruck. Even so, a glance at the foreground reveals only one or two dejected figures. The others appear perplexed or detached. In the background one can spot the face of a woman swooning in ecstasy. See Kirk, "Workers and Nazis in Hitler's Homeland," 37.

57. Schmidl, *März 38*, 182–83, 201, 202, 229.

58. Official statistics indicate that 169,978 Jews lived in Vienna at the time of the Anschluss. Pauley estimates the total number, presumably including Christian converts and dependents, at 180,000. There were also 80,000 "hybrids" or children of mixed-marriages. Most authorities agree that the total Jewish population of Austria was roughly 200,000. Cf. Rosenkranz, *Verfolgung*, 13, 311, and Pauley, *From Prejudice to Persecution*, 346 n. 28.

59. The most prescient analysis is Botz, "Zwischen Akzeptanz und Distanz," 429–55.

60. Caught nearly flat-footed by the Anschluss, Goebbels remained in Berlin where he followed Hitler's triumphal homecoming over the airwaves. Whatever one may think of David Irving's tendentious writings, it is difficult to disagree with his conclusion that "this was no Goebbels spectacular." Cf. Reuth, *Goebbels*, 231–32, and David Irving, *The War Path: Hitler's Germany, 1933–1939* (New York, 1978), 87. For opposite views, see Kreissler, *Der Österreicher und seine Nation*, especially 87–92, and Rathkolb et al., *Die unvertraute Wahrheit: Hitlers Propagandisten in Österreich*.

61. Schmidl, *März 38*, 207, 219, 225–26; Hanisch, *Der lange Schatten des Staates*, 345–46; Pauley, *From Prejudice to Persecution*, 280.

62. Luza, *Austro-German Relations*, 57–58; Botz, "Zwischen Akzeptanz und Distanz," especially 436–40.

63. Thus Weinberg, *The Foreign Policy of Hitler's Germany*, 300. For an exceptionally astute investigation of the April plebiscite, see Hagspiel, *Ostmark*, 35–49.

64. As quoted in Bracher, *The German Dictatorship: The Origins, Structure, and Effects of National Socialism*, 242.

65. For a convincing analysis of Hitler's plebiscitary views, see Zitelmann, *Hitler: Selbstverständnis eines Revolutionärs*, 438–39.

66. Botz, *Der 13. März 38 und die Anschlussbewegung*, 23–27.

67. Two days after Hitler's triumphal reception at Heroes Square, Gauleiter Bürckel cautioned Seyss-Inquart not "to overestimate the mass enthusiasm of the moment." DÖW, *"Anschluss,"* 482.

68. For an excellent case study, see Albrich, " 'Gebt dem Führer euer Ja!,' " 505–36.

69. Brook-Shepherd, *The Austrians*, 332–33.

70. Albrich, " 'Gebt dem Führer euer Ja!,' " 517–18.

71. *New York Times*, 25 March 1938. See also Luza, *Austro-German Relations*, 64.

72. For example, see DÖW, *"Anschluss,"* 429.

73. NA, M 1209, R 7, F 392: Wiley to the Secretary of State, 2 April 1938.

74. Bernbaum, "Nazi Control in Austria," 91; Luza, *Austro-German Relations*, 192–94; Albrich, " 'Gebt dem Führer euer Ja!,' " 519–27.

75. NA, M 1209, R 7, F 390.

76. For solid brief accounts, see Weinberg, *The Foreign Policy of Hitler's Germany*, 300; Luza, *Austro-German Relations*, 64; Brook-Shepherd, *The Austrians*, 330–31; Hagspiel, *Ostmark*, 38–42.

77. Schwarz, "Nazi Wooing of Austrian Social Democracy," 126–30.

78. Luza, *Austro-German Relations*, 70–72.

79. AVA, Rk, Ordner 20, Reichsstatthalterei, Abt. 6: Vienna, 31 March 1938.

80. Ibid.

81. Ibid.

82. Gedye, *Betrayal in Central Europe*, 289.

83. Cf. Luza, *Austro-German Relations*, 66–67, and Neugebauer, "Das NS-Terrorsystem," 163–65.

84. Luza, *Austro-German Relations*, 63.

85. Cf. Eksteins, *Rites of Spring*, 301–31, and Hanisch, *Der lange Schatten des Staates*, 345–47. For additional details, see Luza, *Austro-German Relations*, 63–71; Bernbaum, "Nazi Control in Austria," 88–101; DÖW, *"Anschluss,"* 447–526; Albrich, " 'Gebt dem Führer euer Ja!,' " 505–36.

86. For example, see Zuckmayer, *A Part of Myself*, especially 66–71.

87. DÖW, *"Anschluss,"* 514.

88. For the most comprehensive account, see Domarus, *Hitler*, 2:843–50. See also Botz, *Nationalsozialismus in Wien*, 169–74.

89. Quoted in Shirer, *Nightmare Years*, 316. For different snippets (and assessments) of the speech, see Domarus, *Hitler*, 2:848–49, and Botz, *Nationalsozialismus in Wien*, 172–74.

90. Shirer, *Nightmare Years*, 317; Luza, *Austro-German Relations*, 70–72; Bernbaum, "Nazi Control in Austria," 101.

91. For examples of Nazi pressure at the polling place, see Shirer, *Nightmare Years*, 317; DÖW, *"Anschluss,"* 526; DÖW, *WVOÖ*, 2:264–69.

92. Botz, "Das Ergebnis der 'Volksabstimmung' von 10. April 1938," 95–104; "Schuschniggs geplante 'Volksbefragung' und Hitlers 'Volksabstimmung' in Österreich," 220–43;

"Zwischen Akzeptanz und Distanz," 441–45; "Der 'Anschluss' von 1938 als innerösterreichisches Problem," 10–13; and "War der Anschluss gezwungen?," 9–12.

93. See the revealing collection of oral histories in Erhard and Natter, "'Wir waren alle ja arbeitslos': NS-Sympathisanten deuten ihre Motive," 540–69.

94. Complete returns are reproduced in DÖW, *"Anschluss,"* 524.

95. Botz, "Der 'Anschluss' von 1938 als innerösterreichisches Problem," 3–19.

CHAPTER THREE

1. Pelinka, "The Great Austrian Taboo," 73.

2. Weiss, *Ideology of Death*, 173.

3. Kershaw, *Popular Opinion*, 110.

4. Gellately, *Gestapo and German Society*, 73–74.

5. See Botz's studies "The Changing Patterns of Social Support for Austrian National Socialism (1918–1945)," 202–25; "Strukturwandlungen des österreichischen Nationalsozialismus (1904–1945)," 195–218; and "Arbeiterschaft und österreichische NSDAP-Mitglieder (1926–1945)," 29–48. See also Albrich and Meixner, "Zwischen Legalität und Illegalität," 149–87.

6. Botz, "The Changing Patterns of Social Support for Austrian National Socialism (1918–1945)," 202–15; Hänisch, *NSDAP-Wähler*, 364–80.

7. Ibid., 215–16. In Tyrol, blue-collar workers composed roughly 50 percent of the Illegal Nazi activists. See Albrich and Meixner, "Zwischen Legalität und Illegalität," especially 180–81.

8. Figures in Luza, *Austro-German Relations*, 376.

9. Ibid., 102–3, 117–20; Jagschitz, "Von der 'Bewegung' zum Apparat," 505.

10. For more comprehensive statistics and information, see Luza, *Austro-German Relations*, 114–25, 371–81; Botz, *Nationalsozialismus in Wien*, 213–21; Bukey, *Hitler's Hometown*, 170–78.

11. Botz, "The Changing Patterns of Social Support for Austrian National Socialism (1918–1945)," 217–20.

12. Kater, *The Nazi Party*, 38–44.

13. Botz, "The Changing Patterns of Social Support for Austrian National Socialism (1918–1945)," 222.

14. Luza, *Austro-German Relations*, 117–18.

15. Ibid. For a different interpretation of the data, see Botz, "Arbeiterschaft und österreichische NSDAP-Mitglieder (1926–1945)," 29–48.

16. On the "highly amorphous" structure of the German party, see Orlow, *Nazi Party*, 18.

17. Botz, *Nationalsozialismus in Wien*, 42.

18. Pauley, *Hitler and the Forgotten Nazis*, 52–68, 139–71; Carsten, *Fascist Movements*, 295–314; Black, *Kaltenbrunner*, 69–87.

19. On Leopold, see Williams, "Captain Josef Leopold: Austro-Nazi and Austro-Nationalist?," 57–71; Jedlicka, "Gauleiter Josef Leopold (1889–1941)," 143–61; Pauley, *Hitler and the Forgotten Nazis*, 172–92. See also the insightful analysis of Leopold's tactical objectives in Jagschitz, "NSDAP und 'Anschluss' in Wien 1938," 147–57.

20. Rosar, *Deutsche Gemeinschaft: Seyss-Inquart und der Anschluss*; Haag, "Marginal Men and the Dream of the Reich: Eight Austrian National Catholic Intellectuals, 1918–1938," 339–48; Broucek, *Ein General im Zwielicht*, 268.

21. Black, *Kaltenbrunner*, 87; Carsten, *Fascist Movements*, 301–2, 306; Pauley, *Hitler and the Forgotten Nazis*, 182.

22. Pauley, *Hitler and the Forgotten Nazis*, 179.

23. Black, *Kaltenbrunner*, 80–94; Pauley, *Hitler and the Forgotten Nazis*, 176–80.

24. Luza, *Austro-German Relations*, 62–94; Luza, "Die Strukturen der nationalsozialistischen Herrschaft in Österreich," 471–510; Botz, *Eingliederung*, 73–94.

25. For details of the decision-making process, see Luza, *Austro-German Relations*, 57–94; Botz, *Eingliederung*, 61–178, especially the documents reproduced in 127–78; Botz, *Nationalsozialismus in Wien*, 193–204; Bernbaum, "Nazi Control in Austria," 106–28.

26. Luza, *Austro-German Relations*, 88–94.

27. Ibid.; Botz, *Eingliederung*, 92–99. For biographical data on the Austrian Gauleiter, see Hoffkes, *Hitlers politische Generale*, 58–60, 92–94, 143–45, 166–67, 180–81, 259–63, 351–52. On those who held higher office in the SS more complete information is available in Preradovich, *Österreichs höhere SS-Führer*, 9–10, 35–43, 64–73, 98–104, 163–69.

28. Hanisch, *Der lange Schatten des Staates*, 367–69. Opdenhoff was by no means unsympathetic to a Leopold candidacy, in a number of reports nominating him as Gauleiter in Lower Austria. See Botz, *Eingliederung*, 94–95, 129–59.

29. Parkinson, *Conquering the Past*, 317. See also Luza, *Austro-German Relations*, 63–72.

30. For telling examples, see Zuckmayer, *A Part of Myself*, 49–71.

31. Pauley, *Hitler and the Forgotten Nazis*, 217.

32. Quoted in ibid., 218–19.

33. Hitler's words of assurance to Rainer and Globocnik in 1936. Quoted in Black, *Kaltenbrunner*, 99.

34. Hanisch, *Der lange Schatten des Staates*, 369.

35. Black, *Kaltenbrunner*, 98. The best accounts of Hitler and the post-Anschluss struggle for power in Austria remain Luza, *Austro-German Relations*, 57–94, and Botz, *Eingliederung*, 49–99ff.

36. Luza, *Austro-German Relations*, 63–73, 87–93, 102n.

37. Quoted in Botz, *Nationalsozialismus in Wien*, 162.

38. Ibid., 84.

39. Quoted in Bernbaum, " 'The New Elite,' " 146.

40. Pauley, *Hitler and the Forgotten Nazis*, 217.

41. Ibid., 216–22; Luza, *Austro-German Relations*, 63–77, 92–93, 107; Bukey, "Popular Opinion in Vienna after the Anschluss," 152–56.

42. Luza, *Austro-German Relations*, 67–68, 73–87, 146–50.

43. For the text, see Stadler, *Österreich*, 46.

44. Jagschitz, "NSDAP und 'Anschluss' in Wien 1938," 154–55.

45. Rebecca West's pungent characterization of fascists and fascist movements. West, *Black Lamb and Grey Falcon*, 1:14.

46. The story of the Austrian Legion, a paramilitary force raised in 1933 by Austrian Nazi exiles,

is both labyrinthine and shrouded in great confusion. It merits systematic investigation, even though the effort may yield meager results.

47. Quoted in Hanisch, *Nationalsozialistische Herrschaft*, 72–73.

48. Botz, *Eingliederung*, 96. On the complicated intrigues and machinations leading to Hofer's triumphal return to Innsbruck, see Schreiber, *Die Machtübernahme*, 119–38.

49. Jagschitz, "Von der 'Bewegung' zum Apparat," 497; Botz, *Nationalsozialismus in Wien*, 226–30; AVA, Rk, box 164, folder 322: Bericht an die oberste SA-Führung, 23 July 1938.

50. Walzl, *"Als erster Gau,"* 78–80.

51. Luza, *Austro-German Relations*, 68–72, 92–93, 302–3; Hanisch, *Nationalsozialistische Herrschaft*, 79; Slapnicka, *Oberdonau*, 57–63; AVA, Rk, box 173: Anonymous letters of 27, 28 April, 5, 6, 11, 12, 23, 24, 25 May, 20 June, 8 July 1938.

52. AVA, Rk, box 164, folder 322: "Stimmungsbericht" from Dornbirn, 12 August 1938.

53. Luza, *Austro-German Relations*, 46.

54. Broucek, *Ein General im Zwielicht*, 283.

55. Luza, *Austro-German Relations*, 81.

56. Ibid., 82–83, 136–37, 139–40; Black, *Kaltenbrunner*, 112–13.

57. Quoted in Luza, *Austro-German Relations*, 83.

58. Luza provides the most comprehensive account of the turf struggle in *Austro-German Relations*, 72–150. But see also Bernbaum, "Nazi Control in Austria," 106–49; Rosar, *Deutsche Gemeinschaft*, 299–341; and—for the role of the SS—Black, *Kaltenbrunner*, 104–34. On the infighting in Vienna, see Botz, *Nationalsozialismus in Wien*, 193–293.

59. Langoth, *Kampf um Österreich*, 253–90.

60. Broucek, *Ein General im Zwielicht*, 280–415.

61. Ibid., 286–97.

62. Of the 13,000 men and women employed by the municipality of Vienna only 1,100 (4.5 percent) received pink slips from the Nazis; at least half of the group comprised Jews, the rest visible supporters of the Christian Corporative regime. In Salzburg the story was similar. After five years of wrangling in Germany, Nazi leaders had reached a standoff with the civil service, reluctantly preferring the skills of educated administrators to the zeal of political fanatics and delusional romantics. For this reason the Austrian bureaucracy remained largely unpurged. Feiler, "The Viennese Municipal Civil Service, 1933 to 1950," 195–204; Hanisch, *Nationalsozialistische Herrschaft*, 75–76; Orlow, *Nazi Party*, 18–262; Luza, *Austro-German Relations*, 256–63.

63. Botz, "The Jews of Vienna from the Anschluss to the Holocaust," 188–93; Botz, "The Dynamics of Persecution in Austria," 204; Luza, *Austro-German Relations*, 217–19.

64. PRO/FO: C5441/62/18, Despatch No. 18, 23 May 1938; C6827/62/18, Despatch No. 36, 29 June 1938; C6828/62/18, 1 July 1938.

65. Quoted in Stadler, *Österreich*, 46.

66. Williams, "Aftermath of Anschluss," 131.

67. Weisz, "Geheime Staatspolizei," 78–92; Black, *Kaltenbrunner*, 111.

68. Weisz, "Geheime Staatspolizei," 93. For exact figures see table 3/1 in the appendix: IX, a, 3.

69. PRO/FO: C8826/62/18: Despatch No. 70, 19 August 1938.

70. For more details, see Pauley, *Hitler and the Forgotten Nazis*, 57–103; Jagschitz, "NSDAP und

'Anschluss' in Wien 1938," 147–57; Botz, *Nationalsozialismus in Wien*, 51–67; Luza, *Austro-German Relations*, 157–62.

71. Luza, *Austro-German Relations*, 76–77. For a more detailed account, see Botz, *Nationalsozialismus in Wien*, 51–67, 193–98; Botz, *Eingliederung*, 95–96.

72. Cf. Botz, *Eingliederung*, 95–96, 130–59, and Bernbaum, "Nazi Control in Austria," 167–83.

73. Botz, *Eingliederung*, 140–42.

74. Luza, *Austro-German Relations*, 76–77; Botz, *Eingliederung*, 95–96.

75. Quoted in Botz, *Nationalsozialismus in Wien*, 203.

76. On Globocnik, see ibid., 200–204; Luza, *Austro-German Relations*, 76–77, 110–13.

77. See, for example, Massiczek, *Ich habe meine Pflicht erfüllt*, 30–33.

78. Bernbaum, "Nazi Control in Austria," 184. Luza presents a slightly different version of the story, explaining that it was Göring who first demanded Globocnik's removal. See Luza, *Anglo-German Relations*, 112–13.

79. For an astute analysis of Bürckel's ambiguous attitudes and behavior, see Hagspiel, *Ostmark*, 49–52.

80. Luza, *Austro-German Relations*, 72–76, 102n, 101–6; Jagschitz, "Von der 'Bewegung' zum Apparat," 495; Bernbaum, "Nazi Control in Austria," 175–80; Bernbaum, "'The New Elite,'" 154–57.

81. Bernbaum, "'The New Elite,'" 144–47; Luza, *Austro-German Relations*, 126–50; Broucek, *Ein General im Zwielicht*, 290–309.

82. Historical scholarship has demolished the myth of the domination of Nazi Austria by German elites, but the exact degree of penetration by officials, managers, and officers from the Reich remains to be determined. Two decades ago Gerhard Botz made the sensible suggestion that "German penetration of the administrative apparatus of the Ostmark was less the consequence of a clear personal-political strategy than the outcome of administrative unification and the adoption of Prussian-German administrative rules." While his observation alludes specifically to the civil service, it may apply to other Austrian institutions as well. Recent regional studies make it clear that the German takeover was limited primarily to the economic realm and to a lesser extent to the bureaucracy, where a small number of German administrators were needed to introduce Reich German practices. Even in the security sector Austrians remained largely in control. For the initial debates, see Williams, "Aftermath of Anschluss," 129–44; Bernbaum, "'The New Elite,'" 145–60, and the comments by Peter Burian, Herbert Steiner, Ernst Hanisch, and Gerhard Botz, 161–86—all published as "The Nazi Interlude" in *Austrian History Yearbook* 14 (1978), especially 181 for Botz's quotation. For more recent assessments, see Bukey, "Nazi Rule in Austria," 206–9, and Hagspiel, *Ostmark*, 107–66.

83. For the full details, see Weisz, "Geheime Staatspolizei," 1302–44; Weisz, "Die Gestapo-Leitstelle Wien," 231–34. On the incorporation of professional police officers into the Gestapo in Würzburg and other cities in Bavaria, see Gellately, *Gestapo and German Society*, especially 44–75.

84. PRO/FO: C10692/62/18: St. Clair Gainer to William Strange, 20 September 1938.

85. Stadler, *Österreich*, 49.

86. Luza, *Austro-German Relations*, 93.

87. Quoted in *Red-White-Red Book*, 91. For a more explicit development of this argument, see Bukey, "Popular Opinion in Vienna after the Anschluss," 151–64.

88. Cf. Fest, *Hitler*, 568–70; Orlow, *Nazi Party*, 21–22. Developments in Vienna, perhaps more than any other city in Greater Germany, provide a microcosm of what Hans Mommsen has called the "cumulative radicalization" of the Nazi regime. Mommsen, "Der Nationalsozialismus," 785ff. For an application of this concept to the larger Austrian setting, see Hanisch, *Der lange Schatten des Staates*, 367–79.

89. Luza, *Austro-German Relations*, 92–94; Slapnicka, *Oberdonau*, 57–58; Hanisch, *Nationalsozialistische Herrschaft*, 113.

90. Walzl, *"Als erster Gau,"* 15–29; Karner, *Steiermark*, 19–44; Carsten, *Fascist Movements*, 262–64.

91. Hagspiel reports street clashes in both Klagenfurt and Villach between Nazis and government militiamen, the *Ostmärkischen Sturmscharen*. His account is difficult to square with Walzl's detailed description of a nonviolent takeover. What is indisputable is that once in power Nazi gangs viciously sought out, beat up, and terrorized prominent supporters of the Old Regime, particularly militiamen and functionaries of the Patriotic Front. Cf. Hagspiel, *Ostmark*, 20, and Walzl, *"Als erster Gau,"* 51–66, especially 62–63.

92. Walzl, *"Als erster Gau,"* 58–74.

93. Ibid., 77–79, 89–112.

94. Ibid., 128–34.

95. Carsten, *Fascist Movements*, 308–10, 319–21; Karner, *Steiermark*, 42–44; Gänser, "Kontinuität und Bruch in der Steierischen Landesverwaltung," 126–31.

96. Botz, *Eingliederung*, 118, 132–42; Karner, *Steiermark*, 78–97; Karner, "'. . . Des Reiches Südmark': Kärnten und Steiermark im Dritten Reich 1938–1945," 467–72.

97. On the other hand, Uiberreither had belonged to the Styrian Heimwehr and studied law at the University of Graz. Born in 1908, he was five years younger than both Rainer and Kaltenbrunner, but otherwise shared a common political background, education, and social contacts. That the three men constituted part of a provincial old-boy network is not difficult to surmise. For biographical data, see Hoffkes, *Hitlers politische Generale*, 351–52.

98. Karner, *Steiermark*, 71–105, 293–325.

99. Quoted in Stadler, *Österreich*, 43.

100. Karner, *Steiermark*, 104–5.

101. Carsten, *Fascist Movements*, 293–314, especially 309–10; Schreiber, *Machtübernahme*, 15–35.

102. Quoted in Irving, *The War Path*, 86.

103. Slapnicka, *Oberdonau*, 23–32, 55–64; Bukey, *Hitler's Hometown*, 158–77.

104. Schuster, "Die Entnazifizierung des Magistrates Linz," 91–106; Slapnicka, *Oberdonau*, 57–64; Black, *Kaltenbrunner*, 122–23.

105. On the other hand, roughly a fourth of forty-eight city councillors appointed on 3 February 1939 had belonged to the NSDAP before 1932. Of these, at least seven had been activists for nearly two decades. Cf. Slapnicka, *Oberdonau*, 60; Bukey, *Hitler's Hometown*, 173; and Bart and Puffer, *Die Gemeindevertretung der Stadt Linz vom Jahre 1848 bis zur Gegenwart*, especially the biographies of the councillors listed on 90.

106. Hanisch, *Nationalsozialistische Herrschaft*, 72–85.

107. Schreiber, *Machtübernahme*, 15–35.

108. Ibid., 36–63, 120–26.

109. This is my reading of Schreiber's somewhat contradictory discussion of the matter. Ibid., 121–29.

110. Ibid., 220–226. The proportion of lawyers in Tyrol was twice that of the entire Altreich. Jobs were so scarce, according to the SD, that the average age to begin practice, either in a private firm or the civil service, was thirty-three. Before Hofer's decision to favor the legal profession, there was intense envy of the many Viennese colleagues who had been able to take advantage of the Aryanization Law (which excluded all Jews from the civil service and the practice of law) to reduce their own rate of unemployment by 35 percent. AVA, RStH, box 391, folder 221: "Lagebericht," II-221, 30 July 1938.

111. PRO/FO: C5710/62/18: "Conditions in Western Austria," 7 June 1938.

112. Luza, *Austro-German Relations*, 106–25; Botz, *Nationalsozialismus in Wien*, 413–24.

113. Luza, *Austro-German Relations*, 256–63.

114. Ibid.

115. Feiler, "Viennese Municipal Service," 293–94.

116. Luza, *Austro-German Relations*, 264. Hitler's reasons for appointing Bürckel Gauleiter of Vienna are not altogether clear. The surviving documentation reveals that the Reich commissioner coveted the office and that during a December meeting with the Führer won the support of Seyss-Inquart. As Gauleiter of two provinces, each located at either end of the Reich, Bürckel aimed at retaining a measure of the high status he enjoyed as Reich commissioner once that charge expired on 1 May 1939. Botz, *Nationalsozialismus in Wien*, 421–23.

117. See Rathkolb, *Führertreu und gottbegnadet*, 65–67.

118. Luza estimates that by 1939 Bürckel devoted only 40 percent of his time to his duties in Vienna. Luza, *Austro-German Relations*, 145.

119. For fuller, more textured accounts, see ibid., 144–50; Botz, *Nationalsozialismus in Wien*, 420–27.

120. Bernbaum, "Nazi Control in Austria," 136. In his outstanding recent study Hermann Hagspiel portrays Bürckel as an exceptionally astute politician, a man much more attuned to Austrian demands than the figure depicted in previous accounts. He argues convincingly that the Reich commissioner was well aware of the contradictions confronting him and even outlined the sort of cultural policies that brought his successor, Baldur von Schirach, some success in mollifying the Viennese Nazis. What both men failed to achieve was the oxymoronic conflation of Viennese culture and Prusso-German values demanded by Hitler. Hagspiel, *Ostmark*, 31–39, 49–52, 116–31.

121. The most comprehensive account remains Luza, *Austro-German Relations*, especially 239–45, 264–74. But see also Botz, *Nationalsozialismus in Wien*, 420–29; Bernbaum, "Nazi Control in Austria," 138–42.

122. Quoted in Luza, *Austro-German Relations*, 271. On Mühlmann, see Petropoulos, "The Importance of the Second Rank: The Case of the Art Plunderer Kajetan Mühlmann," 177–221.

123. Quoted in Luza, *Austro-German Relations*, 146.

124. DÖW, doc. 7506: Report of the British Consul General in Vienna, 15 June 1939.

125. Ibid.

126. DÖW, doc. 7495: Copy of Despatch No. 166 to H.M. Ambassador, Berlin, dated 1 August 1939: General political situation in the Ostmark.

127. DÖW, doc. 7495: Copy of Despatch No. 172 to H.M. Ambassador, Berlin, dated 15 August 1939.

128. For this and other comparative insights, see A. J. P. Taylor, *The Habsburg Monarchy, 1809–1918*, 258.

129. Cf. Pauley, *Hitler and the Forgotten Nazis*, 218–22, and Luza, *Austro-German Relations*, 217–27.

CHAPTER FOUR

1. Zitelmann, *Hitler*, 175–98.

2. Kershaw, *Popular Opinion*, 71.

3. Konrad, "Social Democracy's Drift toward Nazism before 1938," 110–36; Schwarz, "Nazi Wooing of Austrian Social Democracy," 125–36; Bukey, *Hitler's Hometown*, 136, 147–48, 185; Bukey, "Nazi Rule in Austria," 211.

4. Hertz, *The Economic Problem of the Danubian States*, 147–50; Rothschild, *Austria's Economic Development*, 51–65; *Statistisches Handbuch für die Republik Österreich* (1938), 18:196–205; Bruckmüller, "Sozialstruktur und Sozialpolitik," 407–13; Stiefel, *Arbeitslosigkeit*, 26–32, 133–48; Karner, *Steiermark*, 294.

5. The Nazis arrested and imprisoned a number of Social Democratic activists immediately following the Anschluss; they also dispatched several prominent leaders to Dachau. Nonetheless, the sum total of those taken into custody appears to have been relatively small. See Kirk, *Nazism and the Working Class in Austria*, 49, 153 n. 4.

6. Luza, *Austro-German Relations*, 151–57; Schwarz, "Nazi Wooing of Austrian Social Democracy," 125–36; Botz, *Nationalsozialismus in Wien*, 129–44; Tálos, "Sozialpolitik 1938–1945," 115–24; Karner, "Zur NS-Sozialpolitik," 257–58; Walser, " 'Treue dem wahren Nationalsozialismus!' Arbeiter in der Vorarlberger NSDAP," 326.

7. Tálos, "Sozialpolitik 1938–1945," 117.

8. Karner, "Zur NS-Sozialpolitik," 257; Kernbauer and Weber, "Österreichs Wirtschaft," 54.

9. Kernbauer and Weber, "Österreichs Wirtschaft," 52–55; Botz, *Nationalsozialismus in Wien*, 299–302; Hautmann and Kropf, *Die österreichische Arbeiterbewegung*, 182; Schausberger, "Der Strukturwandel des ökonomischen Systems, 1938–1945," 151–54; Butschek, *Die österreichische Wirtschaft*, 122.

10. Butschek, *Die österreichische Wirtschaft*, 45–66; Kernbauer und Weber, "Österreichs Wirtschaft," 52–55; Josef Moser, "Der Wandel der Wirtschafts- und Beschäftigungsstruktur einer Region," 202–4; Karner, "Zur NS-Sozialpolitik," 258–59; Tálos, "Sozialpolitik 1938–1945," 130.

11. Botz, *Nationalsozialismus in Wien*, 311–15; Bukey, *Hitler's Hometown*, 186–87; Tálos, "Sozialpolitik 1938–1945," 127–29.

12. Luza, *Austro-German Relations*, 156–57.

13. Karner, "Zur NS-Sozialpolitik," 259.

14. Botz, *Nationalsozialismus in Wien*, 313.

15. Ibid., 290–91; Schwarz, "Nazi Wooing of Austrian Social Democracy," 125. Timothy Kirk points to a smaller working-class population for Vienna, but the figures he draws from the 1939 census still reveal huge concentrations of blue-collar residents in eight of the city's now twenty-two boroughs. Kirk, *Nazism and the Working Class in Austria*, 14; Kirk, "The Austrian Working Class under National Socialist Rule," 55.

16. Konrad, "Social Democracy's Drift toward Nazism," 120–22.

17. See, for example, the reports of the correspondent G. E. R. Gedye in the *New York Times*, 16 March, 22 March, 25 March 1938. See also his *Betrayal in Central Europe*, 283–302.

18. Botz, "'Judenhatz,'" 9–25.

19. Cf. Botz, *Nationalsozialismus in Wien*, 311–25, and Stadler, *Österreich*, 56.

20. Hanisch, "Peasants and Workers," 184. See also the revealing testimony of a trade-union functionary in Feiler, "The Viennese Municipal Service," 181–82.

21. Schwarz, "Nazi Wooing of Austrian Social Democracy," 131.

22. *Deutschland-Berichte der Sozialdemokratischen Partei Deutschlands (Sopade)*, 5:246–47.

23. AVA, Rk, box 19: Globocnik to Gerland, 1 April 1938.

24. DÖW, doc. 5172: Gestapo Vienna to SD RfSS, 31 May 1938.

25. DÖW, doc. 5120: Gestapo Vienna to SD Vienna, 28 June 1938.

26. Botz, *Nationalsozialismus in Wien*, 136.

27. *New York Times*, 23 May 1938.

28. PRO/FO: C6827/62/18: British Consul General in Vienna to British Ambassador in Berlin, 29 June 1938.

29. Luza, *Austro-German Relations*, 162–63.

30. Botz, *Nationalsozialismus in Wien*, 313–16; Williams, "Aftermath of Anschluss," 130–31.

31. Williams, "Aftermath of Anschluss," 134; Kreissler, *Der Österreicher und seine Nation*, 128–32.

32. DÖW, *"Anschluss,"* 605. See also Kirk, *Nazism and the Working Class in Austria*, 58–59.

33. Total Austrian membership rose within a month from 766,000 at the end of June to 1,100,000 by 1 August. Tálos, "Arbeits- und Sozialrecht im Nationalsozialismus—Steuerung der Arbeitsbeziehungen, Integration und Disziplinierung der Arbeiterschaft," 241.

34. AVA, Rk, box 166, folder 327/4700: Hupfauer to Bürckel, 31 August 1938.

35. Cf. Botz, *Nationalsozialismus in Wien*, 323–27, and Mulley, "Modernität oder Traditionalität?," 44.

36. AVA, Rk, box 168, folder 328a: Hupfauer to Bürckel, 16 July 1938.

37. Botz, *Nationalsozialismus in Wien*, 324. For a more skeptical interpretation, see Kirk, *Nazism and the Working Class in Austria*, 50–54.

38. Luza, *Resistance*, 79–80.

39. Garscha, *Die Verfahren vor dem Volksgericht Wien (1945–1955) als Geschichtsquelle*, 47.

40. Luza, *Resistance*, 81.

41. DÖW, doc. 7932: NSDAP Ortsgruppe Neubaugasse, Stimmungsbericht, 23 August 1938.

42. *Deutschland-Berichte der Sozialdemokratischen Partei Deutschlands (Sopade)*, 5:693–94.

43. Luza, *Resistance*, 81.

44. Stadler, *Österreich*, 57–59.

45. Karl Renner, "Die Gründung der Republik Deutsch-Österreich, der Anschluss und die Sudetendeutschen," as quoted in Hanisch, *Der lange Schatten des Staates*, 347.

46. Williams, "Aftermath of Anschluss," 141.

47. AVA, Rk, Ordner 387: Stimmen der Arbeiterschaft Dezember 1938.

48. Ibid.

49. Stadler, *Österreich*, 59–61; Botz, *Nationalsozialismus in Wien*, 465–68.

50. Botz, *Nationalsozialismus in Wien*, 327.

51. For additional details, see Luza, *Austro-German Relations*, 88–125, 138–50.

52. Williams, "Aftermath of Anschluss," 132.

53. Anne O'Hare McCormick, "In Europe: Hitler Does Not Find It Easy to Convert Austria," *New York Times*, 13 February 1939.

54. Anne O'Hare McCormick, "Austria Resists the Vise of the Nazis," *New York Times Magazine*, 12 March 1939, 23.

55. Ibid.

56. PRO/FO: C2406/53/18: Enclosure to Mr. Consul General Gainer's Despatch No. 70 of 15 March [1939].

57. Ibid.

58. Kirk, "The Austrian Working Class under National Socialist Rule," 127.

59. Botz, *Nationalsozialismus in Wien*, 467.

60. Butschek, *Die österreichische Wirtschaft*, 66–71.

61. Botz, *Nationalsozialismus in Wien*, 301, 468–70; Williams, "Aftermath of Anschluss," 133.

62. Botz, *Nationalsozialismus in Wien*, 307–10; AVA, Rk, folder 33: Bericht vom 22. 5. 1939; Luza, *Resistance*, 107–8.

63. DÖW, doc. 1445: Bericht der Urlauber aus der Spinnerei Kulmbach, 16 June 1939.

64. Stadler, *Österreich*, 63–69; Botz, *Nationalsozialismus in Wien*, 470–73.

65. DÖW, doc. 7506: British Consul General Vienna, 15 June 1939.

66. *Red-White-Red Book*, 91.

67. Cf. Kershaw, *Hitler Myth*, 141–42.

68. DÖW, doc. 7506: Reports of Nevile Henderson, Berlin: General situation in Austria. Extract from Despatch No. 162 of 31 July 1939.

69. DÖW, doc. 7495: Despatch No. 172 to Henderson, 15 August 1939.

70. Schöner, *Wiener Tagebücher 1944/45*, 441–44.

71. Botz, *Nationalsozialismus in Wien*, 470–73; Luza, *Resistance*, 108–10.

72. *Red-White-Red Book*, 92.

73. Jeffery, "Center and Periphery in Social Democratic Politics," 9–13; Bukey, *Hitler's Hometown*, 67.

74. Hanisch, "Opposition to Nazism in the Austrian Alps," 185.

75. Jeffery, *Social Democracy in the Austrian Provinces, 1918–1934*; Jeffery, "Center and Periphery in Social Democratic Politics," 28–39; Bukey, *Hitler's Hometown*, 146–48; Konrad, "Social Democracy's Drift toward Nazism before 1938," 110–36.

76. Hanisch, "Opposition to Nazism in the Austrian Alps," 184.

77. *Red-White-Red Book*, 86.

78. Bukey, "Hitler's Hometown under Nazi Rule: Linz, Austria, 1938–1945," 176.

79. Hanisch, "Peasants and Workers," 184–85.

80. Mulley, "Modernität oder Traditionalität?," 44.

81. Luza, *Austro-German Relations*, 57ff.

82. Walser, " 'Treue dem wahren Nationalsozialismus!' Arbeiter in der Vorarlberger NSDAP," 327.

83. Hanisch, "Peasants and Workers," 184–85; Bukey, "Nazi Rule in Austria," 211–12; Erhard and Natter, " 'Wir waren alle ja arbeitslos': NS-Sympathisanten deuten ihre Motive," 547–49.

84. Kepplinger, "Nationalsozialistische Wohnbaupolitik," 265–87.

85. Ibid.; Karner, *Steiermark*, 325–27.

86. Botz, *Nationalsozialismus in Wien*, 162.

87. As quoted in Slapnicka, *Oberdonau*, 53.

88. DÖW, docs. 8353: Unveröffentlichte Manuskripte für das von der Bundesregierung heraus-gegebenen Rot/weiss/rotbuch, Guttaring/St. Veit, May 1946, and 13.114a: Gendar-meriechronik Niklasdorf.

89. Slapnicka, *Oberdonau*, 281–82.

90. Kepplinger, "Nationalsozialistische Wohnbaupolitik," 280; Bukey, *Hitler's Hometown*, 180.

91. Stadler, *Österreich*, 71.

92. Slapnicka, *Oberdonau*, 281–82.

93. Ibid., 181–82; Bukey, *Hitler's Hometown*, 208; DÖW, doc. 17.846: G, Steyr, 1 April, 30 July, 2 August, 3 September 1938; G, Grünburg, 23 July 1938; G, Wolfern, 28 July 1938.

94. Hanisch, *Nationalsozialistische Herrschaft*, 161–65.

95. AVA, Rk, folder 311: Bericht über den Aufbau der Deutschen Arbeitsfront im Gau Nieder-donau, 25 July 1938.

96. Ibid.

97. Kirk, *Nazism and the Working Class in Austria*, 61.

98. DÖW, doc. E 17.846: G, Steyr, 29 July 1938; G, Sierning, 2 August 1938; G, Gleink, 28 Sep-tember 1938; G, Kremsmünster, 26 September 1938.

99. DÖW, doc. E 17.846: LR, Kirchdorf, 5 July, 1 August, 27 September 1938.

100. DÖW, docs. 4212: Gestapo Salzburg to Gestapo Berlin, 29 November 1938, and 17.846: G, Waldneukirchen, 23 September, 24 October 1938; LR, Kirchdorf, 27 September, 28 Octo-ber 1938; G, Weyer, 27 October 1938; G, Steyr, 30 October 1938. Industrial relations in the Steyr Works were certainly unusual for Nazi Germany: the personnel manager was a well-known Social Democrat, who openly favored party cronies over National Socialists. Al-though the SD complained that "there are sections in the *Steyrwerke* today in which only red comrades are taken in or tolerated," the need for skilled munitions workers was so acute that the regime felt it preferable to retain "politically unreliable" workingmen than to scale back operations or to close the plant. See Kirk, *Nazism and the Working Class in Austria*, 61–62.

101. DÖW, doc. 4081: Gestapo Linz to Heydrich, 4 October 1938.

102. DÖW, docs. 4212: Gestapo Salzburg to Gestapo Berlin, 30 December 1938, and E 17.846: G, Spital, 23 November 1938; G, Grünburg, 23 November 1938; G, Kremsmünster, 23 De-cember 1938, 23 January 1939; LR, Kirchdorf, 27 January 1939; G, Wartberg, 22 February 1939.

103. Stadler, *Österreich*, 58–59; Kirk, *Nazism and the Working Class in Austria*, 64; DÖW, doc. 8048: G, Lilienfeld, 20 November 1938; G, Traisen, 5 November 1938; NÖLA/ZR/1939: G, Waidhofen, 27 January 1939; G, Kematen, 25 February 1939; G, Rosenau, 27 March 1939; G, Ybbs, 26 March 1939.

104. Hanisch, "Peasants and Workers," 185.

105. DÖW, doc. 20.387: LR, Zell am See, 31 January 1939.

106. Luza, *Resistance*, 88–110; Hanisch, "Peasants and Workers," 186.

107. DÖW, doc. 17.846: G, Wartberg, 22 April 1939; NÖLA/ZR/1939: G, Ybbs, 26 March 1939; G, Rosenau, 27 March 1939; G, Waidhofen, 27 April 1939; LR, Amstetten, 2 May 1939; G, Waidhofen, 27 August 1939.

108. Luza, *Resistance*, 105–7; WVOÖ, 1:321–22; DÖW, doc. 4081: Gestapo Linz, Lagebericht für die Monate Jänner, Februar, und März 1939, 27 March 1939; Stadler, *Österreich*, 63.

109. Stadler, *Österreich*, 63–64; DÖW, doc. E 17.846: LR, Kirchdorf, 26 July, 29 August 1939; Slapnicka, *Oberdonau*, 258–87; NÖLA/ZR/I/1939: LR, Amstetten 2 May 1939; G, Waidhofen, 27 May, 27 July, 26 August 1939; G, Euratsfeld, 26 July 1939.

110. Hautmann and Kropf, *Die österreichische Arbeiterbewegung*, 106.

111. Schwarz, "Nazi Wooing of Austrian Social Democracy," 131–36.

112. Kirk, "The Austrian Working Class under National Socialist Rule," 136.

113. In his revised dissertation, *Nazism and the Working Class in Austria*, Kirk provides a more circumspect account of the eighteen months following the Anschluss; he now concedes the relative absence of "widespread industrial militancy and direct confrontation with employers" but eschews discussion of the ideological impact of Nazism on labor. Kirk's earlier views evidently reflect those of his doctoral supervisor, Ian Kershaw. Cf. Kershaw, *Popular Opinion*, 66–110; Kirk, "The Austrian Working Class under National Socialist Rule," 98–136; Kirk, *Nazism and the Working Class in Austria*, 48–67. See also Konrad, "Social Democracy's Drift toward Nazism," 110–36; Bukey, "Nazi Rule in Austria," 211–14; Mulley, "Modernität oder Traditionalität?," 44; Tálos, "Sozialpolitik 1938–1945," 115–24; Karner, "Zur NS-Sozialpolitik," 257–58.

114. Botz, "Zwischen Akzeptanz und Distanz," 439.

CHAPTER FIVE

1. Weinzierl, *Prüfstand*, 15–36.

2. Ibid.; Weinzierl, "Kirche und Politik," 437–42, 452–64; Kutschera, *Gföllner*, 47–56.

3. Jeffery, "Center and Periphery in Social Democratic Politics," 12–36; Gulick, *Austria*, 1:554–67; Hanisch, "Der politische Katholizismus," 56–59.

4. Hanisch, "Der politische Katholizismus," 58–63.

5. Weinzierl, "Kirche und Politik," 439–52; Hanisch, "Der politische Katholizismus," 63–66.

6. Weinzierl, "Kirche und Politik," 446–52.

7. Hanisch, "Der politische Katholizismus," 61–62.

8. Ibid., 55–56; Weinzierl, "Kirche und Politik," 437; Lewy, *Catholic Church*, 6.

9. Hanisch estimates that only 10 percent of Viennese Catholics regularly attended mass. Hanisch, "Der politische Katholizismus," 56.

10. Ibid., 64–66; Weinzierl, "Kirche und Politik," 442–51.

11. Weinzierl, *Prüfstand*, 15–74; Weinzierl, "Kirche und Politik," 439–43. For biographies of individual bishops, see Kutschera, *Gföllner*; Jablonka, *Waitz*; Reimann, *Innitzer*; Liebmann, *Innitzer*.

12. Kutschera, *Gföllner*, 93–94; Weinzierl, *Prüfstand*, 37–49.

13. Weinzierl, *Prüfstand*, 54–57.

14. Ibid., 57–73; Liebmann, *Innitzer*, 44–59.

15. Although Pius XI's anti-Nazi encyclical, *Mit brennender Sorge*, caused a sensation when it was read from Catholic pulpits in Germany on Palm Sunday, 21 March 1937, it attracted surprisingly little attention in Austria. See Sauer, "Österreichs Kirchen," 519.

16. For example, see Liebmann, *Innitzer*, 64–65.

17. For details, see Weinzierl, *Prüfstand*, 77–105; Liebmann, *Innitzer*, 65–95; Luza, "Nazi Control of the Austrian Catholic Church," 537–72.

18. Hanisch, *Nationalsozialistische Herrschaft*, 32; Karner, *Steiermark*, 54–55; Liebmann, *Innitzer*, 66–70.

19. The most convincing reconstruction of this momentous meeting—what today would be called a "photo opportunity"—is in Liebmann, *Innitzer*, 70–75. See also Weinzierl, *Prüfstand*, 81–83; Botz, *Nationalsozialismus in Wien*, 119–20; Reimann, *Innitzer*, 114; Fried, *Nationalsozialismus*, 23–24.

20. Liebmann, *Innitzer*, 75–95; Luza, *Austro-German Relations*, 64.

21. Nonetheless, "Innitzer must be seen as the driving force of the political declaration." Hagspiel, *Ostmark*, 39.

22. Liebmann, *Innitzer*, 85–96.

23. DÖW, *"Anschluss,"* 437.

24. The Reich commissioner was by no means disingenuous in this regard. Not only did he enjoy relatively amicable relations with the higher clergy of the Saarland; his sister was married to the brother of Bishop Joseph Wendel of Speyer. Liebmann, *Innitzer*, 66.

25. Ibid., 106–10.

26. Botz, *Nationalsozialismus in Wien*, 123–24; Liebmann, *Innitzer*, 129–38; Rhodes, *The Vatican in the Age of the Dictators*, 150–53.

27. Fried, *Nationalsozialismus*, 28.

28. Lewy, *Catholic Church*, 216.

29. PRO/FO: C6828/62/18: HM Consul General, Vienna, Despatch No. 38, 1 July 1938.

30. Lewy, *Catholic Church*, 217.

31. Kutschera, *Gföllner*, 106–13; Weinzierl, *Prüfstand*, 89–105.

32. Bukey, "Nazi Rule in Austria," 225.

33. See the cynical assessment by the Nazis in their first survey of the popular mood at AVA, Rk, folder 20: Reichsstatthalterei, Abt. 6, Vienna, 31 March 1938.

34. Hanisch, "Austrian Catholicism," 169.

35. Quoted in Rhodes, *The Vatican in the Age of the Dictators*, 152.

36. Liebmann, *Innitzer*, 140–45; Botz, *Nationalsozialismus in Wien*, 343–44; Sauer, "Österreichs Kirchen," 522–23; Weinzierl, *Prüfstand*, 101–2, 106–14.

37. For details of the polycratic infighting, see Luza, "Nazi Control of the Austrian Catholic Church," 543–51; Liebmann, *Innitzer*, 153–73; Sauer, "Österreichs Kirchen," 522–23.

38. The fullest account is Liebmann, *Innitzer*, 145–90. See also Weinzierl, *Prüfstand*, 106–39; Luza, "Nazi Control of the Austrian Catholic Church," 542–47; and Botz, *Nationalsozialismus in Wien*, 343–48.

39. Liebmann, *Innitzer*, 148–52.

40. Ibid., 154–75.

41. Luza, "Nazi Control of the Austrian Catholic Church," 543–47; Botz, *Nationalsozialismus in Wien*, 345–46; Fried, *Nationalsozialismus*, 46–49.

42. Liebmann, *Innitzer*, 169–78; Weinzierl, *Prüfstand*, 125–34; Luza, "Nazi Control of the Austrian Catholic Church," 545–46.

43. For the full text, see Liebmann, *Innitzer*, 178–88.

44. In light of continued declarations of regime support, especially during the Second World War, one must take exception to Erika Weinzierl's notion that the failure to reach a modus vivendi in 1938 marked the end of the church's strategy of appeasement. See Weinzierl, "Österreichs Katholiken und der Nationalsozialismus," 515, as quoted in Botz, *Der Nationalsozialismus in Wien*, 348.

45. The term coined by John Lukacs in his disturbing assessment of the convergence of religion and nationalism in Nazi Europe. Lukacs, *The Last European War*.

46. Liebmann, *Innitzer*, 207–8.

47. Luza, *Austro-German Relations*, 185–86; Luza, *Resistance*, 66–75.

48. On early Catholic resistance groups, see Luza, *Resistance*, 29–59.

49. Hermann Lein, "Das Rosenkranzfest am 7. Oktober 1938," in DÖW, *Jahrbuch 1990*, 51–52.

50. Ibid., 50–55, for the most comprehensive account. But see also Liebmann, *Innitzer*, 190–98, which contains the full text of Innitzer's homily; Weinzierl, *Prüfstand*, 143–44; Botz, *Der Nationalsozialismus in Wien*, 383–84.

51. Lein, "Rosenkranzfest," 50–55. Similar outbursts had occurred in Bavaria the year before, including a stirring ovation for Cardinal Michael Faulhaber at Munich in February 1937. In contrast to the Viennese "Rosary Festival" of 7 October 1938, the Bavarian crowds, although impressive, numbered only several hundred participants. See Kershaw, *Popular Opinion*, 201–5.

52. For the most complete account, see Liebmann, *Innitzer*, 198–208.

53. PRO/FO: C12690/62/18: British Consulate, Vienna, Despatch No. 104, 13 October 1938.

54. *New York Times*, 13 February 1939.

55. Hanisch, "Austrian Catholicism," 168; Sauer, "Österreichs Kirchen," 524–25; Botz, *Nationalsozialismus in Wien*, 388–91.

56. Fest, *Hitler*, 568; Goldinger, "Der Sturm auf das Wiener erzbischöfliche Palais 1938 im Lichte der NS Akten," 16–21; PRO/FO: C13695/62/18, No. 116: British Consulate, Vienna, 7 November 1938.

57. Wistrich, *Antisemitism*, 13–29; Pauley, *From Prejudice to Persecution*, 1–44.

58. Pauley, *From Prejudice to Persecution*, 150–73. Quotation from p. 173.

59. Ibid., 298; Weinzierl, *Zu wenig Gerechte*, 96–97; Freidenreich, *Jewish Politics in Vienna, 1918–1938*, 187; Rosenkranz, *Verfolgung*, 23–24.

60. Weinzierl, *Prüfstand*, 265–67; Weinzierl, *Zu wenig Gerechte*, 97–98; Luza, *Resistance*, 71.

61. Cf. Weinzierl, *Prüfstand*, 258–76; Weinzierl, *Zu wenig Gerechte*, 93–116; Lewy, *Catholic Church*, 274–84; Rhodes, *The Vatican in the Age of the Dictators*, 180.

62. Lukacs, *The Last European War*, 471.

63. For examples, see Weinzierl, *Prüfstand*, 277–86; Weinzierl, *Zu wenig Gerechte*, 11–14.

64. Cf. Liebmann, *Innitzer*, 207–8; Lewy, *Catholic Church*, 283–84; Kershaw, *Popular Opinion*, 253–57, 270–72.

65. Weinberg, *A World at Arms*, 899.

66. Fest, *Hitler*, 568–69.

67. Karner, *Steiermark*, 119.

68. Luza, *Austro-German Relations*, 186–87; Luza, "Nazi Control of the Austrian Catholic Church," 546–47; Weinzierl, *Prüfstand*, 152–55; Botz, *Nationalsozialismus in Wien*, 388–96. The most detailed account of the administrative and financial disestablishment of the Austrian church is in Liebmann, *Innitzer*, 209–26.

69. Hanisch, *Nationalsozialistische Herrschaft*, 103; Hanisch, "Die katholische Kirche," in *WVS*, 2:134; Eichinger, "Die politische Situation im südwestlichen Niederösterreich," 193–94.

70. Eichinger, "Die politische Situation im südwestlichen Niederösterreich," 193–209; Hanisch, *Nationalsozialistische Herrschaft*, 167–70; Hanisch, "Austrian Catholicism," 170–71.

71. Liebmann, *Innitzer*, 210.

72. Luza, "Nazi Control of the Austrian Catholic Church," 548.

73. For the full text of the bishops' letter, see Liebmann, *Innitzer*, 227–35.

74. Some 41,456 Evangelicals also renounced the Christian faith, even though at least two-thirds of the total membership of 331,871 already belonged to the Nazi Party. Luza, *Austro-German Relations*, 187; Sauer, "Österreichs Kirchen," 519.

75. Quoted in Luza, "Nazi Control of the Austrian Catholic Church," 547 n. 23. For the full text of the Nazi report, "Ein Jahr Entkonfessionalisierung der Ostmark," see Liebmann, *Innitzer*, 240–53.

76. *Hitler's Secret Conversations* (20–21 February 1942), 262.

77. *WVT*, 2:102–3.

78. *Red-White-Red Book*, SD, Vienna, 3 July 1939.

79. Ibid.; Williams, "Aftermath of Anschluss," 138–39.

80. Luza, *Resistance*, 35–39.

81. Hanisch, "Austrian Catholicism," 166.

82. Cf. Kershaw, *Popular Opinion*, 223.

CHAPTER SIX

1. Cf. Kershaw, *Popular Opinion*, 33–36, and Bruckmüller, "Sozialstruktur und Sozialpolitik," 389–94.

2. Kershaw, *Popular Opinion*, 34–36, and Bruckmüller, "Sozialstruktur und Sozialpolitik," 392–94.

3. Karner, *Steiermark*, 65, 283–84.

4. Mooslechner and Stadler, "Landwirtschaft und Agrarpolitik," 82–84.

5. For details, see Corni, *Hitler and the Peasants*, 245–68.

6. Mooslechner and Stadler, "Landwirtschaft und Agrarpolitik," 79–81.

7. Cf. Kershaw, *Popular Opinion*, 42–45; Corni, *Hitler and the Peasants*, 143–52; Hanisch, *Nationalsozialistische Herrschaft*, 152; Mooslechner and Stadler, "Landwirtschaft und Agrarpolitik," 74–76.

8. Corni, *Hitler and the Peasants*, 66–115; Mooslechner and Stadler, "Landwirtschaft und Agrarpolitik," 70–73. See also the excellent OSS analysis of June 1945: NA, RG 226, doc. 138849, box 1571: Agriculture and Food Administration in Austria.

9. AVA, Rk, Ordner 211/2260/2: Zwischenbericht, 28 March 1938; DÖW, doc. 17.846: Gendarmerie reports from Gleink, 2 April 1938, Kirchdorf, 3 April 1938; Slapnicka, *Oberdonau*, 281–82.

10. NÖLA/ZR/1938/I: Situationsbericht, Amstetten, 23 March, 28 March, 11 April, 27 April 1938.

11. Slapnicka, *Oberdonau*, 252–53.

12. Cf. Corni, *Hitler and the Peasants*, 220–39; Kershaw, *Popular Opinion*, 55–65.

13. Slapnicka, *Oberdonau*, 158–59; DÖW, doc. 17.846: G, Bad Hall, 2 May 1938.

14. Mooslechner and Stadler, "Landwirtschaft und Agrarpolitik," 85–87; Kershaw, *Popular Opinion*, 57–58; DÖW, doc. 17.846: G, Bad Hall, 2 May 1938.

15. In early June a British observer wrote from Innsbruck: "The peasantry in Tirol are on the whole very detached in their attitude to recent events, and though willing enough to give the new system a fair trial and extremely unlikely to take the political responsibility of showing any opposition, are fundamentally distrustful and ill at ease with the future." PRO/FO: C5710/62/18: Memorandum of Mr. Creswell, "Conditions in Western Austria," 7 June 1938.

16. Slapnicka, *Oberdonau*, 282–83; DÖW, doc. 17.846: G, Steyr, 30 June 1938, G, Reichraming, 29 July 1938, G, Bad Hall, 27 June 1938.

17. The literature on the Austrian church struggle is enormous, but see Weinzierl, *Prüfstand*; Luza, "Nazi Control of the Austrian Catholic Church," 537–72; Hanisch, "Austrian Catholicism," 165–76; Sauer, "Österreichs Kirchen," 517–36. On the church struggle in the Old Reich, see Lewy, *Catholic Church*; Helmreich, *The German Churches under Hitler*; Conway, *Nazi Persecution of the Churches*; Rhodes, *The Vatican in the Age of the Dictators*; Kershaw, *Popular Opinion*, 185–223, 331–57.

18. Hanisch, "Austrian Catholicism," 170.

19. Cf. ibid., 170–75, and Kershaw, *Popular Opinion*, 205–23.

20. Hanisch, "Austrian Catholicism," 171.

21. DÖW, doc. 17.846: G, Kirchdorf, 5 July 1938; Slapnicka, *Oberdonau*, 283.

22. Luza, *Austro-German Relations*, 182–85.

23. AVA, Rk, box 157, folder 3089 (Gauleitung Tirol): Sicherheitspolizei, Innsbruck, 8 July 1938.

24. AVA, Rk, box 157, folder 3089 (Gauleitung Tirol): Hofer to Bürckel, 23 August 1938.

25. Cf. Stadler, *Österreich*, 57–59, and Botz, *Nationalsozialismus in Wien*, 324–63, 465–66.

26. DÖW, doc. 17.846: G, Bad Hall, 12 July 1938; G, Waldneukirchen, 24 July 1938; G, Kirchdorf, 1 August 1938; BH, Steyr, 2 August 1938; G, Ried, 29 August 1938; BH, Steyr, September 1938; G, Bad Hall, 27 September 1938; G, Gleink, 28 September 1938; NÖLA/1938/I/199: BH, Amstetten, 3 October 1938.

27. DÖW, doc. 8339: Pöttsching, 21 September 1938.

28. Slapnicka, *Oberdonau*, 284; DÖW, docs. 8048: G, Türnitz, 16 November 1938; G, Kaunberg, 31 October 1938; G, Lilienfeld, 31 October 1938; and 17.846: G, Sierning, 25 October 1938; G, Bad Hall, 26 October 1938; G, Gleink, 27 October 1938; BH, Steyr, 30 October 1938; NÖLA/ZR/I/1939: BH, Amstetten, 3 October, 2 November, 30 November 1938.

29. Slapnicka, *Oberdonau*, 284–85; DÖW, doc. 8048: G, St. Ägyd, 1 October 1938, Freiland, 30 October 1938, Kaunberg, 31 October 1938, Hainfeld, 1 November 1938, Lilienfeld, 1 November 1938, Traisen, 5 November 1938.

30. Slapnicka, *Oberdonau*, 285; Williams, "Aftermath of Anschluss," 135–36.

31. Mooslechner and Stadler, "Landwirtschaft und Agrarpolitik," 79, 86.

32. Corni, *Hitler and the Peasants*, 253–64.

33. Luza, "Nazi Control of the Austrian Catholic Church," 546–47; Slapnicka, *Oberdonau*, 285–86; NÖLA/ZR/1939: G, Markt Ardagger, 27 January 1939; G, Mauer, 27 January 1939; BH, Amstetten, 3 February 1939. For examples of religious protest in Vorarlberg, see the interesting parish records and photographs in Meusberger, *Bezau*, 261–64.

34. DÖW, doc. E 17.846: G, Spital am Pyhrn, 23 February 1939; NÖLA/ZR/1939: G, Waidhofen, 27 January, 27 February 1939; G, Markt Ardagger, 27 January 1939; G, St. Peter, 10 February 1939.

35. NÖLA/ZR/1939: G, Aschbach, 26 January 1939.

36. Hanisch, "Austrian Catholicism," 170.

37. DÖW, doc. 17.846: G, Kirchdorf, 28 February 1939.

38. DÖW, doc. 17.846: G, Wartberg, 22 February 1939; G, Pettenbach, 23 February 1939; G, Nussbach, 23 February 1939; NÖLA/ZR/1939: G, St. Valentin, 26 February 1939.

39. The number of live births in Austria rose from 12.8 per 1,000 inhabitants in 1937 to 20.7 in 1939. Botz, "Zwischen Akzeptanz und Distanz," 449.

40. DÖW, doc. 17.846: G, Grünburg, 21 March 1939; G, Kremsmünster, 23 March 1939; G, Windischgarsten, 23 March 1939; G, Ried, 25 March 1939; G, Kirchdorf, 27 March 1939; NÖLA/ZR/199/1939: G, Seitenstetten, 25 March 1939; G, Wallsee, 26 February 1939; G, Aschbach, 27 March 1939; G, Ybbsitz, 27 March 1939; G, Markt Ardagger, 27 March 1939; G, St. Peter, 27 March 1939. On reaction in the Altreich, see Kershaw, *Hitler Myth*, 139–41.

41. NÖLA/ZR/199/1939: LR, Amstetten, 2 April 1939.

42. NÖLA/ZR/199/1939: G, Amstetten, 24 April 1939; G, Behamberg, 25 April 1939; G, Seitenstetten, 26 April 1939; G, Strengberg, 27 April 1939; G, Ulmerfeld, April 1939; G, Ybbsitz, 27 April 1939; G, Rosenau, 27 April 1939; DÖW, doc. 17.846: G, Steinbach, 21 April 1939; G, Pettenbach, 22 April 1939; G, Windischgarsten, 23 April 1939.

43. DÖW, doc. 17.846: G, Steinbach am Ziehberge, 21 April 1939.

44. DÖW, doc. 17.846: G, Nussbach, 22 April 1939.

45. NÖLA/ZR/199/1939: G, Euratsfeld, 26 June 1939. In an important study of Nazi rule in Lower Austria Hermann Eichinger writes: "In contrast to measures against the Jews which encountered at least a degree of popular incomprehension, there was never the slightest trace of solidarity with the Gypsies. From the very beginning, every action taken against these people was without exception welcomed. There was no demonstration of sympathy of any kind. People were constantly complaining that the intended regulation of the Gypsy

Question had not yet succeeded." Eichinger, "Die politische Situation im südwestlichen Niederösterreich," 158.

46. For example, Kreissler, *Der Österreicher und seine Nation*, 131–32. See also Williams, "Aftermath of Anschluss," 139–40.

47. Parkinson, *Conquering the Past*, 319. See also Stuhlpfarrer, "Nazism, the Austrians, and the Military," 190–206, and Manoschek and Safrian, "Österreicher in der Wehrmacht," 331–60.

48. DÖW, doc. 17.846: LR, Kirchdorf, 30 May 1939.

49. Hanisch, "Peasants and Workers," 182.

50. Cf. Williams, "Aftermath of Anschluss," 136–37; Hanisch, "Comments," 164–65; Kerschbaumer, *Faszination Drittes Reich*, 34–37.

51. Kerschbaumer, *Faszination Drittes Reich*, 34–41, 60–64; DÖW, doc. 17.858/7: Gendarmerie Chronik Oberdrauburg, 9 November 1939.

52. Kerschbaumer, *Faszination Drittes Reich*, 38–41, 59–60; *Red-White-Red Book*, 88–89.

53. DÖW, doc. 17.846: G, Ried, 19 May 1939.

54. DÖW, docs. 20.387: G, Salzburg, 25 July 1939, and 17.846: G, Windischgarsten, 20 May 1939; G, Steinbach, 20 May 1939; G, Nussbach, 23 June 1939; NÖLA/ZR/199/1939: G, Markt Wallsee, 30 May 1939; LR, Amstetten, 3 June, 2 July 1939; G, Behamberg, 25 June 1939; G, Euratsfeld, 26 June 1939; G, Ybbs, 27 June 1939. On the strikingly similar attitudinal climate in Bavaria, see Kershaw, *Popular Opinion*, 61–65.

55. NÖLA/ZR/199/1939: LR, Amstetten, 3 June 1939; G, Ulmerfeld, 26 June 1939; G, Wolfsbach, 27 June 1939; G, Ybbs, 27 June 1939; G, Rosenau, 27 June 1939.

56. DÖW, doc. 17.846: LR, Kirchdorf a/Krems, 30 May 1939.

57. NÖLA/ZR/199/1939: G, St. Peter, 27 June 1939; Markt Ardagger, 27 June 1939; G, Ried, 23 June 1939; G, Opponitz, June 1939; G, Oed, 27 June 1939; G, Euratsfeld, 26 June 1939; LR, Amstetten, 2 July 1939.

58. DÖW, doc. 17.846: G, Steinbach, 27 June 1939; G, Pettenbach, 22 June 1939; G, Nussbach, 23 June 1939.

59. DÖW, doc. 8351: Abschrift aus der Chronik der Volksschule Luggau von 1939.

60. *Red-White-Red Book*, 89.

61. Luza, *Austro-German Relations*, 187.

62. Klostermann, "Katholische Jugend im Untergrund," 144, 194–96.

63. Hanisch, "Austrian Catholicism," 173.

64. DÖW, doc. 17.846: G, Steyrling, 23 May 1939; G, Wartberg, 22 August 1939.

65. Cf. Slapnicka, *Oberdonau*, 286, and *Red-White-Red Book*, 90.

66. Cf. DÖW, doc. 17.846: G, Wartberg, 22 July 1939; G, Spital, 24 July 1939; doc. 7495: British Consul General Vienna, Extract from Despatch No. 162 of 31 July 1939; *Red-White-Red Book*, 91–92; Williams, "Aftermath of Anschluss," 137–39; Kershaw, *Popular Opinion*, 62–65; Kershaw, *Hitler Myth*, 141–42.

67. DÖW, doc. 17.846: G, Ried, 22 July 1939.

68. DÖW, doc. 17.846: G, Nussbach, 24 July 1939; NÖLA/ZR/199/1939: LR, Amstetten, 2 July 1939; AVA, Rk, box 211: Bürckel (?) to Rainer, 20 July 1939; Williams, "Aftermath of Anschluss," 141.

69. NÖLA/ZR/199/1939: G, Behamberg, 24 July 1939; G, Oed, 25 July 1939; G, Seitenstetten,

26 July 1939; G, Strengberg, 26 July 1939; G, Ybbsitz, 26 July 1939; G, Euratsfeld, 26 July 1939; G, Kematen, 26 July 1939; G, Waidhofen, 27 July 1939; G, Rosenau, 27 July 1939; G, St. Valentin, 28 July 1939; LR, Amstetten, 31 July 1939.

70. DÖW, doc. 17.846: LR, Kirchdorf, 21 August 1939; G, Steyrling, 23 August 1939; NÖLA/ZR/199/1939: G, Seitenstetten, 22 August 1939; G, Wallsee, 25 August 1939.

71. DÖW, doc. 17.846: G, Klaus, 24 August 1939; LR, Kirchdorf, 29 August 1939; doc. 20.387: LR, Zell am See, 3 September 1939; NÖLA/ZR/199/1939: G, Rosenau, 26 August 1939; G, Haag, 26 August 1939; G, Strengberg, 26 August 1939; G, Euratsfeld, 26 July 1939; G, Aschbach, 26 August 1939; G, St. Peter, 27 August 1939; G, Wolfsbach, 1939. See also Slapnicka, *Oberdonau*, 285–87.

72. Hanisch, "Opposition to Nazism in the Austrian Alps," 178.

73. Luza, *Resistance*, 35–36.

74. NÖLA/ZR/199/1939: G, Euratsfeld, 26 May 1939.

75. Hanisch, "Opposition to Nazism in the Austrian Alps," 180.

CHAPTER SEVEN

1. Pauley, *From Prejudice to Persecution*, 318.

2. Botz, "The Jews of Vienna from the Anschluss to the Holocaust," 183.

3. Rosenkranz, "The Anschluss and the Tragedy of Austrian Jewry," 480.

4. Ibid.; Pauley, *From Prejudice to Persecution*, 121–30; Bentwich, "The Destruction of the Jewish Community in Austria," 467.

5. Rosenkranz, *Verfolgung*, 13.

6. Cf. Kershaw, *Popular Opinion*, 224–31; Gold, *Geschichte der Juden in Österreich*; Jonny Moser, *Die Judenverfolgung in Österreich 1938–1945*; Slapnicka, "Zum Antisemitismus Problem in Oberösterreich," 264–67; Fellner, *Antisemitismus in Salzburg 1918–1938*; Walzl, *Die Juden in Kärnten und das Dritte Reich*.

7. The authoritative work is Freidenreich, *Jewish Politics in Vienna*.

8. Rosenkranz, *Verfolgung*, 13.

9. Freidenreich, *Jewish Politics in Vienna*, 205–6; Pauley, *From Prejudice to Persecution*, 277–84; Berkley, *Vienna and Its Jews*, 221–54; Rosenkranz, "The Anschluss and the Tragedy of Austrian Jewry," 479–82.

10. Kershaw, "The Persecution of the Jews and German Popular Opinion in the Third Reich," 261–89; Kater, "Everyday Anti-Semitism in Prewar Nazi Germany: The Popular Bases," 129–59; David Bankier, *The Germans and the Final Solution*, 1–81; Goldhagen, *Hitler's Willing Executioners*, 81–128; Weiss, *Ideology of Death*, 362–79; Friedländer, *Nazi Germany and the Jews*, 125–26, 162–67; Kaplan, *Between Dignity and Despair*, 3–49. Of these works, the thoughtful and highly differentiated assessments of Friedländer and Kaplan come closest to verisimilitude. In contrast, Goldhagen's strident tone and nescience of contradictory evidence undermine a persuasive argument.

11. Janik, review of *From Prejudice to Persecution*, by Bruce F. Pauley, 243.

12. Gedye, *Betrayal in Central Europe*, 284.

13. Ibid. Gedye's estimates may have been exaggerated, but recent research reveals that thousands of Viennese participated in the mob violence. See Safrian and Witek, *Und keiner war dabei*, 195.

14. Stadler, *Österreich*, 27. In a recent article Wolfgang Neugebauer contends that between 50,000 and 76,000 persons were taken into custody, an estimate based on a single ambiguous source. Neugebauer, "Das NS-Terrorsystem," 164. Botz reckons the number of March arrests as between 10,000 and 20,000, but adds that the number of those briefly detained may have been much higher. Botz, *Der Nationalsozialismus in Wien*, 58.

15. Botz, "The Dynamics of Persecution in Austria," 202.

16. Gedye, *Betrayal in Central Europe*, 297.

17. Botz, "The Dynamics of Persecution in Austria," 202.

18. On the tidal wave of anti-Semitic terror in Vienna, see Gedye, *Betrayal in Central Europe*, 270–315, and his *New York Times* articles, 14, 15, and 25 March, 3 April 1938. See also Berkley, *Vienna and Its Jews*, 259–328; Botz, *Der Nationalsozialismus in Wien*, 93–105; Jonny Moser, *Judenverfolgung*, 109–22; Rosenkranz, *Verfolgung*, 20–168; Rosenkranz, "The Anschluss and the Tragedy of Austrian Jewry," 479–546; Bentwich, "The Destruction of the Jewish Community in Austria," 467–98. For memoirs of survivors, see Zuckmayer, *A Part of Myself*, especially 29–94; Hilsenrad, *Brown Was the Danube*, 273–391; Clare, *Last Waltz in Vienna*, especially 158–257; Klüger, *Weiter leben: Eine Jugend*, 7–33; Rudin, *The Way I Remember It*, 33–37.

19. Quoted in Berkley, *Vienna and Its Jews*, 306.

20. Jonny Moser, "Depriving the Jews of Their Legal Rights," 123–24.

21. Pauley is emphatic in arguing that "Aryanization (and also emigration) measures carried out by Austrian Nazis at most only accelerated trends well underway in the Altreich." Botz has long argued this view but appears recently to have become ambivalent, conceding the initiative to the Austrian Nazis and the Viennese mob. Both Hans Safrian and Saul Friedländer have suggested "An Austrian Model" in the evolution of the Holocaust, though the latter discounts the participatory role of the anti-Semitic masses. Pauley, *From Prejudice to Persecution*, 286; Botz, *Wohnungspolitik und Judendeportation in Wien 1938 bis 1945*; Botz, *Nationalsozialismus in Wien*, especially 93–105, 243–59; Botz, "'Judenhatz,'" 9–24; Botz, "The Jews of Vienna from the Anschluss to the Holocaust"; Botz, "The Dynamics of Persecution in Austria," 199–219; Safrian, *Die Eichmann Männer*, 23–67; Friedländer, *Nazi Germany and the Jews*, 240–68.

22. For details of the infighting and confusion, see Safrian, *Die Eichmann Männer*, 30–34.

23. Rosenkranz, "The Anschluss and the Tragedy of Austrian Jewry," 486–90; Botz, "The Dynamics of Persecution in Austria," 204.

24. Quoted in Botz, "The Dynamics of Persecution in Austria," 200.

25. Quoted in Jonny Moser, "Depriving the Jews of Their Legal Rights," 125.

26. For details, see ibid., 125–27; Rosenkranz, "The Anschluss and the Tragedy of Austrian Jewry," 486–90; Rosenkranz, *Verfolgung*, 22, 48–149.

27. For a balanced discussion of the historiographical issues, see David Bankier, *The Germans and the Final Solution*, 1–29, and Friedländer, *Nazi Germany and the Jews*, 162–67. See also Weiss, *Ideology of Death*, 363–79.

28. After examining thousands of Nazi records, Karl Stadler found it impossible to produce even a minimalist sketch. Stadler, *Österreich*, 105.

29. Safrian and Witek, *Und keiner war dabei*, 19–57; Bukey, "Popular Opinion in Vienna after the Anschluss," 156–57.

30. Cf. Bukey, "Popular Opinion in Vienna after the Anschluss," 157, and *New York Times*, 25 March 1938.

31. Berkley, *Vienna and Its Jews*, 259–328; Clare, *Last Waltz in Vienna*, 187–283; Hughes, "Funeral Waltz: Vienna under Nazi Rule, 1938–1939: A Personal Memoir."

32. Botz, "'Judenhatz,'" 17. One eyewitness, Alfred Kessler, takes strong exception to this view, vividly recalling crowds containing a fair share of workers marching in from the industrial suburb of Favoriten to join in the Anschluss hysteria. He concurs, however, that the tone was set by the lower middle class: in the apt words of his father, the late Egon Kessler, "der rasend gewordene Kleinbürger." Conversation with the author, 20 February 1994.

33. Witek, "'Arisierung' in Wien," 205.

34. Safrian and Witek, *Und keiner war dabei*, 195.

35. Denscher, "'Der ewige Jude': Antisemitische Propaganda vom 'Anschluss' bis zum Novemberpogrom 1938," 43–46.

36. AVA, Rk, boxes 173–78, Ordner 338–51.

37. AVA, Rk, box 173, Ordner 338–43.

38. Ibid., especially the letters June–September 1938.

39. Karner, *Steiermark*, 168–71; Bukey, *Hitler's Hometown*, 187–89; Hanisch, *Nationalsozialistische Herrschaft*, 105–11; Köfler, "Tirol und die Juden," 176–78; Walzl, *Die Juden in Kärnten und das Dritte Reich*, 138–49, especially 149; Rosenkranz, *Verfolgung*, 86–94; Rosenkranz, "The Anschluss and the Tragedy of Austrian Jewry," 488–89.

40. For details, see *WVB*, 295–304.

41. Rosenkranz, *Verfolgung*, 92.

42. But see Fellner, "Der Novemberpogrom in Westösterreich," 37; Walzl, *Die Juden in Kärnten*, 147; Kurij, *Nationalsozialismus und Widerstand im Waldviertel*, 151–55.

43. Cf. David Bankier, *The Germans and the Final Solution*, 82–85.

44. DÖW, doc. 17.846: G, Reichraming, 29 July 1938; G, Steyr, 2 August 1938.

45. Weinzierl, *Zu wenig Gerechte*, 107.

46. Bukey, *Hitler's Hometown*, 189.

47. Kurij, *Nationalsozialismus und Widerstand im Waldviertel*, 152.

48. Cf. Kershaw, *Popular Opinion*, 224–77.

49. DÖW, doc. 17.846: G, 23 September 1938.

50. Stubenvoll, *Bibliographie zum Nationalsozialismus in Österreich*, 15–22.

51. DÖW, *Erzählte Geschichte*, 90–163. On the other hand, see the graphic testimony from postwar court records in Witek and Safrian, *Und keiner war dabei*, 22–32.

52. Freidenreich, *Jewish Politics in Vienna*, 202–3; Pauley, *From Prejudice to Persecution*, 275–79.

53. Clare, *Last Waltz in Vienna*, 123. Another Jewish survivor recalled that "German Jews we met in Karlsbad in the mid-1930s had assured us that things were not so bad, that the Nazis' bark was worse than their bite, that one should lie low until this blew over, for the regime

was so extreme that it could not possibly last in a rational society." Furst and Furst, *Home Is Somewhere Else*, 21.

54. Pauley, *From Prejudice to Persecution*, 277; Zweig, *The World of Yesterday*, 402–5.

55. Pauley, *From Prejudice to Persecution*, 277–79; Jonny Moser, "Das Schicksal der Wiener Juden," 172–73.

56. *Documents on German Foreign Policy*, Series D, vol. 1 (docs. 309, 313), 531–35.

57. Jonny Moser, "Das Schicksal der Wiener Juden," 172; Pauley, *From Prejudice to Persecution*, 278–79; Clare, *Last Waltz in Vienna*, 164–68; DÖW, *Erzählte Geschichte*, 99.

58. Conversation with Alfred Kessler, 2 August 1996. Even the crotchety Sigmund Freud was impressed. "At present our government, upright and brave in its own way," he wrote Max Eitingon, "is more energetic in fending off the Nazis than ever before." Quoted in Gay, *Freud*, 617.

59. Clare, *Last Waltz in Vienna*, 171.

60. Pauley, *From Prejudice to Persecution*, 279.

61. Schneider, *Exile and Destruction*, 12.

62. Grunwald, *One Man's America*, 24.

63. Clare, *Last Waltz in Vienna*, 177.

64. DÖW, *Erzählte Geschichte*, 139–40, 100–102.

65. Clare, *Last Waltz in Vienna*, 178. Another survivor, Alfred Kessler, concurs that this single incident also encapsulates his own Anschluss experience. Conversation with the author, 2 August 1996.

66. Botz, "The Jews of Vienna from the Anschluss to the Holocaust," 189; Safrian, *Die Eichmann Männer*, 30–31. In a letter to the author Alfred Kessler, who witnessed the Anschluss as a Viennese "mestizo," explains: "The Austrian Jews, as well as non-Jewish anti-Nazi Austrians, who constituted about 20 per cent of the population, were shell-shocked by 1) the suddenness 2) the entirely spontaneous vehemence and violence on the part of the pro-Nazi Austrians resulting from the Nazi take-over in Austria. Austrian Jews who were non-political (except anti-Nazi) were demoralized, humiliated and desperately trying to rebuild their lives. That sort of psychological condition is rarely conducive to writing objective accounts of the Nazi takeover. Historians among them who attempted it were usually Austrian sentimentalists, putting the blame on greedy German imperialism (or in the case of the monarchist sympathizers, blaming 'Prussian' militarism), from Bismarck onwards. Their perception was distinctly unhistorical, being determined by their psyches, rather than their intellect. I do not find it at all surprising that there are no accounts from them that could ever be remotely acceptable to well-disciplined historians. Those Jews were 'fassungslos' [clueless] when faced by the Nazi takeover, especially its brutality." Alfred Kessler to the author, 6 August 1996.

67. Jonny Moser, "Das Schicksal der Wiener Juden," 178.

68. Gedye, *Betrayal in Central Europe*, 296.

69. Ibid., 299.

70. Jonny Moser "Das Schicksal der Wiener Juden," 177–78.

71. Hofmann, *The Viennese*, 242.

72. Botz, *Nationalsozialismus in Wien*, 103–4. Even Anna Freud considered suicide, but she was dissuaded by her father. Gay, *Freud*, 622.

73. Clare, *Last Waltz in Vienna*, 191–92; Hilsenrad, *Brown Was the Danube*, 273–97.

74. Clare, *Last Waltz in Vienna*, 195; Grunwald, *One Man's Journey*, 27–29; Hilsenrad, *Brown Was the Danube*, 291–302. On the crucial role played by Jewish women in persuading husbands and family members to emigrate from Nazi Germany, see Kaplan, *Between Dignity and Despair*, especially 50–73.

75. Schneider, *Exile and Destruction*, 14.

76. Pauley, *From Prejudice to Persecution*, 282.

77. Ibid., 282–84; Rosenkranz, *Verfolgung*, 39–44.

78. AVA, Rk, box 173, folder 338: Anonymous letters of 11, 27, 28 April and 3, 5 May 1938.

79. Paucker, "Resistance of German and Austrian Jews to the Nazi Regime, 1933–1945," 18.

80. Pauley, *From Prejudice to Persecution*, 282–84; Jonny Moser, "Das Schicksal der Wiener Juden," 180–82. For the most thorough account, see Rosenkranz, *Verfolgung*, 39–58.

81. Schneider, *Exile and Destruction*, 21–23.

82. But see Furst and Furst, *Home Is Somewhere Else*, 29–30.

83. Clare, *Last Waltz in Vienna*, 191. Helen Hilsenrad implies much the same thing in her harrowing memoir of life in Vienna between the German invasion and her family's departure on 22 February 1940. Hilsenrad, *Brown Was the Danube*, 273–391.

84. Jonny Moser, "Österreichs Juden unter der NS-Herrschaft," 191–93; Freidenreich, *Jewish Politics in Vienna*, 206.

85. Quoted in David Bankier, *The Germans and the Final Solution*, 64–65.

86. Ibid., 64–66, 82–85.

87. Rosenkranz, "The Anschluss and the Tragedy of Austrian Jewry," 494–95; Rosenkranz, *Verfolgung*, 157–58; Berkley, *Vienna and Its Jews*, 277–78.

88. The literature on Crystal Night is substantial. For a chilling account of the background and planning of the operation based on recently discovered evidence, see Friedländer, *Nazi Germany and the Jews*, 268–80. See also Graml, *Der 9. November 1938: "Reichskristallnacht"*; Thalmann and Feinermann, *Crystal Night: 9–10 November 1938*; Pehle, *Der Judenpogrom 1938*.

89. Rosenkranz, *"Reichskristallnacht" 9. November 1938 in Österreich*; Rosenkranz, *Verfolgung*, 159–66; Rosenkranz, "The Anschluss and the Tragedy of Austrian Jewry," 495–99; Schmid and Streibel, *Der Pogrom 1938*; Historisches Museum der Stadt Wien, *Der Novemberpogrom*; Feichtenschlager, "Novemberpogrom," 363–87.

90. For details consult the literature in note 89, especially the conflicting estimates of arrests and suicides by Rosenkranz and Feichtenschlager. See also Botz's thoughtful analysis in his *Nationalsozialismus in Wien*, 397–404; "The Dynamics of Persecution in Austria," 207–9; and "'Judenhatz,'" 9–24.

91. Rosenkranz, "The Anschluss and the Tragedy of Austrian Jewry," 495. For a differing view, see Fellner, "Der Novemberpogrom 1938: Bemerkungen zur Forschung," 43–47.

92. For a surviving fragment of the transcript, see Hausjell and Venus, "'... Wie's ihm ums Herz ist,'" 31–33.

93. Quoted in Weinzierl, *Zu wenig Gerechte*, 65.

94. Quoted in Rosenkranz, "The Anschluss and the Tragedy of Austrian Jewry," 497.

95. Quoted in Safrian and Witek, *Und keiner war dabei*, 165 (report of Obersturmführer Riegler).

96. Quoted in Weinzierl, *Zu wenig Gerechte*, 66.

97. DÖW, doc. 1780: SD Unterabschnitt Wien II/112 an den SD Führer des SS-Oberabschnittes Donau, 10 November 1938. Full text in Safrian and Witek, *Und keiner war dabei*, 166–68.

98. Alexander A. Bankier, "'Auch nicht von der Frau Hinterhuber': Zu den ökonomischen Aspekten des Novemberpogroms in Wien," 79.

99. Quoted in Weinzierl, *Zu wenig Gerechte*, 65.

100. Botz, "The Dynamics of Persecution in Austria," 208.

101. Quoted in Weinzierl, *Zu wenig Gerechte*, 65.

102. Full text in Safrian and Witek, *Und keiner war dabei*, 182–85.

103. Full text in ibid., 185–88.

104. Cf. Kershaw, *Popular Opinion*, 268–69; David Bankier, *The Germans and the Final Solution*, 85–88.

105. AVA, Rk, Ordner 387: "Stimmen der Arbeiterschaft Dezember 1938."

106. Which is not to deny that individual spectators and bystanders expressed disgust and humanitarian concern. Weinzierl, *Zu wenig Gerechte*, 66–67; Feichtenschlager, "Novemberpogrom," 375–77, 386 n. 87; Berkley, *Vienna and Its Jews*, 309–11; Kershaw, *Popular Opinion*, 269–71.

107. Fest, *Hitler*, 568. On the other hand, the inhabitants of many small towns in Hesse and Franconia also participated in the assault on the Jews; in other localities public disapproval of the pogrom was not as uniform as once thought. That the number of Jews arrested or murdered in Austria was proportionate to that of Greater Germany as a whole deserves consideration as well. Goldhagen, *Hitler's Willing Executioners*, 100–101; Weiss, *Ideology of Death*, 371–73; Friedländer, *Nazi Germany and the Jews*, 295–98; Pauley, *From Prejudice to Persecution*, 288.

108. Quoted in Rosenkranz, "The Anschluss and the Tragedy of Austrian Jewry," 498.

109. Quoted in ibid. For a full account of the events in Innsbruck, see Gehler, "Murder on Command: The Anti-Jewish Pogrom in Innsbruck 9th–10th November 1938," 119–33.

110. Ibid., 497–99; Rosenkranz, *Verfolgung*, 160–67; Rosenkranz, "The Anschluss and the Tragedy of Austrian Jewry," 497–98.

111. Full text in *WVT*, 1:451–53.

112. Quoted in Bukey, *Hitler's Hometown*, 189. For details and the full text, see Gold, *Geschichte der Juden in Österreich*, 60.

113. DÖW, doc. 17.846: LR, Steyr, 30 November 1938; LR, Kirchdorf, 23 November 1938; G, Hinterstoder, 23 November 1938.

114. Quoted in Rosenkranz, *Verfolgung*, 162.

115. NÖLA/ZR/1939: LR, Amstetten, 1 January 1939.

116. Quoted in Czeitschner, Czernin, and Schmiederer, "'Einige Sekunden blieb alles still,'" 72.

117. Quoted in Rosenkranz, "The Anschluss and the Tragedy of Austrian Jewry," 498.

118. Quoted in Rosenkranz, *Verfolgung*, 161.

119. Karner, *Steiermark*, 172; Walzl, *Die Juden in Kärnten*, 219.

120. For example DÖW, doc. 15.349: Antisemitismus in Salzburg (oral history collection); Botz, "'Judenhatz,'" 19; Botz, "The Dynamics of Persecution in Austria," 208; Walzl, *Die Juden in Kärnten*, 220–21.

121. See Chapter 5.

122. *Trial of the Major War Criminals before the International Tribunal*, XXVIII, 499ff.

123. David Bankier, *The Germans and the Final Solution*, 85–100; Kershaw, *Popular Opinion*, 268–77; Kershaw, "The Persecution of the Jews and German Popular Opinion in the Third Reich," 278–89; Pauley, *From Prejudice to Persecution*, 288.

124. Botz, "The Jews of Vienna from the Anschluss to the Holocaust," 183–91; Botz, "The Dynamics of Persecution in Austria," 208–33.

125. This account summarizes Jonny Moser, "Depriving the Jews of Their Legal Rights," 127–32, but see also Rosenkranz, *Verfolgung*, 163–67.

126. DÖW, doc. 9539: Berichte des SA-Streifendienstes an den Gauleiter Bürckel über die vom SA-Streifendienst festgestellten Übergriffe gegen Juden und deren Eigentum in der Zeit 3 August 1938–3 Jänner 1939.

127. Botz, "The Dynamics of Persecution in Austria," 208–9.

128. Botz, "The Jews of Vienna from the Anschluss to the Holocaust," 191.

129. Botz, "The Dynamics of Persecution in Austria," 208–10.

130. Ibid.

131. Ibid., 210.

132. Ibid.

133. C. Gwyn Moser, "Jewish *U-Boote* in Austria, 1938–1945," 53–62.

134. Schleunes, *The Twisted Road to Auschwitz*; Kershaw, *Popular Opinion*, 277.

CHAPTER EIGHT

1. There is no comprehensive account of life in Austria during the Second World War, but see the outstanding local study by Albrich and Gisinger, *Im Bombenkrieg*, and the essays in Neugebauer, *Österreicher und der zweite Weltkrieg*. The two best eyewitness accounts are Franziska Berger, *Tage wie schwarze Perlen*, and Schöner, *Wiener Tagebuch*. Material on wartime conditions can be found also in Hagspiel, *Ostmark*, 58–101; Luza, *Austro-German Relations*, 264–366; Tálos, *NS-Herrschaft*; Stadler, *Österreich*, 116–407; and Kreissler, *Der Österreicher und seine Nation*, 189–371. See also the interesting technical study by Beer and Karner, *Der Krieg aus der Luft*.

2. Cf. Shirer, *Berlin Diary*, 197–202; Steinert, *Hitler's War*, 50–51; Stokes, "SD," 278–79; Kershaw, *Hitler Myth*, 14–43; Bukey, *Hitler's Hometown*, 208–9; Slapnicka, *Oberdonau*, 286–87; and Hanisch, *Nationalsozialistische Herrschaft*, 63.

3. Schöner, *Wiener Tagebuch*, 1 September 1939, 444.

4. DÖW, doc. 17.846: LR, Kirchdorf, 22 September 1939, and Ried, 20 September 1939; Schöner, *Wiener Tagebuch*, 5 September 1939, 445–46.

5. DÖW, doc. 17.846: LR, Kirchdorf, 22 September 1939, and Ried, 20 September 1939 and docs. 202–12: Stimmungsberichte von Ortsgruppen der NSDAP an das Kreispropagandaamt IX, September 1939; AVA, Rk, Ordner 387: Täglicher Stimmungsbericht des SD, 16, 20, 26, 27 September, 2, 5 October 1939. On the resurgence of popular anti-Semitism in Vienna, see Safrian, *Die Eichmann Männer*, 68–72. For graphic examples of dissenting views, see Kirk, *Nazism and the Working Class in Austria*, 121–25.

6. AVA, Rk, Ordner 387: Täglicher Stimmungsbericht des SD, 5 October 1939.

7. Boberach, *Meldungen*, 3:492 (24 November 1939); DÖW, docs. 201, 203: Stimmungsbericht von Ortsgruppen der NSDAP (Neu-Gersthof, 19 November 1939, Edelhof, 13 November 1939), and E 17.846: Landrat and police reports for November from Micheldorf, Steyrling, Steinbach, and Ried; NÖLA/ZR/I/1939: Landrat reports for November from Ybbs and Wolfsbach.

8. DÖW, doc. 17.846: LR, Pettenbach, 13 November 1939. Cf. doc. 20.387: LR, Tamsweg, 28 November 1939: "It goes without saying that the attempt on the Führer's life aroused extraordinary excitement in all layers of the populace. It was most severely condemned by the entire people, and not one instance of a contrary expression has become known."

9. Kirk, *Nazism and the Working Class in Austria*, 117.

10. Butschek, *Die österreichische Wirtschaft*, 72–85; Tálos, "Sozialpolitik," 129.

11. For example, DÖW, doc. 17.846: LR, Kirchdorf, 25 September, 4 December 1939; G, Pettenbach, 9 October 1939; NÖLA/ZR/I/1939: LR, Amstetten, 24 December 1939; G, Waidhofen, 27 December 1939. Also AVA, Rk, Ordner 387: Täglicher Inlandsbericht des SD, 2, 5 October, 4, 5 November 1939.

12. Kirk, "The Austrian Working Class under National Socialist Rule," 139–64; Butschek, *Die österreichische Wirtschaft*, 72–73, 124.

13. Kirk, *Nazism and the Working Class in Austria*, 88–93.

14. Ibid., 162–64; Boberach, *Meldungen*, 3:634 (18 December 1939).

15. Stadler, *Österreich*, 123–38; Stokes, "SD," 387–89; AVA, Rk, Ordner 322: SD Stimmungsbericht, 10 May 1940; and Luza, *Austro-German Relations*, 268.

16. AVA, Rk, Ordner 387: SD Wochenbericht, 8 April 1940. Presumably, the new salary schedule fostered inequities in the other professions as well.

17. Freudenberger and Luza, "National Socialist Germany and the Austrian Industry, 1938–1945," 73–75.

18. Luza, *Austro-German Relations*, 264–65.

19. NÖLA/ZR/I/1940, especially the police report from Behamberg, 24 February 1940. DÖW, doc. 16.114: Amtsgericht-Leonfelden an das Landgericht Linz, 3 February 1940; doc. 20.387: LR, Tamsweg 28 November, 29 December 1939; LR, Hallein, 29 December 1939; LR, Zell am See, 30 December 1939, 26 January 1940; and Film 97: Reports of the General-staatsanwalt (GStA) and Oberlandesgericht (OLG), Linz, 9 January, 23 February, 1 March, and 26 April 1940.

20. Freund and Perz, "Industrialisierung durch Zwangsarbeit," 100–101.

21. Karner, *Steiermark*, 335–36; Albrich and Gisinger, *Im Bombenkrieg*, 110; Slapnicka, *Oberdonau*, 164; Kirk, *Nazism and the Working Class in Austria*, 73.

22. Slapnicka, *Oberdonau*, 164. See also Stadler, *Österreich*, 276–84.

23. Bukey, *Hitler's Hometown*, 190–91.

24. Quoted in Gellately, *The Gestapo and German Society*, 224. For another version of the regulations, see *WVOÖ*, 2:477.

25. For details on the German setting, see Gellately, *The Gestapo and German Society*, 222–44.

26. *WVOÖ*, 2:477–79; NÖLA/ZR/Ia-10/1940: Police report, Behamberg, 24 February 1940.

27. Stadler, *Österreich*, 283.

28. Cited in Hanisch, *Nationalsozialistische Herrschaft*, 159.

29. NÖLA/ZR/Ia-10/1940: Police reports, Behamberg, 24 February 1940, Euratsfeld, 24 February 1940; *WVOÖ*, 2:477–78; Hanisch, *Nationalsozialistische Herrschaft*, 158; Stadler, *Österreich*, 282–83; Gellately, *The Gestapo and German Society*, 222–24.

30. AVA, Rk, box 164: Situation report of SD-Leitabschnitt, Vienna, 15, 20, 22, 27, 29, 30 May 1940; Baird, *The Mythical World of Nazi War Propaganda, 1939–1945*, 82–83.

31. NÖLA/ZR/I/1940: Police reports from Rosenau, 28 June, St. Pantaleon, 27 June, Oed, 26 June, and Waidhofen an der Ybbs, 27 June 1940.

32. AVA, Rk, box 164: Situation report of SD-Leitabschnitt, Vienna, 15, 20, 22, 27, 29, 30 May 1940.

33. AVA, Rk, box 164: Situation report of SD-Leitabschnitt, Vienna, 22 May 1940; DÖW: docs. 201, 1179, 1189.

34. *Red-White-Red Book*, 103–6.

35. On both Hitler's resolve to keep Vienna firmly under Reich German control and his ambivalent but hostile attitude toward the metropolis, see Stadler, "Provinzstadt im Dritten Reich," 15–21; Schausberger, "Hitler und Österreich: Einige Anmerkungen zur Hitler-Interpretation," 363–77; and, above all, the dictator's own angry testimony, as recorded by Goebbels on 24 June 1943, in Wortmann, *Baldur von Schirach: Hitlers Jugendführer*, 216–20.

36. *New York Times*, 28 November 1940.

37. AVA, RStH, box 388: SD, Vienna, 21 October 1940; *Red-White-Red Book*, 105–6.

38. Luza, *Austro-German Relations*, 264–311, and for the Hitler quotation, 297, and *New York Times*, 28 November 1940.

39. Luza, *Austro-German Relations*, 297–352, and Wortmann, *Schirach*, 187–229.

40. Wortmann, *Schirach*, 205–6, and for the quotation, Conot, *Justice at Nuremberg*, 423.

41. Wortmann, *Schirach*, 187–215; Luza, *Austro-German Relations*, 304–30; Luza, *Resistance*, 129.

42. Fred Taylor, *Goebbels Diaries*, 267.

43. Rosenkranz, *Verfolgung*, 297–301. For a succinct account of the Holocaust in Austria, see Albrich, "Holocaust und Schuldabwehr vom Judenmord zum kollektiven Opferstatus," 40–106.

44. David Bankier, *The Germans and the Final Solution*, 132.

45. Rosenkranz, *Verfolgung*, 297–301; Safrian, *Die Eichmann Männer*, 120–22. For the quotation, see Weinzierl, *Zu wenig Gerechte*, 114–15.

46. Czedik, *Uns fragt man nicht*, 36.

47. Cf. Kershaw, *Hitler Myth*, 156–58, and NÖLA/ZR/II/1940: LR and police reports from Euratsfeld, Ybbsitz, Wallsee, and Waidhofen.

48. Luza, *Austro-German Relations*, 186–92; Luza, "Nazi Control of the Austrian Catholic Church," 559–64; Conway, *Nazi Persecution of the Churches*, 393–97.

49. Fr. Ludwig Leuprecht to Apostolic Administrator in Innsbruck, 12 March 1941, *WVT*, 2:265–66.

50. Luza, *Austro-German Relations*, 190–91; Eichinger, "Die politische Situation im südwestlichen Niederösterreich," 203–7; *WVS*, 2:269–70; Slapnicka, *Oberdonau*, 211–24; Kershaw, *Popular Opinion*, 332–34.

51. Conway, *Nazi Persecution of the Churches*, 393–97.

52. For a full account of the T4 euthanasia program, see Friedlander, *The Origins of Nazi Genocide*. For information on killing operations in Austria, see Neugebauer, "Von der Rassenhygiene zum Massenmord," 263–85; Neugebauer, "Vernichtung von 'Minderwertigen'—Kriegsverbrechen?," 121–43; Horwitz, *In the Shadow of Death*, 55–82.

53. Scharpf to Jury, 3 April 1941, in *WVNÖ*, 3:672–73.

54. *WVS*, 2:575.

55. Horwitz, *In the Shadow of Death*, 61–62.

56. Ernst Hanisch and Hans Spatzenegger, "Die katholische Kirche," in *WVS*, 2:135. See also the documents in the same volume, 591–97.

57. Kershaw, *Popular Opinion*, 334–40; Steinert, *Hitler's War*, 80–83; Conway, *Nazi Persecution of the Churches*, 276–84; Helmreich, *The German Churches under Hitler*, 352–61; Horwitz, *In the Shadow of Death*, 57. According to the SD, Galen's letter was openly read and circulated in Austrian churches. DÖW, doc. 17.845/1: SD, Linz, 29 September 1941.

58. Friedlander, *The Origins of Nazi Genocide*, 150.

59. Boberach, *Meldungen*, 7:2481–83 (3 July 1941).

60. Jagschitz, "Von der 'Bewegung' zum Apparat," 515.

61. Sauer, "Österreichs Kirchen," 524–25.

62. Schausberger, *Rüstung in Österreich 1938–1945*, 34–36, 69–71, 84, 190–98.

63. DÖW, doc. 17.846: SD, Linz, 21 March 1941, and Fred Taylor, *Goebbels Diaries*, 265–66.

64. Fred Taylor, *Goebbels Diaries*, 265–66.

65. Kepplinger, "Aspekte nationalsozialistischer Herrschaft in Oberösterreich," 428; Karner, *Steiermark*, 326.

66. Karin Berger, "Die innere Front," 59–66, and *Zwischen Eintopf*, 116.

67. Luza, *Austro-German Relations*, 278–90; Hanisch, *Nationalsozialistische Herrschaft*, 114; Kerschbaumer, *Faszination Drittes Reich*, 151–259; Karner, *Steiermark*, 189–205; Slapnicka, *Oberdonau*, 66–94.

68. Kershaw, *Hitler Myth*, 158–59; DÖW docs. 17.846: SD, Linz, 26 April, 24 June 1941, and 17.858/6: Kärnten-Gendarmerie, Galizien, April 1941; Karner, *Steiermark*, 128; and Luza, *Austro-German Relations*, 177. In the face of considerable evidence to the contrary, August Walzl has argued that ordinary Carinthians were so outraged by removals of the Slovenian minority to concentration camps that they actually broke with the Nazi regime. Robert Knight's painstaking analysis of the documentation exposes Walzl's contention as both ludicrous and "deeply unconvincing." Cf. Walzl, *"Als erster Gau,"* 291, 305, and Knight "Carinthia and Its Slovenes: The Politics of Assimilation, 1945–1960," 44–54.

69. Kershaw, *Hitler Myth*, 173.

70. Slapnicka, *Oberdonau*, 288–90; Bukey, *Hitler's Hometown*, 209; Kirk, *Nazism and the Working Class in Austria*, 125–26.

71. Schöner, *Wiener Tagebuch*, 449–51.

72. DÖW, Film 97: GStA, Innsbruck, 22 July 1941; OÖLA, Pol. Akten, box 69: SD, Linz, 27 June, 31 July, 29 August 1941.

73. Steinert, *Hitler's War*, 118–22; Boberach, *Meldungen*, 7:2442–43 (26 June 1941), 2529 (17 July 1941); Franklin D. Roosevelt Library, Hyde Park, N.Y., President's Secretary File, Consular Reports Relating to Conditions in Occupied Countries 1941, part 1, box 72: "Conditions in

the Vienna Consular District," 6 August 1941. I am grateful to Günter Bischof for providing me with a copy of this important document.

74. Steinert, *Hitler's War*, 127–29; OÖLA, Pol. Akten, box 69: SD, Linz, 29 September 1941; Luza, *Resistance*, 130; DÖW, Film 97: GStA, Graz, 1 September 1941, and Innsbruck, 29 September 1941. In his study of Austrian labor Kirk details the upsurge of "railway accidents; electrical short circuits; severed cables and belts; and rural fires." Acknowledging widespread sabotage, he makes the telling point that "not all industrial accidents were sabotage, not all sabotage was politically motivated." Kirk, "The Austrian Working Class under National Socialist Rule," 175.

75. DÖW, Film 97: GStA, Innsbruck, 1 December 1941. See also Kershaw, *Hitler Myth*, 174–75.

76. Steinert, *Hitler's War*, 128.

77. Ibid., 130; Kershaw, *Hitler Myth*, 174–75.

78. Steinert, *Hitler's War*, 131–32; Kershaw, *Hitler Myth*, 174–78.

79. Luza, "Nazi Control of the Austrian Catholic Church," 563–64; Kershaw, *Popular Opinion*, 34–57; OÖLA, Pol. Akten, box 69: SD, Linz, 27 September 1941.

80. Eichinger, "Die politische Situation im südwestlichen Niederösterreich," 206–7.

81. NÖLA/ZR/Ia-10/1942: LR, St. Pantaleon, 27 January 1942, Euratsfeld, 26 February 1942.

82. *WVS*, 2:130–31.

83. Quoted in Sauer, "Österreichs Kirchen," 529.

84. In a memorandum to the U.S. Department of State the American vice-consul in Vienna wrote: "As might be expected, the most influential members of the upper classes of Viennese society are representatives of the old nobility, whose influence is out of proportion to their numbers. This group is largely monarchist and clerical in political conviction, and has been characterized by its contempt for the national socialists and its fear of the communists. There can be little doubt that the decision to fight Russia received the whole-hearted approbation of this group, and represents perhaps the first development of the present war which has received its approval." Franklin D. Roosevelt Library, Hyde Park, N.Y., President's Secretary File, Consular Reports Relating to Conditions in Occupied Countries, part 1, box 72: Memorandum prepared by Vice Consul Theodore J. Hohenthal, Vienna, Germany, 6 August 1941.

85. Naderer, "Dr. Josef Cal. Fliesser: Bischof von Linz," 89; Naderer, "Die Haltung Bischof Fliesser und der Nationalsozialismus," 87–90; Slapnicka, *Oberdonau*, 223–24.

86. Jeffery, "Konsens und Dissens im Dritten Reich mit einer Fallstudie über Oberösterreich," 129–47; and Hanisch, "Bäuerliches Milieu und Arbeitermilieu in Alpengauen: Ein historischer Vergleich," 583–98; "Austrian Catholicism," 165–76; and "Westösterreich," 437–56.

87. NÖLA/ZR/Ia-10/1942: LR, Melk, 7 January; LR, St. Pölten, 4 January; LR, Scheibbs, 15 January 1942.

88. Kershaw, *Hitler Myth*, 176; Steinert, *Hitler's War*, 148; NÖLA/ZR/Ia-10/1942: LR, Wiener Neustadt, 10 January 1942; and Riedmann, *Tirol*, 1067.

89. AVA, RStH, box 391: SD, Innsbruck, 12 January 1942; NÖLA/ZR/Ia-10/1942: LR, Melk, 7 January 1942; LR, Wiener Neustadt, 10 January 1942.

90. NÖLA/ZR/Ia-10/1942: LR, Eisenstadt, 13 January 1942.

91. Steinert, *Hitler's War*, 150; NÖLA/ZR/Ia-10/1942: LR, Tulln, 9 January 1942; LR, Amstet-

ten, 2 January 1942; LR, Eisenstadt, 13 January 1942; AVA, RStH, box 391: SD, Innsbruck, 12 January 1942.

92. Boelcke, *Secret Conferences*, 209; NÖLA/ZR/Ia-10/1942: LR, Wiener Neustadt, 10 February 1942; LR, Zwettl, 2 February 1942; AVA, RStH, box 391: SD, Innsbruck, 2 February 1942.

93. NÖLA/ZR/Ia-10/1942: LR, St. Pölten, 4 March 1942; AVA, RStH Wien, box 391: SD, Innsbruck, 13 April 1942; Riedmann, *Tirol*, 1069.

94. AVA, RStH, box 391: SD, Innsbruck, 30 March 1942; Riedmann, *Tirol*, 1067; Boelcke, *Secret Conferences*, 219.

95. NÖLA/ZR/Ia-10: LR, Kematen, 26 March, Waidhofen, 26 March, Amstetten, 24 March 1942; AVA, RStH, box 391: SD, Innsbruck, 23 March, 20 April 1942.

96. Steinert, *Hitler's War*, 157.

97. Riedmann, *Tirol*, 1069; NÖLA/ZR/Ia-10/1942: LR, Wolfsbach, 26 February, 27 March, 27 May 1942; LR, Ybbsitz, 26 February 1942; Gendarmerieposten, Waidhofen an der Ybbs, 26 April 1942; Ortsgruppenleiter, St. Valentin, 27 April 1942, *WVT* (doc. 332), 164, and (doc. 342), 168.

98. NÖLA/ZR/Ia-10/1942: LR, Amstetten, 24 April 1942.

99. Kershaw, *Hitler Myth*, 182–84; Steinert, *Hitler's War*, 158–60; AVA, RStH, box 391: SD, Innsbruck, 27 April, 4 May 1942; NÖLA/ZR/Ia-10/1942: Gendarmerieposten, Wolfsbach, 27 April 1942; LR, Amstetten, 4 May 1942.

100. NÖLA/ZR/Ia-10/1942: LR, Euratsfeld, 26 May, and Seitenstetten, 28 May 1942.

101. AVA, RStH, box 391: SD, Innsbruck, 18 May, 1, 8, 22 June, 6, 13 July 1942; DÖW, doc. 12.320: LR, Vorchdorf, 21 May, Laakirchen, 22 June 1942; NÖLA/ZR/Ia-10/1942: LR, Waidhofen, 25 June, Rosenau, 27 June, and Haidershofen, 27 June 1942.

102. DÖW, doc. 12.320: LR, Laakirchen, 20 May, Grünau, 22 May, Gmunden, 1 June, Mittendorf, 24 June 1942; NÖLA/Ia-10/1942: LR, Behamberg, 26 May, Opponitz, 27 May 1942; AVA, RStH Wien, box 391: SD, Innsbruck, 18 May, 1 June (for reaction to Heydrich's death), 22, 29 June 1942.

103. Steinert, *Hitler's War*, 160–66; NÖLA/Ia–10/1942: LR, Behamberg, 27 June, Amstetten, 26 August 1942; AVA, RStH Wien, box 391: SD, Innsbruck, 22, 29 June, 6, 13, especially 27 July 1942.

104. NÖLA/ZR/Ia-10/1942: LR and police reports from Seitenstetten, Ybbsitz, Waidhofen, St. Peter, Wolfsbach, St. Valentin, Haag, Behamberg, Hollenstein, Amstetten, Ulmerfeld, Ardagger, Kematen, Wallsee, 23–27 July, especially Ulmerfeld, 23 July, and Wallsee, 25 July 1942; AVA, RStH Wien, box 391: SD, Innsbruck, 20 July, 3 August 1942.

105. AVA, RStH Wien, box 391: SD, Innsbruck, 10 August 1942.

106. AVA, RStH Wien, box 388: SD, Vienna, 20 July 1942.

107. Ibid. For more information on the deportations from Vienna, see Rosenkranz, *Verfolgung*, 291–94.

108. Quoted in Stadler, *Österreich*, 291.

109. Steinert, *Hitler's War*, 132–47; Kershaw, *Popular Opinion*, 359–72; Horwitz, *In the Shadow of Death*, 52; DÖW, doc. 12.320: LR, St. Wolfgang, 22 April, 12 August 1942.

110. AVA, RStH Wien, box 391: SD, Innsbruck, 4, 10 May 1943.

111. Stadler, *Österreich*, 386.

112. NÖLA/ZR/Ia-10/1942: Landrat and police reports, August–October 1942; DÖW, Film 97: GStA, Innsbruck, 22 September 1942, and doc. 12.320: LR, Gmunden, 1 June 1942.

113. DÖW, doc. 12.320: LR, Laakirchen, 22 June 1942.

114. AVA, RStH, box 391: SD, Innsbruck, 31 August, 7, 14 September 1942.

115. Boelcke, *Secret Conferences*, 276.

116. AVA, RStH, box 391: SD, Innsbruck, 21 September 1942.

117. AVA, RStH, box 391: SD, Innsbruck, 20 June, 6, 20 July 1942; Kershaw, *Popular Opinion*, 320–22; DÖW, doc. 12.320: LR, Gmunden, 1 June 1942.

118. AVA, RStH, box 391: SD, Innsbruck, 10 August 1942.

119. GStA, Innsbruck, 29 July 1942, quoted in Albrich and Gisinger, *Im Bombenkrieg*, 64.

120. AVA, RStH, box 391: SD, Innsbruck, 20 July, 3 August, 28 September 1942.

121. AVA, RStH Wien, box 391: DÖW, Film 97: SD, Innsbruck, 28 September 1942; GStA, Innsbruck, 22 September 1942; Domarus, *Hitler*, 4:1913–24; Kershaw, *Hitler Myth*, 185–86; Steinert, *Hitler's War*, 168.

122. Czedik, *Uns fragt man nicht*, 70–71; AVA, RStH Wien, box 391: SD, Innsbruck, 2 November 1942. On 26 October 1942 a Japanese carrier group operating in the Solomon Islands scored a Pyrrhic victory by sinking the USS *Hornet* and severely damaging the *Enterprise* in the Battle of Santa Cruz.

123. Domarus, *Hitler*, 4:1933–44; AVA, RStH, box 391: SD, Innsbruck, 9, 16, 23 November 1942.

124. AVA, RStH, box 391: SD, Innsbruck, 7 December 1942; NÖLA/ZR/Ia-10/1942: LR, Melk, Scheibbs, Krems, Wiener Neustadt, and Eisenstadt, December 1942; NA, T 81, R 6: SD, Linz, 29 November, 7, 14 December 1942.

125. NA, T 81, R 6: SD, Linz, 14 December 1942; AVA, RStH, box 391: SD, Innsbruck, 14 December 1942.

126. AVA, RStH, box 391: SD, Innsbruck, 14 December 1942; NA, T 81, R 7: SD, Linz, 21, 28 December 1942, 4, 11 January 1943; Beck, *Under the Bombs*, 18–21. Evidence of the cheerful holiday atmosphere prevailing in Vienna and Wagrain, near Salzburg, can be found in Czedik, *Uns fragt man nicht*, 75–81.

127. AVA, RStH, box 391: SD, Innsbruck, 11, 18, 25 January 1943; Beck, *Under the Bombs*, 21–24; NA, T 81, R 7: SD, Linz, 18, 25, 30 January 1943.

128. AVA, RStH Wien, box 391: SD, Innsbruck, 8 February 1943; NA, T 81, R 6: SD, Linz, 8 February 1943; NÖLA/ZR/Ia-10/1943: LR, Eisenstadt, 5 February, Scheibbs, 8 February, Tulln, 10 February, Lilienfeld, 12 February 1943; Czedik, *Uns fragt man nicht*, 84–85. It is not without significance that both Stadler and Kreissler, in their studies of the development of Austrian opposition to German rule, misconstrue the devastating impact of the Stalingrad debacle on popular morale. See Stadler, *Österreich*, 293–303, and Kreissler, *Der Österreicher und seine Nation*, 290–92. For reactions in the Old Reich, see Boberach, *Meldungen*, 12:4750–52, 4760–63; Steinert, *Hitler's War*, 184–90; Kershaw, *Hitler Myth*, 189–95; Beck, *Under the Bombs*, 28–30, 33–37.

129. In the twenty-one months between 30 September 1940 and 25 June 1942 the number of people taken into "protective custody" by the Viennese Gestapo more than doubled from 465 to 1,083; aside from Jews, most of them were monarchists, priests, or Communists.

Whether there were more acts of resistance, as measured by arrests for political crimes, in Austria than elsewhere in Greater Germany is a subject in need of systematic investigation. The available evidence shows a dramatic increase of cases brought before Special Courts in both Munich and Vienna in 1942. The public prosecutor in Vienna in explaining an upsurge of arrests for defeatism and "malicious practices," however, took pains to point out that his expanded caseload was the result of a centralization of venue from the provinces to his courtroom. AVA, Staatspolizei Wien (Gestapo), boxes 1–2: Gestapo, Vienna, 30 September 1940, 25 June 1942; Kershaw, *Hitler Myth*, 187; DÖW, Film 97: GStA, Vienna, 30 January 1943.

130. Jagschitz, "Von der 'Bewegung' zum Apparat," 505–6, 515–16 n. 84; Luza, *Austro-German Relations*, 187.

CHAPTER NINE

1. Luza, *Austro-German Relations*, 330–32; Fredborg, *Behind the Steel Wall*, 184; Schärf, *Österreichs Erneuerung 1945–1955*, 23–25. For examples of pro-Austrian outbursts, see *WVNÖ*, 3:568–77; *WVT*, 1:282, 300; Slapnicka, *Oberdonau*, 292.

2. The foremost exponents of this interpretation are Stadler, *Österreich*, especially 293–303, and Kreissler, *Der Österreicher und seine Nation*, 286–99. See also Maass, *Country without a Name*, 62–69.

3. Fredborg, *Behind the Steel Wall*, 180.

4. Ibid.

5. Ibid., 180–87, 247–49. Quotations from pp. 184, 247.

6. Ibid., 187.

7. NA, M 1209, R 29, F 63–260: Records of the Department of State Relating to the Internal Affairs of Austria, Decimal File 863, especially "News from Austria," American Legation, Stockholm, 31 May 1943.

8. NA, M 1209, R 29, F 93–94: "The Feelings of the Austrian Population," Istanbul, 13 April 1943, and F 155–56: "What People Think about Austria," 2 August 1943.

9. NA, M 1209, R 29, F 113: "News from Austria," Stockholm, 31 May 1943. For a similar impression, see the handwritten report of the Austrian resistance fighter Josef Meisel after his harrowing escape from Auschwitz at DÖW, doc. 841: "Bericht über die Situation in Österreich."

10. NA, M 1209, R 29, F 107–8, 112, 123: "News from Austria," 31 May 1943.

11. Ibid., F 107–30; F 93–94: "The Feelings of the Austrian People"; and F 155–56: "What People Think about in Austria," Istanbul, 12 August 1943.

12. NA, M 1209, R 29, F 95: Johnson (Stockholm) to State Department, 27 July 1943.

13. Luza, *Austro-German Relations*, 288, 335–39.

14. DÖW, Film 97: GStA, Vienna, to Thierack, 1 July 1943.

15. NA, M 1209, R 29, F 124: "News from Austria."

16. Steinert, *Hitler's War*, 184–257; Kershaw, *Hitler Myth*, 192–95; Orlow, *Nazi Party*, 411–20; Stadler, *Österreich*, 293–313; and Boberach, *Meldungen*, 14:5403–7.

17. Stadler, *Österreich*, 296.

18. For example, NA, T 81, R 6, F 13343: SD, Linz, 20 February 1943.

19. Stadler, *Österreich*, 285.

20. *WVNÖ*, 3:552–53.

21. Kershaw, *Popular Opinion*, 321.

22. Ibid., and Steinert, *Hitler's War*, 187–89.

23. AVA, RStH, box 391: SD, Innsbruck, 8, 15, 22 February 1943; NA, T 81, R 6: SD, Linz, 8, 19 February 1943; NÖLA/ZR/Ia-10/1943: LR, Lilienfeld, 12 February 1943, and Polizeidirektor, Wiener Neustadt, 10 February 1943.

24. Steinert, *Hitler's War*, 121.

25. AVA, RStH, box 391: SD, Innsbruck, 22 February 1942; NA, T 81, R 6: SD, Linz, 8, 20 February 1943.

26. Cf. Kershaw, *Popular Opinion*, 308ff., and Karin Berger, "'Hut ab vor Frau Sedlmayer!,'" 150.

27. AVA, RStH, box 391: SD, Innsbruck, 1 March 1943.

28. Butschek, *Die österreichische Wirtschaft*, 86–87; Freudenberger and Luza, "National Socialist Germany and the Austrian Industry, 1938–1945," 73–100; Kernbauer and Weber, "Österreichs Wirtschaft," 57–64; Karin Berger, *Zwischen Eintopf*, 23.

29. AVA, RStH, box 391: SD, Innsbruck, 1, 15 March 1943.

30. NA, T 81, R 6: SD, Linz, 8 March 1943; AVA, RStH, box 391: SD, Innsbruck, 22 March 1943; NÖLA/ZR/Ia-10/1943: Polizeidirektor, St. Pölten, 5 April 1943.

31. AVA, RStH, box 391: SD, Innsbruck, 22, 29 March 1943; NA, T 81, R 6: SD, Linz, 8 March 1943.

32. NA, T 81, R 6: SD, Linz, 13, 29 March, 7 April 1943. On the persistence of the Führer myth in Austria, see Hanisch, "Ein Versuch den Nationalsozialismus zu verstehen," 157–58. For isolated examples of disenchantment, see Meusberger, *Bezau*, 269. On Hitler's last hometown visit to Linz, see Speer, *Spandau*, 170–75.

33. NA, T 81, R 6: SD, Linz, 8, 19 February, 8 March 1943; Stadler, *Österreich*, 294–303; Luza, *Austro-German Relations*, 330–32. The resistance fighter Fritz Molden recalls a meeting with his parents in early summer 1943 on the Bavarian Chiemsee in which his father "thought the war could not last more than a year at the outside. Various straws in the wind had led him to believe that the Allies would restore Austrian independence." Molden, *Exploding Star*, 131.

34. NA, M 1209, R 29: "Styria—the Land of Sorrow," *Allehanda*, 16 January 1944.

35. *WVNÖ*, 3:568–77; *WVT*, 1:282, 300; AVA, RStH, box 391: SD, Innsbruck, 15, 29 March, 12 April 1943.

36. Robert Knight, "At the Gates of the Underworld," *Times Literary Supplement*, 21–27 July 1989, p. 797.

37. Without dissociating herself from the war effort, Maria Czedik experienced a "most wonderful dream" shortly after Stalingrad. According to her diary entry, "St. Stephens was bathed with pure candlelight from within. The bells began to peal, and you could hear singing from inside. The war was over; once again there was an Austria; and everyone fell weeping and praying to their knees." Czedik, *Uns fragt man nicht*, 86–87.

38. Beck, *Under the Bombs*, 37; Kershaw, *Hitler Myth*, 187, 195.

39. Albrich and Gisinger, *Im Bombenkrieg*, 77.

40. DÖW, Film 97: GStA, Graz, 27 January 1943.

41. Kershaw, *Hitler Myth*, 194–96.

42. NA, RG 226, Records of the OSS, entry (E) 16, box 0617, doc. 54103: "Internal Austrian Public Opinion," 17 January 1944.

43. Cf. Hanisch, "Versuch," 157–58, and Kershaw, *Hitler Myth*, 92. For examples, however, of anti-Hitler outbursts in Austria, see *WVT*, 2:280–81, 284–85, 288–89, 290; *WVOÖ*, 1:428, 435–36, 441; *WVNÖ*, 3:550–54; *WVS*, 2:390–92.

44. DÖW, Film 97: GStA, Graz, 29 March 1943; NA, T 81, R 6: SD, Linz, 29 March, 23 April, 5 May 1943; NÖLA/ZR/Ia-10/1943: LR, Wiener Neustadt, 8 April 1943.

45. AVA, RStH, box 391: SD, Innsbruck, 29 March, 12, 19, 27 April, 4, 10 May 1943; NA, T 81, R 6: SD, Linz, 7, 21 April 1943; NÖLA/ZR/Ia-10/1943: LR, Scheibbs, May 1943.

46. NÖLA/ZR/Ia-10/1943: LR, Zwettl, 9 June, Baden, 10 June, Wiener Neustadt, 12 June 1943; AVA, RStA, box 391: SD, Innsbruck, 4, 10, 24 May 1943.

47. For example, see Slapnicka, *Oberdonau*, 290–91, and DÖW, Film 97: GStA, Vienna, 1 July 1943. On the other hand, for evidence of a decline of subversive activities, see *WVNÖ*, 3:598.

48. Steinert, *Hitler's War*, 220–22, 230–32; NA, T 81, R 6: SD, Linz, 26 May 1943; DÖW, Film 97: OLG, 29 March 1943; Stadler, *Österreich*, 303–4; *WVNÖ*, 2:423–27; *WVT*, 1:396–99; and *WVOÖ*, 2:427–39.

49. DÖW, Film 97: GStA, Vienna, 1 July 1943.

50. Ibid.

51. *WVW*, 2:25–27, and *WVNÖ*, 3:572–73. On the upsurge of juvenile protest, see Gerbel, Mejstrik, and Sieder, "Wiener Arbeiterjugendlichen," 243–68. For the *Altreich*, see Peukert, *Inside Nazi Germany*; Peukert, "Youth in the Third Reich," 25–40.

52. Peukert, "Youth in the Third Reich," 37.

53. Gerbel, Mejstrik, and Sieder, "Wiener Arbeiterjugendlichen," 245–55.

54. Ibid., 255–59; Boberach, *Meldungen*, 11:4056 (10 August 1942).

55. Gerbel, Mejstrik, and Sieder, "Wiener Arbeiterjugendlichen," 259–63; *WVNÖ*, 3:572–73.

56. Gerbel, Mejstrik, and Sieder, "Wiener Arbeiterjugendlichen," 267 n. 32.

57. Steinert, *Hitler's War*, 213. See also Kershaw, *Hitler Myth*, 201–7.

58. AVA, RStH, box 391: SD, Innsbruck, 12, 21 June 1943.

59. AVA, RStH, box 391: SD, Innsbruck, 28 June 1943; Albrich and Gisinger, *Im Bombenkrieg*, 94–107.

60. AVA, RStH, box 391: SD, Innsbruck, 5, 12 July 1943.

61. AVA, RStH, box 391: 19, 26 July 1943; Albrich and Gisinger, *Im Bombenkrieg*, 97–107.

62. Albrich and Gisinger, *Im Bombenkrieg*, 103–7; NA, M 1209, R 29: "News from Austria," 13.

63. Steinert, *Hitler's War*, 215.

64. Quoted in Albrich and Gisinger, *Im Bombenkrieg*, 112.

65. AVA, RStH, box 391: SD, Innsbruck, 2 August 1943.

66. AVA, RStH, box 391: SD, Innsbruck, 9 August 1943.

67. Ibid.

68. AVA, RStH, box 391: SD, Innsbruck, 16 August 1943.

69. Schausberger, *Rüstung in Österreich*, 121, 131; NÖLA/Ia-10/14/1943: LR, St. Pölten, 8 September 1943, and Police Director, Wiener Neustadt, 7 September 1943.

70. Steinert, *Hitler's War*, 224–25; Beck, *Under the Bombs*, 92–94; NÖLA/Ia-10/14/1943: LR, Tulln, 9 September 1943; LR, Melk, 7 September 1943; LR, Scheibbs, 10 September 1943; AVA, RStH, box 391: SD, Innsbruck, 30 August 1943.

71. AVA, RStH, box 391: SD, Innsbruck, 6, 13 September 1943.

72. Domarus, *Hitler*, 4:2035–39; Steinert, *Hitler's War*, 225–26; Kershaw, *Hitler Myth*, 211; Beck, *Under the Bombs*, 92–94.

73. Lochner, *Goebbels Diaries*, 447.

74. Steinert, *Hitler's War*, 225.

75. Ibid., 225–26; Kershaw, *Hitler Myth*, 221; NÖLA/ZR/Ia-10/14/1943: LR, Baden, 11 October 1943; LR, Wiener Neustadt, 9 October 1943; AVA, RStH, box 391: SD, Innsbruck, 13, 20 September 1943. See also Albrich and Gisinger, *Im Bombenkrieg*, 116–19.

76. Albrich and Gisinger, *Im Bombenkrieg*, 116–18; Riedmann, *Tirol*, 1076–78.

77. Beck, *Under the Bombs*, 92–94; Steinert, *Hitler's War*, 226–27; Albrich and Gisinger, *Im Bombenkrieg*, 121; AVA, RStH, box 391: SD, Innsbruck, 5, 12, 19, 26 October 1943. See also NÖLA/ZR/Ia-10/14/1943: LR, Gänserndorf, 9 November 1943.

78. AVA, RStH, box 391: SD, Innsbruck, 12, 19, 26 October 1943.

79. OÖLA, Pol. Akten, OÖ 12/36: SD, Linz, 2 November 1943.

80. Beck, *Under the Bombs*, 93–94.

81. NÖLA/Ia-10/14/1943: LR, Korneuburg, 12 October 1943; LR, Scheibbs, 3 November 1943.

82. AVA, RStH, box 391: SD, Innsbruck, 19, 26 October 1943; NÖLA/ZR/Ia-10/14/1943: LR, Wiener Neustadt, 14 October 1943; LR, Korneuburg, 11 November 1943.

83. AVA, RStH, box 391: SD, Innsbruck, 2 November 1943.

84. AVA, RStH, box 391: SD, Innsbruck, 12 October 1943; NÖLA/ZR/Ia-10/14/1943: LR, Wiener Neustadt, 14 October 1943; LR, St. Pölten, 4 November 1943; LR, Melk, 6 November 1943; LR, Baden, 13 November 1943; Franziska Berger, *Tage wie schwarze Perlen*, 32–51.

85. AVA, RStH, box 391: SD, Innsbruck, 26 October 1943.

86. NÖLA/ZR/Ia-10/14/1943: LR, Neunkirchen, 10 October 1943.

87. Domarus, *Hitler*, 4:2050–59.

88. Steinert, *Hitler's War and the Germans*, 229; Beck, *Under the Bombs*, 94–95; Kershaw, *Hitler Myth*, 211–13.

89. Kershaw, *Hitler Myth*, 212.

90. AVA, RStH, box 391: SD, Innsbruck, 9 November 1943.

91. NÖLA/ZR/Ia-10/14/1943: LR, Krems, 15 November 1943; Zwettl, 10 December 1943; St. Pölten, 9 November 1943; Lilienfeld, 11 December 1943; Korneuburg, 15 December 1943; Horn, 9 December 1943; Amstetten, 3 December 1943; Oberpullendorf, 15 December 1943; Scheibbs, 8 December 1943.

92. NÖLA/ZR/Ia-10/14/1943: LR, Tulln, 9 December 1943.

93. Müller, *Hitler's Justice*, 142–46.

94. On this issue, especially the need for a comparative perspective, see Bukey, "Nazi Rule in Austria," 228–33.

95. Stadler, *Österreich*, 352.

96. AVA, Rk, Gestapo, box 5: Tagesberichte, 1942–43. The monthly reports are also available at the DÖW, docs. 8476–79.

97. Translated and quoted in Koch, *In the Name of the Volk*, 158.

98. Kirk, *Nazism and the Working Class in Austria*, 99–102. In this meticulous examination of cases brought against indigenous Austrians for labor offenses, the author writes that "it is generally difficult to see any pattern in [their] behaviour." Much of the discontent in the industrializing West he attributes to the fact "that the regime had underestimated the unwillingness of people to be uprooted and separated from their families." He acknowledges the existence of autochthonous resistance groups, but urges caution in assessing their activities and motives. In contrast, Hagspiel emphasizes the prominent role played by Viennese Czechs in anti-Nazi sabotage. Cf. ibid., 93–108, and Hagspiel, *Ostmark*, 215.

99. Luza, *Resistance*, 140–42; Neugebauer, "Widerstand und Opposition," 549.

100. Horwitz, *In the Shadow of Death*, 95.

101. Steinert, *Hitler's War and the Germans*, 227–28; Beck, *Under the Bombs*, 95–96. In a report to the Reich minister of justice on 10 February 1944 the public prosecutor in Linz indicated a "healthy response" to the publication of death sentences by the People's Court. DÖW, Film 97: GStA, Linz, 10 February 1944. The journal entries of Franziska Berger, however, provide ample evidence of the rising climate of fear among ordinary Austrians. Berger, *Tage wie schwarze Perlen*, 56–66.

102. Cf. Stadler, *Österreich*, 293–303, and AVA, RStH, box 391: SD, Innsbruck, 12, 19, 26 October, 29 December 1943.

103. F. Parkinson, "Epilogue," in Parkinson, *Conquering the Past*, 317.

104. On the Moscow Declaration, see Keyserlingk, *Austria in World War II*, 123–56. For the actual text, 152.

105. Ibid., 154.

106. Boberach, *Meldungen*, 15:5996 (8 November 1943).

107. Cf. NÖLA/ZR/Ia-10/23/1943 and 1944: Landrat and police reports, November 1943–August 1944, and Kreissler, *Der Österreicher und seine Nation*, 299–301.

108. AVA, RStH, box 391: SD, Innsbruck, 16 November 1943. The Moscow Declaration did not contain such language.

109. NA, RG 226, E 16, box 0617, doc. 54103: OSS, 17 January 1944.

110. NA, RG 226, E 16, box 24, doc. XL2001: "Interview with Prisoner of War D.," 25 October 1944.

111. Kreissler, *Der Österreicher und seine Nation*, 299–301, and Luza, *Resistance*, 197.

112. For example, see *WVNÖ*, 2:81–82 and 3:576–77.

113. Kreissler, *Der Österreicher und seine Nation*, 302.

114. Even after the end of the war the bishop of Linz refused to honor the memory of the peasant-pacifist Franz Jägerstätter, beheaded in 1943 for resisting service in the German armed forces: "I consider the greater heroes to be those exemplary young Catholic men, seminarians, priests, and heads of families who fought and died in heroic fulfillment of duty and in the firm conviction that they were fulfilling the will of God at their post, just as the Christian soldiers in the armies of the heathen emperor had done." Maislinger, "Franz Jägerstätter," 180–81.

115. *WVNÖ*, 2:569; Slapnicka, *Oberdonau*, 292; and NÖLA/ZR/Ia-10/23/1944: Landrat and police reports from Scheibbs, 5 June 1944, Neunkirchen, 17 June 1944, and Oberpullendorf, 14 July 1944.

116. OÖLA, Pol. Akten, Sch. 80: GStA, Linz, to Thierack, 5 June 1944.

117. NA, RG 226, E 16, box 0807, doc. 69480: "Austria: Attitudes to Germany, the War and the Future," 23 April 1944.

CHAPTER TEN

1. For details, see Albrich and Gisinger, *Im Bombenkrieg*, 142–46.

2. Ibid. Boberach, *Meldungen*, 15:6189 (27 December 1943); AVA, RStH, box 391: SD, Innsbruck, 20, 29 December 1943.

3. Albrich and Gisinger, *Im Bombenkrieg*, 146–55.

4. NÖLA/ZR/Ia-10/1944: LR, Zwettl, 10 February 1944; LR, Lilienfeld, 7 March 1944.

5. Kershaw, *Hitler Myth*, 207–10. Conversely, Kirk demonstrates that most arrests for "slandering the Führer" took place in blue-collar neighborhoods. "It was here," he argues, "that the criticism was most emphatic, most vituperative and most personal." Kirk, *Nazism and the Working Class in Austria*, 118. Given the absence of comparative data, one must regard this as a questionable judgment.

6. Albrich and Gisinger, *Im Bombenkrieg*, 140, 157–62; NÖLA/ZR/Ia-10/1944: LR, Wiener Neustadt, 7 February 1944; LR, Krems, 9 February 1944; NA, RG 226, E 16, box 170, doc. XL1270: SD, Salzburg, 2 February 1944.

7. See *WVS*, 2:359, and *WVNÖ*, 3:598–600. Writing to the minister of justice on 10 February 1944, the public prosecutor in Linz referred to cases before the People's Court as "obscene slander of the Führer." DÖW, Film 97: GStA, Linz, 10 February 1944.

8. NÖLA/ZR/Ia-10/1944: LR, Zwettl, 10 February 1944; LR, Baden, 16 February 1944.

9. NÖLA/ZR/Ia-10/1944: LR, Eisenstadt, 12 February 1944. Similar sentiments can be found in a report filed three days earlier in Salzburg, a document also expressing renewed concern with the situation in Italy. NA, RG 226, E 16, box 170, doc. XL1270: SD, Salzburg, 9 February 1944.

10. For details, see Ulrich, *Der Luftkrieg über Österreich 1939–1945*, 14–15, and Albrich and Gisinger, *Im Bombenkrieg*, 172–74.

11. Steinert, *Hitler's War*, 234–37; NÖLA/ZR/Ia-10/23/1944: Gänserndorf, 7 February 1944, Lilienfeld, 7 March 1944, Wiener Neustadt, 7 March 1944, Baden, 16 February 1944; and OÖLA, Pol. Akten, Sch. 80: GStA, Linz, 5 June 1944. On the other hand, the county executive in Mistelbach wrote that most of the farming population discounted the Luftwaffe's raids on London and disparaged a "successful end to the war." NÖLA/ZR/Ia-10/23/1944: LR, Mistelbach, 28 June 1944.

12. Boberach, *Meldungen*, 15:6596–98.

13. NÖLA/ZR/Ia-10/23/1944: St. Pölten, 8 July 1944.

14. NA, T 77, R 1037, F 6509660: Wehrkreiskommando XVII, Vienna, to OKW, 21 July 1944; Czedik, *Uns fragt man nicht*, 106; NÖLA/ZR/Ia-10/23/1944: LR and police reports from St. Pölten, 8 July 1944, Wiener Neustadt, 6 July 1944, and Scheibbs, 7 July 1944. See also Boberach, *Meldungen*, 17:6631–34.

15. NÖLA/ZR/Ia-10/23/1944: LR, Eisenstadt, 11 July 1944.

16. NÖLA/ZR/Ia-10/23/1944: Oberpullendorf, 14 July 1944.

17. NÖLA/ZR/Ia-10/23/1944: Lilienfeld, 9 August 1944.

18. NÖLA/ZR/Ia-10/23/1944: Landrat report, Wiener Neustadt, 9 August 1944.

19. Boberach, *Meldungen* 17:6651 (14 July 1944).

20. As claimed by Jedlicka, *Der 20. Juli 1944 in Österreich*, 12.

21. Kreissler, *Der Österreicher und seine Nation*, 315.

22. Preradovich, *Grossdeutschland 1938*; Manoschek and Safrian, "Österreicher in der Wehrmacht," 331–60; Höbelt, "Österreicher in der deutschen Wehrmacht 1938 bis 1945," 417–32.

23. Jedlicka, *Der 20. Juli 1944 in Österreich*, 50–92, and Hoffmann, *The History of the German Resistance, 1933–1945*, 465–70, 457–59.

24. NÖLA/ZR/Ia-10/23/1944: LR and police reports for August 1944 from Wiener Neustadt, Oberpullendorf, Neubistritz, Lilienfeld, Krems, Korneuburg, Horn, Gmünd, Eisenstadt, Bruck an der Leitha, Waidhofen an der Thaya, Gänserndorf, Hollabrunn, Mistelbach, Melk, and Zwettl.

25. Ringler, *Illusion einer Jugend*, 121.

26. DÖW, Film 97: GStA, Linz, 7 August 1944.

27. DÖW, Film 97: GStA, Vienna, 1 October 1944.

28. Stadler, *Österreich*, 337.

29. Bukey, *Hitler's Hometown*, 213; Hanisch, *Nationalsozialistische Herrschaft*, 234; and NÖLA/ZR/Ia-10/23/1944: Landrat and police reports for August from Gmünd, Oberpullendorf, Amstetten, and Melk.

30. Quoted in Jedlicka, *Der 20. Juli 1944 in Österreich*, 92.

31. Czedik, *Uns fragt man nicht*, 112.

32. NÖLA/ZR/Ia-10/23/1944: LR, Eisenstadt, 15 August 1944.

33. Jedlicka, *Der 20. Juli 1944 in Österreich*, 96–97.

34. Ibid., 95–98.

35. Ibid., 100.

36. DÖW, doc. 8570: Frauenfeld to Schirach, 4 September 1944.

37. Czedik, *Uns fragt man nicht*, 117.

38. NA, RG 226, E 16, box 23, doc. XL1824: "Austrian Intelligence," 5 October 1944. See also Luza, *Austro-German Relations*, 336–38.

39. NA, T 77, R 1037, F 6509660: Wehrkreiskommando XVII, Vienna, 21 July 1944; Boberach, *Meldungen*, 17:6657; DÖW, Film 97: OLG, Vienna, 4 July 1944; GStA, Vienna, 1 October 1944; Slapnicka, *Oberdonau*, 292–93; Franziska Berger, *Tage wie schwarze Perlen*, 87–118; Albrich and Gisinger, *Im Bombenkrieg*, 219–20.

40. Schöner, *Wiener Tagebuch*, 25–34.

41. Ibid., 32–86.

42. Bernhard, *Gathering Evidence*, 88, 91, 93, 104.

43. DÖW, Film 97: GStA, Vienna, 1 October 1944; OLG, 1 November 1944; GStA, Graz, 29 October 1944; OLG, Graz, 30 November 1944; Slapnicka, *Oberdonau*, 293–94; Hanisch, *Nationalsozialistische Herrschaft*, 247–48.

44. Luza, *Resistance*, 27–154.

45. Ibid., 158–226.

46. DÖW, Film 97: GStA, Vienna, 1 October 1944.

47. Kreissler, *Der Österreicher und seine Nation*, 153–54, 210, 233–45; Stadler, *Österreich*, 153–239, 357–83; Voges, "Klassenkampf in der 'Betriebsgemeinschaft,'" 329–83.

48. Kirk, *Nazism and the Working Class in Austria*, 93–134; Kirk, "The Austrian Working Class under National Socialist Rule," 191–218. Quotation from p. 201.

49. NA, RG 226, E 16, box 23, doc. XL1824: "Austrian Intelligence," 5 October 1944.

50. NA, RG 226, E 16, box 24, doc. XL2102: "Austrian Intelligence," 31 October 1944.

51. Ibid.

52. Ibid.

53. Luza, *Resistance*, 159. Timothy Kirk has drawn a more brutal conclusion. "The Austrian resistance," he writes, "is a construct imposed after 1945 on the more heterogeneous and ambivalent realities of opposition, resistance and consent during the years of occupation; it has been a rationalization of events determined to a large extent by the conditions of the Moscow declaration and the necessity of distancing Austria from a defeated Nazi Germany. If Austrians resisted they did so primarily not as Austrians, but as Communists, Socialists, Roman Catholics, Jehovah's Witnesses and so on, and this continued to be true up to the last months of the war. Links were forged, but there was a great deal of mutual suspicion." Kirk, *Nazism and the Working Class in Austria*, 140.

54. DÖW, Film 97: OLG, 30 November 1944.

55. DÖW, doc. 7266: SD, Vienna, 17 October 1944; Film 97: OLG, Vienna, 7 November 1944, 22 January and 8 March 1945; NÖLA/ZR/Ia-10/23/1945: Lagebericht für Jänner 1945. The substance of these reports is corroborated in much greater detail in Schöner, *Wiener Tagebuch*, 61–85.

56. DÖW, doc. 7266: SD, Vienna, 13 December 1944.

57. Slapnicka, *Oberdonau*, 293–94. The prevailing defeatism in Linz is well documented in Franziska Berger, *Tage wie schwarze Perlen*, 72–73, 102–10, 133–34.

58. NA, RG 226, E 16, doc. 102066: OSS, 16 November 1944.

59. DÖW, doc. 7266: SD, Vienna, 22 January and 8 March 1945; NÖLA/ZR/Ia-10/23/1945: Lagebericht für Jänner 1945.

60. Hanisch, "Versuch," 161. See also the diary entry of 28 February 1945 in Franziska Berger, *Tage wie schwarze Perlen*, 139–41.

61. Horwitz, *In the Shadow of Death*, 124–43.

62. Ibid., 133.

63. NÖLA/ZR/Ia-10/23/1945: Landrat and police reports for February and March 1945, especially from Korneuburg, 14 March, and Eisenstadt, 19 February and 3 March.

64. DÖW, doc. 7266: SD, Vienna, 22 January 1945; NA, T 77, R 1037: Wehrkreiskommando XVII, II a/W Pro, Vienna, 20 January 1945.

65. Schöner, *Wiener Tagebuch*, 95.

66. Vassiltchikov, *Berlin Diaries, 1940–1945*, 243.

67. Ibid., 248.

68. Ibid., 253–55.

69. Ibid., 256.

70. Ibid., 242–72, and Luza, *Austro-German Relations*, 343–45.

71. Luza, *Austro-German Relations*, 345.

72. Jedlicka, *Der 20. Juli 1944 in Österreich*, 102–3.

73. Ibid., and Luza, *Austro-German Relations*, 345.

74. Luza, *Austro-German Relations*, 345.

75. Schöner, *Wiener Tagebuch*, 86–105.

76. Quoted in Maass, *Country without a Name*, 133.

77. Schöner, *Wiener Tagebuch*, 108–30.

78. Ibid., 130–42.

79. Ibid., 136–42.

80. Horwitz, *In the Shadow of Death*, 144–63. Quotation from p. 149.

81. Ibid., 156.

82. Ibid., 159.

83. Quoted in Pauley, *From Prejudice to Persecution*, 301.

84. Beer and Karner, *Der Krieg aus der Luft*, 327–30; Hanisch, "An Attempt to 'Understand' National Socialism," 47.

85. Stadler, *Österreich*, 404; Hanisch, *Nationalsozialistische Herrschaft*, 250.

86. Stadler, *Österreich*, 404–5.

EPILOGUE

1. Luza, *Austro-German Relations*, 352. These figures do not include the approximately 140,000 prisoners killed or worked to death on Austrian soil at Hartheim, Am Steinhof, and the Mauthausen concentration camp complex.

2. Quoted in Knight, *"Ich bin dafür,"* 75.

3. Luza, *Austro-German Relations*, 349–52; Brook-Shepherd, *The Austrians*, 377–83; Hanisch, *Der lange Schatten des Staates*, 399–407.

4. For details, see Stiefel, *Entnazifizierung in Österreich*, 247–58.

5. Tweraser, *US Militärregierung*, 174–242.

6. Luza, *Austro-German Relations*, 355–58. For incisive overviews of the politics of memory in postwar Austria, see Bischof, "Die Intrumentalisierung der Moskauer Erklärung nach dem 2. Weltkrieg," 345–66; Bischof, "Founding Myths," 302–41.

7. Quoted in Herf, *Divided Memory*, 217.

8. Parkinson, *Conquering the Past*, 323.

9. Schneider, *Exile and Destruction*, 159.

10. Clare, *Berlin Days*, 209.

11. Katzenstein, *Disjoined Partners*, 166.

12. Hanisch, *Der lange Schatten des Staates*, 399–425; Bischof, "Founding Myths," 303–8.

13. In 1956, polling data indicated that only 49 percent of the Austrian people thought that they belonged to a distinctive nation or were developing into one. Within fifteen years, the figure had climbed to 82 percent; by 1990 only 10 percent disagreed. Cf. Steiner, *Politics in Austria*, 156, and Brook-Shepherd, *The Austrians*, 428.

14. Tweraser, *US Militärregierung*, 242. Elsewhere in Austria, 41 percent of the adult population thought that Nazism had been a good idea badly carried out, a figure roughly comparable to that of respondents in the American occupation zone in Germany. Wagnleitner, *Understanding Austria*, 338.

15. Pelinka, "SPÖ, ÖVP, and the 'Ehemaligen': Isolation or Integration?," 245–56.

16. Markovits, "Austrian-German Relations in the New Europe: Predicaments of Political and National Identity Formation," 107.

17. Reiterer, *Nation und Nationalbewusstsein in Österreich*, 61, 132–37; Parkinson, *Conquering the Past*, 323; Brook-Shepherd, *The Austrians*, 427–28.

18. Pauley, *From Prejudice to Persecution*, 301–3; Schneider, *Exile and Destruction*, 159–67; Albrich, *Exodus durch Österreich*; Albrich, "Holocaust und Schuldabwehr," 61–64.

19. Pauley, *From Prejudice to Persecution*, 301.

20. Quoted in Wagnleitner, *Understanding Austria*, 119.

21. Ibid., 247–58; Tweraser, *US Militärregierung*, 276–85.

22. Schneider, *Exile and Destruction*, 163; Pauley, *From Prejudice to Persecution*, 307–10; Sternfeld, *Betrifft: Österreich: Von Österreich betroffen*, 110–15; Knight, *"Ich bin dafür,"* 243.

23. Pauley, "Austria," 492–507; Albrich, "Holocaust und Schuldabwehr," 61–85.

24. Herzstein, *Waldheim*.

25. Pauley, "Austria," 499–506.

26. Ibid., 495–508; Brook-Shepherd, *The Austrians*, 429–54.

27. Uhl, *Zwischen Versöhnung und Verstörung*; Sully, "The Waldheim Connection," 294–312; Pauley, "Austria," 493–95.

28. Pauley, "Austria," 506–7. The best survey of contemporary Austria is Pelinka, *Austria: Out of the Shadow of the Past*.

BIBLIOGRAPHY

UNPUBLISHED DOCUMENTS

Allgemeines Verwaltungsarchiv (AVA), Vienna
  Reichskommissar für die Wiedervereinigung Österreichs mit dem Deutschen Reich
    (Rk), boxes 19, 20, 157, 164, 166, 168, 173–78, 211, 322, 387, 388, 391
  Reichsstatthalter Wien (RStH), boxes 388, 391
Dokumentationsarchiv des österreichischen Widerstandes (DÖW), Vienna
  Documents 202–12, 1179, 1189, 1445, 1780, 4081, 4212, 5120, 5172, 7266, 7495, 7506,
    7932, 8048, 8339, 8351, 8353, 8570, 12.320, 15.349, 16.114, 17.846, 17.858/6,
    20.387, Film 97
National Archives (NA), Washington, D.C.
  Record Group 226, Records of the Office of Strategic Services, entry 16, boxes 23, 24,
    0617, 1571
  Records of the Department of State Relating to Internal Affairs of Austria, 1930–44,
    microcopy 1209, reels 6–7, 29
  World War II Collection of Seized Enemy Records filmed at Alexandria, Virginia
    Microcopy T-77, Records of Headquarters, German Armed Forces, High Command
    Microcopy T-81, Records of the National Socialist German Labor Party, reels 6–7
    Microcopy T-84, Miscellaneous German Collections
Niederösterreiches Landesarchiv (NÖLA), Vienna
  ZR Ia-10 (1938–45)
Oberösterreichisches Landesarchiv (OÖLA), Linz
  Politische Akten, 1933–45, box 69
Public Record Office (PRO), London
  Foreign Office Political and Diplomatic Files: FO 371 (1938–39)
Franklin D. Roosevelt Library, Hyde Park, N.Y.
  President's Secretary File, Consular Reports Relating to Conditions in Occupied
    Countries

PUBLISHED DOCUMENTS

"Anschluss 1938": Eine Dokumentation. Edited by the Dokumentationsarchiv des
  österreichischen Widerstandes. Vienna: Österreichischer Bundesverlag, 1988.
Archives of the Holocaust: An International Collection of Selected Documents. 22 vols. Edited by
  Henry Friedlander and Sybil Milton. New York: Garland Publishing, 1990–93.

Deutschland-Berichte der Sozialdemokratischen Partei Deutschlands (Sopade): 1934–1940. 7 vols. Frankfurt am Main: Petra Nettelbeck, 1980.

Documents on German Foreign Policy. Series D, 1937–45, vol. 1. Washington, D.C.: U.S. Government Printing Office, 1951.

Erzählte Geschichte: Jüdische Schicksale: Berichte von Verfolgten. 3 vols. Edited by the Dokumentationsarchiv des österreichischen Widerstandes. Vienna: Österreichischer Bundesverlag, 1993.

Hitler: Reden und Proklamationen 1932–1945: Kommentiert von einem deutschen Zeitgenossen. 4 vols. Edited by Max Domarus. Wiesbaden: R. Löwit, 1973.

Hitler's Secret Conversations, 1941–1944. Edited by H. R. Trevor Roper. New York: Farrar, Straus and Young, 1953.

Justice for Austria! Red-White-Red Book: Description, Documents and Proofs to the Antecedents and History of the Occupation of Austria (from Official Sources). Part 1. Vienna: Austrian State Print House, 1947.

Meldungen aus dem Reich: Die Geheimen Lageberichte des Sicherheitsdienstes der SS 1938–1945. 17 vols. Edited by Heinz Boberach. Herrsching: Pawlak Verlag, 1984.

Statistisches Handbuch für die Republik Österreich. Edited by Bundesamt für Statistik. Vols. 16–18. Vienna: Österreichische Staatsdruckerei, 1936–38.

Trial of the Major War Criminals before the International Tribunal. XXVIII. Nuremberg: n.p., 1947.

Widerstand und Verfolgung in Burgenland 1934–1945: Eine Dokumentation. Edited by the Dokumentationsarchiv des österreichischen Widerstandes. Vienna: Österreichischer Bundesverlag, 1979.

Widerstand und Verfolgung in Niederösterreich 1934–1945: Eine Dokumentation. 3 vols. Edited by the Dokumentationsarchiv des österreichischen Widerstandes. Vienna: Österreichischer Bundesverlag, 1987.

Widerstand und Verfolgung in Oberösterreich 1934–1945: Eine Dokumentation. 2 vols. Edited by the Dokumentationsarchiv des österreichischen Widerstandes. Vienna: Österreichischer Bundesverlag, 1982.

Widerstand und Verfolgung in Salzburg 1934–1945: Eine Dokumentation. 2 vols. Edited by the Dokumentationsarchiv des österreichischen Widerstandes. Vienna: Österreichischer Bundesverlag, 1991.

Widerstand und Verfolgung in Tirol 1934–1945: Eine Dokumentation. 3 vols. Edited by the Dokumentationsarchiv des österreichischen Widerstandes. Vienna: Österreichischer Bundesverlag, 1984.

Widerstand und Verfolgung in Wien 1934–1945: Eine Dokumentation. 3 vols. Edited by Herbert Steiner, Peter Eppel, and Johann Holzner. Vienna: Österreichischer Bundesverlag, 1975.

NEWSPAPERS

Manchester Guardian, 1938–39
New York Times, 1938–41

The Times, 1938–39

Völkischer Beobachter (Wiener Ausgabe), 1938–40

MEMOIRS, ARTICLES, AND SECONDARY VOLUMES

Albrich, Thomas. *Exodus durch Österreich: Die jüdischen Flüchtlinge 1945–1948*. Innsbruck: Haymon Verlag, 1987.

———. " 'Gebt dem Führer euer Ja!' Die NS-Propaganda in Tirol für die Volksabstimmung am 10. April 1938." In *Tirol und der Anschluss: Voraussetzungen, Entwicklungen, Rahmenbedingungen 1918–1938*, edited by Thomas Albrich, Klaus Eisterer, and Rolf Steininger, 505–37. Innsbruck: Haymon Verlag, 1988.

———. "Holocaust und Schuldabwehr: Vom Judenmord zum kollektiven Opferstatus." In *Österreich im 20. Jahrhundert: Vom Zweiten Weltkrieg bis zur Gegenwart*, edited by Rolf Steininger and Michael Gehler, 39–106. Vienna, Cologne, and Weimar: Böhlau Verlag, 1997.

———. "Vom Vorurteil zum Pogrom: Antisemitismus von Schönerer bis Hitler." In *Österreich im 20. Jahrhundert: Von der Monarchie bis zum Zweiten Weltkrieg*, edited by Rolf Steininger and Michael Gehler, 309–66. Vienna, Cologne, and Weimar: Böhlau Verlag, 1997.

Albrich, Thomas, and Arno Gisinger. *Im Bombenkrieg: Tirol und Vorarlberg 1943–1945*. Innsbruck: Haymon Verlag, 1992.

Albrich, Thomas, and Wolfgang Meixner. "Zwischen Legalität und Illegalität: Zur Mitgliederentwicklung, Alters- und Sozialstruktur der NSDAP in Tirol und Vorarlberg vor 1938." *Zeitgeschichte* 22 (1995): 149–87.

Andics, Hellmut. *Der Staat, den keiner wollte: Österreich von der Gründung der Republik bis zur Moskauer Deklaration*. Vienna and Munich: Molden, 1968.

Baird, Jay W. *The Mythical World of Nazi War Propaganda, 1939–1945*. Minneapolis: University of Minnesota Press, 1974.

Bankier, Alexander A. " 'Auch nicht von der Frau Hinterhuber': Zu den ökonomischen Aspekten des Novemberpogroms in Wien." In *Der Novemberpogrom 1938: Die "Reichskristallnacht" in Wien*, edited by Historisches Museum der Stadt Wien, 70–83. Vienna: Eigenverlag der Museen der Stadt Wien, 1988.

Bankier, David. *The Germans and the Final Solution: Public Opinion under Nazism*. Oxford: Oxford University Press, 1992.

Bart, Richard, and Emil Puffer. *Die Gemeindevertretung der Stadt Linz vom Jahre 1848 bis zur Gegenwart*. Linz: Gutenberg, 1968.

Beck, Earl R. *Under the Bombs: The German Home Front, 1942–1945*. Lexington: University of Kentucky Press, 1986.

Beer, Siegfried, and Stefan Karner. *Der Krieg aus der Luft: Kärnten und Steiermark 1941–1945*. Graz: Weishaupt, 1992.

Bell, P. M. H. *John Bull and the Bear: British Public Opinion, Foreign Policy and the Soviet Union, 1941–1945*. London: Edward Arnold, 1990.

———. *The Origins of the Second World War in Europe*. London: Longman, 1986.

Bentwich, Norman. "The Destruction of the Jewish Community in Austria, 1938–1942." In *The Jews of Austria: Essays on Their Life, History and Destruction*, edited by Josef Fraenkel, 467–78. London: Vallentine, Mitchell, 1967.

Berger, Franziska. *Tage wie schwarze Perlen: Tagebuch einer jungen Frau Oberösterreich 1942–1945*. Grünbach: Franz Steinhaußl, 1989.

Berger, Karin. "'Hut ab vor Frau Sedlmayer!' Zur Militarisierung und Ausbeutung der Arbeit von Frauen in nationalsozialistischen Österreich." In *NS-Herrschaft in Österreich 1938–1945*, edited by Emmerich Tálos, Ernst Hanisch, and Wolfgang Neugebauer, 141–61. Vienna: Verlag für Gesellschaftskritik, 1988.

———. "Die innere Front." In *Österreicher und der zweite Weltkrieg*, edited by Wolfgang Neugebauer, 59–66. Vienna: Österreichischer Bundesverlag, 1989.

———. *Zwischen Eintopf und Fliessband: Frauenarbeit und Frauenbild im Faschismus: Österreich 1938–1945*. Vienna: Verlag für Gesellschaftskritik, 1984.

Berkley, George. *Vienna and Its Jews: The Tragedy of Success, 1880s–1980s*. Lanham, Md.: Madison Books, 1988.

Bernbaum, John A. "Nazi Control in Austria: The Creation of the Ostmark, 1938–1940." Ph.D. dissertation, University of Maryland, 1972.

———. "'The New Elite': Nazi Leadership in Austria, 1938–1945." *Austrian History Yearbook* 14 (1978): 145–60.

Bernhard, Thomas. *Gathering Evidence: A Memoir*. New York: Knopf, 1985.

Bischof, Günter. "Founding Myths and Compartmentalized Past: New Literature on the Construction, Hibernation, and Deconstruction of World War II Memory in Postwar Austria." *Contemporary Austrian Studies* 5 (1997): 302–41.

———. "Die Instrumentalisierung der Moskauer Erklärung nach dem 2. Weltkrieg." *Zeitgeschichte* 20, nos. 11–12 (1993): 345–66.

Black, Peter. *Ernst Kaltenbrunner: Ideological Soldier of the Third Reich*. Princeton: Princeton University Press, 1984.

Blanning, T. C. W. *Joseph II*. London: Longman, 1994.

Boelcke, Willi A., ed. *The Secret Conferences of Dr. Goebbels: The Nazi Propaganda War, 1939–43*. New York: Dutton, 1970.

Botz, Gerhard. "Der 'Anschluss' von 1938 als innerösterreichisches Problem." *Aus Politik und Zeitgeschichte: Beilage zur Wochenzeitung "Das Parlament."* B9/88 (26 February 1988): 3–19.

———. "Arbeiterschaft und österreichische NSDAP-Mitglieder (1926–1945)." In *Arbeiterschaft und Nationalsozialismus in Österreich*, edited by Rudolf G. Ardelt and Hans Hautmann, 29–48. Vienna: Europaverlag, 1990.

———. "The Changing Patterns of Social Support for Austrian National Socialism (1918–1945)." In *Who Were the Fascists? Social Roots of European Fascism*, edited by Stein Ugelvik Larsen, Bernt Havet, and Jan P. Myklebust, 202–25. Bergen: Bergen Universitetsforlaget, 1980.

———. "Eine deutsche Geschichte 1938 bis 1945? Österreichische Geschichte zwischen Exil, Widerstand und Verstrickung." *Zeitgeschichte* 14, no. 1 (1986): 19–37.

——. *Der 13. März 38 und die Anschlussbewegung: Selbstaufgabe, Okkupation und Selbstfindung Österreichs 1918–1945*. Vienna: Dr. Karl Renner Institut, 1978.

——. "The Dynamics of Persecution in Austria, 1938–45." In *Austrians and Jews in the Twentieth Century: From Franz Joseph to Waldheim*, edited by Robert S. Wistrich, 199–233. New York: St. Martin's Press, 1992.

——. *Die Eingliederung Österreichs in das Deutsche Reich: Planung und Verwirklichung des politisch-administrativen Anschlusses (1938–1940)*. Vienna: Europaverlag, 1976.

——. "Das Ergebnis der 'Volksabstimmung' von 10. April 1938." In *Wien 1938: Forschungen und Beiträge zur Wiener Stadtgeschichte: Sonderreihe der Wiener Geschichtsblätter*, 95–104. Vienna: Verein für die Geschichte der Stadt Wien, 1988.

——. "Hitlers Aufenthalt in Linz in März 1938 und der Anschluss." *Historisches Jahrbuch der Stadt Linz 1970* (1971): 185–214.

——. "The Jews of Vienna from the Anschluss to the Holocaust." In *Jews, Antisemitism and Culture in Vienna*, edited by Ivar Oxaal, Michael Pollack, and Gerhard Botz, 185–204. London: Routledge and Kegan Paul, 1987.

——. "'Judenhatz' und 'Reichskristallnacht' im historischen Kontext: Pogrome in Österreich und in Osteuropa um 1900." In *Der Pogrom 1938: Judenverfolgung in Österreich und Deutschland: Dokumentation eines Symposium der Volkshochschule Brigittenau*, edited by Kurt Schmid and Robert Streibel, 9–25. Vienna: Picus Verlag, 1990.

——. *Nationalsozialismus in Wien: Machtübernahme und Herrschaftssicherung 1938/39*. Vienna: Obermayer, 1988.

——. "Schuschniggs geplante 'Volksbefragung' und Hitlers 'Volksabstimmung' in Österreich." In *Anschluss 1938: Protokoll des Symposiums in Wien am 14. und 15. März 1978*, edited by Rudolf Neck and Adam Wandruszka, 220–43. Vienna: Verlag für Geschichte und Politik, 1981.

——. "Strukturwandlungen des österreichischen Nationalsozialismus (1904–1945)." In *Politik und Gesellschaft im alten und neuen Österreich: Festschrift für Rudolf Neck zum 60. Geburtstag*, edited by Isabella Ackerl et al., 2:195–218. Munich: Oldenbourg, 1981.

——. "Stufen der Ausgliederung der Juden aus der Gesellschaft: Die österreichischen Juden vom 'Anschluss' zum 'Holocaust.'" *Zeitgeschichte* 14, nos. 9–10 (1987): 359–78.

——. "War der Anschluss gezwungen?" In *Fünfzig Jahre danach—Der "Anschluss" von innen und aussen gesehen: Beiträge zum Internationalen Symposion von Rouen, 29. Februar–4. März 1988*, edited by Felix Kreissler, 97–119. Vienna: Europaverlag, 1989.

——. *Wohnungspolitik und Judendeportation in Wien 1938 bis 1945: Zur Funktion des Antisemitismus als Ersatz nationalsozialistische Sozialpolitik*. Vienna: Geyer-Edition, 1975.

——. "Zwischen Akzeptanz und Distanz: Die österreichische Bevölkerung und das NS-Regime nach dem 'Anschluss.'" In *Österreich, Deutschland und die Mächte: Internationale und österreichische Aspekte des "Anschlusses" vom März 1938*, edited by Gerald Stourzh and Brigitta Zaar, 429–69. Vienna: Akademie der Wissenschaften, 1990.

Boyer, John. *Political Radicalism in Late Imperial Vienna: Origins of the Christian Social Movement, 1848–1897*. Chicago: University of Chicago Press, 1981.

Bracher, Karl Dietrich. *The German Dictatorship: The Origins, Structure, and Effects of National Socialism*. New York: Praeger, 1970.

Brandstötter, Rudolf. "Dr. Walter Riehl und die Geschichte der DNSAP in Österreich." Ph.D. dissertation, University of Vienna, 1968.

Brook-Shepherd, Gordon. *The Anschluss*. Philadelphia: J. P. Lippincott, 1953.

———. *The Austrians: A Thousand-Year Odyssey*. London: Harper Collins, 1996.

Broszat, Martin, Elke Fröhlich, and Artur Grossmann, eds. *Bayern in der NS-Zeit*. 6 vols. Munich: Oldenbourg, 1977–83.

Broucek, Peter, ed. *Ein General im Zwielicht: Die Erinnerungen Edmund Glaises von Horstenau*. Vol. 3, *Deutscher bevollmächtiger General in Kroaten und Zeuge des Unterganges des "Tausendjähriges Reich."* Vienna: Böhlau, 1988.

Bruckmüller, Ernst. "Sozialstruktur und Sozialpolitik." In *Österreich 1918–1938: Geschichte der Ersten Republik*, edited by Erika Weinzierl and Kurt Skalnik, 1:381–435. Graz: Verlag Styria, 1983.

Bukey, Evan Burr. "The Austrians and the 'Ostmark' 1938–1945." In *Ungleiche Partner? Österreich und Deutschland in ihrer gegenseitigen Wahrnehmung. Historisch Analysen und Vergleiche aus dem 19. und 20. Jahrhundert*, edited by Michael Gehler, Rainer F. Schmidt, Harm-Hinrich Brandt, and Rolf Steininger, 513–31. Stuttgart: Franz Steiner Verlag, 1996.

———. "Die Heimatfront: Von der 'Ostmark' zu den 'Alpen- und Donaugauen' 1939–1945." In *Österreich im 20. Jahrhundert: Von der Monarchie bis zum Zweiten Weltkrieg*, edited by Rolf Steininger and Michael Gehler, 465–98. Vienna, Cologne, and Weimar: Böhlau, 1997.

———. *Hitler's Hometown: Linz, Austria, 1908–1945*. Bloomington: Indiana University Press, 1986.

———. "Hitler's Hometown under Nazi Rule: Linz, Austria, 1938–1945." *Central European History* 16, no. 2 (June 1983): 171–86.

———. "Nazi Rule in Austria." *Austrian History Yearbook* 22 (1992): 202–33.

———. "Popular Opinion in Vienna after the Anschluss." In *Conquering the Past: Austrian Nazism Yesterday and Today*, edited by F. Parkinson, 151–64. Detroit: Wayne State University Press, 1989.

Burke, Peter. *History and Social Theory*. Ithaca, N.Y.: Cornell University Press, 1992.

Butschek, Felix. *Die österreichische Wirtschaft 1938 bis 1945*. Stuttgart: G. Fischer, 1978.

Buttinger, Joseph. *In the Twilight of Socialism: A History of Revolutionary Socialists in Austria*. New York: F. A. Praeger, 1953.

Calder, Angus. *The People's War: Britain, 1939–1945*. New York: Pantheon Books, 1971.

Carsten, F. L. *Fascist Movements in Austria: From Schönerer to Hitler*. London: Sage Publications, 1977.

———. *The First Austrian Republic, 1918–1938: A Study Based on British and Austrian Documents*. Hants: Gower/Maurice Temple Smith, 1986.

———. *Revolution in Central Europe, 1918–1919*. Berkeley: University of California Press, 1972.

Clare, George. *Berlin Days*. London: Macmillan, 1989.

———. *Last Waltz in Vienna: The Rise and Destruction of a Family*. New York: Holt, Rinehart and Winston, 1980.

Connely, John. "The Uses of *Volksgemeinschaft*: Letters to the NSDAP Kreisleitung Eisenach, 1939–40." *Journal of Modern History* 62 (1996): 899–930.

Conot, Robert E. *Justice at Nuremberg*. New York: Harper and Row, 1983.

Conway, John. *The Nazi Persecution of the Churches, 1933–1945*. New York: Basic Books, 1968.

Corni, Gustavo. *Hitler and the Peasants: Agrarian Policy of the Third Reich, 1930–1939*. New York: Berg, 1990.

Czedik, Maria. *Uns fragt man nicht: Ein Tagebuch 1941–1945*. Vienna: Jugend und Volk, 1988.

Czeitschner, Burgl, Hubertus Czernin, and Ernst Schmiederer. " 'Einige Sekunden blieb alles still.' " *Profil*, no. 45, 7 November 1988, 62–86.

Davidson, W. Phillips. "Public Opinion." In *International Encyclopedia of the Social Sciences*, 13:188–93. New York: Macmillan, 1968.

Denscher, Bernhard. " 'Der ewige Jude': Antisemitische Propaganda vom 'Anschluss' bis zum Novemberpogrom 1938." In *Der Novemberpogrom 1938: Die "Reichskristallnacht" in Wien*, edited by Historisches Museum der Stadt Wien, 43–52. Vienna: Eigenverlag der Museen der Stadt Wien, 1988.

Edmondson, C. Earl. *The Heimwehr and Austrian Politics, 1918–1936*. Athens: University of Georgia Press, 1978.

Eichinger, Hermann. "Die politische Situation im südwestlichen Niederösterreich 1934 bis 1945." Ph.D. dissertation, University of Vienna, 1986.

Eksteins, Modris. *Rites of Spring: The Great War and the Birth of the Modern Age*. New York: Anchor Books, 1989.

Epstein, Klaus. *The Genesis of German Conservatism*. Princeton: Princeton University Press, 1966.

Erhard, Benedikt, and Bernhard Natter. " 'Wir waren alle ja arbeitslos': NS-Sympathisten deuten ihre Motive." In *Tirol und der Anschluss: Voraussetzungen, Entwicklungen, Rahmenbedingungen 1918–1938*, edited by Thomas Albrich, Klaus Eisterer, and Rolf Steininger, 540–69. Innsbruck: Haymon Verlag, 1988.

Eubank, Keith, ed. *The Road to World War II: A Documentary History*. New York: Crowell, 1973.

Falter, Jürgen W., and Dirk Hänisch. "Wahlerfolge und Wählerschaft der NSDAP in Österreich von 1927 bis 1932: Soziale Basis und Parteipolitische Herkunft." *Zeitgeschichte* 15, no. 2 (1988): 223–44.

Feichtenschlager, Norbert. "Der Novemberpogrom 1938 in Wien." *Zeitgeschichte* 11, nos. 11–12 (1994): 363–87.

Feiler, Margaret. "The Viennese Municipal Civil Service, 1933 to 1950: A Case Study in Bureaucratic Resiliency." Ph.D. dissertation, Columbia University, 1964.

Fellner, Günter. *Antisemitismus in Salzburg 1918–1938*. Vienna: Veröffentlichen der Historische Institut der Universität Salzburg, 1979.

———. "Der Novemberpogrom in Westösterreich." In *Der Pogrom 1938: Judenverfolgung in Österreich und Deutschland*, edited by Kurt Schmid and Robert Streibel, 34–41. Vienna: Picus, 1990.

———. "Der Novemberpogrom 1938: Bemerkungen zur Forschung." *Zeitgeschichte* 16, no. 2 (1988–89): 35–58.

Fest, Joachim. *Hitler*. New York: Harcourt, Brace, Jovanovich, 1974.

Fredborg, Avrid. *Behind the Steel Wall: A Swedish Journalist in Berlin*. New York: Viking, 1944.

Freidenreich, Harriet Pass. *Jewish Politics in Vienna, 1918–1938*. Bloomington: Indiana University Press, 1991.

Freudenberger, Herbert, and Radomir Luza. "National Socialist Germany and the Austrian Industry, 1938–1945." In *Austria since 1945*, edited by William E. Wright, 73–100. Minneapolis: University of Minnesota Press, 1982.

Freund, Florian. "Kriegswirtschaft, Zwangsarbeit und Konzentrationslager in Österreich." In *Österreicher und der zweite Weltkrieg*, edited by Wolfgang Neugebauer, 101–19. Vienna: Österreichischer Bundesverlag, 1989.

Freund, Florian, and Bertrand Perz. "Industrialisierung durch Zwangsarbeit." In *NS-Herrschaft in Österreich 1938–1945*, edited by Emmerich Tálos, Ernst Hanisch, and Wolfgang Neugebauer, 95–114. Vienna: Verlag für Gesellschaftskritik, 1988.

Fried, Jakob. *Nationalsozialismus und katholische Kirche in Österreich*. Vienna: Wiener Dom Verlag, 1947.

Friedlander, Henry. *The Origins of Nazi Genocide: From Euthanasia to the Final Solution*. Chapel Hill: University of North Carolina Press, 1995.

Friedländer, Saul. *Nazi Germany and the Jews: The Years of Persecution, 1933–1939*. New York: Harper Collins, 1997.

Furst, Desider, and Lilian R. Furst. *Home Is Somewhere Else: Autobiography in Two Voices*. Albany: State University of New York Press, 1994.

Gänser, Gerlad. "Kontinuität und Bruch in der Steierischen Landesverwaltung." *Historisches Jahrbuch der Stadt Graz* 18–19 (1988): 126–31.

Garscha, Winfried R. *Die Verfahren vor dem Volksgericht Wien (1945–1955) als Geschichtsquelle*. Vienna: Dokumentationsarchiv des österreichischen Widerstandes, 1993.

Gay, Peter. *Freud: A Life for Our Time*. New York: Norton, 1988.

Gedye, G. E. R. *Betrayal in Central Europe: Austria and Czechoslovakia: The Fallen Bastions*. New York: Harper, 1939.

Gehl, Jürgen. *Germany and the Anschluss, 1931–1938*. London: Oxford University Press, 1963.

Gehler, Michael. "Murder on Command: The Anti-Jewish Pogrom in Innsbruck 9th–10th November 1938." *Leo Baeck Institute Yearbook* 38 (1993): 119–33.

Gellately, Robert. "Denunciations in Twentieth Century Germany: Aspects of Self-Policing in the Third Reich and the German Democratic Republic." *Journal of Modern History* 62, no. 4 (1996): 931–67.

———. *The Gestapo and German Society: Enforcing Racial Policy, 1933–1945*. Oxford: Oxford University Press, 1991.

Gellately, Robert, and Sheila Fitzpatrick. "Introduction to the Practice of Denunciation in Modern European History." *Journal of Modern History* 62, no. 4 (1996): 747–67.

Gellott, Laura. "Recent Writings on the Ständestaat, 1934–1938." *Austrian History Yearbook* 26 (1995): 207–38.

Gerbel, Christian, Alexander Mejstrik, and Reinhard Sieder. "Die 'Schlurfs': Verweigerung und Opposition von Wiener Arbeiterjugendlichen im 'Dritten Reich.'" In *NS-Herrschaft in Österreich 1938–1945*, edited by Emmerich Tálos, Ernst Hanisch, and Wolfgang Neugebauer, 243–68. Vienna: Verlag für Gesellschaftskritik, 1988.

Gold, Hugo. *Geschichte der Juden in Österreich: Ein Gedenkbuch*. Tel Aviv: Olamenu, 1971.

Goldhagen, Daniel Jonah. *Hitler's Willing Executioners: Ordinary Germans and the Holocaust.* New York: Alfred A. Knopf, 1996.

Goldinger, Walter. *Geschichte der Republik Österreich.* Vienna: Verlag für Geschichte und Politik, 1962.

———. "Der Sturm auf das Wiener erzbischöfliche Palais 1938 im Lichte der NS Akten." *Geschichte und Gegenwart* 1 (1989): 16–21.

Graml, Hermann. *Der 9. November 1938: "Reichskristallnacht."* Bonn: Bundeszentrale für Heimatdienst, 1956.

Gruber, Helmut. *Red Vienna: Experiment in Working Class Culture, 1919–1934.* Oxford: Oxford University Press, 1991.

Grunwald, Henry. *One Man's America: A Journalist's Search for the Heart of His Country.* New York: Doubleday, 1997.

Guderian, Heinz. *Panzer Leader.* New York: Ballantine Books, 1952.

Gulick, Charles A. *Austria from Habsburg to Hitler.* 2 vols. Berkeley: University of California Press, 1948.

Haag, John. "Marginal Men and the Dream of the Reich: Eight Austrian National Catholic Intellectuals, 1918–1938." In *Who Were the Fascists? Social Roots of European Fascism,* edited by Stein Ugelvik Larsen, Bernt Havet, and Jan P. Myklebust, 339–48. Bergen: Universitetsforlaget, 1980.

Hagspiel, Hermann. *Die Ostmark: Österreich im Großdeutschen Reich 1938 bis 1945.* Vienna: Braumüller, 1995.

Hall, Kay B., ed. *World War II: From the Battle Front to the Home Front: Arkansans Tell Their Stories.* Fayetteville: University of Arkansas Press, 1995.

Hamann, Brigitte. *Hitlers Wien: Lehrjahre eines Diktators.* Munich: Piper, 1996.

Hänisch, Dirk. *Die österreichischen NSDAP-Wähler: Eine empirische Analyse ihrer politischen Herkunft und ihres Sozialprofils.* Vienna, Cologne, and Weimar: Böhlau, 1998.

Hanisch, Ernst. "An Attempt to 'Understand' National Socialism." *Austria Today* 13, no. 2 (1987): 9–10, 46–49.

———. "Austrian Catholicism: Between Accommodation and Resistance." In *Conquering the Past: Austrian Nazism Yesterday and Today,* edited by F. Parkinson, 165–89. Detroit: Wayne State University Press, 1989.

———. "Bäuerliches Milieu und Arbeitermilieu in den Alpengauen: Ein historischer Vergleich." In *Arbeiterschaft und Nationalsozialismus in Österreich,* edited by Rudolf G. Ardelt and Hans Hautmann, 583–98. Vienna: Europaverlag, 1990.

———. "Comments." *Austrian History Yearbook* 14 (1978): 164–65.

———. *Der lange Schatten des Staates: Österreichische Gesellschaftsgeschichte im 20. Jahrhundert.* Vienna: Ueberreuter, 1994.

———. *Nationalsozialistische Herrschaft in der Provinz: Salzburg im Dritten Reich.* Salzburg: Schriftenreihe des Landespressebüro, 1983.

———. "Peasants and Workers in Their Environment: Nonconformity and Opposition to National Socialism in the Austrian Alps." In *Germans against Nazism: Nonconformity, Opposition, and Resistance in the Third Reich: Essays in Honour of Peter Hoffmann,* edited by Francis R. Nicosia and Lawrence D. Stokes, 175–90. New York: Berg, 1990.

———. "Der politische Katholizimus als ideologischer Träger des 'Austrofaschismus.'" In *"Austrofaschismus": Beiträge über Politik, Ökonomie und Kultur 1934–1938*, edited by Emmerich Tálos and Wolfgang Neugebauer, 53–73. Vienna: Verlag für Gesellschaftskritik, 1984.

———. "Ein Versuch den Nationalsozialismus zu verstehen." In *Das grosse Tabu: Österreichs Umgang mit seiner Vergangenheit*, edited by Anton Pelinka and Erika Weinzierl, 154–62. Vienna: Verlag der österreichischen Staatsdruckerei, 1987.

———. "Westösterreich." In *NS-Herrschaft in Österreich 1938–1945*, edited by Emmerich Tálos, Ernst Hanisch, and Wolfgang Neugebauer, 437–56. Vienna: Verlag für Gesellschaftskritik, 1988.

———. "Zur Frühgeschichte des Nationalsozialismus in Salzburg (1913–1925)." *Mitteilungen der Gesellschaft für Salzburger Landeskunde* 117 (1977): 371–410.

Hausjell, Fritz, and Theo Venus. "'. . . Wie's ihm ums Herz ist': Eine Radioreportage zum Judenpogrom 'Reichskristallnacht' ausgestrahlt vom Sender Wien am 10. November 1938: Eine Dokumentation." *Medien und Zeit* 3 (March 1988): 31–33.

Hautmann, Hans, and Rudolf Kropf. *Die österreichische Arbeiterbewegung vom Vormärz bis 1945: Sozialökonomische Ursprünge ihrer Ideologie und Politik*. Vienna: Europaverlag, 1974.

Helmreich, Ernst Christian. *The German Churches under Hitler: Background, Struggle, and Epilogue*. Detroit: Wayne State University Press, 1979.

Herf, Jeffrey. *Divided Memory: The Nazi Past in the Two Germanies*. Cambridge, Mass.: Harvard University Press, 1997.

Hertz, Friedrich. *The Economic Problem of the Danubian States: A Study of Economic Nationalism*. London: Howard Fertig, 1947.

Herzstein, Robert E. *Waldheim: The Missing Years*. New York: Arbor House, 1988.

Hilsenrad, Helen. *Brown Was the Danube*. New York: T. Yoseloff, 1966.

Historisches Museum der Stadt Wien, ed. *Der Novemberpogrom 1938: Die "Reichskristallnacht" in Wien*. Vienna: Eigenverlag der Museen der Stadt Wien, 1988.

———. *Wien 1938*. Vienna: Österreichischer Bundesverlag, 1988.

Höbelt, Lothar. "Österreicher in der deutschen Wehrmacht 1938 bis 1945." *Truppendienst* 5 (1989): 417–32.

Hoffkes, Karl. *Hitlers politische Generale: Die Gauleiter des Dritten Reiches: Ein biographisches Nachschlagwerk*. Tübingen: Graebert Verlag, 1986.

Hoffmann, Peter. *The History of the German Resistance, 1933–1945*. Cambridge, Mass.: MIT Press, 1977.

Hofmann, Paul. *The Viennese: Splendor, Twilight, and Exile*. New York: Anchor Books, 1989.

Horwitz, Gordon J. *In the Shadow of Death: Living Outside the Gates of Mauthausen*. New York: Free Press, 1990.

Hughes, Walter. "Funeral Waltz: Vienna under Nazi Rule, 1938–1939: A Personal Memoir." Lecture, Faculty of Languages, Polytechnic of Central London, 23 January 1987.

Hutton, Patrick H. "The History of Mentalities: The New Map of Cultural History." *History and Social Theory* 20, no. 3 (1981): 237–59.

Ingrao, Charles. *The Habsburg Monarchy, 1618–1815*. Cambridge: Cambridge University Press, 1994.

Jablonka, Hans. *Waitz: Bischof unter Kaiser und Hitler*. Vienna: Wiener Dom Verlag, 1971.

Jagschitz, Gerhard. "NSDAP und 'Anschluss' in Wien 1938." In *Wien 1938: Forschungen und Beiträge zur Wiener Stadtgeschichte: Sonderreihe der Wiener Geschichtsblätter*, 147–63. Vienna: Verein für die Geschichte der Stadt Wien, 1978.

——. *Der Putsch: Die Nationalsozialisten in Österreich*. Graz: Verlag Styria, 1976.

——. "Von der 'Bewegung' zum Apparat: Zur Phänomenologie der NSDAP 1938 bis 1945." In *NS-Herrschaft in Österreich 1938–1945*, edited by Emmerich Tálos, Ernst Hanisch, and Wolfgang Neugebauer, 487–516. Vienna: Verlag für Gesellschaftskritik, 1988.

Janik, Allan. Review of *From Prejudice to Persecution*, by Bruce F. Pauley. *Central European History* 28, no. 2 (1995): 243.

Jedlicka, Ludwig. "Gauleiter Josef Leopold." In *Geschichte und Gesellschaft: Festschrift für Karl R. Stadler zum 60. Geburtstag*, edited by Gerhard Botz, Hans Hautmann, and Helmut Konrad, 143–61. Vienna: Europaverlag, 1974.

——. *Der 20. Juli 1944 in Österreich*. Vienna: Verlag Herold, 1965.

Jeffery, Charlie. "Center and Periphery in Social Democratic Politics in the Austrian First Republic, 1918–1934." Leicester University Discussion Papers in Politics, No. P 93/2. June 1993.

——. "Konsens und Dissens im Dritten Reich mit einer Fallstudie über Oberösterreich." *Zeitgeschichte* 19, nos. 5–6 (1992): 129–47.

——. *Social Democracy in the Austrian Provinces, 1918–1934: Beyond Red Vienna*. London: Leicester University Press, 1995.

Jelavich, Barbara. *Modern Austria: Empire and Republic, 1815–1986*. Cambridge: Cambridge University Press, 1987.

Johnston, William M. *The Austrian Mind: An Intellectual and Social History, 1848–1938*. Berkeley: University of California Press, 1972.

Kann, Robert A. *A History of the Habsburg Empire, 1526–1918*. Berkeley: University of California Press, 1974.

Kaplan, Marion A. *Between Dignity and Despair: Jewish Life in Nazi Germany*. Oxford: Oxford University Press, 1998.

Karner, Stefan. "'. . . Des Reiches Südmark': Kärnten und Steiermark im Dritten Reich 1938–1945." In *NS-Herrschaft in Österreich 1938–1945*, edited by Emmerich Tálos, Ernst Hanisch, and Wolfgang Neugebauer. Vienna: Verlag für Gesellschaftskritik, 1988.

——. *Die Steiermark im Dritten Reich 1938–1945: Aspekte ihrer politischen, wirtschaftlich-sozialen und kulturellen Entwicklung*. Graz: Leykam Verlag, 1986.

——. "Zur NS-Sozialpolitik gegenüber der österreichischen Arbeiterschaft." In *Arbeiterschaft und Nationalsozialismus in Österreich*, edited by Rudolf G. Ardelt and Hans Hautmann, 255–63. Vienna: Europaverlag, 1990.

Kater, Michael. "Everyday Anti-Semitism in Prewar Nazi Germany: The Popular Bases." *Yad Vashem Studies* 16 (1984): 129–59.

——. *The Nazi Party: A Social Profile of Members and Leaders, 1919–1945*. Cambridge, Mass.: Harvard University Press, 1983.

Katzenstein, Peter J. *Disjoined Partners: Austria and Germany since 1815*. Berkeley: University of California Press, 1976.

Kepplinger, Brigitte. "Aspekte nationalsozialistischer Herrschaft in Oberösterreich." In *NS-Herrschaft in Österreich 1938–1945*, edited by Emmerich Tálos, Ernst Hanisch, and Wolfgang Neugebauer, 417–36. Vienna: Verlag für Gesellschaftskritik, 1988.

——. "Nationalsozialistische Wohnbaupolitik in Oberösterreich." In *Arbeiterschaft und Nationalsozialismus in Österreich*, edited by Rudolf G. Ardelt and Hans Hautmann, 265–87. Vienna: Europaverlag, 1990.

Kernbauer, Gert, and Fritz Weber. "Österreichs Wirtschaft 1938 bis 1945." In *NS-Herrschaft in Österreich 1938–1945*, edited by Emmerich Tálos, Ernst Hanisch, and Wolfgang Neugebauer, 49–67. Vienna: Verlag für Gesellschaftskritik, 1988.

Kernbauer, Hans, Eduard März, and Fritz Weber. "Die wirtschaftliche Entwicklung." In *Österreich 1918–1938: Geschichte der Ersten Republik*, edited by Erika Weinzierl and Kurt Skalnik, 1:366–70. Graz: Verlag Styria, 1983.

Kerschbaumer, Gert. *Faszination Drittes Reich: Kunst und Alltag der Kulturmetropole Salzburg*. Salzburg: Otto Müller Verlag, 1988.

Kershaw, Ian. *The Hitler Myth: Image and Reality in the Third Reich*. Oxford: Oxford University Press, 1987.

——. "The Persecution of the Jews and German Popular Opinion in the Third Reich." *Leo Baeck Institute Yearbook* 26 (1981): 261–89.

——. *Popular Opinion and Political Dissent in the Third Reich: Bavaria, 1933–1945*. Oxford: Oxford University Press, 1983.

Keyserlingk, Robert H. *Austria in World War II: An Anglo-American Dilemma*. Montreal: McGill-Queen's University Press, 1988.

Kirk, Timothy. "The Austrian Working Class under National Socialist Rule: Industrial Unrest and Political Dissent in the 'People's Community.'" Ph.D. dissertation, University of Manchester, 1988.

——. *Nazism and the Working Class in Austria: Industrial Unrest and Political Dissent in the National Community*. Cambridge: Cambridge University Press, 1996.

——. "Workers and Nazis in Hitler's Homeland." *History Today* 46, no. 7 (July 1996): 36–42.

Kitchen, Martin. *The Coming of Austrian Fascism*. London: Croom Helm, 1980.

Klemperer, Klemens von. "The Habsburg Heritage: Some Pointers for a Study of the First Austrian Republic." In *The Austrian Socialist Experiment: Social Democracy and Austromarxism, 1918–1934*, edited by Anson Rabinbach, 11–20. Boulder, Colo.: Westview Press, 1985.

——. *Ignaz Seipel: Christian Statesman in a Time of Crisis*. Princeton: Princeton University Press, 1972.

Klostermann, Ferdinand. "Katholische Jugend im Untergrund." In *Das Bistum Linz im Dritten Reich*, edited by Rudolf Zinnhobler, 138–92. Linz: OLV, 1979.

Kluge, Ulrich. *Der österreichische Ständestaat 1934–1938: Entstehung und Scheitern*. Munich: Oldenbourg, 1984.

Klüger, Ruth. *Weiter leben: Eine Jugend*. Munich: Oldenbourg, 1996.

Knight, Robert. "Carinthia and Its Slovenes: The Politics of Assimilation, 1945–1960." Unpublished manuscript.

——. *"Ich bin dafür, die Sache in die Länge zu ziehen": Wortprotokolle der österreichischen Bundesregierung von 1945–52 über die Entschädung der Juden.* Frankfurt am Main: Athenäum, 1988.

Koch, H. W. *In the Name of the Volk: Political Justice in Hitler's Germany.* New York: St. Martin's Press, 1989.

Köfler, Grete. "Tirol und die Juden." In *Tirol und der Anschluss: Voraussetzungen, Entwicklungen, Rahmenbedingungen,* edited by Thomas Albrich, Klaus Eisterer, and Rolf Steininger, 169–82. Innsbruck: Haymon Verlag, 1988.

Konrad, Helmut. "Social Democracy's Drift toward Nazism before 1938." In *Conquering the Past: Austrian Nazism Yesterday and Today,* edited by F. Parkinson, 110–36. Detroit: Wayne State University Press, 1989.

Kreissler, Felix. *Der Österreicher und seine Nation: Ein Lernprozess mit Hindernissen.* Vienna: Böhlau, 1984.

Kulka, Otto Dov, and Aron Rodrigue. "The German Population and the Jews of the Third Reich: Recent Publication and Trends in Research on German Society and the 'Jewish Question.'" *Yad Vashem Studies* 16 (1984): 365–86.

Kurij, Robert. *Nationalsozialismus und Widerstand im Waldviertel: Die politische Situation 1938–1945.* Horn: Waldviertler Heimatbund, 1987.

Kutschera, Richard. *Johannes Maria Gföllner: Bischof dreier Zeitenwenden.* Linz: Oberösterreichischer Landesverlag, 1972.

Langoth, Franz. *Kampf um Österreich: Erinnerungen eines Politikers.* Wels: Welsermühl, 1951.

Lazarsfeld, Paul. "An Episode in the History of Social Research: A Memoir." In *The Intellectual Migration: Europe and America, 1930–1960,* edited by Donald Fleming and Bernard Bailyn, 270–337. Cambridge, Mass.: Harvard University Press, 1969.

Lein, Hermann. "Das Rosenkranzfest am 7. October 1938." In *Dokumentationsarchiv des österreichischen Widerstandes, Jahrbuch 1990:* 50–55.

Lewy, Guenter. *The Catholic Church and Nazi Germany.* New York: McGraw-Hill, 1964.

Liebmann, Maximilian. *Theodor Innitzer und der Anschluss: Österreichs Kirche 1938.* Graz, Vienna, and Cologne: Styria, 1988.

Lochner, Louis, ed. *The Goebbels Diaries, 1942–1943.* New York: Doubleday, 1948.

Low, Alfred D. *The Anschluss Movement, 1918–1938: Background and Aftermath. An Annotated Bibliography of German and Austrian National Socialism.* New York: Garland, 1984.

——. *The Anschluss Movement, 1931–1938, and the Great Powers.* Boulder, Colo.: East European Monographs, 1985.

Lukacs, John. *Historical Consciousness or the Remembered Past.* New York: Harper and Row, 1968.

——. *The Last European War: September 1939 / December 1941.* New York: Anchor Press Doubleday, 1976.

Luza, Radomir. *Austro-German Relations in the Anschluss Era.* Princeton: Princeton University Press, 1975.

——. "Nazi Control of the Austrian Catholic Church, 1939–1941." *Catholic Historical Review* 62 (1977): 537–72.

——. *The Resistance in Austria, 1938–1945.* Minneapolis: University of Minnesota Press, 1984.

———. "Die Strukturen der nationalsozialistischen Herrschaft in Österreich." In *Österreich, Deutschland und die Mächte: Internationale und österreichische Aspekte des "Anschlusses" vom März 1938*, edited by Gerald Stourzh and Brigitta Zaar, 471–510. Vienna: Akademie der Wissenschaften, 1990.

Maass, Walter B. *Country without a Name: Austria under Nazi Rule, 1938–1945*. New York: Unger, 1979.

McGrath, William J. *Dionysian Art and Populist Politics in Austria*. New Haven: Yale University Press, 1974.

Maislinger, Andreas. "Franz Jägerstätter." In *Conquering the Past: Austrian Nazism Yesterday and Today*, edited by F. Parkinson, 177–89. Detroit: Wayne Sate University Press, 1989.

Manoschek, Walter. *"Serbien ist judenfrei": Militärische Besatzungspolitik und Judenvernichtung in Serbien 1941–1942*. Munich: Oldenbourg, 1993.

Manoschek, Walter, and Hans Safrian. "Österreicher in der Wehrmacht." In *NS-Herrschaft in Österreich 1938–1945*, edited by Emmerich Tálos, Ernst Hanisch, and Wolfgang Neugebauer, 331–60. Vienna: Verlag für Gesellschaftskritik, 1988.

Markovits, Andrei S. "Austrian-German Relations in the New Europe: Predicaments of Political and National Identity Formation." *German Studies Review* 19, no. 1 (1996): 91–111.

Marx, Julius. *Die österreichische Zensur im Vormärz*. Munich: Oldenbourg, 1959.

Marx, Karl. *The Eighteenth Brumaire of Louis Bonaparte*. In *Surveys from Exile*. New York: Random House, 1973.

Massiczek, Albert. *Ich habe meine Pflicht erfüllt: Von der SS in den Widerstand*. Vienna: Junius, 1989.

Mattl, Siegfried. "Die Finanzdiktatur: Wirtschaftspolitik in Österreich 1933–1938." In *"Austrofaschismus": Beiträge über Politik, Ökonomie und Kultur 1934–1938*, edited by Emmerich Tálos and Wolfgang Neugebauer, 133–59. Vienna: Verlag für Gesellschaftskritik, 1984.

Meusberger, Wilhelm. *Bezau: Geschichte–Gesellschaft–Kultur*. Lochau: Russ-Druck, 1995.

Mikoletzky, Hanns L. *Österreich im 20. Jahrhundert*. Vienna: Österreichischer Bundesverlag, 1962.

Miller, James William. *Engelbert Dollfuss als Agrarfachmann: Eine Analyse bäuerlicher Führungsbegriffe und österreichische Agrarpolitik 1918–1934*. Vienna and Cologne: Böhlau, 1989.

Molden, Fritz. *Exploding Star: A Young Austrian against Hitler*. New York: William Morrow, 1979.

Mommsen, Hans. "Der Nationalsozialismus." In *Meyers Enzyklopädisches Lexikon*. Vol. 16. Mannheim: Bibliographisches Institut, 1976.

Mooslechner, Michael, and Robert Stadler. "Landwirtschaft und Agrarpolitik." In *NS-Herrschaft in Österreich 1938–1945*, edited by Emmerich Tálos, Ernst Hanisch, and Wolfgang Neugebauer, 69–94. Vienna: Verlag für Gesellschaftskritik, 1988.

Moser, C. Gwyn. "Jewish *U-Boote* in Austria, 1938–1945." *Simon Wiesenthal Center Annual* 2 (1985): 53–62.

Moser, Jonny. "Depriving the Jews of Their Legal Rights in the Third Reich." In

November 1938: From "Reichskristallnacht" to Genocide, edited by Walter H. Pehle, 127–32. New York: Berg, 1991.

———. *Die Judenverfolgung in Österreich 1938–1945*. Vienna: Monographien zur Zeitgeschichte, 1966.

———. "Österreichs Juden unter der NS-Herrschaft." In *NS-Herrschaft in Österreich 1938–1945*, edited by Emmerich Tálos, Ernst Hanisch, and Wolfgang Neugebauer, 185–98. Vienna: Verlag für Gesellschaftskritik, 1988.

———. "Das Schicksal der Wiener Juden in den März- und Apriltagen 1938." In *Wien 1938*, edited by Historisches Museum der Stadt Wien, 172–82. Vienna: Österreichischer Bundesverlag, 1988.

Moser, Josef. "Der Wandel der Wirtschafts- und Beschäftigungsstruktur einer Region während der nationalsozialistischen Herrschaft am Beispiel Oberösterreichs." In *Arbeiterschaft und Nationalsozialismus in Österreich*, edited by Rudolf G. Ardelt and Hans Hautmann, 201–30. Vienna: Verlag für Gesellschaftskritik, 1990.

Müller, Ingo. *Hitler's Justice: The Courts in the Third Reich*. Cambridge, Mass.: Harvard University Press, 1991.

Mulley, Karl-Dieter. "Modernität oder Traditionalität? Überlegungen zum sozialstrukturellen Wandel in Österreich 1938 bis 1945." In *NS-Herrschaft in Österreich 1938–1945*, edited by Emmerich Tálos, Ernst Hanisch, and Wolfgang Neugebauer, 25–48. Vienna: Verlag für Gesellschaftskritik, 1988.

Naderer, Anton. "Dr. Josef Cal. Fliesser: Bischof von Linz." Ph.D. dissertation, University of Vienna, 1972.

———. "Die Haltung Bischof Fliesser und der National Sozialismus." In *Das Bistum Linz im Dritten Reich*, edited by Rudolf Zinnhobler, 74–107. Linz: Oberösterreichischer Landesverlag, 1979.

Neck, Rudolf, and Ludwig Jedlicka, eds. *Das Jahr 1934: 12 Februar: Protokoll des Symposiums in Wien am 5. Februar 1974*. Vienna: Verlag für Geschichte und Politik, 1975.

———. *Das Juliabkommen von 1936: Vorgeschichte, Hintergründe und Folgen*. Munich: Oldenbourg, 1977.

Neugebauer, Wolfgang. "Das NS-Terrorsystem." In *NS-Herrschaft in Österreich 1938–1945*, edited by Emmerich Tálos, Ernst Hanisch, and Wolfgang Neugebauer, 163–83. Vienna: Verlag für Gesellschaftskritik, 1988.

———. "Vernichtung von 'Minderwertigen'—Kriegsverbrechen?" In *Österreicher und der zweite Weltkrieg*, edited by Wolfgang Neugebauer, 121–43. Vienna: Österreichischer Bundesverlag, 1989.

———. "Von der Rassenhygenie zum Massenmord." In *Wien 1938*, edited by Historisches Museum der Stadt Wien, 263–85. Vienna: Österreichischer Bundesverlag, 1988.

———. "Widerstand und Opposition." In *NS-Herrschaft in Österreich 1938–1945*, edited by Emmerich Tálos, Ernst Hanisch, and Wolfgang Neugebauer, 537–52. Vienna: Verlag für Gesellschaftskritik, 1988.

———, ed. *Österreicher und der zweite Weltkrieg*. Vienna: Österreichischer Bundesverlag, 1989.

Orlow, Dietrich. *The History of the Nazi Party: 1933–1945*. Pittsburgh: University of Pittsburgh Press, 1973.

Parkinson, F., ed. *Conquering the Past: Austrian Nazism Yesterday and Today*. Detroit: Wayne State University Press, 1989.

Paucker, Arnold. "Resistance of German and Austrian Jews to the Nazi Regime, 1933–1945." *Leo Baeck Institute Yearbook* 40 (1995): 3–20.

Pauley, Bruce F. "Austria." In *The World Reacts to the Holocaust*, edited by David S. Wyman, 473–513. Baltimore: Johns Hopkins University Press, 1996.

——. *From Prejudice to Persecution: A History of Austrian Anti-Semitism*. Chapel Hill: University of North Carolina Press, 1992.

——. *The Habsburg Legacy, 1867–1939*. New York: Holt, Rinehart and Winston, 1972.

——. *Hitler and the Forgotten Nazis: A History of Austrian National Socialism*. Chapel Hill: University of North Carolina Press, 1981.

——. "The Social and Economic Background of Austria's Lebensunfähigkeit." In *The Austrian Socialist Experiment: Social Democracy and Austromarxism, 1918–1934*, edited by Anson Rabinbach, 21–37. Boulder, Colo.: Westview Press, 1985.

Pehle, Walter H., ed. *Der Judenpogrom 1938: Von der "Reichskristallnacht" zum Völkermord*. Frankfurt: Fischer, 1988.

Pelinka, Anton. *Austria: Out of the Shadow of the Past*. Boulder, Colo.: Westview Press, 1998.

——. "The Great Austrian Taboo: The Repression of the Civil War." *New German Critique*, no. 43 (1988): 69–81.

——. "SPÖ, ÖVP, and the 'Ehemaligen': Isolation or Integration?" In *Conquering the Past: Austrian Nazism Yesterday and Today*, edited by F. Parkinson, 245–56. Detroit: Wayne State University Press, 1989.

Petropoulos, Jonathan. *Art as Politics in the Third Reich*. Chapel Hill: University of North Carolina Press, 1996.

——. "The Importance of the Second Rank: The Case of Art Plunderer Kajetan Mühlmann." *Contemporary Austrian Studies* 4 (1996): 177–201.

Peukert, Detlev J. K. *Inside Nazi Germany: Conformity, Opposition, and Racism in Everyday Life*. New Haven: Yale University Press, 1987.

——. "Youth in the Third Reich." In *Life in the Third Reich*, edited by Richard Bessel, 25–49. Oxford: Oxford University Press, 1987.

Preradovich, Nikolaus von. *Grossdeutschland 1938: Traum, Wirklichkeit, Tragödie*. Leoni am Starnberger See: Druffel Verlag, 1987.

——. *Österreichs höhere SS-Führer*. Berg am See: Kurt Vowinckel Verlag, 1987.

Rabinbach, Anson. *The Crisis of Austrian Socialism: From Red Vienna to Civil War*. Chicago: University of Chicago Press, 1983.

Rath, R. John, and Carolyn Schum. "The Dollfuss-Schuschnigg Regime: Fascist or Authoritarian?" In *Who Were the Fascists? Social Roots of European Fascism*, edited by Stein Ugelvik Larsen, Bernt Havet, and Jan P. Myklebust. Bergen: Universitetsforlaget, 1980.

Rathkolb, Oliver. *Führertreu und gottbegnadet: Künstlereliten im Dritten Reich*. Vienna: Österreichischer Bundesverlag, 1991.

Rathkolb, Oliver, Wolfgang Duchowitsch, Fritz Hausjell, and Hannes Haas. *Die unvertraute Wahrheit: Hitlers Propagandisten in Österreich*. Salzburg: Muller, 1988.

Reimann, Viktor. *Innitzer: Kardinal zwischen Hitler und Rom*. Vienna, Munich, and Zurich: Verlag Fritz Molden, 1967.

Reiterer, Albert F. *Nation und Nationalbewusstsein in Österreich: Ergebnisse einer empirischen Untersuchung*. Vienna: Verband der wissenschaftlichen Gesellschaften Österreichs, 1988.

Reuth, Ralf Georg. *Goebbels*. New York: Harcourt Brace, 1993.

Rhodes, Anthony. *The Vatican in the Age of the Dictators, 1922–1945*. New York: Holt, Rinehart and Winston, 1973.

Riedmann, Josef. *Das Bundesland Tirol 1918–1970 (Geschichte des Landes Tirol 4/II)*. Bozen, Innsbruck, and Vienna: Tyrolia Verlag, 1988.

Ringler, Ralf Roland. *Illusion einer Jugend: Lieder, Fahnen und das bittere Ende: Hitler Jugend in Österreich: Ein Erlebnisbericht*. St. Pölten: Verlag Niederösterreiches Pressehaus, 1977.

Rosar, Wolfgang. *Deutsche Gemeinschaft: Seyss-Inquart und der Anschluss*. Vienna: Europa Verlag, 1971.

Rosenkranz, Herbert. "The Anschluss and the Tragedy of Austrian Jewry 1938–1945." In *The Jews of Austria: Essays on Their Life, History and Destruction*, edited by Josef Fraenkel, 479–575. London: Vallentine, Mitchell, 1967.

———. *"Reichskristallnacht" 9. November 1938 in Österreich*. Vienna: Europa Verlag, 1968.

———. *Verfolgung und Selbstbehauptung: Die Juden in Österreich 1938–1945*. Vienna: Herold, 1978.

Rothschild, K. W. *Austria's Economic Development between Two Wars*. London: Frederick Muller, 1947.

Rudin, Walter. *The Way I Remember It*. London: London Mathematical Society, 1997.

Safrian, Hans. *Die Eichmann Männer*. Vienna: Europaverlag, 1993.

Safrian, Hans, and Hans Witek. *Und keiner war dabei: Dokumente des alltäglichen Antisemitismus in Wien*. Vienna: Picus, 1988.

Sauer, Walter. "Österreichs Kirchen 1938–1945." In *NS-Herrschaft in Österreich 1938–1945*, edited by Emmerich Tálos, Ernst Hanisch, and Wolfgang Neugebauer, 517–36. Vienna: Verlag für Gesellschaftskritik, 1988.

Schärf, Adolf. *Österreichs Erneuerung 1945–1955*. Vienna: Verlag der Wiener Volksbuchverhandlung, 1960.

Schausberger, Norbert. *Der Griff nach Österreich: Der Anschluss*. Munich: Jugend und Volk, 1978.

———. "Hitler und Österreich: Einige Anmerkungen zur Hitler-Interpretation." *Österreich in Geschichte und Literatur* 28, no. 6 (1984): 363–77.

———. *Rüstung in Österreich 1938–1945: Eine Studie über die Wechselwirkung von Wirtschaft, Politik und Kriegsführung*. Vienna: Verlag Brüder Hollinek, 1970.

———. "Der Strukturwandel des ökonomischen Systems 1938–1945." In *Arbeiterschaft und Nationalsozialismus in Österreich*, edited by Rudolf G. Ardelt and Hans Hautmann, 151–68. Vienna: Europaverlag, 1990.

Schleunes, Karl A. *The Twisted Road to Auschwitz: Nazi Policy towards German Jews, 1933–1939*. Chicago: University of Chicago Press, 1970.

Schmid, Kurt, and Robert Streibel, eds. *Der Pogrom 1938: Judenverfolgung in Österreich und Deutschland*. Vienna: Picus, 1990.

Schmidl, Erwin A. *März 38: Der deutsche Einmarsch in Österreich.* Vienna: Österreichischer Bundesverlag, 1988.

——. "Die militärische Situation in Tirol im März 1938." In *Tirol und der Anschluss: Voraussetzungen, Entwicklungen, Rahmenbedingungen 1918–1938,* edited by Thomas Albrich, Klaus Eisterer, and Rolf Steininger, 481–504. Innsbruck: Haymon Verlag, 1988.

Schneider, Gertrude. *Exile and Destruction: The Fate of Austrian Jews, 1938–1945.* Westport, Conn.: Praeger, 1995.

Schöner, Josef. *Wiener Tagebuch 1944/45.* Vienna, Cologne, and Weimar: Böhlau, 1992.

Schorske, Carl E. *Fin-de-Siècle Vienna: Politics and Culture.* New York: Knopf, 1980.

Schreiber, Horst. *Die Machtübernahme: Die Nationalsozialisten in Tirol 1938/1939.* Innsbruck: Haymon Verlag, 1994.

——. *Wirtschafts- und Sozialgeschichte der Nazizeit in Tirol.* Innsbruck: Österreichischer Studien Verlag, 1994.

Schuster, Walter. "Die Entnazifizierung des Magistrates Linz." *Historisches Jahrbuch der Stadt Linz* (1995): 87–205.

Schwarz, Robert. "Nazi Wooing of Austrian Social Democracy between Anschluss and War." In *Conquering the Past: Austrian Nazism Yesterday and Today,* edited by F. Parkinson, 125–36. Detroit: Wayne State University Press, 1989.

Shirer, William L. *Berlin Diary: The Journal of a Foreign Correspondent, 1934–1941.* New York: Penguin, 1979.

——. *The Nightmare Years: 1930–1940.* Boston: Little, Brown, 1984.

Simon, Walter B. "Democracy in the Shadow of Imposed Sovereignty: The First Republic of Austria." In *The Breakdown of Democratic Regimes: Europe,* edited by Juan L. Linz and Alfred Stepan, 80–121. Baltimore: Johns Hopkins University Press, 1978.

Sked, Alan. *The Decline and Fall of the Habsburg Monarchy, 1815–1918.* London: Longman, 1989.

Slapnicka, Harry. *Oberösterreich als es "Oberdonau" hiess (1938–1945).* Linz: Oberösterreichischer Landesverlag, 1978.

——. "Zum Antisemitismus Problem in Oberösterreich." *Zeitgeschichte* 11–12 (1974): 264–67.

Smelser, Ronald M. "Hitler and the DNSAP: Between Democracy and Gleichschaltung." *Bohemia: Jahrbuch des Collegium Carolinum* 20 (1979): 137–55.

Speer, Albert. *Spandau: The Secret Diaries.* New York: Macmillan, 1976.

Stadler, Karl. *Österreich 1938–1945 im Spiegel der NS Akten.* Vienna: Herold Verlag, 1966.

——. "Provinzstadt im Dritten Reich." In *Nationalsozialismus in Wien: Machtübernahme und Herrschaftssicherung 1938/39,* edited by Gerhard Botz, 15–21. Vienna: Obermayer, 1988.

Steiner, Kurt. *Politics in Austria.* Boston: Little, Brown, 1972.

Steinert, Marlis. *Hitler's War and the Germans: Public Mood and Attitude during the Second World War.* Athens: Ohio University Press, 1977.

Steininger, Rolf. "Der Anschluss—Stationen auf dem Weg zum März 1938." In *Tirol und der Anschluss: Voraussetzungen, Entwicklungen, Rahmenbedingungen 1918–1938,* edited by Thomas Albrich, Klaus Eisterer, and Rolf Steininger, 9–42. Innsbruck: Haymon Verlag, 1988.

Sternfeld, Albert. *Betrifft: Österreich: Von Österreich betroffen.* Freistadt: Löcker Verlag, 1990.

Stiefel, Dieter. *Arbeitslosigkeit: Soziale, politische und wirtschaftliche Auswirkungen—am Beispiel Österreichs 1918–1938.* Berlin: Duncker und Humblot, 1979.

——. *Entnazifizierung in Österreich.* Vienna: Europaverlag, 1981.

——. *Die grosse Krise in einem kleinen Land: Österreichische Finanz- und Wirtschaftspolitik 1929–1938.* Vienna: Böhlau, 1988.

Stokes, Lawrence Duncan. "The 'Sicherheitsdienst' (SD) of the 'Reichsfuehrer' SS and German Public Opinion, September 1939–June 1941." Ph.D. dissertation, Johns Hopkins University, 1972.

Stubenvoll, Karl. *Bibliographie zum Nationalsozialismus in Österreich: Eine Auswahl.* Vienna: Kammer für Arbeiter und Angestellte für Wien, 1992.

Stuhlpfarrer, Karl. "Nazism, the Austrians, and the Military." In *Conquering the Past: Austrian Nazism Yesterday and Today,* edited by F. Parkinson, 190–206. Detroit: Wayne State University Press, 1989.

Sully, Melanie A. "The Waldheim Connection." In *Conquering the Past: Austrian Nazism Yesterday and Today,* edited by F. Parkinson, 294–312. Detroit: Wayne State University Press, 1989.

Tálos, Emmerich. "Arbeits- und Sozialrecht im Nationalsozialismus—Steuerung der Arbeitsbeziehungen, Integration und Disziplinierung der Arbeiterschaft." In *Arbeiterschaft und Nationalsozialismus in Österreich,* edited by Rudolf G. Ardelt and Hans Hautmann, 231–54. Vienna: Europaverlag, 1990.

——. "Sozialpolitik 1938–1945." In *NS-Herrschaft in Österreich 1938–1945,* edited by Emmerich Tálos, Ernst Hanisch, and Wolfgang Neugebauer, 115–40. Vienna: Verlag für Gesellschaftskritik, 1988.

Tálos, Emmerich, Herbert Dachs, Ernst Hanisch, and Anton Staudinger, eds. *Handbuch des politischen Systems Österreichs 1918–1933.* Vienna: Manz, 1995.

Tálos, Emmerich, Ernst Hanisch, and Wolfgang Neugebauer, eds. *NS-Herrschaft in Österreich 1938–1945.* Vienna: Verlag für Gesellschaftskritik, 1988.

Tálos, Emmerich, and Wolfgang Neugebauer, eds. *"Austrofaschismus": Beiträge über Politik, Ökonomie und Kultur 1934–1938.* Vienna: Verlag für Gesellschaftskritik, 1984.

Taylor, A. J. P. *The Habsburg Monarchy, 1809–1918: A History of the Austrian Empire and Austria Hungary.* New York: Harper and Row, 1965.

Taylor, Fred, ed. *The Goebbels Diaries, 1939–1941.* New York: Putnam, 1983.

Thalmann, Rita, and Emmanuel Feinermann. *Crystal Night: 9–10 November 1938.* London: Thames and Hudson, 1974.

Thorne, Christopher. *The Approach of War, 1938–39.* London: Macmillan–St. Martins, 1967.

Tweraser, Kurt. "Carl Beurle and the Triumph of German Nationalism in Austria." *German Studies Review* 4, no. 3 (1981): 403–26.

——. *US Militärregierung Oberösterreich 1945–1950.* Linz: Oberösterreichischer Landesarchiv, 1995.

Uhl, Heidemarie. *Zwischen Versöhnung und Verstörung: Eine Kontroverse um Österreichs historische Identität fünfzig Jahre nach dem "Anschluß."* Vienna, Cologne, and Weimar: Böhlau, 1992.

Ulrich, Johann. *Der Luftkrieg über Österreich 1939–1945*. Vienna: Heeresgeschichtliches Museum, 1982.

Unger, Aryeh L. "The Public Opinion Reports of the Nazi Party." *Public Opinion Quarterly* 29 (1965–66): 565–82.

Vassiltchikov, Marie. *Berlin Diaries, 1940–1945*. New York: Knopf, 1987.

Voges, Michael. "Klassenkampf in der 'Betriebsgemeinschaft': Die 'Deutschland Berichte' der Sopade (1934–1940) als Quelle zum Widerstand der Industriearbeiter im Dritten Reich." *Archiv für Sozialgeschichte* 21 (1982): 329–83.

Wagner, Dieter and Gerhard Tomkowitz. *Anschluss: The Week Hitler Seized Austria*. New York: St. Martin's Press, 1971.

Wagnleitner, Reinhold. *Understanding Austria: The Political Reports of Martin F. Herz, Political Officer of the US Legation in Vienna, 1945–1948*. Salzburg: Wolfgang Neugebauer Verlag, 1984.

Walser, Harald. " 'Treue dem wahren Nationalsozialismus!' Arbeiter in der Vorarlberger NSDAP." In *Arbeiterschaft und Nationalsozialismus in Österreich*, edited by Rudolf G. Ardelt and Hans Hautmann, 317–34. Vienna: Europaverlag, 1990.

Walzl, August. *"Als erster Gau . . ." Entwicklungen und Strukturen des Nationalsozialismus in Kärnten*. Klagenfurt: Universitätsverlag Carinthia, 1992.

———. *Die Juden in Kärnten und das Dritte Reich*. Klagenfurt: Universitätsverlag Carinthia, 1987.

Wandruszka, Adam. "Österreichs politische Struktur." In *Geschichte der Republik Österreich*, edited by Heinrich Benedict, 369–82. Vienna: Verlag für Geschichte und Politik, 1954.

Weinberg, Gerhard. *The Foreign Policy of Hitler's Germany*. Vol. 2, *Starting World War II, 1937–1939*. Chicago: University of Chicago Press, 1980.

———. *A World at Arms: A Global History of World War II*. Cambridge: Cambridge University Press, 1994.

Weinzierl, Erika. "Kirche und Politik." In *Österreich 1918–1938: Geschichte der Ersten Republik*, edited by Erika Weinzierl and Karl Skalnik, 1:437–96. Graz, Vienna, and Cologne: Verlag Styria, 1983.

———. *Prüfstand: Österreichs Katholiken und der Nationalsozialismus*. Mödling: Verlag St. Gabriel, 1988.

———. *Zu wenig Gerechte: Österreicher und Judenverfolgung 1938–1945*. Graz: Verlag Styria, 1969.

Weiss, John. *Ideology of Death: Why the Holocaust Happened in Germany*. Chicago: Ivan R. Dee, 1996.

Weisz, Franz. "Die Geheime Staatspolizei, Staatspolizeistelle Wien 1938–1945: Organisation, Arbeitsweise, personale Angelegenheiten." Ph.D. dissertation, University of Vienna, 1991.

———. "Die Gestapo-Leitstelle Wien." *Wiener Geschichtsblätter* 47 (1992): 231–34.

West, Rebecca. *Black Lamb and Grey Falcon: A Journey through Yugoslavia*. 2 vols. New York: Viking, 1941.

Whiteside, Andrew. *Austrian National Socialism before 1918*. The Hague: Martinus Nijhoff, 1962.

———. "Nationaler Sozialismus in Österreich vor 1918." *Vierteljahrshefte für Zeitgeschichte* 9 (1961): 333–59.

———. *The Socialism of Fools: Georg Ritter von Schönerer and Austrian Pan-Germanism*. Berkeley: University of California Press, 1975.

Williams, Maurice. "The Aftermath of Anschluss: Disillusioned Germans or Budding Austrian Patriots?" *Austrian History Yearbook* 14 (1978): 129–44.

———. "Captain Josef Leopold: Austro-Nazi and Austro-Nationalist?" In *Conquering the Past: Austrian Nazism Yesterday and Today*, edited by F. Parkinson, 57–71. Detroit: Wayne State University Press, 1989.

Wiltschegg, Walter. *Die Heimwehr: Eine unwiderstehliche Volksbewegung?* Munich: Oldenbourg, 1985.

Wistrich, Robert S. *Antisemitism: The Longest Hatred*. New York: Pantheon Books, 1991.

Witek, Hans. "'Arisierungen' in Wien: Aspekte nationalsozialistischer Enteignungspolitik 1938–1940." In *NS-Herrschaft in Österreich 1938–1945*, edited by Emmerich Tálos, Ernst Hanisch, and Wolfgang Neugebauer, 199–216. Vienna: Verlag für Gesellschaftskritik, 1988.

Wortmann, Michael. *Baldur von Schirach: Hitlers Jugendführer*. Cologne: Böhlau, 1982.

Zitelmann, Rainer. *Hitler: Selbstverständnis eines Revolutionärs*. Stuttgart: Klett-Cotta, 1987.

Zuckmayer, Carl. *A Part of Myself*. New York: Carroll & Graf, 1984.

Zweig, Stefan. *The World of Yesterday*. New York: Viking, 1945.

Nazi Party: surveillance by, x–xi; in Germany, 43; occupational composition of, 45; *Social Darwinism* of, 60, 70; appeal to working class, 71, 76, 80, 85, 91; social policy of, 72, 74, 91; working class members of, 80, 87, 92; security organs of, 91; working-class goals of, 91–92; Catholic laity on, 95; and Catholic bishops, 95–96; settlement with Catholic Church, 100–102; attacks on Catholic Church, 106–9, 117–18, 121, 126–28, 129, 165, 170; agricultural policy of, 113–19; rural opinion on, 121–23, 128, 129–30; de-Christianization campaign, 126–28; wartime sentiment on, 184, 188–89, 201; alienation of youth from, 195; refugees' criticism of, 201; wartime resentment of, 201, 222–23; postwar sentiment on, 230
— Austrian: in 1932 elections, 10, 12; before Anschluss, 12–14, 44–46; use of terrorism, 13; banning of, 13, 47, 48; German nationalists in, 14; and Dollfuss, 14, 44; during Dollfuss-Schuschnigg regime, 20; factions in, 21, 47–49, 50, 66; at start of Anschluss, 26; popular support for, 33–34, 43; attitudes of, 43; professionals in, 44; membership of, 44–47, 167, 193, 228; of post-Anschluss era, 45–47, 49; occupational composition of, 46, 47; effect of July Putsch on, 47; Carinthian influence in, 48–49, 53, 61, 62; Bürckel's reorganization of, 49–50; disillusionment with Anschluss, 51, 52
— Viennese, 51; in pre-Anschluss elections, 13; disillusionment of, 55–60, 70, 77, 161; arrest of members, 56; dissension among, 56; leadership of, 56–57; and Bürckel, 58; in the provinces, 60–66; indebtedness of, 66; under Reich Civil Service Act, 67; on eve of war, 69–70; and Social Democrats, 78; radicalism of, 134; anti-Semitic violence by, 143–44; cultural policies of, 167; administration of city, 215–16; de-Nazification of members, 229–30
Nazi Women's Aid Society, 126
Nazi Women's Association, 121
Neubacher, Hermann, 57, 68; rehiring of activists, 72
Nibelungen Works, 221
Night of the Generals, 213–15

Nohel, Gustav, 64
Norway: Austrian troops in, 160
NSDAP. *See* Nazi Party
Nuremberg racial laws, 110, 138; extension to Austria, 135
Nussbach, 123; religious observances in, 127

O5 (resistance group), 218
Old Fighters, 46, 48; exclusion from rewards, 52, 53, 64; in Tyrol-Vorarlberg, 61; among Kreisleiter, 61–62; morale of, 67; rehiring of, 87; during World War II, 161
Opdenhoff, Christian, 51, 52, 61; appointees of, 62; in Gauleiter crisis, 68
Operation Barbarossa, 169
Operation Blue, 176
Order of Teutonic Knights, 101
OSS, xii; in Switzerland, 208; and Austrian resistance, 218
Österreichische Kampffront, 142
Österreichische Volkspartei (ÖVP, Austrian People's Party), 229, 232
Ostmark. *See* Austria
Ostmark Law (1939), 68
Ottomans, 3, 4

Pacelli, Eugenio Cardinal, 96, 98
Pan-German movement, 6
Papen, Franz von: belief in moderates, 13; as ambassador to Vienna, 15, 140
Particularism, 55; in provinces, 193; Bavarian, 209
Patent of Toleration, 22
Patriotic Front (Dollfuss regime), 14; peasants in, 117
Patriotism, Austrian, 155; wartime revival of, 192–93, 199; Allied appeal to, 207–8, 209
Pauley, Bruce, 13, 22, 23
Pawlowski, Wladimir von, 148
Pearl Harbor: attack on, 172
Peasant League, 9
Peasants: farm legislation for, 115; flight from land, 115, 116–17, 122, 125, 129; political indifference of, 117; opinion of Anschluss, 121
People's Court (Volksgerichtshof): in Vienna, 188; in Berlin, 205
Perl, Estra, 141
Peter, Sara Gertrud, 178